THE FINANCIAL TIMES GUIDE TO BOND AND MONEY MARKETS

PEARSON

At Pearson, we believe in learning – all kinds of learning for all kinds of people. Whether it's at home, in the classroom or in the workplace, learning is the key to improving our life chances.

That's why we're working with leading authors to bring you the latest thinking and best practices, so you can get better at the things that are important to you. You can learn on the page or on the move, and with content that's always crafted to help you understand quickly and apply what you've learned.

If you want to upgrade your personal skills or accelerate your career, become a more effective leader or more powerful communicator, discover new opportunities or simply find more inspiration, we can help you make progress in your work and life.

Pearson is the world's leading learning company. Our portfolio includes the Financial Times and our education business, Pearson International.

Every day our work helps learning flourish, and wherever learning flourishes, so do people.

To learn more, please visit us at **www.pearson.com/uk**

The Financial Times

With a worldwide network of highly respected journalists, *The Financial Times* provides global business news, insightful opinion and expert analysis of business, finance and politics. With over 500 journalists reporting from 50 countries worldwide, our in-depth coverage of international news is objectively reported and analysed from an independent, global perspective.

To find out more, visit **www.ft.com/pearsonoffer/**

THE FINANCIAL TIMES GUIDE TO BOND AND MONEY MARKETS

GLEN ARNOLD

Harlow, England • London • New York • Boston • San Francisco • Toronto • Sydney
Auckland • Singapore • Hong Kong • Tokyo • Seoul • Taipei • New Delhi
Cape Town • São Paulo • Mexico City • Madrid • Amsterdam • Munich • Paris • Milan

PEARSON EDUCATION LIMITED
Edinburgh Gate
Harlow CM20 2JE
United Kingdom
Tel: +44 (0)1279 623623
Web: www.pearson.com/uk

First edition published 2015 (print and electronic)

ISBN: 978-0-273-79179-9 (print)
      978-0-273-79180-5 (PDF)
      978-1-292-00542-3 (eText)
      978-0-273-79181-2 (ePub)

British Library Cataloguing-in-Publication Data
A catalogue record for the print edition is available from the British Library

Library of Congress Cataloging-in-Publication Data
Arnold, Glen.
  The Financial Times guide to bond and money markets / Glen Arnold
    pages cm
  Includes index.
  ISBN 978-0-273-79179-9 (print) -- ISBN 978-0-273-79180-5 (PDF) --
  ISBN 978-1-292-00542-3 (eText) -- ISBN 978-0-273-79181-2 (ePub)
  1. Bonds--Handbooks, manuals, etc.   2. Money market--Handbooks, manuals, etc.
  3. Investments--Handbooks, manuals, etc.   I. Title.
  HG4651.A76 2015
  332.63'23--dc23

                                                                    2015020242

10 9 8 7 6 5 4 3 2 1
19 18 17 16 15

Front cover image © Kord.com/Getty Images

Print edition typeset in 9.5/14pt Stone Serif ITC Pro by 35
Print edition printed by Ashford Colour Press Ltd, Gosport

NOTE THAT ANY PAGE CROSS REFERENCES REFER TO THE PRINT EDITION

CONTENTS

PART 4
VALUING BONDS AND MONEY MARKET INSTRUMENTS 309

PART 5
SOME VARIATIONS ON A BOND THEME 381

ABOUT THE AUTHOR

Glen Arnold, PhD, has held positions of Professor of Investment and Professor of Corporate Finance, but came to the conclusion that academic life was not nearly as much fun as making money in the financial markets. As a wealthy investor in his early 50s, Glen now spends most of his time running his own portfolio (www.glen-arnold-investments.co.uk) and a property development company from his office in the heart of rural Leicestershire. He is happy to share his ideas with fellow enthusiasts and so writes a regular *Deep Value Shares* newsletter on the investment website ADVFN.

Glen is the author of the number one best-selling investment book *The Financial Times Guide to Investing* as well as the investing classics *The Financial Times Guide to Value Investing, The Great Investors* and *Get Started in Shares*. He wrote the market-leading university textbooks *Corporate Financial Management, Modern Financial Markets and Institutions* and *Essentials of Corporate Financial Management*. He is also the author of three definitive books on finance: *The Financial Times Guide to Banking, The Financial Times Handbook of Corporate Finance* and *The Financial Times Guide to the Financial Markets*. All these books are available from Pearson Education.

PREFACE

Everybody's life is touched by financial markets. This was painfully brought home to us when markets built on badly thought-through finance collapsed, triggering the long recession in 2008. Millions were thrown out of work, wages were cut, governments went bust and interest rates were slashed. Clearly we all need to have some acquaintance with what these financial instruments are and how these markets work.

This book is a simple, easy-to-follow guide to bond and money markets, which assumes no prior knowledge of finance. The emphasis is on gaining an understanding of the underlying concepts in the first half of the book, the importance of these markets and ideas in the practical world of finance. Later I introduce those elements of quantitative finance that are absolutely essential. This way, I hope, the essence of this technical subject is explained without bamboozling the reader with an overload of mathematics.

It explains:

- the jargon used in the debt markets
- the wide variety of bond markets, from sovereign bonds to junk
- the vital role of money market instruments, ranging from commercial paper to interbank lending
- the valuation of these securities and how value changes as interest rates change.

Who might find the book useful?

- Market professionals needing a succinct, down-to-earth guide to throw light into an area of knowledge that they know they need to fulfil their roles effectively and advance their careers.
- People working at banks, insurance companies, lawyers' offices and accounting firms needing to develop a good working knowledge of key financial terms and functioning of the main markets.

- University students needing more depth on bond and money markets than is provided by their main course texts.
- Those curious minds who realise they need to understand the financial markets to comprehend the modern economy.
- Private investors who might consider putting some of their savings in these markets.

I hope you enjoy the book.

Glen Arnold

ACKNOWLEDGEMENTS

Susan Henton, my personal assistant, helped tremendously with this book. I thank her for her thoughtful, diligent and meticulous contributions to so many sections.

I would also like to thank Christopher Cudmore, my editor at Pearson Education, for his enthusiasm, encouragement and support for this project.

The production team at Pearson did a great job of turning a raw manuscript into a book. I would like to thank Lisa Robinson, Melanie Carter, Vivienne Church, Jen Halford and Kelly Miller.

Publisher's acknowledgements

We are grateful to the following for permission to reproduce copyright material:

Table 2.11 courtesy of FTSE Group; tables 2.5, 2.6, 2.7, 3.1, 3.2, 3.5, 5.3, 5.4, 7.2, 7.3 and 11.2 courtesy of Thomson Reuters; table 9.6 courtesy of Moody's Investors Service; table 9.7 courtesy of Standard & Poor's; table 10.1 courtesy of Euro Repo Index.

Figures 3.3, 3.4 and 3.5 courtesy of Agence France Trésor; figure 3.6 courtesy of Bundesrepublik Deutschland Finanzagentur; figures 4.6 and 4.7 courtesy of www.advfn.com; figure 8.2 courtesy of the European Central Bank; figures 15.3, 15.5, 15.6 and 15.7 courtesy of the European Covered Bond Council.

All *Financial Times* articles © The Financial Times Limited. All Rights Reserved, except Article 7.2, printed courtesy of Andrew Macdowall.

In some instances we have been unable to trace the owners of copyright material, and we would appreciate any information that would enable us to do so.

PART 1
AN OVERVIEW

CHAPTER 1
INTRODUCTION TO BOND AND MONEY MARKETS

Bond and money markets are vital parts of the global financial infrastructure. They provide financing requirements for, and are essential to, the daily financial management of governments as well as thousands of corporations and financial institutions. They also provide alternative sources of investment returns for savers. A country's economic strength will be reflected in the value placed by the financial markets on its government-issued borrowing instruments. Similarly, the financial strength of a corporation or a bank is indicated by the rates of return it has to offer to borrow in the bond or money markets.

The difference between bond markets and money markets is a time or maturity issue. The **term to maturity** (or simply **term** or **maturity** or **tenor**) is the length of time remaining until the borrower pays the stated amount to the lender who owns the bond or money market instrument. Generally, money market instruments have maturity dates of one year or less, and bond markets deal in instruments with maturities in excess of one year.

As you can see from the extract from the annual accounts of the giant drinks company Diageo (Table 1.1), a firm requires good understanding of a great many different debt instruments to carry out the efficient management of its financing requirements, and it is crucial that this aspect of running a firm is expertly executed. The debt instruments employed by Diageo are typical of those used by large corporations, ranging from a simple bank overdraft to the more esoteric hedging instruments, and may be in different currencies and have different maturity dates. At this stage the titles of these instruments are going to seem confusing jargon, but by the end of the book you will have a sound understanding of terms such as commercial paper, medium-term notes and interest rate hedging.

To keep track of all its financial instrument obligations and to ensure that a company has sufficient finance for its needs throughout a year at the lowest cost is a skilful undertaking and requires a complete understanding of the

Table 1.1

	Repayment date	Currency	Year end interest rates %	2013 £ million	2012 £ million
Bank overdrafts	On demand	Various	Various	111	38
Commercial paper	–	US dollar	Various	–	23
Bank and other loans	Various	Various	Various	163	165
Credit support obligations	2013	Various	Various	72	130
Guaranteed bonds 2013	2013	US dollar	5.2	–	478
Guaranteed bonds 2013	2013	US dollar	5.5	–	382
Guaranteed bonds 2013	2013	Euro	5.5	983	–
Guaranteed bonds 2014	2014	US dollar	7.375	529	–
Fair value adjustment to borrowings	–	–	–	–	14
Borrowings due within one year and bank overdrafts				**1,858**	**1,230**
Guaranteed bonds 2013	2013	Euro	5.5	–	926
Guaranteed bonds 2014	2014	US dollar	7.375	–	514
Guaranteed bonds 2014	2014	Euro	6.625	853	805
Guaranteed bonds 2015	2015	US dollar	5.3	493	477
Guaranteed bonds 2015	2015	US dollar	3.25	328	318
Guaranteed bonds 2016	2016	US dollar	5.5	394	381
Guaranteed bonds 2016	2016	US dollar	0.625	492	–
Guaranteed bonds 2017	2017	US dollar	5.75	820	794
Guaranteed bonds 2017	2017	US dollar	1.5	655	633
Guaranteed bonds 2018	2018	US dollar	1.125	424	–
Guaranteed bonds 2020	2020	US dollar	4.828	400	379
Guaranteed bonds 2022	2022	US dollar	2.875	653	631
Guaranteed bonds 2022	2022	US dollar	8.0	196	189
Guaranteed bonds 2023	2023	US dollar	2.625	883	–
Guaranteed bonds 2035	2035	US dollar	7.45	264	255
Guaranteed bonds 2036	2036	US dollar	5.875	391	377
Guaranteed bonds 2042	2042	US dollar	4.25	325	314
Guaranteed bonds 2043	2043	US dollar	3.875	322	–
Medium term notes	2018	US dollar	4.85	132	127
Bank and other loans	Various	Various	Various	21	44
Fair value adjustment to borrowings	–	–	–	187	235
Borrowings due after one year				**8,233**	**7,399**
Total borrowings before derivative financial instruments				**10,091**	**8,629**
Fair value of foreign currency forwards and swaps	–	–	–	(205)	(210)
Fair value of interest rate hedging instruments				–	(3)
Total borrowings after derivative financial instruments				**9,886**	**8,416**

Source: Diageo plc, Annual Report 2013, Note 17

complexities of the bond and money markets. If a firm can achieve efficient management of its financing requirements, its customers may also benefit through lower prices. If a firm mismanages its financing, and has to pay exorbitant interest rates on the money it needs to borrow, then these inefficiencies may well result in higher consumer prices or company liquidation.

Structure of the book

The first seven chapters of this book provide an introduction to the bond markets, followed by four chapters describing the different money markets. Only when you have a firm grasp of the nature of these instruments do we look at the mathematical structures required for bond and money valuations. Thus maths is reserved for Chapters 12 to 14.

Then, in Chapters 15 and 16, we examine some of the more unusual securities that have evolved from the markets, such as bonds where the interest paid to investors depends on monthly mortgage payments from thousands of home owners, or the trading of agreements to notionally deposit money and notionally receive interest at a future date.

Finally, we consider the importance of central banks to the workings of these markets and how the authorities try to control inflation through altering interest rates in the money and bond markets.

Bonds

The concept of governments, companies and other institutions borrowing funds to invest in long-term projects and operations is a straightforward one, yet in today's sophisticated capital markets, with their wide variety of financial instruments and forms of debt, the borrowing and lending decision can be bewildering. Is the domestic bond market or the Eurobond market the better choice? On what terms, fixed- or floating-rate interest, with collateral or unsecured? And what about high-yield bonds or convertibles? The variety of methods of providing long-term finance is almost infinite.

A **bond** is a long-term contract in which the bond holder lends money to the bond issuer.[1] Basically, bonds may be regarded as merely IOUs with pages of legal clauses expressing the promises made. In return for the loan of money,

---

[1] Also called the **debtor** or **borrower**.

the issuer promises to make predetermined payments in the future which consist of an interest component, known as the **coupon** (usually regularly, once or twice a year), and the payment of a capital sum, the **face value** (**par value** or **nominal value**) of the bond, at the end of the bond's life. Straightforward bonds like this are known as **plain vanilla bonds** (or **conventional bonds**), but bonds come in a variety of types. Some do not promise a capital repayment, they just keep paying the coupon in perpetuity. Others do not offer a regular coupon, just a lump sum at the end of a period of time; these are known as **zero coupon bonds**. Some bonds have features such as floating rates of interest, 'bullet' or 'balloon' payments (all explained later).

Primary and secondary markets

Bond issuers obtain funding by issuing new bonds on the **primary market**, where the sale is usually handled by one or a syndicate of dealers and/or brokers, who earn commission by selling the issue to investors. After this initial sale, the bonds may be traded on the **secondary market** between investors, either through stock exchanges for listed bonds or, more likely, over the counter. **Over the counter (OTC) trading** is trading carried out between two parties directly (dealer-to-dealer or dealer-to-investor) as opposed to **exchange trading** which is carried out on a highly regulated public market. Bonds may change hands several times before their maturity.

The secondary markets are sometimes very **liquid**; that is, those organisations lending their surpluses to borrowers by buying bonds are able to get at their capital (turn it into cash) by selling quickly to other investors without the risk of reducing the price significantly, and the transaction costs of releasing the cash are low. But most corporate bonds have pretty poor liquidity, with most primary market investors buying them and then holding until maturity, resulting in very few secondary market trades.

Shorts, mediums and longs

Bonds with up to five years left until they mature and pay their **principal** (the amount that the issuer agreed to pay the owner at the maturity date) are generally known as **shorts**, but the boundary lines are often blurry; **medium-dated** (**intermediate**) bonds generally have remaining maturities of between 5 and 12 or 15 years; **longs** are bonds with remaining maturities of over 12 years. An alternative classification is **ultra-shorts**, up to 3 years; shorts, 3–7 years; mediums, 7–15 years; and longs, over 15 years. The time to maturity for bonds when they are first issued is generally between 5 and 30 years, but it should be noted that a bond is classified during its life according to the time remaining to maturity, not the maturity when it was issued, so a 30-year bond which has only 4 years left until it matures, is a short.

A number of firms have issued bonds with a longer than usual maturity date – IBM and Reliance of India have issued 100-year bonds, as have Coca-Cola and Walt Disney (Disney's was known as the 'Sleeping Beauty bond'). There are even some 1,000-year bonds in existence – Canadian Pacific Corporation is paying a dividend of 4% on a 1,000-year bond issued in 1883 by the Toronto Grey and Bruce Railway and due to be repaid in 2883.

Bonds, equity, bank loans and overdrafts compared

Both bonds and equities (shares in companies) are generally **negotiable** securities, i.e. they can be traded on financial markets. The advantage a bond possesses over a share is that the investor is *promised* a return. Bond investors are exposed to less risk than share investors because the promise is backed up by a series of legal rights, e.g. the right to receive the annual interest before the equity (share) holders receive any dividend. So in a bad year (e.g. no profits) bond investors are far more likely to receive a payout than shareholders. This is usually bolstered by rights to seize company assets if the company reneges on its commitment to pay coupons or redeem bonds at maturity. If things go very badly for the firm, there is a greater chance of saving the investors' investments if they are holding its bonds rather than its shares, because on liquidation the holders of debt-type financial securities are paid from the proceeds raised by selling off the assets first, before shareholders receive anything.

Offsetting these plus points are the facts that bond holders do not (usually) share in the increase in value created by an extraordinarily successful business, and there is an absence of any voting control over the management of the company.

For a company, bonds offer the advantage of long-term borrowing, often with a constant interest rate for, say, 15 years; the original lenders cannot withdraw the capital they lent from the company or increase the interest rate (this is the most common case, but, given the potential for innovation here, there are bonds that allow these things). An overdraft may have a variable interest rate and can be withdrawn at short notice, leaving the company in need of finance. It also has to be renewed, maybe every six months, and there is a real danger that the lender will refuse to '**roll over**' (continue) the debt at a future renewal date, or may demand a much higher interest rate to continue the lending.

Term loans from banks are often more difficult to obtain in the size required by larger companies, and they frequently cost more over the lifetime of the loan. Of course, bank overdrafts and loans have the advantage that they are available even to the smallest firms, whereas the bond market is generally open for large firms only.

Fixed-interest securities

Bonds are often referred to collectively as **fixed-interest securities**. Most bonds are indeed fixed rate, offering regular coupon amounts agreed at the outset, but some are variable, with the interest rising or falling every few months depending on a benchmark interest rate (e.g. Libor, the London Interbank Offered Rate – discussed in Chapter 8). Other bonds vary the interest paid for a particular three or six months depending on all sorts of factors, e.g. the rate of inflation or the price of copper. Nevertheless they are all lumped together as fixed interest to contrast these types of loan instrument with equities that do not carry a promise of a return.

Fluctuating values

The value of a bond – the price at which it is trading between investors on the secondary market – may fluctuate considerably during its life, and this value reflects the changes in the prevailing interest rate. Bonds are usually issued, but not always, with a nominal value of £100 or $1,000 (or €1,000, etc.). They may have any nominal value, but typical 'lots' are 100, 1,000, 10,000 and 50,000 of, say, pounds, euros or dollars. A five-year £100 bond issued with a coupon of 5% means that it will pay £5 per year, which is 5% of its nominal value of £100. After five years have expired, the issuer will have made five payments of the £5 coupon to the current holder, or ten of £2.50 if it pays semi-annual (every six months) interest, and the eventual holder receives the nominal value of £100 at the end of the term.

If, during those five years, the interest rate that investors demand for bonds of a similar risk class and time to maturity rises, the market value of the bond will fall to compensate for its **coupon rate** of only 5%, so that its rate of return reflects the prevailing interest rate.

To put it simply, if a five-year £100 bond is issued with a coupon of 5% and market interest rates for bonds with similar risk and length of time to maturity remain at 5% for the five-year life of the bond, its value will remain at £100 throughout its life. However, this is unlikely to be the case, as the value of a bond will fluctuate throughout its life to take into account the prevailing rate of interest. Interest rates may change daily and the value of bonds changes accordingly. If interest rates on alternative, equally risky bonds rise to 6% when the bond has three years left to maturity, the bond will be a less attractive investment were it still to be offered for sale at £100. It is offering the following deal: in one year receive £5, in two years another £5, and in three years £100 plus the final £5 coupon, i.e. 5% at a time when other bonds offer 6% for the same risk and maturity.

For investors to obtain the current going rate of 6%, the bond must offer secondary market traders £5 per year plus a capital gain over the next three years. This will occur if the price of the bond drops to £97.327 (take this on trust for now, you will be able to calculate this yourself after reading Chapter 13). At this price, investors gain £2.673 by buying at £97.327 and receiving £100 on maturity three years later.

The capital gain is worth £2.673 ÷ £97.327 = 2.746% over three years, or 0.915% per year. Add that to the coupon of £5 per year on an investment that cost £97.327, which in percentage terms works out at 5.137% per year, £5 ÷ £97.327 = 5.137%, and you obtain (approximately) the 6% that investors in bonds of this risk class and maturity are now requiring. These are rough calculations to give you the gist, precision comes in Chapter 13 – then you'll see how the overall rate of return does work out at exactly 6% once we take into account the timing of compounding (interest received on the interest in the three years).

So the bond selling in the secondary market is rather like a bank account that offers the following deal: you put £97.327 into the bank account and the bank pays you 6% interest per year. Each year you withdraw £5. At the end of three years your bank account contains £100. However, while a bank account might produce this type of deal if you agree to hold your money there for the full three years, the bond has the advantage that you can choose to sell the bond to another investor at any point during the three years.

Conversely, if general interest rates that investors are now accepting for this risk class fall to 2% when the bond has three years to maturity, then it will seem an attractive investment at £100, because it is offering a better rate of interest than is current, and its price will rise to £108.652. Investors are accepting a capital loss of £8.652 over the three years but being compensated with three lots of £5.

In both these cases, the bond will still be worth its face value (£100) at the end of its life.

The size of the bond markets

Bonds are the most significant financial instruments in the world today, with more than $90,000,000,000,000 ($90 trillion) in issue in 2013 – see Figure 1.1.[2] To put this number into perspective, the UK's annual output (gross domestic product, GDP) for one year is about £1.5 trillion.

Bonds come in all shapes and sizes, from UK government bonds to Chinese company bonds. Of this vast volume of $90 million million bonds[3] outstanding

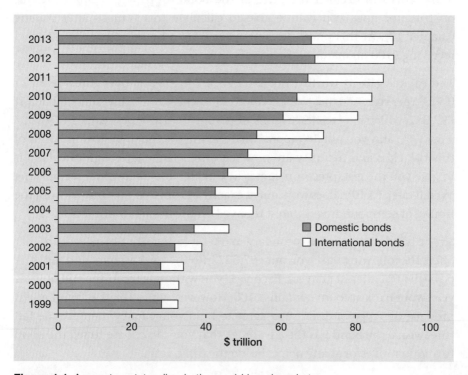

Figure 1.1 Amounts outstanding in the world bond market

Source: Data from the Bank for International Settlements

---

[2] Included in the BIS figures for domestic bonds are a small fraction of money market instruments.
[3] This includes all currencies, even though they are summed in US dollars.

(not yet redeemed – the capital has not been repaid), about $70 trillion are issued in the **domestic** bond markets of countries, that is issued within the country in its currency by resident issuers, under the jurisdiction of the authorities there. In addition to these domestic bonds there are another $20 trillion of bonds issued outside the domestic markets on the **international** bond markets. These are issued outside the market where the borrower resides. These can either be outside the jurisdiction of the country in whose currency the bond is denominated – thus a bond denominated in pounds sterling but issued in Switzerland is outside of the control of London regulators and government (a **Eurobond**) – or issued by foreigners in a country's currency in and under the rules of that country (a **foreign bond**).

Most bonds are bought by investment institutions such as pension funds, insurance companies, etc. When bonds are bought and sold on the secondary markets between investors the returns in the market place can be quite volatile. See Figure 1.2 for US government bonds and US shares (stocks), which

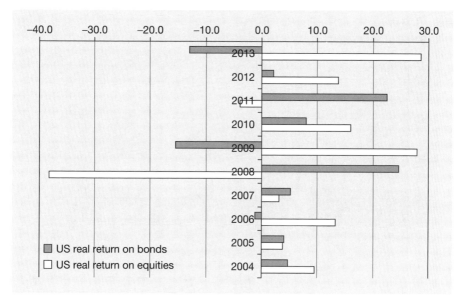

Figure 1.2 A comparison between real (inflation removed) annual returns on US government bonds and US equities (calculated by imagining that each year bonds or shares are bought on 1 January and sold on 31 December and taking into account both income (interest or dividends) and capital gains or losses over the year resulting from selling to another investor at the end of the year)

Source: Data from Barclays Equity Gilt Study 2014

shows some large ups and downs over a ten-year period. As we saw in the example of the 5% coupon bond, if the rates of return investors demand from bonds in the future rise, then the price of the bond can fall, sometimes dramatically as in the case of 2013. Thus there are years when bond prices fall by a larger percentage than the percentage coupon rate, resulting in an overall negative return for the year for an investor who buys at the beginning of the year and sells at the end.

It might be difficult to discern from this figure, with it being only for a ten-year period and one subject to a severe shock in 2008, that it is generally the case that bond returns are less volatile than share returns. This is better illustrated in Figure 1.3, which shows the returns on UK government bonds (gilts) over each of the years from 1900 to 2013. These are not interest rates that the government paid, rather they are the combination of the cash coupon received

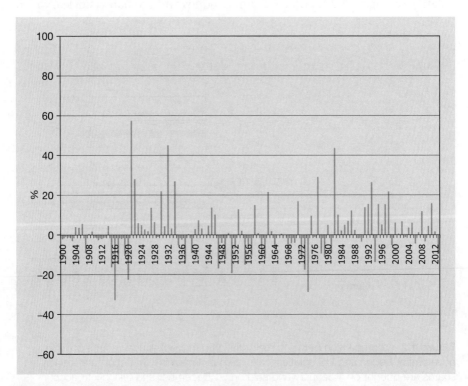

Figure 1.3 UK annual real gilt returns 1900–2013, percentage (real means after excluding inflation)

Source: Data from Barclays Equity Gilt Study 2014

as a percentage of the secondary market price at the start of the year, plus the capital gain or loss in the secondary market over 365 days for bonds with 15 or 20 years to run before the government redeems them.

Note that there are many years where the return was negative. However, a comparison with the equity markets' returns shows that government bond returns were far less volatile than equity returns – see Figure 1.4. Shares quite often show annual returns up and down more than 15%; bonds show this relatively infrequently.

Governments issue bonds to finance the gap between what they raise in taxes and what they spend. Bonds from strong nations, such as the UK, the USA or Germany, are considered (almost) risk free with regard to the likelihood of the issuer not paying coupons and/or the principal, or breaching some other condition in the agreement, i.e. **default risk**, and so give relatively low rates of return because of their small risk factor. If a country is in economic trouble, with high levels of borrowing, investors may become nervous that they will

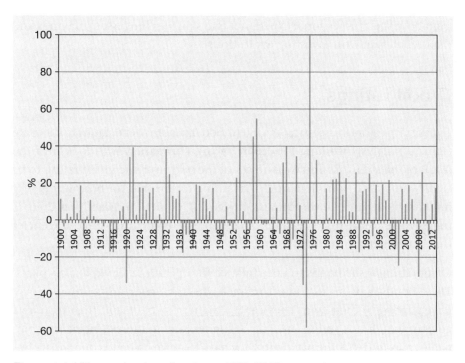

Figure 1.4 UK annual real equity returns 1900–2013, percentage

Source: Data from Barclays Equity Gilt Study 2014

not receive their coupon payments and the return of the principal, and therefore be less willing to hold these bonds unless they offer higher interest rates. This happened to Greece, Spain, Portugal and Ireland in 2011, causing their bonds to be deemed a riskier investment and investors to require higher rates of interest to invest in them.

Bond issuance

Financial institutions, usually an investment bank, may assist a firm to issue bonds. This is known as **underwriting** and they generally guarantee to the issuer that the entire issue will be sold. They then try to sell the bonds to investors, taking the risk that they may not be able to sell the whole issue. Alternatively they may act as a distribution agent for the issuer, trying to sell on a **best-efforts** basis, but not guaranteeing the sale. A third possibility is that the investment bank organises a **private placement** where one or more large financial institutions are lined up to receive the whole of a forthcoming bond issue. Companies, by paying commission to the financial institutions, benefit from both their professional experience and skill in selling issues of bonds and their reputation with investing institutions.

Credit ratings

To assist investors in assessing the likelihood of a borrower defaulting there are teams of analysts working for **credit rating companies** who look into the detail of the strengths and weaknesses of the borrower and give a rating to its creditworthiness – a triple-A, AAA, Aaa rating means that the borrower is very unlikely to default. Lower ratings, single-A, B, C or D, indicate that there is progressively more risk of default. Details about credit ratings and the agencies that issue them are in Chapter 5.

Corporations issue bonds to raise finance for operations or expansion plans. These bonds may be rated in accordance with their company's rating or may have a rating of their own. They carry a higher risk of default than reputable government bonds and so must pay a higher rate of interest. However, companies may find that the payments they have to make on bond coupons are less than they would have to pay for a similar size loan from a bank. They may also find that it is easier to raise large amounts of money by means of a securities issue, whereas a bank may not be in a position to offer the total amount required. When a company issues bonds, it has some control over what covenants or restrictions are placed on the issue. **Covenants** are conditions with which the bond issuer must comply (such as limiting the amount of debt a company can take on).

Securitised and covered bonds

Banks are the main issuers of **securitised** or **covered bonds**, bonds which are secured on assets from the regular and predictable income which companies receive from sources such as mortgages, loans, leases, trade receivables, credit card payments, etc.

Securitised bonds are issued by an entity separate from the owner of the cash flow and therefore can have a separate credit rating which may well be a higher rating than the company/bank as a whole is given. Thus, for example, a bank might set up a separate company which receives monthly income from 1,000 house mortgage payers. This separate company issues bonds secured against the mortgage rights it holds, and the bond interest is paid out of the mortgage receipts from 1,000 households. The interest on these bonds may be fixed at the time of issue or floating relative to a benchmark interest rate such as Libor, a standard rate of interest for loans.

Covered bonds are secured on the cash flows from mortgages, public sector loans or other loan receipts, but the assets (e.g. 1,000 mortgage rights) remain on the balance sheet of the issuer, usually a bank or financial institution, which retains control over them. Thus the covered bond holder has the security of both the assigned assets, e.g. the cash inflows from 1,000 mortgages, and the promise from the issuing firm to make good any shortfall if the securitised assets are not sufficient. Covered bonds usually are perceived as very low risk due to the reliability of the assets they can draw on.

Some technical terms for bonds

- **Yield** is the return achieved from the bond. There is a whole host of different yields. The two main ones are:
  - **Current yield** (also called **interest yield**, **flat yield**, **income yield**, **simple yield**, **annual yield** or **running yield**) is the annual income

received divided by price of the instrument. In our earlier example with a bond offering a £5 annual coupon and selling in the secondary market for £97.327, the current yield is £5 ÷ £97.327 = 5.137%.

● **Yield to maturity** (also called **redemption yield** or **gross redemption yield**) is the most important and is the one quoted in bond charts and tables. It is the annual rate of return offered on the bond taking into account all remaining coupon payments and the capital gain or loss on the bond between its current price and the redemption face value. For our example bond offering £5 per year and a capital gain over three years of £100 minus £97.327 the yield to maturity is 6%. An explanation of yields and the calculations is in Chapters 12 and 13.

● **Put option** can be added to the bond holder's set of rights in the initial agreement. It gives the holder the right but not the obligation to demand that the issuer redeems the bond before its normal maturity date, i.e. to sell it back to the issuer at a price that was fixed when the bond was first issued. If interest rates have risen, resulting in the bond price falling, an investor might seek to sell the bond to the issuer at the agreed price. The mere existence of the right to receive full payment for the bond without recourse to selling in the secondary market generally ensures that the price remains above par value. This extra advantage for the holder has to be paid for – usually achieved by the issuer offering a lower yield in the first place.

● **Call option (callable bond)** gives the bond issuer the right but not the obligation to repurchase the bonds from the holder at a defined price; the issuer can insist that the bond holder sell at a price at certain dates during the life of the bond. Issuers may exercise this option if they no longer need the funding or if they think they could reissue replacement bonds at a more favourable yield rate (this may happen if market interest rates for this risk class and time to maturity have fallen since the bond was first issued, i.e. the bond price has risen). They are also aware that some bonds place tight covenant restrictions on the firm so it is useful to be able to buy them back and issue less restrictive bonds in their place. Finally, exercising the call may permit the firm to adjust its financial **leverage** (that is the amount of debt relative to shareholders' equity capital) by reducing its debt. For these call privileges the issuer will pay a higher coupon rate from the outset. In other words, the bond will be sold for less than it would without the call feature (and this also applies to secondary market prices). The fact that the bonds can be called back for redemption at any time is obviously not something bond holders favour without offsetting compensation, especially when the bond price would otherwise have risen significantly above the par value.

- Usually bonds are set up with a **bullet structure**, where regular payments made reflect the interest only and the whole of the principal amount (face value) is repaid at maturity. **Balloon interest** means that the coupons paid on a long-term bond rise over time. Thus bonds issued to finance the construction of a wind turbine field might pay low coupons in the early years when income is poor and expenses high, but then, after the first three years, the coupons grow larger.

- **Principal** is the amount that will be repaid on maturity, typically £100, £1,000 or $1,000. It has various names: **face value**, **par value**, **face amount**, **redemption value** or **maturity value**.

- **Coupon rate** is the amount of interest paid per year expressed as a percentage of the principal. Typically it is paid twice a year, or semi-annually, but it could be paid more or less frequently than this. It is also known as **interest rate**, **dividend** or **nominal rate**.

- **Zero coupon** is when a bond does not pay interest/coupon payments, but is redeemed for face value at maturity. The return that an investor receives on these bonds is achieved by buying the bonds at a discounted price which is less than face value. So a five-year zero coupon bond that will be redeemed at £100 might be selling at £60 today. Using the discounted purchase price and the time to redemption, it is possible to work out the annual yield during the life of the bond, which in this case works out at 10.76% (see Chapter 13 for the calculations).

- **Convertible** bonds can be converted at the insistence of the holder into shares or other securities of the issuing company, usually equity shares.

- **Floating-rate notes (FRNs)** (also called **variable-rate notes**) have a variable coupon reset on a regular basis, usually every three or six months, in relation to a benchmark or reference rate. The typical term for an FRN is about 5–12 years.

- **Bond funds** are collective investment vehicles which enable small/retail investors as well as major financial institutions to invest in a broad portfolio of bonds. Some are listed on stock markets, others are traded over the counter in tailor-made deals.

Money markets

Money markets are a source of short-term finance for governments, corporations and other organisations. There are times when these organisations are in need of funds for merely a day, a week or the next three months. They thus need a place where they can borrow to make up a shortfall; the money markets fulfil this role. Banks are an alternative source of short-term finance, but in many cases the money markets are cheaper and involve less hassle.

At other times an organisation may have surplus funds and instead of keeping that money as cash or in current accounts at banks, earning little or no interest, it chooses to lend it out to those needing short-term funds by purchasing money market instruments from them.

While we, as individuals, borrow to make up shortfalls or lend surpluses (e.g. by withdrawing or depositing money in our bank accounts) and do so in tens, hundreds or maybe thousands of pounds or euros, governments and companies borrow or lend in millions of pounds or euros. Thus the money markets are termed **wholesale markets** rather than **retail markets**.

Interest often comes from discount pricing

When manufacturing firms, financial institutions, governments, etc. find themselves in need of short-term funds they often sell an instrument which carries the promise to pay, say, £10 million in 30 days from now. For many of the money market instruments the purchaser of that promise will not pay as much as £10 million because they want to receive an effective interest rate for lending. So they might pay, say, £9.9 million. Thus the security is sold for less than face value. The **discount** is the difference between face value and purchase price. The yield, the rate of interest gained by the holder, occurs when the instrument reaches maturity and the face value is paid by the issuer to the holder. In this case the return, if the instrument is held to maturity, i.e. for 30 days, would be £100,000, which equates to 1.01% (£100,000 ÷ £9,900,000 = 1.01%). To compare returns on different financial securities, it is necessary to work out the annual rate, which is explained in Chapters 12 and 14.

(Note that while most money market securities are issued at a discount, this is not true of all of them. Certificates of deposit and **interbank deposits** (banks lending for short periods to each other), for example, are issued at their face value and then redeemed at a higher value.)

Secondary trading in the money markets

With many money market instruments the original purchaser is able to sell the instrument in the secondary market on to another investor before maturity if they want to raise some cash themselves; thus these securities are said to be liquid or negotiable. So, staying with the example, after 20 days the original lender might sell this promise to pay £10 million in a further 10 days for, say, £9.96 million. Thus a profit can be made by trading the instruments on the secondary market before they reach the redemption date – in this case £60,000.

However, it must be noted that a loss may be incurred by selling in the secondary market. If, say, the original lender can only attract buyers at a price of £9.87 million then it makes a £30,000 loss. This low price may occur if, say, interest rates on similar financial instruments with 10 days to maturity are now yielding a higher rate of return because lenders have become more wary and are demanding higher rates of return to compensate for higher risk – a lot can change in the financial markets in 20 days. The potential secondary market purchaser would be silly to pay a price higher (receive a lower yield) than the going market rate for this particular issue when there are better deals to be had – i.e. the potential buyer has an **opportunity cost** (the return on the best alternative use of their investment money) and so the best the original lender can get is £9.87 million, if it has to sell. If it can avoid selling for another 10 days then it will receive the full £10 million from the borrower/issuer.

The discount and rate of interest (yield) earned are dependent on the risk level and the maturity of the instrument. The maturity is the length of time between issue of the instrument (start of borrowing) and the time it is redeemed when money due is paid (**original maturity**), or the length of time between when a security is priced or purchased in the secondary market and the date of redemption (**current maturity**). The maturity length can vary from overnight (borrowing for just 24 hours) to 3 months to 1 year (or more, occasionally). Interest is measured in percentage points, which are further divided into **basis points (bps)**. One basis point equals 1/100 of a percentage point.

There are various types of money market instruments:

- **Treasury bills** are government-issued money market instruments. Most governments round the world issue Treasury bills, often at government-run auctions, and some countries' bills are regarded as 'risk-free', better defined as the lowest chance of default compared with all other financial securities. There is a strong secondary market in these bills, and their secondary market price (and hence their yield) will fluctuate according to current conditions. (There is more on Treasury bills in Chapter 9.)

- **Commercial paper** is a very popular way of raising money for large, well-regarded companies. For example, a corporation wishes to borrow £100 million for two months. It issues commercial paper with a face value of £101 million, payable in 60 days' time. A purchaser is prepared to accept the promise of the company to pay out in 60 days and so buys some of the commercial paper, paying £25 million for one-quarter of the total issue at a discount to the face value. In 60 days' time, the purchaser collects £25.25 million from the corporation. It has earned £250,000 in return for lending the corporation £25 million. (More detail on commercial paper can be found in Chapter 9.)

- **Repurchase agreements (repos)** are a way of borrowing for a few days using a **sale and repurchase agreement** in which securities (e.g. government bonds) are sold for cash at an agreed price with a promise to buy back the securities at a specified (higher) price at a future date. The interest on the agreement is the difference between the initial sale price and the agreed buy-back, and because the agreements are usually collateralised (secured) by government-backed securities such as Treasury bills, the interest rate is lower than a typical unsecured loan from a bank. If the borrower defaults on its obligations to buy back on maturity the lender can hold on to or sell the securities. Banks and other financial institutions use repos very regularly to borrow money from each other. Companies do use the repo markets, but much less frequently than the banks. (There is more on repos in Chapter 10.)

- **Local authority issues** are short-term instruments issued by local authorities to finance capital expenditure and cash flow needs. They tend to be regarded as relatively safe investments. There is a strong market in local authority bills and bonds in many European countries, notably France,

Italy and Germany, where individual federal states issue them regularly. There are also many bill issues by companies close to governments, e.g. the French railway, SNCF, or the German postal service, Deutsche Bundespost.

- **Certificates of deposit (CDs)** are issued by banks when funds are deposited with them by other banks, corporations, individuals or investment companies. The certificates state that a deposit has been made (a **time deposit**) and that at the maturity date the bank will pay a sum higher than that originally deposited. The maturities are typically one to four months and can be negotiable or non-negotiable. (You can find more on this in Chapter 10.) There is a penalty on the saver withdrawing the money before the maturity date (they are **term securities**). A company with surplus cash can put it into a negotiable CD knowing that if its situation changes and it needs extra cash, it can sell the CD for cash in a secondary market.

- **Bills of exchange** and **banker's acceptances** are commercial financial instruments, often linked to international trade (exports), which enable corporations to obtain credit or raise money and to trade with corporations at low risk of financial inconvenience or loss. Once issued, they may be traded on the secondary markets. (There is more on these instruments in Chapter 11.)

The markets in short-term money

Money markets exist all over the world as a means of facilitating business. **Domestic money market** means that the funds are borrowed and lent in the country's home currency and under the authority of the country's regulators. There are also money markets outside the jurisdiction of authorities of the currency of their denomination – these are the **Euro money markets**. This is nothing to do with the currency in Europe: they were termed 'Euro markets' long before the euro was dreamed up.

Money markets are used by a wide variety of organisations, from treasury departments of corporations to banks and finance companies (e.g. raising large sums in the money markets to then provide hundreds of loans to people wanting to buy cars on hire purchase deals). Pension funds and insurance companies maintain a proportion of their investment funds in liquid, low-risk form (they lend on the money markets) to meet unpredictable cash outflows, e.g.

following a hurricane. These markets are also used by central banks to influence interest rates charged throughout the economy – for example, changing base rates at banks through the central bank conducting repo deals in the market will have a knock-on effect on mortgage rates or business loan rates.

In the modern era, rather than having one or a few market locations or buildings in which money market instruments are bought and sold, we have organisations arranging deals over the telephone and then completing them electronically. The process of bringing buyers and sellers together is assisted by the many brokers and dealers who tend to operate from the trading rooms of the big banks and specialist trading houses – they regularly trade money market securities in lots worth tens of millions of pounds, dollars, etc. Some of them act as **market makers**, maintaining an inventory of securities and advertising prices at which they will sell and, slightly lower, prices at which they will buy. By providing these middle-man services they assist the players in the market to quickly find a counterparty willing to trade, thus enhancing liquidity. They are said to be traders in **STIR products**, that is **short-term interest rate products**.

Some of the trades are simply private deals with legal obligations to be enforced by each side, but some are conducted through a **central clearing house**, with each party responsible for reporting the deal to the clearing house, which settles the deal by debiting the account of the buyer and crediting the account of the seller. The clearing house then holds the security on behalf of the buyer. The risk of a counterparty reneging on the deal (**counterparty risk**) is reduced by trading through a clearing house because the clearing house itself usually becomes a guarantor to each party.

Case study

Vodafone

You can get some idea of the importance of money markets to companies from Table 1.2 showing investment amounts taken from Vodafone's annual reports. Vodafone keeps a large amount of cash and cash equivalents in reserve: over £7 billion in 2013. **Cash equivalents** are not quite cash but they are so liquid that they are **near-cash** (**near-money** or **quasi-money**). They are financial assets that can easily be sold to raise cash, or which are due to pay back their capital value in a few days, with low risk regarding the amount of cash they will release. These are mostly money market instruments.

Vodafone keeps such a large quantity of money available in this highly liquid and low-risk form so that it can supply its various business units with the cash they need for day-to-day operations or for regular investment projects. Also, it is useful to have readily accessible money to be able to take advantage of investment opportunities as they fleetingly appear (e.g. the purchase of a company). Alternatively, the cash and near-cash is there because the company has recently had a major inflow – perhaps it sold a division or has had bumper profits – and it has not yet allocated the money to its final uses, such as paying billions in dividends to shareholders, launching a new product, buying another company or simply paying a tax bill. In the meantime that money might as well be earning Vodafone some interest, so the money that is surplus to the immediate needs of Vodafone's various business units is gathered together and temporarily lent to other organisations in the money markets.

Vodafone also uses the money markets to borrow money. For example, at 2013 year-end it had more than £4 billion owing to purchasers of its commercial paper. This was borrowed (and had to be repaid) in sterling, US dollars, euros and Japanese yen. But this is not the half of it. Vodafone had arrangements with banks to borrow via commercial paper as much as US$15 billion and £5 billion at any one time. The banks committing to this deal will generally make arrangements for other investors to supply this finance if Vodafone wishes to borrow this way to meet short-term liquidity requirements at any point in the year.

Table 1.2 Money market holdings and cash taken from Vodafone's annual reports, 2008–2013

Cash and cash equivalents	2013 £m	2012 £m	2011 £m	2010 £m	2009 £m	2008 £m
Cash at bank and in hand	1,396	2,762	896	745	811	451
Money market funds	3,494	3,190	5,015	3,678	3,419	477
Repurchase agreements	2,550	600	–	–	648	478
Commercial paper	–	–	–	–	–	293
Short term securitised investments	183	586	–	–	–	–
Other	–	–	341	–	–	–
Cash and cash equivalents as presented in the balance sheet (statement of financial position)	7,623	7,138	6,252	4,423	4,878	1,699

Money market funds

Despite the wholesale nature of the money markets entailing the transacting of large sums of money – usually £500,000 or $1,000,000 is the minimum transaction size – it is possible for private individuals with funds available for lending in thousands of pounds/euros/dollars rather than hundreds of thousands to participate in the money markets. They can do so via **money market funds** administered by financial institutions and set up to invest in money market instruments by pooling the savings of many people.

Corporations may also deposit money in money market funds to obtain good rates of interest through professional management of the fund. They also value being able to withdraw their money from the fund without the need to deal with the selling of the underlying securities in the secondary markets – in most cases investors in money market funds can gain access to their money within hours: 'same-day' access. It is also possible to put in place a **sweep facility** so that money is automatically transferred from a bank account (paying little interest) if it exceeds a stated balance to a money market account (paying more interest) and vice versa – this can be done at the end of each day.

With much of the rest of the financial sector, money markets went through a crisis in 2008. A money market fund, Reserve Primary Fund, had invested a substantial proportion of its funds in Lehman Brothers' short-term debt. When Lehman Brothers went bust the fund was unable to return to investors the amount they had paid into it. This **'breaking of the buck'** is a great sin in the money market world – all money market funds are supposed to be incredibly safe. What made it worse was the subsequent freezing-up of credit markets: investors in funds could not withdraw their money at short notice as per the agreement. The market became illiquid because the money market funds could not find buyers for the securities they held and so could not raise cash at the moment when a high proportion of their investors clamoured to withdraw cash.

A proposal was floating around the corridors of power of the European Commission in 2014 to reform the rules for money market funds. In Europe there is over €450 billion invested in **constant net asset value** (CNAV) or **fixed-value money market funds** which promise the return of a euro/dollar put in, while paying out the interest they receive from Treasury bills, etc. to investors. The **variable net asset value** (VNAV) money market sector is even larger. These funds fluctuate in value each day depending on the market value of the underlying investments; they may go below the initial €1 value. The proposal is to force CNAV funds to hold 3% of their assets in cash as a buffer against 'runs' by investors, so that those wanting their money returned quickly can have it without too much strain caused by funds having to sell securities in a hurry.

However, there were howls of protest that the loss of interest on 3% of the fund was too much to bear at a time when money market funds were struggling to make even a 0.1% return in a year for investors because interest rates were so low – see Article 1.1. In 2015 the politicians decided to abandon the 3% buffer rule. Instead they insist that most CNAV funds switch to a 'low-volatility NAV', which means they can only hold money market instruments which mature within 90 days. The other 10% of CNAV are allowed to escape this rule if they are aimed purely at 'retail' investors or if they invest 99.5% of their assets in government debt. (In the article, 'AUM' is assets under management – the amount they are investing for others.)

In July 2014 the regulator in the US, the Securities and Exchange Commission (SEC), gained the power to force some CNAV funds to scrap their fixed $1-a-share price structure, permitting the fund to continue even if the underlying money market investments, e.g. commercial paper, add up to less than $1 per share. This applies to funds invested in corporate debt and municipal (local authority) debt. Those that buy only federal government debt or are sold only to retail investors are exempt, so they stay as CNAV funds.

Article 1.1

Money funds at risk of big drop in assets

By Christopher Thompson and Stephen Foley

Financial Times November 21, 2013

Global money market funds are projected to lose around a third of their assets under management next year as the combined forces of record low interest rates and new regulations batter the multi-trillion dollar industry.

Incoming rules from regulators in the US and Europe could trigger outflows of at least 30%, according to Moody's, the credit rating agency. Under US and European regulators' proposals money market funds are potentially moving from a stable $1 or €1 net asset value to one that will fluctuate according to the market value of the underlying investments.

'If the regulation comes in as proposed we expect a 30% or higher decline of AUM because of the likely switch to "variable net asset values" by most managers,' said Yaron Ernst, a managing director of global managed investments at Moody's.

Money market funds, which act as reservoirs of easy-to-access cash, are a crucial source of short-term financing for banks and companies worldwide. They are used by corporates and others to diversify short-term cash holdings and are widely perceived as low risk.

'We are overwhelmingly invested in senior bank debt of less than three months' maturity . . . the default risk on those assets is almost non-existent according to long-term studies,' said Martin Curran, a senior portfolio manager at Royal Bank of Scotland. 'With variable net asset values a corporate cash manager puts £1 into a MMF to pay his bills, but it might not repay £1 the day after – he can't afford to be in that position, and particularly if he's managing millions of them.'

In the US, the Securities and Exchange Commission has proposed limiting investors' ability to withdraw their cash from money market funds during times of market stress, and is currently weighing whether this idea is better than a floating NAV, or whether it can combine the two. The changes would only affect part of the industry. The SEC plans to exempt funds that invest only in super-safe government securities, and those targeted at retail investors, who are seen as less likely to start a run on a fund.

The gloomy Moody's prognosis comes as low interest rates, which squeeze funds' already wafer-thin margins, have led to declines in assets under management for many funds.

'Fees have already been waived for more than a year by most MMF managers, which reflects the stress on the industry's business model,' said Mr Ernst.

Euro-denominated money market funds shed €127bn of assets between June 2011–13 according to Moody's figures. HSBC estimates that the US industry has seen assets decline from $4tn in 2009 to about $2.7tn.

Regulators say they want to bolster money market funds and avoid a run on the market in the event of a financial crisis, which would lead to global finance freezing up.

PART 2
BOND MARKETS

CHAPTER 2
GOVERNMENT BONDS

Most governments issue bonds in their domestic currency to raise money when their tax receipts are less than their expenditure. There is a robust international market for these bonds when the national currency is strong and stable, such as the currencies in Figure 2.1; this data from the International Monetary Fund (IMF) shows the percentage of foreign currencies kept in reserve by 144 reporting countries.[1] These currencies are known as **hard currencies**, that is, they are from countries where there is relative economic and political stability and the currencies are widely accepted in payment for goods or services.

If the national currency is unstable or weak for whatever reason the government may be able to issue bonds denominated in a foreign hard currency, usually the US dollar. This makes them more attractive to investors because they are viewed as less risky than **domestic currency bonds** because the government is committed to paying interest and principal in, say, the US dollar, regardless of inflation or exchange rate movement in that country. Bonds issued by a government either in the country's own currency or in another currency are usually known as **sovereign bonds**.

Following the round of financial crises, most governments have had to issue more bonds to permit **deficit spending** (i.e. not raising enough in taxes to cover outgoings to boost the economy). Statistics from *The Economist* from a range of countries show the enormous amount of debt some countries

---

[1] **Foreign currency reserves** or **foreign exchange reserves** (**FOREX reserves** or **FX reserves**) are held by the national central bank or other monetary authority. They usually consist of a range of hard foreign currency and bonds issued by other governments (popular usage of the term usually also includes gold reserves, shares and the ability to draw money from the IMF). These are saved to reduce the risk of not being able to pay off international debt obligations, thus increasing the confidence of overseas creditors that the country will not default. They also allow the purchase of the domestic currency, thus influencing monetary policy and exchange rates.

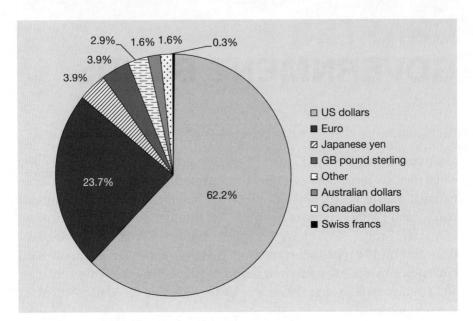

Figure 2.1 Currency composition of foreign exchange reserves 2013

Source: Data from www.imf.org

owe – see Figure 2.2. For every person in Italy, the government owes more than $39,000. It is even worse in Japan, where the government owes over $98,000 per person. In both cases the debt is mostly bought domestically rather than lent by foreigners, and so the risk of a foreign lenders' strike or a major outflow of interest payments is less worrisome. Nevertheless, that is an awful lot of borrowing.

Bonds issued by reputable governments are the most secure (least risky) in the world because they are very aware of the need to maintain a good reputation for paying their debts on time. Furthermore, for countries able to issue in their own currencies, should there be a cash flow difficulty, they are able to print more money or to raise taxes, to ensure they have the means to pay the bonds' coupons or the bonds' redemption value. But if money creation is taken too far, raised inflation may be the result, putting off potential lenders in that currency.

We first look at the UK government bond market to get a feel for the workings of these markets and then, in Chapter 3, consider the US, French, German, Japanese, Chinese and emerging (underdeveloped) government bond markets.

Canada total: $1,633bn Per person: $46,498	UK total: $2,525bn Per person: $39,691	Sweden total: $194bn Per person: $20,067
Russia total: $202bn Per person: $1,436	Netherlands total: $579bn Per person: $34,386	Denmark total: $150bn Per person: $26,476
Japan total: $12,331bn Per person: $98,246	USA total: $13,646bn Per person: $43,049	France total: $2,423bn Per person: $37,801
Germany total: $2,794bn Per person: $34,212	China total: $1,624bn Per person: $1,212	Spain total: $1,067bn Per person: $22,906
Italy total: $2,405bn Per person: $39,289	Malaysia total: $210bn Per person: $7,158	Portugal total: $279bn Per person: $26,101
India total: $1,267bn Per person: $1,024	Brazil total: $1,576bn Per person: $8,007	Australia total: $398bn Per person: $17,038
Chile total: $23bn Per person: $1,332	Argentina total: $194bn Per person: $4,652	N Zealand total: $76bn Per person: $16,557
Global total: $53,503bn Per person: $7,643		

Figure 2.2 Total public debt for a selection of countries: total amount outstanding in $USbn

UK gilts

In most years, in common with other countries in the world, the British government does not raise enough in taxes to cover its expenditure – see Figure 2.3, which shows the amount the UK public sector (central and local government) had to borrow between 2000 and 2014 to make up this deficit and to maintain stability and restore confidence. Note the significant rise following the 2008 financial crisis as the government borrowed to cover falling tax receipts, boost aggregate demand and bail out the banks.

In addition to these 'net borrowing' amounts the UK government issues new debt instruments to raise money simply to repay old debts that become due. Thus, the **gross borrowing (gross issuance)** is actually much larger – of the order of an extra £50–60 billion per year.

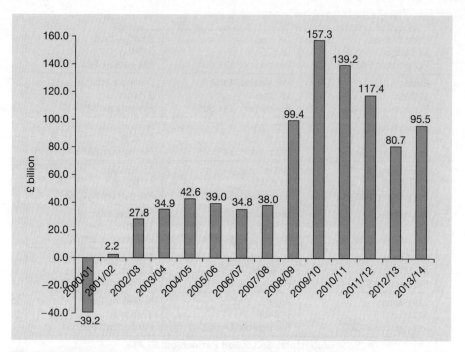

Figure 2.3 UK public sector (central and local government) net borrowing 2000–2014 (the difference between expenditure and revenue)

Source: ONS Public Sector Finances, March 2014 www.ons.gov.uk/ons/dcp171778_360531.pdf

While most of the gap between UK government receipts and expenditure is covered by selling bonds to investors, the government may also borrow via its **National Savings and Investments** arm, such as through premium bonds, and raise income from selling off assets, e.g. Royal Mail shares, Lloyds Bank shares.

UK government bonds are called gilts because in the old days they were very attractive certificates with gold-leaf edges (**gilt-edged securities**). Lending to the UK government by buying gilts is one of the safest forms of lending in the world; the risk of the UK government failing to pay is inconceivably small – it has never done so, although a few doubts did creep in following the high government spending during 2010–2011 when the volume of gilts outstanding grew enormously – see Figure 2.4. There are so many gilts held by investors and financial institutions that they equal more than 75% of the amount of output that UK citizens produce in one year (GDP).

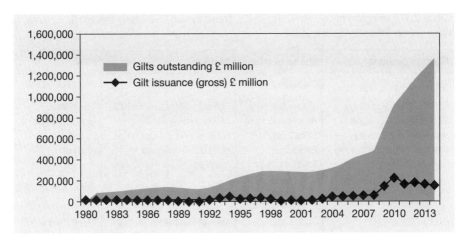

Figure 2.4 The amount of UK government gilts in issue up to 2014 and gross issuance (includes gilts sold to replace maturing gilts being redeemed)

Source: Debt Management Office www.DMO.gov.uk

Issuing gilts

The UK government issues most gilts through auction via the **Debt Management Office (DMO)** and each issue receives a unique identification number, an **ISIN (International Securities Identification Number)**. Gilts are issued with a par (face) value of £100. This is the amount guaranteed to be paid on maturity to the holder, who may or may not be the original purchaser. Their maturity can be 5, 10, 30, 40, 50 and recently 55 years, and during the time to maturity they pay a twice-yearly coupon, the amount of which reflects the current and expected future rates of interest at the time of issue.

Most are conventional bonds, but since 1981 gilts have been issued which offset the effect of inflation; the coupons and principal paid on these are linked to the Retail Prices Index (RPI) over the life of the bond and are known as **index-linked gilts**. Table 2.1 gives examples of conventional and index-linked gilts.

In March 2014 there were 72 gilts in issue with a total outstanding value (including inflation uplift for index-linked gilts) of about £1.4 trillion and of varying maturities – see Figure 2.5. The maturity of a gilt is measured by the remaining time left to redemption.

Table 2.1 Examples of two gilts, the 4¼% Treasury Gilt 2039 and the 2½% Index-linked Treasury Stock 2024

Coupon amount	Name of gilt	Maturity	ISIN
4¼%	Treasury Gilt	2039	GB00B3KJDS62
£100 × 4¼% ÷ 2. Thus £2.125 will be paid on set dates at 6 monthly intervals to the gilt holder	Those issued in recent years are called Treasury Stocks or Treasury Gilts	The gilt will mature in 2039 at which time the final coupon and the par value of £100 will be paid to the holder	The ISIN is a unique number identifying each gilt
2½%	Index-linked Treasury Stock	2024	GB0008983024
£100 × 2½% ÷ 2. Thus £1.25 plus an increase to take inflation into account will be paid on set dates at 6 monthly intervals to the gilt holder	Those issued in recent years are called Treasury Stocks or Treasury Gilts	The gilt will mature in 2024 at which time the final coupon and the par value of £100 plus an increase to take inflation into account will be paid to the holder	The ISIN is a unique number identifying each gilt

Source: www.DMO.gov.uk

The UK authorities define the maturities of gilts as:

- ultra-short conventional   up to 3 years
- short conventional   3–7 years
- medium conventional   7–15 years
- long conventional   15–50 years
- ultra-long conventional   over 50 years
- undated
- index-linked   various

An analysis of the 72 gilts in issue is as follows:

- 40 conventional, with more than £1 trillion of nominal value.
- 24 index-linked, with over £300 billion of nominal value (including the inflation uplift). Of that total, 19 are subject to an inflation uplift in the coupon with a three-month inflation indexation lag (a coupon payable today is raised by inflation that occurred up to a date three months ago) and 5 (issued before 2000) subject to an inflation uplift lagged by eight months. The coupon and principal payment of these is increased according to the

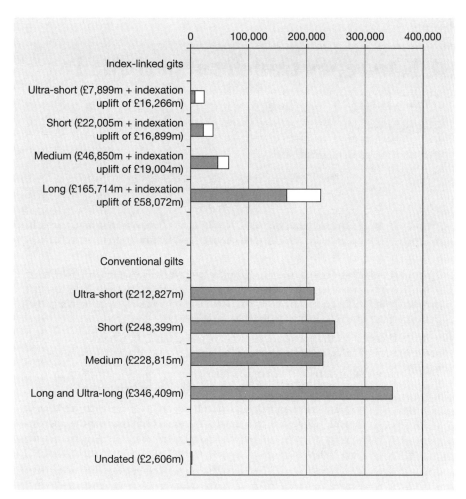

Figure 2.5 UK gilts in issue 12 March 2014, in millions of pounds
Source: DMO, Quarterly Review January–March 2014

change in the RPI. The RPI is published monthly by the Office for National Statistics and measures the change in price of a representative basket of retail goods and services.

● Eight undated older gilts issued between 1853 and 1946 with no redemption date. They pay their coupons in perpetuity, but can be redeemed at the discretion of the government – see Article 2.1. Most pay semi-annual coupons but some pay interest each quarter. Their nominal value is £2.6 billion.

● More than 170 STRIPS of gilts (discussed later in this chapter).

Article 2.1

UK to repay tranche of perpetual war loans

By Elaine Moore

Financial Times October 31, 2014

One of Britain's oldest and most unusual national debts is to be repaid, marking the end of an era for a government bond that can trace its lineage back to the 18th century.

As Europe marks the centenary of the Great War, the Treasury has announced it will redeem bonds issued in 1927 by then chancellor Winston Churchill to refinance money borrowed to fund it.

Around 11,200 investors hold the 4% Consolidated Loan, the vast majority of whom are individuals with less than £10,000. Now the government is seeking to take advantage of falling borrowing costs on global capital markets by refinancing the debt at a time when long-dated gilt yields are at a 60-year low.

The '4% Consols', as the bonds are known, are perpetual gilts which have no fixed redemption date, giving the government the right to repay them at any time.

On February 1 all investors will be repaid their principal, marking the first time in almost 70 years that the British government has repaid a perpetual bond.

'This is a great example of pragmatic and attentive debt management on the part of the UK government. I hope that this move is the first of many to cut the interest bill and save taxpayers money,' said Toby Nangle, head of multi-asset allocation at Threadneedle Asset Management, who has argued that the UK could save £300m by exercising its right to call the larger £2bn perpetual 'War Loan'. Threadneedle is the second-biggest holder of the bond.

The government said it was looking into the practicalities of repaying the loan, which has a 3.5% coupon and trades below face value.

'Some investors had doubted whether the 3.5% coupon war loan would ever be bought back by the Treasury but this is now clearly on the table,' said Michael Riddell at M&G Investments, which also holds the bonds.

The UK has one of the world's oldest government debt markets and the consolidation of bonds over the years means that the debt redeemed has its origin in the South Sea Bubble crisis of 1720 and the Napoleonic and Crimean wars.

On Twitter, George Osborne, the chancellor, wrote: 'We'll redeem £218m of 4% Consols, including debts incurred because of the South Sea Bubble. Another financial crisis we're clearing up after.'

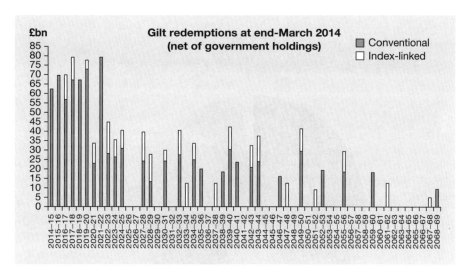

Figure 2.6 When gilts will be redeemed

Source: DMO, Quarterly Review January–March 2014 www.dmo.gov.uk/documentview.aspx?docname=publications/quarterly/jan-mar14.pdf&page=Quarterly_Review

The average maturity for conventional gilts currently outstanding is about 15 years, and for index-linked is 21 years – see Figures 2.6 and 2.7.

When gilts are sold by the government with a nominal value of £100, only the 20 Gilt-edged Market Makers (GEMMs)[2] can submit competitive bids at the auction. They may do this for themselves or for their clients. For conventional gilts, all those who bid above the minimum needed to sell the bonds pay the price they bid (a **multiple price auction**). For index-linked gilts the pricing at the conclusion of the auction is different: all bidders pay the same lowest accepted price rather than each paying the price at which they bid (a **uniform price auction**).[3] In return for exclusive access to auctions GEMMs must commit

---

[2] GEMMs are a group of commercial banks/financial institutions/brokers, the number of which has varied between 20 and 30, and at the time of writing is 20.

[3] The index-linked market has fewer similar gilts already trading in the secondary market to allow investors to gauge where to pitch their bid, therefore they face the danger of over-pricing if they have to pay the price they offer. This 'winner's curse' problem is off-putting to investors and so to attract them, the DMO prices all index-linked bonds at a level that will sell the bonds – even if a particular investor bids a very high price it will pay the same as the other successful bidders. The conventional gilt market is much more liquid, with many more comparators for bidders to gauge where to pitch their bids, and so the winner's curse disincentive does not have much of an impact, thus the DMO can get away with charging higher prices to some buyers.

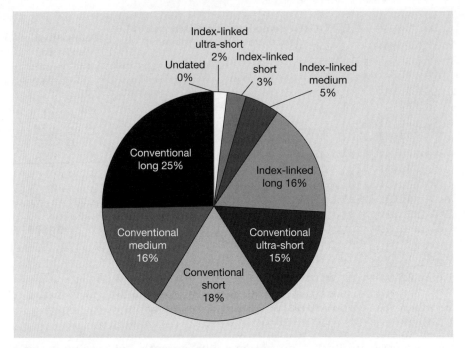

Figure 2.7 Gilts in issue 12 March 2014

Source: DMO, Quarterly Review January–March 2014

to making a secondary market for gilts by providing continuous prices at which they will buy or sell for the gilts in which they deal.

As well as GEMMs submitting competitive bids at the auction, they can take up the **post-auction option facility (PAOF)**, which enables successful bidders to acquire up to an extra 10% of their allocation at the average accepted (strike) price at conventional auctions and at the single clearing (strike) price at index-linked auctions.

Following an auction GEMMs can trade in the secondary market directly with investors, making available advertised prices between 8am and 5pm every business day in all those gilts in which they are recognised as market maker. They quote two prices: the **bid** price is the price at which they will buy, the **offer** price is their selling price. The difference between the bid price and the offer price is known as the **dealer's spread**, i.e. their potential profit. They are also able to trade gilts anonymously with each other through **interdealer brokers (IDBs)**, who act as intermediaries for GEMMs. IDBs are required to post deals done on their screens for all other GEMMs to see. Below is the list of GEMMs and interdealer brokers at the time of writing.

GEMMs	Interdealer brokers
† Barclays Bank plc	BGC Brokers L.P.
BNP Paribas (London branch)	BrokerTec Europe Limited
Citigroup Global Markets Limited	Dowgate
Credit Suisse Securities	GFI Securities Limited
Deutsche Bank AG (London branch)	ICAP WCLK Limited
Goldman Sachs International Bank	Tullett Prebon Gilts
† HSBC Bank plc	
* Jefferies International Limited	
JPMorgan Securities plc	
Lloyds TSB Bank plc	
Merrill Lynch International	
Morgan Stanley & Co. International plc	
Nomura International plc	
Royal Bank of Canada Europe Limited	
† Royal Bank of Scotland	
Santander Global Banking & Markets UK	
Scotiabank Europe plc	
Société Générale Corporate & Investment Banking	
* The Toronto-Dominion Bank (London branch)	
UBS Limited	

† STRIPS market participant
* Retail GEMM

Table 2.2 shows details for the gilts issued over a one-month period. Note a strange phenomenon in 2014: index-linked issues could be sold at a yield of less than zero before taking into account the inflation uplift, e.g. while the '⅛% Index-linked Treasury Gilt 2019' has a nominal coupon yield of positive one-eighth of 1% per year, it sold at a price of £105.83. The capital loss of £5.83 over the five years (because it will be redeemed at £100 (plus inflation)) means that the yield will be negative 0.918% per annum before inflation uplift. This is an indication that investors were so desperate to invest in 'safe-haven' assets with both high default protection and some inflation protection that they accepted returns guaranteeing a real-terms reduction of capital value. **Bid to cover ratio** means the amount investors offered to buy relative to the amount offered for sale.

Table 2.2 Examples of the results of gilt auctions

Auction date	Gilt name	Indexation lag for index-linked gilts	Amount issued (£m nominal)	Bid to cover ratio at auction	Average accepted price (£)	Yield at average accepted price (%)
12 June 2014	0⅛% Index-linked Treasury Gilt 2019	3 months	1,469.76	2.78	105.830	−0.918
10 June 2014	2¾% Treasury Gilt 2024		3,250.00	2.04	99.383	2.820
3 June 2014	1¾% Treasury Gilt 2019		4,028.42	1.61	99.095	1.936
28 May 2014	0¼% Index-linked Treasury Gilt 2052	3 months	1,209.97	2.56	112.068	−0.065
15 May 2014	4½% Treasury Gilt 2034		2,181.56	2.00	118.591	3.243

Source: www.dmo.gov.uk

Primary market for retail investors

As well as being able to buy gilts in the secondary market through GEMMs, individuals may bid at auctions providing they have applied for and been accepted into the **Approved Group of Investors**.[4] The DMOs auction calendar is published up to a year in advance (see www.dmo.gov.uk), but greater details of the gilts to be offered for sale are announced a week or so beforehand. Approved Group investors can then obtain a prospectus and application form. They may make one *non-competitive bid* per auction between £1,000 and £500,000 (nominal prices) and they pay the average price set by the successful competitive bidders for conventional gilts and the lowest accepted price for index-linked gilts. Each bid must be a multiple of £1,000. Buyers send payment large enough to more than cover the cost – the exact amount will not be known beforehand as this depends on the results of the competitive auction. After the auction refunds are made for the difference between the amount sent and the amount actually paid.

Investors wishing to bid for more than £500,000 nominal in a competitive bid must submit their bids through a GEMM stating the price they wish to pay. If

---

[4] A piece of bureaucracy designed to exclude money launderers and other financial criminals. Application forms are available from the DMO. The approval process takes a few days.

the bid is below the price required to sell the gilts available they will receive no bonds, or only a proportion of those bid for.

Syndication and mini-tenders

Some gilts are sold by **syndication**, a process whereby the DMO appoints a group of investment banks to manage the sale of the bonds on its behalf. **Lead managers** and **co-lead managers** (the chosen banks) market the issue to investors. They '**build a book**', that is, they converse with potential investors and gain indications of offers for the bonds. When the size of the book (serious offers) reaches the DMO's sale objectives, the book is closed and bonds are allocated to investors at the prices previously discussed. In the period following the financial crisis the DMO increased the use of syndications significantly because it had to sell a vast quantity of gilts and the banks were capable of actively finding buyers.

Mini-tenders also take place between the major auctions. They are smaller issues which supplement the main auction sales, and are designed to tap into emerging pockets of demand for particular gilts.

Supplementary issues

If a gilt already in issue is 'supplemented' (more issued) it keeps the same ISIN number – see Table 2.3, where we can see the details of a 3¾% Treasury Gilt with a redemption date of 2021, issued originally on 18 March 2011 with an initial issuance of £2.75 billion and paying a coupon of £3.75 annually in two equal semi-annual payments made on fixed dates six months apart; with gilt GB00B4RMG977 these payments are on 7 March and 7 September each year.

Since it was first sold, the government raised more money with this gilt, ending up with a total issuance of nearly £28 billion. The purchase (market) price of a gilt varies, depending on the coupon offered, the general level of interest rates in the markets, dealers' perception of future interest rates, and present and expected inflation rates. For gilt GB00B4RMG977 the initial price was £100.80 and the subsequent prices varied between £98.91 and £114.49. At maturity it will be worth £100 and as a gilt approaches maturity its price will become ever nearer to its par value.

Table 2.3 Issuance details of Treasury gilt GB00B4RMG977

Gilt name	ISIN code	Issue date	Clean price at issue (£)	Yield at issue (%)	Nominal amount issued (£ million)	Cumulative total amount in issue (£ million)
3¾% Treasury Gilt 2021	GB00B4RMG977	18-Mar-2011	100.80	3.657	2,750.000	2,750.000
3¾% Treasury Gilt 2021	GB00B4RMG977	06-Apr-2011	98.91	3.878	3,807.112	6,557.112
3¾% Treasury Gilt 2021	GB00B4RMG977	03-Jun-2011	102.88	3.414	3,603.787	10,160.899
3¾% Treasury Gilt 2021	GB00B4RMG977	06-Jul-2011	102.03	3.510	3,572.947	13,733.846
3¾% Treasury Gilt 2021	GB00B4RMG977	02-Sep-2011	108.59	2.762	3,000.000	16,733.846
3¾% Treasury Gilt 2021	GB00B4RMG977	05-Oct-2011	113.37	2.239	3,574.970	20,308.816
3¾% Treasury Gilt 2021	GB00B4RMG977	19-Oct-2011	N/A	N/A	440.000	20,748.816
3¾% Treasury Gilt 2021	GB00B4RMG977	02-Dec-2011	111.85	2.382	3,298.400	24,047.216
3¾% Treasury Gilt 2021	GB00B4RMG977	12-Jan-2012	114.49	2.084	3,282.568	27,329.784
3¾% Treasury Gilt 2021	GB00B4RMG977	17-Jul-2012	N/A	N/A	379.000	27,708.784

Source: www.dmo.gov.uk

From the **clean price** (the price of the gilt excluding any accrued interest since the last coupon was paid – see later in the chapter) and yield at issue we can gain an impression of how the prevailing rate of interest for securities with a similar risk and maturity changed over the period March 2011 to January 2012, falling 157 basis points. Indeed, interest rates usually change daily, even if usually by very small amounts.

Who buys gilts?

Table 2.4 shows that the main purchasers of gilts are outside of the UK. Also, in recent years, one buyer has gone from being quite small to being dominant: the Bank of England bought large amounts of gilts on the secondary market to lower interest rates and try to revive the post-crisis economy (see Chapter 16 for a discussion of this 'quantitative easing').

Table 2.4 Distribution of UK gilt holders December 2013

(£ millions) at end	Q3 2013	Q4 2013
Overseas	393,937	413,104
Bank of England (Asset Purchase Facility)	373,561	367,486
Insurance companies and pension funds	370,019	365,027
Monetary Financial Institutions*	122,458	133,349
Other financial institutions and other	88,779	89,882
Households	16,882	12,093
Local authorities and public corporations	2,206	2,155
TOTAL	**1,367,842**	**1,383,096**

* 'Monetary Financial Institutions' replaced the 'Banks' and 'Building Societies' categories in January 2011 and excludes Bank of England holdings.

Source: DMO, Quarterly Review January–March 2014 www.dmo.gov.uk/documentview.aspx?docname= publications/quarterly/jan-mar14.pdf&page=Quarterly_Review

Article 2.2 discusses the operations of the DMO, with particular reference to the necessity to sell gilts to overseas investors.

Article 2.2

Hard times force UK seller of gilts on a globe-trotting journey

By Elaine Moore

Financial Times May 21, 2014

In a modest office beneath the shadow of one of London's newest skyscrapers, the man responsible for selling Britain's debt to investors around the world is explaining why he has stopped spending so much time at his desk.

'I think that since the crisis, I have gone out to Asia at least once a year,' says Robert Stheeman. 'That didn't happen before – [I] barely travelled. But the investor base is more diverse now.'

The UK's unprecedented need to borrow hundreds of billions of pounds from the markets since the financial crisis has pushed Mr Stheeman, a 54-year-old former investment banker, into the limelight over the past few years. As chief executive of the UK's Debt Management Office he is charged with ensuring the country is able to borrow as much as it needs at the lowest rate possible.

The UK's centuries-old system of raising funds by selling bonds – known as gilts after the gilded edges of the old paper certificates – has created one of the most liquid markets in the world.

Keeping up a dialogue with gilt investors is no longer a case of inviting pension funds and insurance companies for tea at the DMO's London office. Mr Stheeman must instead go out into the world to sell – hence the trips to Asia.

International investors are now the largest holders of UK debt, with £413bn – just under a third of the total – as of December. Keeping those investors engaged is not simply a matter of air miles, and the job is made more challenging by the fact that the UK does not know exactly who its overseas investors are.

Many of the central banks and sovereign wealth funds that now buy large volumes of gilts do so through nominee accounts, which do not reveal the underlying investor. 'We have an idea who they are,' he says. 'Although they don't like to show their hand.'

Composed and fond of answering a question with the aid of a chart, Mr Stheeman personifies the stability he wants investors to associate with the market. But he acknowledges substantial changes in the past decade.

In 2004–5, the country raised £50bn through gilts sales. Six years later, at the peak of the crisis in 2009, the UK had to convince the markets to absorb gilts worth £228bn. This financial year, it plans to raise £127bn.

The rise of overseas investors has also necessitated a change of strategy. Pension funds and insurance companies face liabilities in the future and want long-term investments. Overseas buyers prefer short-term investments. The result is that the number of short-dated bonds issued by the UK has grown rapidly since 2008.

'One concept I try to convey to [the government] is that we can't force people to buy our debt,' says Mr Stheeman. 'What we can do is to put in place a framework that makes it attractive to invest in.'

There have been occasions since the crisis began when the allure of gilts seemed under threat. Following the introduction of the Bank of England's gilt purchasing programme – known as Quantitative Easing – a bond auction drew fewer bids than expected for the first time in years. A few years later, credit rating agencies stripped the UK of its triple A grade, citing sluggish economic growth.

Despite these stumbling blocks, demand has remained strong as investors have sought the relative haven of UK government debt.

What he is certain about is that the UK's need to raise very large amounts of money will remain for years to come.

'The debt stock has increased so dramatically that it cannot go back to pre-crisis levels for a long time,' he says. 'Not for a generation.'

Gilts remain the main way in which the UK government finances the shortfall between what it spends and what it receives in tax revenues, and borrowing costs have been falling steadily since the 1980s when they exceeded 16%. Yields are expected to rise when the BoE finally raises interest rates above 0.5%.

Prices and returns

The coupons on different conventional gilts can have a wide range, from 1% to 8¾%. This often reflects just how much interest rates have fluctuated in the past; the coupon percentages were (roughly) the rates of interest that the government had to offer at the time of issue. These original percentages are on the face value only and are not the rates of return offered on the gilt to a buyer in the secondary market today. So, if we take an undated (with no redemption date, going on for ever) gilt offering a coupon of 2.5% on the nominal value of £100, we may find that investors are buying and selling this bond at a price of £50, not at its nominal value of £100, but still receiving the coupon of £2.50. This gilt therefore offers an investor today a yield of 5%.

If we take a redeemable Treasury 10% with five years to maturity currently selling in the secondary market at £120 we glean that it pays a coupon of £10 per year (10% of the nominal value of £100). And investors in the secondary market will receive a current yield of £10 per year for each £120 paid, which equates to 8.33%, worked out as follows:

$$\text{Interest yield} = \frac{\text{Coupon rate}}{\text{Market price}} = \frac{£10}{£120} \times 100 = 8.33\%$$

Accounting for the capital loss over the next five years: the investor pays £120 but will receive only £100 at maturity, a loss of £4 per year over the five years, or as a percentage of what the investor pays £4/£120 × 100 = 3.33% per year. The yield to maturity, YTM (redemption yield), is approximately

8.33% – 3.33% = 5% (greater precision comes in Chapter 13). The general rules are:

- If a dated gilt is trading below £100 the purchaser will receive a capital gain between purchase and redemption and so the YTM is greater than the current yield.
- If a dated gilt is selling at more than £100 a capital loss will be made if held to maturity and so the YTM is below the current yield.

Of course, these capital gains and losses are based on the assumption that the investor buys the gilt and then holds it to maturity. In reality many investors sell their bonds a few days or months after purchase, in which case they may make capital gains or losses dependent not on what the government pays on maturity but on the market price another investor is prepared to offer. This, in turn, depends on general economic conditions, in particular projected general inflation over the life of the gilt: investors will not buy a gilt offering a 5% redemption yield over five years if future inflation is expected to be significantly higher than this.

As we have seen, bond prices and yields move in opposite directions. If our five-year gilt purchased for £120 offering a coupon of 10% with an approximate redemption yield of 5% is trading in an environment where general interest rates for that risk level rise to 6% because of an increase in inflation expectations, investors will no longer be interested in buying this gilt for £120, because at this price it yields only 5%. Demand will fall, resulting in a price reduction until the bond yields 6% – the bond's market value will then be £116.85 (see calculation method in Chapter 13). A rise in yield goes hand in hand with a fall in price.

Quotes

Tables 2.5, 2.6 and 2.7, from the *Financial Times*, show the 'mid-prices' half way between the bid and the offer prices of the government-approved dealers, GEMMs.

Remember, the current redemption yield shown in the *FT* is relevant only if you are an investor on that particular day paying the price shown. This figure may change daily, reflecting interest rate changes. However, holders

Table 2.5 Gilts – UK cash market on 9 June 2014 – conventional gilts, maturity terms under 15 years

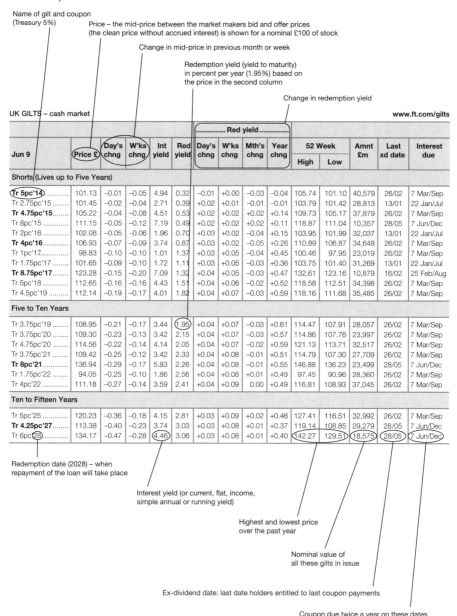

Name of gilt and coupon (Treasury 5%)

Price – the mid-price between the market makers bid and offer prices (the clean price without accrued interest) is shown for a nominal £100 of stock

Change in mid-price in previous month or week

Redemption yield (yield to maturity) in percent per year (1.95%) based on the price in the second column

Change in redemption yield

Redemption date (2028) – when repayment of the loan will take place

Interest yield (or current, flat, income, simple annual or running yield)

Highest and lowest price over the past year

Nominal value of all these gilts in issue

Ex-dividend date: last date holders entitled to last coupon payments

Coupon due twice a year on these dates

Source: Thompson Reuters

Table 2.6 Gilts – UK cash market on 9 June 2014 – conventional gilts, maturity terms over 15 years

www.ft.com/gilts

Jun 9	Price £	Day's chng	W'ks chng	Int yield	Red yield	...........Red yield............				52 Week		Amnt £m	Last xd date	Interest due
						Day's chng	W'ks chng	Mth's chng	Year chng	High	Low			
Over Fifteen Years														
Tr 4.75pc'30	119.83	−0.45	−0.32	3.95	3.19	+0.03	+0.07	+0.02	+0.34	126.11	115.50	28,716	28/05	7 Jun/Dec
Tr 4.25pc'32	113.35	−0.45	−0.33	3.73	3.26	+0.03	+0.07	+0.02	+0.30	118.75	109.05	34,598	28/05	7 Jun/Dec
Tr 4.5pc'34	117.01	−0.48	−0.37	3.83	3.34	+0.03	+0.07	+0.02	+0.26	122.28	112.57	25,501	26/02	7 Mar/Sep
Tr 4.25pc'36	113.37	−0.49	−0.38	3.73	3.38	+0.03	+0.06	+0.03	+0.24	118.17	108.92	25,952	26/02	7 Mar/Sep
Tr 4.75pc'38	122.49	−0.54	−0.43	3.86	3.39	+0.03	+0.06	+0.03	+0.20	127.24	117.68	24,601	28/05	7 Jun/Dec
Tr 4.25pc'39	113.94	−0.51	−0.41	3.71	3.42	+0.03	+0.05	+0.03	+0.18	117.87	109.28	19,280	26/02	7 Mar/Sep
Tr 4.5pc'42	119.28	−0.56	−0.45	3.76	3.43	+0.03	+0.05	+0.04	+0.14	123.05	114.24	26,001	28/05	7 Jun/Dec
Tr 3.25pc'44	95.86	−0.49	−0.39	3.37	3.48	+0.03	+0.05	+0.04	+0.10	98.22	90.69	23,778	13/01	22 Jan/Jul
Tr 4.25pc'46	115.63	−0.59	−0.49	3.66	3.45	+0.03	+0.05	+0.04	+0.10	118.71	109.84	20,873	28/05	7 Jun/Dec
Tr 4.25pc'49	116.75	−0.62	−0.54	3.62	3.43	+0.03	+0.05	+0.04	+0.05	120.05	110.52	19,301	28/05	7 Jun/Dec
Tr 3.75pc'52	106.49	−0.59	−0.51	3.50	3.44	+0.03	+0.05	+0.04	+0.03	109.48	100.30	19,761	13/01	22 Jan/Jul
Tr 4.25pc'55	118.68	−0.66	−0.56	3.56	3.41	+0.03	+0.05	+0.04	+0.02	122.22	111.43	23,416	28/05	7 Jun/Dec
Tr 4pc'60	113.86	−0.67	−0.57	3.49	3.40	+0.03	+0.05	+0.04	+0.01	117.49	106.48	18,764	13/01	22 Jan/Jul
Undated														
Cons 4pc ....*	97.09	−0.62	−0.53	4.09	4.12‡	+0.03	+0.05	+0.04	+0.01	99.91	90.45	257	22/01	1 Feb/Aug
War Ln 3.5pc	83.57	−0.52	−0.45	4.16	4.19‡	+0.03	+0.05	+0.03	+0.10	85.52	77.76	1,938	21/05	1 Jun/Dec
Cn 3.5pc'61 Aft .....*	81.43	−0.49	−0.42	–	4.30‡	+0.03	+0.05	+0.03	+0.10	83.84	77.71	17	23/03	1 Apr/Oct
Tr 3pc'66 Aft ....*	68.36	−0.41	−0.35	4.36	4.39‡	+0.03	+0.05	+0.03	+0.10	70.42	64.91	40	26/03	5 Apr/Oct
Cons 2.5pc ....*	58.57	−0.36	−0.31	4.24	4.27‡	+0.03	+0.05	+0.03	+0.10	60.43	55.54	177	26/03	5 Ja/Ap/Jul/Oc
Tr 2.5pc ....*	59.69	−0.37	−0.32	4.16	4.19‡	+0.03	+0.05	+0.03	+0.10	61.59	56.64	287	23/03	1 Apr/Oct

Source: Thomson Reuters

Table 2.7 Gilts – UK cash market on 9 June 2014 – index-linked

The real (after inflation removal) rates of return on the basis of assumed inflation of 5% and 3% (these days the real return is negative).

www.ft.com/gilts

Jun 9	Price £	Day's chng	W'ks chng	Int yield (1)	Red yield (2)	Red yield Day's chng	W'ks chng	Mth's chng	Year chng	52 Week High	Low	Amnt £m	Last xd date	Interest due
Index-linked														
2.5pc'16.............(81.6)	336.93	-0.14	-0.17	-2.27	-1.77	+0.02	+0.07	+0.15	+0.20	345.22	336.33	7,899	15/01	26 Jan/Jul
1.25pc'17† (193.725)	109.62	-0.08	-0.09	-1.46	-1.46	+0.02	+0.07	+0.08	+0.33	114.45	109.06	11,846	13/05	22 May/Nov
2.5pc'20.............(83.0)	362.83	-0.41	-0.19	-0.94	-0.76	+0.02	+0.08	+0.10	+0.47	375.79	357.72	6,579	07/04	16 Apr/Oct
1.875pc'22† (205.65806)	120.53	-0.17	-0.08	-0.50	-0.50	+0.02	+0.08	+0.06	+0.40	127.41	118.43	15,743	13/05	22 May/Nov
0.125pc'24............	103.77	-0.15	-0.04	-0.26	-0.26	+0.02	+0.08	+0.07	+0.37	108.33	100.08	8,688	12/03	22 Mar/Sep
2.5pc'24 (97.7)	330.58	-0.47	-0.13	-0.37	-0.26	+0.02	+0.07	+0.08	+0.36	342.13	319.33	6,821	08/01	17 Jan/Jul
1.25pc'27† (194.06667)	119.09	-0.24	-0.13	-0.15	-0.15	+0.02	+0.06	+0.05	+0.28	125.35	115.11	14,170	13/05	22 May/Nov
0.125pc'29............	102.67	-0.22	-0.15	-0.06	-0.06	+0.01	+0.06	+0.04	+0.23	106.59	98.14	14,229	12/03	22 Mar/Sep
4.125pc'30.......(135.1)	313.69	-0.69	-0.50	-0.17	-0.09	+0.02	+0.06	+0.05	+0.26	326.00	302.44	4,841	13/01	22 Jan/Jul
1.25pc'32† (217.13226)	124.55	-0.35	-0.34	-0.07	-0.07	+0.02	+0.05	+0.04	+0.19	130.42	119.51	12,760	13/05	22 May/Nov
0.75pc'34......(235.20)	115.36	-0.34	-0.32	-0.02	-0.02	+0.02	+0.05	+0.04	+0.15	119.44	109.97	12,458	12/03	22 Mar/Sep
2pc'35............(173.6)	206.07	-0.58	-0.58	-0.10	-0.04	+0.02	+0.05	+0.04	+0.16	210.39	194.33	9,084	15/01	26 Jan/Jul
1.125pc'37† (202.24286)	127.51	-0.44	-0.48	-0.04	-0.04	+0.02	+0.05	+0.05	+0.11	132.09	121.33	12,132	13/05	22 May/Nov
0.625pc'40† (216.52258)	116.68	-0.46	-0.50	-0.02	-0.02	+0.02	+0.05	+0.06	+0.08	120.10	109.89	11,438	12/03	22 Mar/Sep
0.75pc'47† (207.76667)	126.34	-0.63	-0.74	-0.03	-0.03	+0.02	+0.05	+0.06	+0.02	131.17	117.56	11,687	13/05	22 May/Nov
0.5pc'50† (213.40000)	119.43	-0.63	-0.72	-0.04	-0.04	+0.02	+0.05	+0.06	-0.01	124.32	110.25	11,351	12/03	22 Mar/Sep
0.25pc'52............	110.54	-0.66	-0.74	-0.03	-0.03	+0.02	+0.05	+0.06	-0.02	115.27	101.04	9,002	12/03	22 Mar/Sep
1.25pc'55† (192.20000)	155.48	-0.88	-0.97	-0.07	-0.07	+0.02	+0.05	+0.06	-0.02	162.14	143.00	10,169	13/05	22 May/Nov
0.375pc'62............	121.86	-0.88	-1.03	-0.07	-0.07	+0.02	+0.05	+0.05	-0.03	127.99	109.00	12,480	12/03	22 Mar/Sep

All UK Gilts are Tax free to non-residents on application. xd Ex dividend. Closing mid-prices are shown in pounds per £100 nominal of stock. Weekly percentage changes are calculated on a Friday to Friday basis. A full list of Gilts can be found daily on ft.com/bond&rates. † Rump gilts Prospective real redemption rate on projected inflation of (1) 5% and (2) 3% (b) Figures in parentheses show RPI base for indexing (ie 8 months prior to issue and, for gilts issued since September 2005, 3 months prior to issue) and have been adjusted to reflect rebasing of RPI to 100 in January 1987. Conversion factor 3.945. RPI for Jan 2012: 238.0 and for Oct 2012 245.6. For those bonds indicated, with a 3m lag, the 'clean' price shown has no inflation adjustment. The yield is calculated using no inflation assumption.

Source: Thomson Reuters

of the gilt to maturity will receive the yield that was obtainable at the time of purchase.

Redemption yields for gilts are quoted daily online by the Debt Management Office at www.dmo.gov.uk. Other sources of information on prices, and on the gilts market generally, are websites, e.g. www.bloomberg.com, www. fixedincomeinvestor.co.uk, www.hl.co.uk, www.londonstockexchange.com, www.selftrade.co.uk, www.iii.co.uk and www.fitchratings.com.

Investors buying and selling gilts in the secondary market

Institutional investors in bonds deal directly with the GEMMs (the **primary dealers**). Non-institutional investors can buy or sell gilts through brokers, who contact the GEMMs, dealing on the telephone or online. They need to state the nominal value of the gilts they want to deal and whether they want to trade **at best** (the best price currently in the market) or with **a limit** on the price they are prepared to pay (or sell for). High street banks, some building societies, independent financial advisers and even some solicitors and accountants will buy or sell gilts for clients.

The **settlement day**, the date on which transfer of gilt and payment occur, is usually the next business day after the trade is conducted (T+1), although other settlement dates may be negotiated between the buyer/seller and the GEMM. The CREST system run by Euroclear organises the transfer between investors and maintains records of ownership transferred in the secondary market, usually an electronic record rather than paper certificates. (Euroclear also does this for another 30 bond markets internationally.)

Retail investors can also buy and sell gilts in the primary and secondary markets via the DMO's **Gilt Purchase and Sales Service** using Computershare (www-uk. computershare.com). It is first necessary to fill in forms to become an Approved Group of Investors member. The investor is not able to specify the price or a maximum/minimum price at which the purchase/sale of gilts is to be made.

Computershare maintains the main **register of holdings** of gilts under contract from HM Treasury. It will send out coupons ('dividends') and redemption monies to arrive on the due dates.

Since 2010 retail investors have been able to buy and sell gilts and other bonds through the London Stock Exchange's electronic **Order book for Retail Bonds (ORB)** where lots can be very small (minimum £1) and the costs of trading are relatively low. The London Stock Exchange authorises dedicated market makers to state bid/offer prices (some are GEMMs). Buyers and sellers are able to set limits on the prices they are willing to pay/accept or simply ask a broker to trade at the current market price. Small investors can now see ORB gilt prices on free financial websites (e.g. www.advfn.com, www.londonstockexchange.com).

Other ways for small investors to gain exposure to the gilt (and/or corporate bond) market is to buy units in a unit trust or shares in an investment trust that specialises in the type of bonds they are interested in. They gain professional management and diversification but will pay fees (sometimes more than 1% per year, which is a lot as a proportion of the annual interest on gilts of, say, 3% or 4%). Exchange traded funds are another alternative. Collective bond funds such as these are discussed in *The Financial Times Guide to Investing* (Glen Arnold, 2014, Pearson).

Taxation on gilts

The investor's tax bracket influences the return they receive. Currently there are four tax brackets applying to a person's marginal taxable income and capital gains. The interest on gilts is taxed but the capital gains are not, thus higher-rate tax payers are better off if they select gilts with a greater proportion of the total return coming from capital gains rather than coupons. The *Financial Times* provides a helpful table (Table 2.8) showing the best value gilts in terms of after-tax returns in the four tax brackets. Note that the 'GRY' (gross redemption yield) shown here is actually a yield calculated after the deduction of tax. So, for example, looking at other databases on 13 June 2014, the gross redemption yield (before tax deduction) for the Treasury 1.75% 2022 is 2.62%, whereas in the so-called 'GRY' shown in Table 2.8 it is 1.68% for the 40% tax bracket investor and 1.59% for the 45% tax bracket investor. Again note the way in which the prices of index-linked bonds were pushed so high in 2014 that they all provide a negative return after tax and assuming inflation of 3%.

Table 2.8 Gilt issues: best value versus tax status

	Stock	Price	GRY %	Real yield %
Non Taxpayers				
Conventional 1–5 Years	Treasury 4.5 2019	112.84	1.68	
Conventional 5–15 Years	Treasury 4.25 07 Dec 2027	115.29	2.88	
Conventional >15 Years	Treasury 3.25 2044	97.88	3.35	
Index Linked 1–5 Yrs	TSYI/L 3MO 1.25 2017 Rg	110.08		−1.53
Index Linked >5 Yrs	TSYI/L 0.125 2044	105.89		−0.07
20% Taxpayers				
Conventional 1–5 Years	Treasury 1.25 2018	98.72	1.32	
Conventional 5–15 Years	Treasury 2.75 2024	100.83	2.11	
Conventional >15 Years	Treasury 3.25 2044	97.88	2.70	
Index Linked 1–5 Yrs	TSYI/L 3MO 1.25 2017 Rg	110.08		−1.77
Index Linked >5 Yrs	TSYI/L 0.125 2044	105.89		−0.09
40% Taxpayers				
Conventional 1–5 Years	Treasury 1.25 2018	98.72	1.07	
Conventional 5–15 Years	Treasury 1.75 2022	95.18	1.68	
Conventional >15 Years	Treasury 3.25 2044	97.88	2.05	
Index Linked 1–5 Yrs	TSYI/L 3MO 1.25 2017 Rg	110.08		−2.01
Index Linked >5 Yrs	TSYI/L 0.125 2044	105.89		−0.12
45% Taxpayers				
Conventional 1–5 Years	Treasury 1.25 2018	98.72	1.00	
Conventional 5–15 Years	Treasury 1.75 2022	95.18	1.59	
Conventional >15 Years	Treasury 3.25 2044	97.88	1.88	
Index Linked 1–5 Yrs	TSYI/L 3MO 1.25 2017 Rg	110.08		−2.07
Index Linked >5 Yrs	TSYI/L 0.125 2044	105.89		−0.12

Best performing bonds are selected on highest yield for each marginal tax rate based on closing mid price.
Gilts exclude double-dated and rump issues. Prices quoted as £ per £100 nominal. For Inflation-linked gilts:
year-on-year inflation.
GRY = Gross Redemption Yield. Data compiled on: May 30th 2014
Source: Barclays plc

Cum-dividend and ex-dividend

Between each six-monthly coupon payment the interest accrues on a daily basis. When you buy a gilt you are entitled to the interest that has accrued since the last coupon. You will receive this when the next coupon is paid. That is, you buy the gilt **cum-dividend**. Gilts (and other bonds) are quoted at clean prices (**flat prices**) – that is, quoted without taking account of any accrued interest. However, the buyer will pay the clean price plus the accrued interest value (called the **dirty price** or **full price** or **invoice price** or **full accrual price**) and will receive all of the next coupon. So, if you buy a gilt four months before the next coupon is due, you would pay the clean price, say £101, plus 60 days' accrued interest, i.e. two months of accrued coupon since the last was paid. The accrued interest for a bond that pays coupons every six months is calculated by taking the annual coupon and dividing it by two to obtain the half-yearly coupon. This number is then multiplied by the fraction of the half-year that has already passed. So, if the bond pays an annual coupon of 7% and is currently quoted at a clean price of £101, the dirty price is:[5]

Dirty price

= clean price

$$+ \left\{ \frac{\text{annual coupon}}{2} \times \frac{\text{Actual number of days since last coupon payment}}{\text{Actual number of days in coupon period}} \right\}$$

Dirty price = £101 + (£7/2 x 60/182) = £102.1538

If you bought just before the coupon is to be paid, the situation is different. There would not be enough time to change the register to make sure that the coupon goes to the new owner (you). To allow for this problem a gilt switches from being quoted cum-dividend to being **ex-dividend (xd)** a few days (usually seven) before an interest payment. If you buy during the ex-dividend period, the person you buy from will receive the coupon from the issuer and this will be reflected in the price you pay.

Index-linked gilts

There is a danger with conventional gilts – inflation risk. Say, for example, that you, along with the rest of the gilt-buying community, think that inflation over the next ten years will average 2.5%. As a result you buy ten-year gilts that have a redemption yield of 4.8%, giving a comfortable real income over and above the expected cost-of-living increases. However, two years later inflation starts to take off (oil prices quadruple, or the government goes on a spending spree). Now investors reckon that inflation will average 6% over the following eight years. As a result your gilt yield will fail to maintain your capital in real terms.

---

[5] Note that the 'actual number of days since last coupon payment' is to the settlement day, when the buyer actually takes possession of the bond (the day of the deal is usually one day before settlement day).

With UK government index-linked stocks the coupon amount and the nominal value to be paid on redemption are adjusted according to the Retail Prices Index. The deal here is that the gilt initially offers to pay £100 at the end of its term, say ten years away. It also offers to pay a low coupon, say 0.25%. The key thing about index-linked bonds is that neither the capital sum on maturity nor the coupon stays at these levels unless inflation is zero over the next ten years.

Suppose inflation is 4% over the first year of the bond's life. The payout on maturity would rise to £104. However, this inflation-linked uplift happens every year (more specifically, the uplift for inflation occurs every six months). So, if over the ten years the inflation measure has risen by 60%, the payout on the bond is £160. This means that you can buy just as many goods and services at the end with the capital sum as at the beginning of the bond's life (if you paid £100). Furthermore, the coupon rate also rises through the years if inflation is positive. So after the inflation experience in the first year, the coupons for the first six months of the second year go up by 4%, (£0.25 ÷ 2) × (1 + 0.04) to £0.13. The situation is slightly more complicated than this in that the inflation figures used are those for three months preceding the relevant coupon dates, but this example illustrates the principle.[6]

Any future rises in inflation lead to further growth in the coupon, so that the last coupon will be 60% larger than the initial coupon rate if inflation over the ten years accumulates to 60%, paying £0.40 per £100 nominal.

Because most investors hold index-linked gilts to maturity secondary market trading is thin and dealing spreads are wider than for conventional gilts.

Many governments now issue index-linked bonds – a sample is shown on the *Financial Times* website, see Table 2.9. '**Break even inflation**' means the rate of inflation that would make the returns from conventional gilts and index-linked gilts the same. This is implied by the difference between gross redemption yield on conventional government bonds and the pre-inflation–uplift return offered on an index-linked gilt of the same maturity. That is, if you observe the gross redemption yield from a conventional gilt to be 2.8% over ten years, and you know that the capital repayment and coupons from a ten-year index-linked bond are increased by inflation, what inflation rate would be required so that the index-linked bond return would also be 2.8%, given its

---

[6] For bonds issued prior to July 2005 the lag is eight months.

Table 2.9 Index-linked bonds issued by a number of governments

	Price	Yield		Month return	Break even inflation*	Value Stock
	Jun 11	Jun 11	Jun 10			
Can 4.25% '21	130.98	0.09	0.07	−0.79	2.08	5.2
Fr 2.25% '20	115.88	−0.32	−0.35	0.17	0.98	20.0
Swe 0.25% '22	100.45	0.27	0.27	0.10	1.35	26.4
UK 2.5% '16	336.71	−1.74	−1.75	−0.22	2.63	7.9
UK 2.5% '24	330.17	−0.24	−0.24	−0.97	3.07	6.8
UK 2% '35	206.13	−0.04	−0.03	−1.17	3.42	9.1
US 0.625% '21	103.84	0.08	0.07	−1.30	2.11	35.8
US 3.625% '31	137.97	0.74	0.73	−2.05	2.25	16.8

Representative stocks from each major market
* Diff between conventional and IL bond. † Local currencies. ‡ Total market value. In line with market convention, for UK Gilts inflation factor is applied to price, for other markets it is applied to par amount.
Source: Merrill Lynch Global Bond Indices

current price and coupon?[7] 'Value stock' means the volume in issue expressed in the local currency, e.g. the UK 2.5% 2016 has £7.9 billion in issue.

Inflation-linked bond issues are taking off across Europe – see Article 2.3.

Article 2.3

Europe on track to sell record amounts of inflation-linked debt

By Elaine Moore

Financial Times June 12, 2014

Europe is on course to sell more government debt linked to inflation than ever before, in spite of the looming risk of deflation across the region. So far this year the supply of bonds tied to eurozone inflation has reached €52.9bn, more than two-thirds of the entire supply of inflation-linked bonds in 2013 and close to the full year's supply in 2012.

[7] This is far from an agreed scientific way of estimating the market's expectations of future inflation. Many other factors play a role in pushing yields on gilts up or down – for example, pension funds may increase their buying of linkers (index-linked bonds) to better match their liabilities, thereby encouraging higher prices and lowering yields.

On Wednesday, France issued its largest inflation-linked bond since the financial crisis began, selling €3.5bn of 15-year debt. France is the exception within inflation-linked bond issuers because it sells bonds tied to the Europe-wide measure of goods and services as well as one connected to domestic inflation.

Clearly inflation in Europe is extremely low but there is a lot of discussion in the markets about whether it will stay that way and the strength of appetite for inflation-linked bonds shows that not all investors think it will.

The latest inflation-tied debt issuance, which was sold via BNP Paribas, Crédit Agricole, HSBC, Nomura and Société Générale, was notable for the level of interest it drew from UK and domestic investors, said one banker. The bond was priced to yield 20 basis points more than the country's existing inflation-linked note which matures in July 2027.

Inflation-linked bonds have performed poorly for investors in recent years, as global inflation stayed low. However, they are seen as a hedge against the possibility of inflation increases.

'Demand is high for inflation protection at these levels,' said Jonathan Gibbs, a fund manager at Standard Life Investments. 'Investors with liabilities linked to inflation, such as pension funds, will be using the opportunity to buy into these bonds.'

In May, Spain issued its first inflation-linked bond, which attracted orders of more than €20bn. Last week Germany added €1bn to its existing inflation-linked bond due to mature in 2023.

STRIPS

Some conventional gilts, following issuance by the government and trading on the secondary market, can be stripped. A gilt STRIPS (the letters stand for **Separate Trading of Registered Interest and Principal Securities**) occurs when the gilt is separated from its coupons and the gilt and its coupons all become zero coupon bonds. Thus a five-year gilt could become eleven separate zero coupon bonds, each with its own ISIN, one for each six-monthly coupon plus the original bond. Twenty-nine gilts have been stripped, resulting in 164 separately traded instruments, and the STRIPS have a value of around £1.8 billion. They are traded at a discount to their redemption value and once stripped can be reconstituted. Only GEMMs can strip gilts.

Table 2.10 UK government STRIPS, some examples

Gilt name	Redemption date	Clean price (£)	Dirty price (£)	Redemption yield (%)
4% Treasury Principal Strip 07 March 2022	07 March 2022	82.094598	82.094598	2.565673
Treasury Coupon Strip 07 March 2022	07 March 2022	82.094598	82.094598	2.565673
Treasury Coupon Strip 07 June 2022	07 June 2022	81.283016	81.283016	2.610852
1¾ Treasury Principal Strip 07 September 2022	07 September 2022	80.473389	80.473389	2.654188
Treasury Coupon Strip 07 March 2024	07 March 2024	75.730615	75.730615	2.874803

Source: DMO, 10 June 2014 www.dmo.gov.uk/

The motivation for stripping is that investing institutions might offer a higher price because they can obtain the exact maturity profile and interest rate they are looking for. The problem with conventional coupon-paying bonds is that long-term buy-and-hold investors have to reinvest the money paid as a coupon, say half way to maturity. What reinvestment interest rate might you get three or four years down the line? It might be more or less than the yield to maturity that you originally bought into, which distorts the overall return received. With STRIPS the rate of return is fixed for the full term because there is only one payout. Table 2.10 shows some of the STRIPS available – details are updated daily on the DMO website. Of course, the clean and the dirty market prices are the same because there are no payments made each six months, therefore no coupon interest is accruing day by day.

Islamic UK government bonds

The UK government is determined to make London a world centre for the issuance of bonds that comply with sharia law (see Chapter 7 for more detail). In 2014 it pioneered western government sovereign borrowing in sukuk – see Article 2.4. It will not pay interest because this is forbidden under sharia, but it will pay annual profit.

Article 2.4

UK sukuk bond sale attracts £2bn in orders

By Elaine Moore and Thomas Hale

Financial Times June 25, 2014

Britain has become the first western country to issue an Islamic bond, attracting orders of more than £2bn from global investors for its sale of sharia-compliant debt.

London's maiden 'sukuk' will pay out profits based on the rental income from three government-owned properties in lieu of interest, which is forbidden under Islamic religious law.

The £200m sale, which comes days before the start of Ramadan, was heavily over-subscribed by investors in the UK, Middle East and Asia, attracting orders of £2.3bn – 10 times higher than the amount sold.

British grocer Tesco issued a sukuk in 2007 through its Malaysian arm and Ocado, the independent online grocer, borrowed £10m in a sharia-compliant loan in 2009. Some of the UK's largest property companies have already expressed interest in the idea of raising finance through Islamic bonds said one banker, but so far only one domestic company – small Yorkshire-based manufacturer International Innovative Technologies – has borrowed money in the UK via a bond that complies with Islamic religious rules.

South Africa and Hong Kong have stated interest in planning Islamic bonds of their own and Luxembourg is expected to issue a €200m bond this year.

'The issuance of a UK sovereign sukuk sets a precedent for the western financial world with the high demand hopefully encouraging further issuance from western countries and corporates,' said Humphrey Percy, chief executive of The Bank of London and The Middle East.

The UK's five year Islamic bond will pay out an annual 'profit' of 2.036%, set at the same rate as the yield on the UK's equivalent five-year government bond.

HSBC, Malaysia's CIMB, Qatar's Barwa Bank, National Bank of Abu Dhabi and Standard Chartered were responsible for marketing the bond. According to HSBC more than a third of the issuance went to UK investors, with the remaining bonds sold in the Middle East and Asia.

The sale is small in terms of overall sukuk issuance, which has exceeded $21bn this year according to Dealogic, but was popular with Islamic investors in search of high grade debt.

Fixed-interest indices

The FTSE (owned by the London Stock Exchange) creates indices for a variety
of securities. The 'FTSE Actuaries UK Gilts Index Series' provides an indication
of returns on bonds of various classes over time. Table 2.11 shows the performance over one month and one year of collections of bonds, e.g. a representative group of twelve bonds with less than five years to maturity. The column
labelled 'Total return' includes both interest payments that the bond accrues

Table 2.11 Gilts – UK FTSE actuaries indices

Price Indices Fixed Coupon	Jun 16	Day's chge %	Total Return		Return 1 month	Return 1 year	Yield
1 Up to 5 years (12)	99.62	−0.05	2282.80		−0.44	−0.25	1.49
2 5–10 years (9)	172.49	−0.04	2963.71		−1.09	−1.55	2.39
3 10–15 years (4)	190.35	−0.02	3324.36		−1.46	−1.65	3.00
4 5–15 years (13)	176.16	−0.03	3047.63		−1.19	−1.48	2.63
5 Over 15 years (15)	255.06	+0.16	3531.54		−1.44	+1.56	3.38
6 Irredeemables (1)	354.85	+0.18	4112.78		−1.85	+2.75	4.17
7 All stocks (41)	160.93	+0.03	2872.10		−1.04	−0.04	3.05

Index-Linked	Jun 16	Day's chge %	Month chge %	Year's chge %	Total Return	Return 1 month	Return 1 year
1 Up to 5 years (2)	319.07	−0.01	−0.65	−2.01	2376.40	−0.65	−0.06
2 Over 5 years (21)	489.18	+0.11	−2.00	−0.27	3568.47	−2.00	+0.70
3 5–15 years (7)	413.78	+0.00	−1.41	−2.84	3090.17	−1.41	−1.48
4 Over 15 years (14)	569.60	+0.17	−2.31	+0.99	4088.01	−2.31	+1.75
5 All stocks (23)	461.40	+0.09	−1.85	−0.31	3403.30	−1.85	+0.81

Yield indices	Jun 16	Jun 13	Yr ago		Jun 16	Jun 13	Yr ago
5 yrs	2.02	2.00	1.15	20 yrs	3.36	3.37	3.12
10 yrs	2.84	2.83	2.17	45 yrs	3.39	3.41	3.45
15 yrs	3.20	3.21	2.78	Irred	4.17		

	....Inflation 0 %....				....Inflation 5%....			
Real yield	Jun 16	Dur yrs	Jun 13	Yr ago	Jun 16	Dur yrs	Jun 13	Yr ago
Up to 5 yrs	−1.09	2.56	−1.09	−1.51	−1.72	2.57	−1.72	−2.06
Over 5 yrs	−0.06	21.21	−0.06	−0.15	−0.10	21.32	−0.09	−0.18
5–15 yrs	−0.20	9.35	−0.20	−0.61	−0.31	9.38	−0.31	−0.73
Over 15 yrs	−0.04	27.45	−0.03	−0.07	−0.06	27.52	−0.05	−0.09
All stocks	−0.08	19.26	−0.07	−0.18	−0.12	19.40	−0.12	−0.22

FTSE is making a number of enhancements to the FTSE Actuaries UK Gilts Index Series which are effective from 28 April 2014.
Please see the FTSE website for more details: www.markets.ft.com

Source: FTSE Group

and the payments that have actually been made which are reinvested in the index as well as capital gain or loss. The base value for the total return index is a figure that was set years ago, equal to the total market value of the group of gilts at the base (starting) date divided by the starting index value at that date (often 100) but which is subsequently adjusted to allow for changes in the constituents of the group and the nominal amounts of the constituent gilts.

The table also shows the average yield to maturity currently available to a buyer of this group of gilts. The price indices, in the second column, labelled 'Jun 16' (the day of the download), is an arithmetically weighted index based on the dirty price and weighted by the nominal amount outstanding (it does not allow for that part of the return from coupons).

The 'real yield' (after deduction of inflation) for the index-linked securities (final section) is shown for bonds with a variety of maturities and is based on different assumptions with regard to future inflation.[8] 'Dur yrs' is the length of the duration in years, a measure related to price volatility of the collection of bonds (see Chapter 13).

---

[8] A greater range of real yields based on assumptions of future annual inflation rates of 0%, 3%, 5% and 10% can be seen at www.ftse.com.

CHAPTER 3
GOVERNMENT BONDS AROUND THE WORLD

Having covered the main characteristics of government bonds in the last chapter we now briefly describe a few other significant national markets. There is also an overview of developing country bonds. Finally, this chapter covers bonds issued by local authorities, such as in the US municipal bond market, and by organisations that while not strictly government owned have a close relationship with the central government.

Sovereign bond risk and return

Most countries issue government bonds which are similar in format to UK gilts and each country and their bonds are given a credit rating by one of the credit rating agencies. The three biggest and best-known agencies are Moody's, Standard & Poor's and Fitch, but there are others; recently the Chinese agency Dagong has made headlines by downgrading the UK and the US. The rating they give indicates the relative risk of default – see Figure 3.1 for some of Standard & Poor's credit ratings in June 2014. Only a handful of countries are regarded as very safe, 'triple A' rated – all of the AAA-rated countries are shown in Figure 3.1, along with countries on a slightly lower rating, AA or A, and those with a greater degree of risk. Triple A ratings allow countries to issue at a low real (after allowing for anticipated inflation) yield. Other countries, such as Greece and Uganda, are regarded as having more risk and so will have to pay a high-risk premium (a higher rate on the coupon) to entice investors to buy their bonds. Credit ratings are discussed further in Chapter 5.

As communications have become easy and international flows of investment money commonplace, all bond markets worldwide are interconnected and interest rates have become linked. So, in general, bonds pay similar rates of interest if they carry the same risk (and inflation is anticipated to be the same). Table 3.1 shows the interest rates for a few of the bonds of the leading

The triple As (AAAs)
Australia
Canada
Denmark
Finland
Germany
Hong Kong
Luxembourg
Norway
Singapore
Sweden
Switzerland
UK

Some double As (AAs)
Austria
Belgium
Chile
China
France
Japan
Netherlands
New Zealand
Saudi Arabia
Taiwan
USA

Some single As
Ireland
Israel
Malaysia
Poland
Thailand
Trinidad and Tobago

Some triple Bs (BBBs)
Brazil
India
Italy
Russia
South Africa
Spain
Turkey

Some rated lower than triple B
Argentina
Greece
Indonesia
Kenya
Pakistan
Uganda
Ukraine
Vietnam
Zambia

Figure 3.1 Credit ratings for some countries

Source: Data from Standard & Poor's website June 2014 www.standardandpoors.com/ratings/sovereigns/
ratings-list/en/us/?sectorName=null&subSectorCode=&start=0&range=50

Table 3.1 Benchmark government bonds on 11 June 2014

Jun 11	Red date	Coupon	Bid price	Bid yield	Day chg yield	Wk chg yield	Month chg yld	Year chg yld
Australia	06/16	4.75	103.94	2.71	−0.03	0.01	0.01	0.19
	04/24	2.75	91.23	3.80	0.00	0.04	–	0.44
Austria	09/16	4.00	108.67	0.14	−0.01	0.04	−0.07	−0.18
	10/24	1.65	99.41	1.70	0.04	0.11	0.03	−0.28
Belgium	03/16	2.75	104.66	0.13	0.00	−0.03	−0.11	−0.23
	06/24	2.60	106.63	1.87	0.07	−0.08	−0.16	−0.52
Canada	05/16	1.00	99.86	1.08	0.01	0.00	0.02	−0.09
	06/24	2.50	101.37	2.35	0.01	0.01	−0.02	0.15
Denmark	11/16	2.50	105.74	0.12	−0.03	0.00	−0.05	−0.24
	11/23	1.50	100.68	1.41	0.01	−0.03	−0.10	−0.25
Finland	04/16	1.75	103.05	0.08	0.01	−0.03	−0.10	−0.19
	04/24	2.00	103.43	1.61	0.06	−0.05	−0.12	−0.26
France	02/16	2.25	103.63	0.11	0.00	−0.02	−0.10	−0.22
	05/19	1.00	101.88	0.61	0.04	−0.10	−0.21	−0.45
	05/24	2.25	104.50	1.75	0.05	−0.06	−0.15	−0.43
	05/45	3.25	107.81	2.87	0.06	−0.02	−0.06	−0.32
Germany	06/16	0.25	100.41	0.04	−0.02	−0.02	−0.09	−0.16
	04/19	0.50	100.38	0.42	0.01	−0.05	−0.15	−0.23
	05/24	1.50	100.87	1.41	0.03	−0.01	−0.05	−0.20
	07/44	2.50	103.45	2.34	0.04	0.03	−0.04	−0.08
Greece	02/24	2.00	81.97	5.78	0.02	−0.60	−0.32	−3.91
	02/34	2.00	69.16	6.72	−0.01	−0.35	−0.20	−2.48
Ireland	06/19	4.40	116.84	0.94	0.02	−0.24	−0.34	−1.68
	03/24	3.40	108.37	2.44	0.01	−0.18	−0.23	−1.65
Italy	05/16	2.25	103.06	0.64	0.07	−0.17	−0.14	−1.22
	05/19	2.50	104.95	1.45	0.14	−0.25	−0.23	−1.77
	03/24	4.50	114.60	2.79	0.08	−0.21	−0.16	−1.52
	09/44	4.75	113.33	4.03	0.09	−0.12	−0.03	−0.94
Japan	06/16	0.10	100.03	0.09	0.00	0.00	0.00	−0.04
	03/19	0.20	100.08	0.18	0.00	0.00	−0.01	−0.11
	06/24	0.60	99.95	0.61	0.00	−0.01	0.00	−0.24
	03/34	1.50	100.63	1.46	0.01	0.01	−0.02	−0.20
Netherlands	04/16	–	99.82	0.10	0.00	−0.03	−0.08	−0.16
	07/24	2.00	103.14	1.63	0.07	−0.04	−0.12	−0.31
New Zealand	03/19	5.00	103.91	4.09	0.05	0.12	0.09	–
	04/23	5.50	107.67	4.45	0.05	0.16	0.17	0.81
Norway	05/19	4.50	112.06	1.91	0.01	−0.07	−0.18	0.25
	03/24	3.00	102.92	2.66	0.03	−0.03	−0.13	0.38
Portugal	02/16	6.40	108.92	0.98	0.07	−0.18	−0.14	−2.20
	02/24	5.65	118.93	3.33	−0.05	−0.34	−0.21	−2.89
Spain	04/16	3.25	104.98	0.57	0.05	−0.16	−0.16	−1.53
	04/24	3.80	109.89	2.64	0.06	−0.22	−0.27	−1.94
Sweden	07/16	3.00	105.14	0.50	−0.02	−0.05	−0.14	−0.42
	11/23	1.50	97.22	1.82	0.00	−0.04	−0.09	0.12
Switzerland	03/16	2.50	104.54	−0.11	–	−0.01	0.10	−0.13
	06/24	1.25	104.62	0.77	0.06	0.03	−0.05	−0.04
UK	01/15	2.75	101.41	0.44	0.02	0.04	–	0.06
	07/19	1.75	98.83	1.99	0.02	0.06	−0.02	0.79
	09/23	2.25	96.22	2.71	0.02	0.07	0.02	0.56
	01/44	3.25	95.85	3.48	0.00	0.03	0.02	0.04
US	05/16	0.38	99.89	0.43	0.01	0.03	0.05	0.11
	05/19	1.50	99.07	1.70	0.02	0.06	0.07	0.57
	05/24	2.50	98.78	2.64	0.03	0.05	0.02	0.43
	05/44	3.38	98.28	3.47	0.02	0.04	0.00	0.10

Redemption date April 2024

Coupon – the amount paid each year as a percentage of the nominal value of the bond, 2.5 per cent

Bid price – the price at which a market maker will buy from an investor should they wish to sell. In the case of a UK government bond with a unit nominal value of £100 the price is £101.41

Bid yield – the yield to redemption based on the market's bid price, 2.71 per cent

Yield changes over one day, week, month or year.

London close.
Yields: Local market standard Annualised yield basis. Yields shown for Italy exclude withholding tax at 12.5 per cent payable by non-residents.
Source: Thomson Reuters

government issuers when issuing in their currency. **Benchmark securities** are those used as market indicators, the bedrock yields. In the bond market the usual benchmarks are the prices and yields of bonds with 2 years, 5 years, 10 years and 30 years to redemption. These issues tend to be more liquid (traded more) than other bonds.

The *Financial Times* website also has a table displaying the **spreads** on ten-year benchmark bonds. That is, the number of percentage points of gross redemption yield above the ten-year German government bond (Bund) and above the ten-year US government bond (Treasury bond or T-bond) offered on a ten-year government bond from another country. Thus, Table 3.2 shows an investor in New Zealand government bonds (denominated in NZ$) will receive 3.06% per year more than an investor in German bonds (in euros) and 1.83% more than an investor in US bonds (in US$). The additional yield may compensate for greater anticipated inflation, greater perceived risk (such as exchange rate change risk) or other factors, e.g. the relative tendency for central banks to push down ten-year bond yields through their quantitative easing programmes (buying bonds, pushing up their prices and lowering their yields – see Chapter 16).

Table 3.2 Government bonds – spreads over ten-year bonds and US Treasuries

Jun 11	Bid Yield	Spread vs Bund	Spread vs T-Bonds		Bid Yield	Spread vs Bund	Spread vs T-Bonds
Australia	3.80	+2.42	+1.19	Netherlands	1.63	+0.25	−0.98
Austria	1.70	+0.32	−0.91	New Zealand	4.45	+3.06	+1.83
Belgium	1.87	+0.47	−0.76	Norway	2.66	+1.27	+0.04
Canada	2.35	+0.94	−0.29	Portugal	3.33	+1.95	+0.72
Denmark	1.41	+0.02	−1.21	Spain	2.64	+1.25	+0.02
Finland	1.61	+0.22	−1.01	Sweden	1.82	+0.43	−0.80
France	1.75	+0.36	−0.87	Switzerland	0.77	−0.62	−1.85
Germany	1.41	−	−1.23	UK	2.71	+1.33	+0.10
Greece	5.72	+4.34	+3.11	US	2.64	+1.23	−
Ireland	2.44	+1.05	−0.18	Yields: annualised basis.			
Italy	2.79	+1.40	+0.17				
Japan	0.61	−0.78	−2.01				

Source: Thomson Reuters

US Treasury bills, notes and bonds

The **Bureau of the Fiscal Service**, part of the United States Department of the Treasury, is responsible for managing US government securities. It borrows money from investors by issuing securities backed by the full faith and credit of the US government. It also administers **TreasuryDirect**, which offers online electronic dealings (purchasing and redeeming) to individual investors as well as financial institutions. The largest investors in US Treasuries are China and Japan, which wax and wane with respect to keenness to hold US debt – see Article 3.1.

Article 3.1

Foreign investors dump Treasuries at record pace

By Tracy Alloway and Vivianne Rodrigues

Financial Times August 15, 2013

Worries over the end of the Federal Reserve's bond-buying programme spurred foreign investors to sell US Treasuries at the fastest pace on record in June.

The Treasury showed that outflows of longer-term US securities, which include government debt as well as equities, reached $66.9bn in June. Foreign investors sold $40.8bn worth of Treasury bonds, the highest monthly sell-off on record.

June's sell-off in US securities coincided with a wider downturn in fixed income markets as investors fretted over the future of the US central bank's 'quantitative easing' policy; deflating asset prices and roiling many big market participants.

The central bank could start to 'taper' its unprecedented monetary stimulus later this year and end bond purchases in 2014, Ben Bernanke, Fed chairman, said in June.

A decision to wind down the central bank's emergency economic policies would indicate that the US economy is recovering but could also spur more bouts of market volatility, analysts say.

After selling Treasuries in May, private foreign accounts based in the Caribbean, Belgium and Luxembourg – a proxy for hedge funds – bought back a combined $19bn of US government debt in June.

'I wouldn't be surprised to see a big swing back in flows when July figures come out,' said Mr Miller [director of fixed-income strategy at GMP Securities]. 'There's only so much large holders of Treasuries can sell, [as] they all need to keep exposure to the Treasury market, given its depth and liquidity.'

China remained the biggest investor of US government bonds but pared back its holdings by $21bn to $1.28tn between May and June. Japan, the second-biggest investor, cut its holdings by $20bn to $1.08tn.

Total outflows of $66.9bn surpassed the $59bn seen in November 2008, just after the collapse of Lehman Brothers which sparked the global financial crisis.

Source: Alloway, T. and Rodrigues, V. (2013) Foreign investors dump Treasuries at record pace, *Financial Times*, 15 August.

The US Public Debt stood at nearly $17.5 trillion in February 2014. But about $5 trillion of that was accounted for by one area of government owing another area of government money, thus the net amount (owing external investors) was around $12.5 trillion. Nearly $12 trillion of Treasury-issued marketable securities are held by outside investors, including notes, bills, bonds and TIPS (explained on page 67) – see Figure 3.2. Most of the rest is owned by government-managed trust funds and savings bonds.

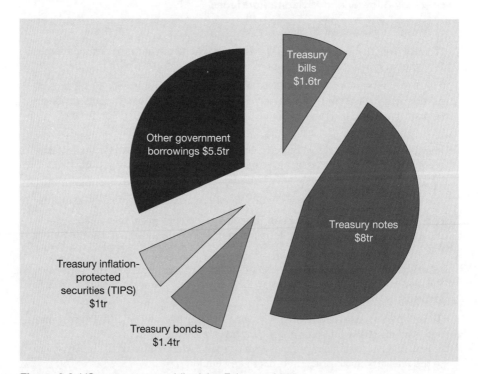

Figure 3.2 US government public debt, February 2014

US Treasury securities are initially sold at government-run auctions; the auction bids are based on the yield amount and every bidder pays the same price, which is set by the auction. The securities are issued electronically, although some older ones exist in paper form. At the auctions, only banks, brokers or dealers may make competitive bids, up to a maximum of 35% of the total amount on offer, and they are allocated some, or all, of the requested amount. Individuals may participate in the auctions through TreasuryDirect or through a broker (or bank), up to a maximum of $5 million, and they are guaranteed to receive the amount requested, but they will pay the price that is the outcome of the competitive bid auction. At the close of the auction all non-competitive bids are accepted, followed by competitive bids starting with the lowest yield, until the amount of bids accepted reaches the sum the government wishes to raise at that particular auction, and that yield becomes the accepted bid.

Treasury bills (T-bills) range in maturity from 1 day to 52 weeks, with 4-week (28 days), 13-week (91 days) and 26-week (182 days) bills being the most common. They are sold at a discount to par value by auction every week, except for the 52-week bills which are auctioned every 4 weeks. They are **zero coupon** securities, i.e. they do not pay a dividend; any gain for an investor results from the difference between the purchase price and the selling price.

Treasury notes have a coupon payable every six months. They have a maturity of two, three, five, seven or ten years and are sold at roughly monthly intervals. Notes are sold in increments of $100. The minimum purchase is $100.

Treasury bonds are auctioned every few months, have maturities greater than 10 years (usually 30 years) and pay interest twice per year. Bonds are sold in increments of $100. The minimum purchase is $100. Notes and bonds are referred to collectively as **Treasury coupon securities**.

Treasury inflation-protected securities (TIPS) are index-linked bonds whose principal value is adjusted according to changes in the **Consumer Price Index (CPI)**. They have maturities of 5, 10 or 30 years and interest is paid twice yearly at a fixed rate on the inflation-adjusted amount. TIPS are sold in increments of $100. The minimum purchase is $100. If an investor buys in the primary market $100,000 of TIPS offering a 2% annual coupon (1% per six months) with 10 years to maturity, and inflation in the first six months is 1.5%, the principal amount rises to $101,500. The first semi-annual coupon will be 1% of the new principal amount, i.e. $1,015. The upward adjustment of principal amount for inflation occurs before each of the subsequent coupon payments, thus raising the coupon by the CPI. At maturity the investor will receive the final principal amount including adjustment for ten years of inflation. To protect against deflation the holder receives at maturity the adjusted principal or the original principal, whichever is greater.

Treasury floating-rate notes (FRNs) were introduced in January 2014. Auctions of FRNs take place each month, with original issues in January, April, July and October, and **reopenings** in the other months, that is, the auction of additional amounts of a previously issued security. They pay quarterly a rate of interest that varies according to the rates on 13-week T-bills (a slightly higher rate is given – 'spread over bills'). FRNs are sold in increments of $100. The minimum purchase is $100. Article 3.2 explains that the US Treasury has chosen to introduce FRNs as a way of attracting lenders worried that interest rates might rise unexpectedly over the life of the bond (a fixed-rate bond would then fall in price, but with the coupons rising on the FRN, it may maintain its price).

Article 3.2

Why Uncle Sam needs some novel sweeteners for its bonds

By Gillian Tett

Financial Times January 31, 2014

This week the US government delivered two pieces of noteworthy news. One caused a splash: the Federal Reserve announced another $10bn cut in its monthly bond purchases, the second time it has tapered. Cue Twitter alerts and headlines.

But the real drama came a few hours earlier, when Uncle Sam successfully sold $15bn of two-year floating-rate notes to investors in the first innovation in federal debt for 16 years. The sale of these bonds that reset according to market rates – thus avoiding any losses if rates rise – attracted a startling $85bn of orders; not that you would have noticed from following the media, whether social or mainstream.

On one level this disparity is no surprise. Government bond auctions tend to be technical affairs. The Fed's taper, by contrast, is replete with drama for global investors, particularly since it could trigger more volatility for emerging markets.

But investors and taxpayers would be foolish to ignore the 'floaters'. What they show is the degree to which Treasury officials are hunting for ways to ensure the US can keep selling its debt to global investors when interest rates rise. And the outcome of those discreet experiments could prove critical to whether that much-debated taper will play out smoothly – or not.

The issue at stake partly revolves around the manner in which the Treasury sells government debt. In the past this was done in a straightforward way: bonds carried fixed interest rates, and most of these were either short-term bills or 10-year ones. Until recently US officials saw little reason to change this approach as demand was sky high.

But now a business-as-usual course is starting to look dangerously complacent. Never mind the fact that the US debt pile has doubled to $17tn in the past decade; and ignore recent fiscal fights and the threat of a new debt-ceiling showdown. The other challenge haunting the Treasury is the maturity profile of the debt.

In the past three decades this maturity has averaged 58 months, meaning it must be renewed almost every five years. During the financial crisis it declined to four years – half the average maturity of most European countries. That produced one oft-ignored benefit: because the Fed has kept rates ultra-low, total interest costs have not risen as fast as total debt. Just like a homeowner on a floating mortgage, low rates have meant low monthly interest payments for the Treasury. Indeed, interest payments now represent 6% of federal outlays; two decades ago it was 15%.

But this benefit comes with a sting that mortgage borrowers know well: if rates increase, interest payments could balloon. And if investors panic about inflation, higher rates or fiscal sustainability, that squeeze could be more intense.

The good news is that the Treasury is aware of this danger, and trying to prepare. In recent months it has had success in raising the average maturity profile by selling more long-term bonds. This stands at 66.7 months, and officials say that by 2020 it could reach 80.

Treasury officials are also trying to help the market absorb future rate rises by offering a more flexible range of instruments. This week's experiment with floaters is one move. However, the Treasury is also selling inflation-protected bonds and officials are getting more proactive about asking large investors – including Asian buyers – what moves will keep them purchasing Treasuries. In March 2014 there were 32 bills being traded, 219 Notes, 64 Bonds, 38 TIPS and 321 STRIPS. Treasuries interest payments are exempt from local and state taxes, but not from federal income taxes.

Source: Tett, G. (2014) Why Uncle Sam needs some novel sweeteners for its bonds, *Financial Times*, 31 January.

US STRIPS

Treasury STRIPS are similar to UK STRIPS, sold at a discount with maturities of 9 months to 30 years. US government notes and bonds may be converted to STRIPS by financial institutions and government securities brokers and dealers, who create STRIPS after purchasing the non-stripped notes or bonds.

They then ask the Federal Reserve (US central bank) to record the separation of coupons and face value with separate number identifiers on its computer system. The individual coupons and principal can then be traded as zero coupon securities by dealers. The minimum face amount needed to strip a fixed-principal note or bond or a TIP is $100 and any par amount to be stripped above $100 must be in a multiple of $100. STRIPS may be **reconstituted** – this might be worthwhile if the package of zero coupon STRIPS is selling in the market at less than the complete Treasury security.

Secondary market

US government bills, notes and bonds are traded in an active and liquid secondary market (in an over-the-counter market rather than on a formal exchange), with dealers posting bid (buying) and ask (selling) prices, and trades conducted over the telephone or by electronic communication. The central actors in the secondary market are the primary dealers (largest banks and brokerages in New York, Tokyo and London), which often act as market makers. Notes and bonds usually trade in $1,000 denominations. Settlement normally takes place one business day after a trade. Primary dealers also trade with each other directly or through interdealer brokers who match up buyers and sellers, usually with the advantage of anonymity for the participants. Retail investors buy or sell through banks and brokerage firms.

Prices for notes and bonds are quoted as a combination of whole dollars and as a fraction of a dollar. This may be in decimal terms, i.e. a fraction of 100, but more often the fraction used is 1/32nd of a dollar. Thus a US Treasury bond price has two parts: (1) the **handle**, that is, the main number (the first), and (2) the **32nds**, that is, the number expressed as a fraction of 32. This can be confusing because a decimal point might be used to separate the handle from the 32nds, despite the fact that the number that follows is not a fraction of 100 but of 32.

Table 3.3 shows the prices of US Treasury notes and bonds of varying maturities on 27 March 2014. The price for a $1,000 five-year note consists of (a) 99 and (b) 19¾ of 32. (Thankfully our numbers are separated by a dash rather than a decimal point.) To convert into a percentage to determine the dollar amount for the bond we first divide 19¾ by 32. This equals 0.6171875. We then add that amount to 99 (the handle), which equals 99.6171875. So, 99–19¾ equals 99.6171875% of the par value. If the par is $1,000, then the price is $996.171875.

Table 3.3 Prices of US Treasury notes and bonds, 27 March 2014

	Coupon	Price	Yield
2-year	0.375	99–27½	0.45%
5-year	1.625	99–19¾	1.71%
10-year	2.75	100–14½	2.70%
30-year	3.625	101–15½	3.54%

Source: Data from Bloomberg.com www.bloomberg.com/markets/rates-bonds/government-bonds/us/

This price, which is slightly lower than the face value, demonstrates that the current interest rates (market yields) are higher than the coupon yield of 1.625%, $1.625 per $100. Often notes and bond prices are quoted just with a yield figure, as it is then possible to work out what the market price would be. (These calculations are explained in Chapter 13.) Some very active issues may be quoted in 64ths of a point – in this case a + sign is added to the 32nds. Some traders/writers use even more convoluted and confusing conventions and fractions. It is definitely a weird system, time honoured, but weird.

French bonds

The French Treasury, Agence France Trésor (AFT), is responsible for borrowing to finance the public debt – for 2013 this figure was €169 billion. With this added to the total, France owed investors a sum equal to more than 90% of annual output. Most of this was raised by selling medium- and long-term securities. AFT sells by auction on fixed dates government bonds with a face value of €1 and a minimum bid of €1 million. Any institution affiliated to Euroclear France[1] and holding an account with the Banque de France (the central bank) is eligible to bid at the auctions, and they are able to sell the securities on to retail investors. Bids are made and the Treasury accepts the bids from the highest downwards until the target amount is achieved. Bidders pay varying prices according to their bids. The bonds issued are as follows:

BTFs (bons du Trésor à taux fixe et à intérêts précomptés) are government bills with which the government covers its short-term cash position fluctuations. They have a maturity of one year or less and are auctioned every Monday.

---

[1] A system for settling trades in securities: the simultaneous transfer of cash to the seller for payment and securities to the buyer. It also performs the functions of safekeeping and asset servicing ('**custody**') of these securities.

BTANs (bons du Trésor à intérêts annuels) are auctioned on the third Thursday of each month and are two- to five-year bonds with a fixed annual rate of interest. Since the 1st of January 2013, new benchmark securities created on medium-term (maturities of two and five years) are issued under the form of OAT (Obligation Assimilable du Trésor), as it is the case for long-term securities (10 years and more). The specific name of BTAN for medium-term securities has indeed no more the utility it had originally. Existing BTAN continue to be tapped in order to maintain their liquidity.

OATs (obligations assimilables du Trésor) are auctioned on the first Thursday of each month and range in maturity from 7 to 50 years. They are mostly fixed rate, but some have floating rates, pegged to the TEC 10, an index of long-term government bond yields; these are called TEC 10 OATs (because the yield on a bond with close to ten years to redemption is used). There are some index-linked bonds, linked either to the domestic consumer price index, OATi, or to the eurozone price index, OAT€i. Once issued OATs may be supplemented by further issues. Interest is paid once per year. OATs may be STRIPS.

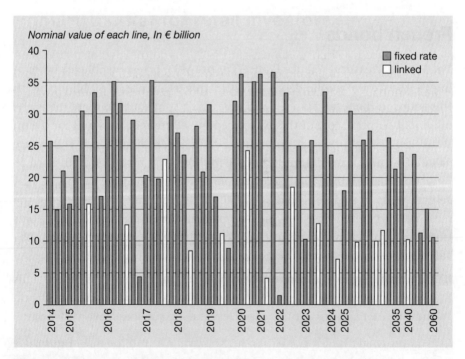

Figure 3.3 French government fixed-rate and index-linked bonds in issue by redemption year. Nominal amounts in € billion in April 2014

Source: Agence France Trésor, Monthly Bulletin, May 2014 www.aft.gouv.fr/documents/%7BC3BAF1F0-F068-4305-821D-B8B2BF4F9AF6%7D/publication/attachments/23525.pdf

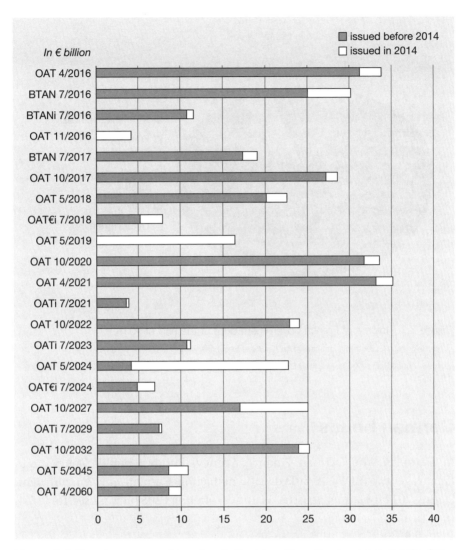

Figure 3.4 French government bond maturity dates. Securities issued during the first quarter of 2014 and total issuance

Source: Agence France Trésor, Monthly Bulletin, May 2014 www.aft.gouv.fr/documents/%7BC3BAF1F0-F068-4305-821D-B8B2BF4F9AF6%7D/publication/attachments/23525.pdf

In 2014 the total of these bonds in issue was over €1.4 trillion – see Figures 3.3 and 3.4. Primary dealers commit to market making in OATs in an OTC market.

Note that the majority of French debt is held by non-residents – see Figure 3.5.

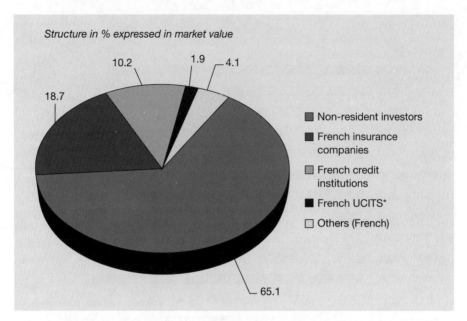

Figure 3.5 Holders of French government debt at the end of 2013

* Undertakings in Collective Investment in Transferable Securities

Source: Agence France Trésor, Monthly Bulletin, May 2014 www.aft.gouv.fr/documents/%7BC3BAF1F0-F068-4305-821D-B8B2BF4F9AF6%7D/publication/attachments/23525.pdf

German bonds

In Germany, the German Finance Agency, Bundesrepublik Deutschland Finanzagentur (BDF), is tasked with managing German government debt. During 2014 it planned to issue securities totalling €205 billion – see Table 3.4.

Table 3.4 German securities issues for 2014

Security	Share 2014	Volume 2014 €bn
Schaetze 2Y	25.4%	52
Bobl 5Y	23.4%	48
Bund 10Y	26.3%	54
Bund 30Y	3.4%	7
Capital market	78.5%	161
Bubill 6M	10.7%	22
Bubill 12M	10.7%	22
Money market	21.5%	44

Source: Data from www.deutsche-finanzagentur.de

The BDF sells via pre-announced auctions arranged by the Bundesbank, the German central bank, with 6-month, 12 -month, 2-, 5-, 10- and 30-year maturities, with a nominal value of €1 and a minimum bid of €1 million. Only the 37 members of the Bietergruppe Bundesemissionen (Bund Issuance Auction Group) can place bids at the auctions. Bids may be competitive or non-competitive. Competitive bids are made as a percentage of the nominal price and successful bidders pay the actual price bid, with bids being accepted from the highest downwards. Non-competitive bids are settled at the weighted average price of accepted bids. A detailed auction timetable is available from the BDF (www.deutsche-finanzagentur.de). The bills are discount securities and the bonds pay interest once per year.

Unverzinsliche Schätzanweisungen (Bubills) have maturities of 6 and 12 months. They are auctioned most months and generally account for less than 5% of German government securities outstanding in the secondary market.

Bundesschatzanweisungen (Schaetze) are two-year Federal Treasury notes. New Schaetze are issued four times a year, thus at any one time there are eight in issue. They made up about 11% of government debt in 2013.

Bundesobligationen (Bobls) are five-year Federal Notes. There are 3 new Bobl auctions per year and 15 series of Bobls are in issue. Bobls account for about 21% of German government securities outstanding in the secondary market.

Bundesanleihen (Bunds) are 10- and 30-year Federal bonds and form the majority of German government debt, around 60%. There are about 40 bunds in issue. In 2014 three new 10-year bunds were issued, each with a volume of €18 billion. Three issues of 30-year bunds add up to €7 billion. Some bunds may be stripped.

The total amount of German government securities outstanding was over €1.1 trillion at the beginning of 2014 – see Figure 3.6, which shows the total value of bunds, etc., even if they have only a year or two left to redemption. There is considerable trading on the secondary market, at over five times the amount of securities in issue traded each year. The yield to maturity offered on German government bonds usually forms the reference or benchmark interest rate for other borrowings in the euro currency. In other words, it is the lowest rate available, with other interest rates described as so many basis points above, say, the ten-year bund rate.

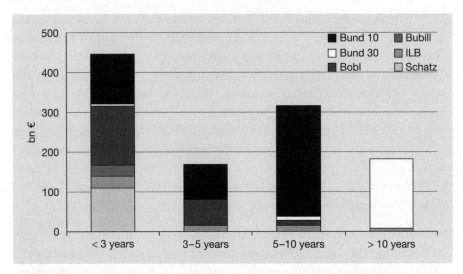

Figure 3.6 The remaining time to maturity of German government securities, December 2013

Source: Bundesrepublik Deutschland Finanzagentur www.deutsche-finanzagentur.de/en/institutional/secondary-market

During the darkest days of the eurozone financial crisis investors were so concerned about default risk that they were willing to pay very high prices for government bonds from those countries perceived to be safest. They did this to such an extent that the yield fell to below zero (the capital loss over the holding period outweighed the coupon income). Then with deflation came widespread holding of negative yield bonds – see Article 3.3.

Article 3.3

Investors be warned: the bond market must turn some time

By John Authers

Financial Times February 27, 2015

Records were made to be broken. There were plenty of headlines for new equity highs this week, particularly the first new record close in 15 years for the UK's FTSE 100. But a high after 15 years does not necessarily trigger much cause for alarm. Even if this is not an obvious time to buy UK stocks, it is hard to make the case that they are overblown.

But then comes the bond market. Here, history suggests that prices have entered into new and undiscovered territory. But because that territory is so new, history has few precedents to help predict what might happen next.

This week's publication of the annual Barclays equity-gilt study demonstrated that UK gilts have outperformed stocks over the past 25 years – a remarkable outcome that implies that bonds' outperformance cannot be sustained. Over the longer term, as Neil Collins details elsewhere in these pages, equities have comfortably outperformed.

But by the standards of government bonds, UK gilts are not that impressive. Negative yields, meaning that investors are in effect paying the government for the privilege of looking after their money, are now available on bonds from Germany and Switzerland. This sounds crazy. Why would anyone do this?

In fact, negative yields can be explained by a number of factors. First, there is the fear of deflation. If you think the buying power of money will decline, it makes sense to buy a bond whose value will also decline.

Second, there is second-guessing the actions of central banks. If they will be buying at whatever price, then buy bonds, even at a negative yield, and sell to them later. The European Central Bank is about to launch into indefinite bond purchases, and the Bank of Japan is in the midst of a continuing bond-buying campaign. They can print money so they can be relied on to buy.

Third, there are demographics. As populations age, so it makes sense for more people to buy bonds that provide an income in retirement, and for more pension funds to buy them so that they can afford to make guarantees for the future. This is particularly true when governments change regulations to force them to do so, thereby arguably forcing them to lend cheap to the state.

Fourth, there is supply. There are fewer safe assets than there used to be. US mortgage-backed debt is, naturally, no longer considered to be in that category; the number of corporations with the top triple-A credit rating is also now negligible; and government bonds issued by peripheral eurozone countries are now regarded as very risky.

Hence, naturally enough, the few truly safe assets that are left become even more valuable – to the point where investors will even accept a negative yield.

Finally there is demand. Foreign exchange reserve managers have steadily bought bonds, particularly Treasuries, as insurance against crises. China's huge build-up of Treasury bonds, which arguably kept rates artificially low, was dubbed a 'savings glut' as long as a decade ago. Now, the eurozone's huge and growing trade surplus should deepen that savings glut – and force bond yields down.

In the short term, it is eminently possible for bonds' price rise to continue, even though they have reached a historic extreme. The experience of last year, when substantially nobody was ready for bond yields to pivot downwards once again, makes that clear.

Richard Batley, economist at Lombard Street Research, points out that the money coming from the ECB and the Bank of Japan will be more than enough to counteract any decline in the balance sheet of the Federal Reserve, according to their announced plans.

But investors may have learnt the wrong lesson from 2014. Yes, bond yields can continue to fall, and even go negative. But that does not mean that they can never reverse.

Demographics have helped bonds (and equities) for the past three decades, and are in the process of reversing in the western world and even in China. Once there are fewer savers as a proportion of the population, and more people gradually selling bonds as they live into their retirement, so this will be a big headwind for bond prices. And at some point, central banks will stop offering their support, even if that point is still in the future.

And the pain when they do could be considerable. Investors have grown accustomed to low or even negative interest rates, and have developed a range of securities to act as a proxy for the safe income-producers that government bonds used to be. Look at the growth of real estate or infrastructure investing, for example, or the popularity of high-yielding dividend stocks.

All of these assets would be affected if and when the bond market finally turns.

And the steady exit of banks from fixed-income markets, under pressure from regulators, means that they would not be there to ease the process as bonds finally turn. There have been a few indicators in the past two years that the bond market is vulnerable to short and sharp turns – such as the 'taper tantrum' in spring 2014, when yields rose, or last October's 'flash crash', when they fell.

The chief warning of the Barclays study, even though history provides so few precedents, is that the bond market must turn at some point, and that when it does that turn could be violent.

Japanese bonds

The Japanese Ministry of Finance issues **Japanese government bonds** (**JGBs**), paying interest semi-annually. In March 2014, the Japanese government had outstanding debt of ¥1,025 trillion ($10 trillion). Medium- and long-term bonds made up nearly 80% of this. Auctions take place regularly (usually monthly) according to a published calendar. Maturities on JGBs can be 2, 5, 10, 20, 30 or 40 years. Inflation-indexed JGBs are also issued for 10-year maturities and floating-rate JGBs for 15-year maturities. Japanese institutions purchase the majority (about 70%) of these bonds (see Figure 3.7), but retail investors are able to purchase 3-, 5- and 10-year bonds.

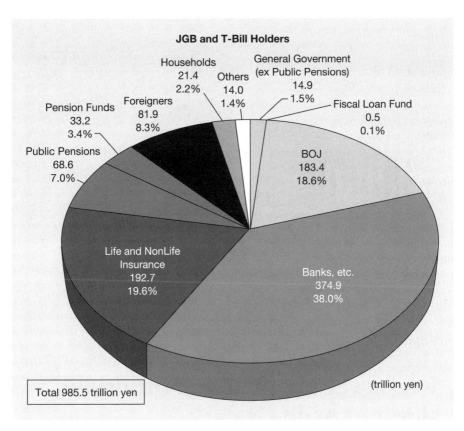

Figure 3.7 Breakdown of holders of Japanese government bonds and T-bills, December 2013 (BOJ is Bank of Japan, the central bank)

Source: Japanese Ministry of Finance www.mof.go.jp/english/jgbs/publication/newsletter/jgb2014_05e.pdf

The unit face values of JGBs are:

- ¥10,000 for JGBs for retail investors (3-year fixed rate, 5-year fixed rate, 10-year floating rate)
- ¥50,000 for 2-, 5-, 10-, 20-, 30- and 40-year
- ¥100,000 for 10-year inflation indexed, 15-year floating rate.

Many JGBs are traded in the over-the-counter secondary market, but trade has been severely constrained by the impact of the enormous quantity of buying by the central bank – see Article 3.4. Foreign investors are encouraged, but still hold less than 10%. A few are traded on the Tokyo Stock Exchange and other exchanges. The average time to maturity of bonds and T-bills combined is seven and a half years – see Figure 3.8.

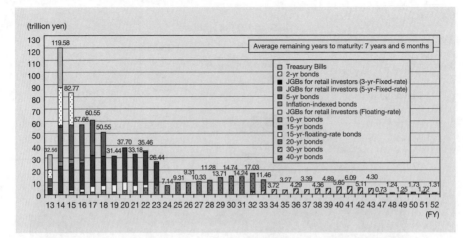

Figure 3.8 Time-to-maturity structure of outstanding Japanese government bonds in December 2013 – for redemption years stretching from 2013 to 2052

Source: Japanese Ministry of Finance www.mof.go.jp/english/jgbs/publication/newsletter/jgb2014_05e.pdf

Article 3.4

Kuroda always looks on the bright side, but reality is dark

By Ben McLannahan

Financial Times June 11, 2014

For Bank of Japan governor Haruhiko Kuroda, things are always looking up.

The 2% target for inflation will be met before long, he keeps saying. Growth in the economy is well above potential. And liquidity in the bond market is 'not very low'.

Really? People actually in the Y854tn ($8.4tn) Japanese government bond (JGB) market – the world's second largest – tend to give a different story. Dealers say the BoJ's commitment to buy up about 70% of net issuance by the government has forced almost everyone else out, and institutions complain that they cannot buy or sell when they want to. In fact, in the fiscal year to March, the turnover of JGBs fell to a record low. One risk of such a gummed-up market is that it sends out false signals. At the moment, for example, the 10-year yield seems stuck at about 0.6%, while core inflation – excluding the recent tax increase – is about 1.3%.

A second, more serious risk is that thin trading magnifies the effects of a sudden sell-off. In March, the market wobbled after the BoJ said it would buy fewer bonds than expected. Given that reaction, how can the bank dare to hint about an exit from its buying policy?

Credit Suisse has already calculated that, if the bank keeps buying bonds at its current rate, it will hold nearly 40% of all outstanding five to 10-year JGBs by next March – nearly double its current share.

 Source: McLannahan, B. (2014) Kuroda always looks on the bright side, but reality is dark, *Financial Times*, 11 June.

Chinese bonds

China's government bond market was established in 1950, but that experiment by the Communist Party was closed down in 1958. With the economic reforms of the 1980s the Chinese bond market was re-established and is now one of the largest in the world, having grown exponentially during the 21st century. Unlike most debt markets the Chinese one is generally closed to foreign issuers, investors and intermediaries, except for investments via **qualified foreign institutional investors (QFIIs)**, which are a select few foreign financial institutions allowed to invest in the Chinese securities market. Even then, they can do so only up to their quota limit.

The amount of bonds (government plus corporate) outstanding at the end of 2013 was over Rmb 35 trillion (about £3.4 trillion) – see Article 3.5.

The bond market is split into three roughly equal portions: (1) government bonds consisting of Treasury bonds and bills, savings bonds and local government bonds, and central government bonds; (2) policy bank bonds, issued by the Agricultural Development Bank of China, China Development Bank and Export–Import Bank of China; and (3) corporate bonds, most of which are issued by state-owned enterprises and a few private corporate entities and financial institutions (they also issue medium-term notes, commercial paper).

There are two main types of government bonds traded in China:

● Treasury bonds – these have maturities up to 50 years. They are issued at auctions with no set pattern of issuance
● financial bonds – these are issued by banks and financial institutions and are heavily backed by government-owned or controlled institutions. They are traded in the interbank markets.

Wary of foreign investment and control, most domestic debt is still purchased by state-owned or state-controlled financial institutions, thus concentrating risk in quasi-government-owned institutions instead of spreading it among many investors. The secondary market is very thin.

Article 3.5

China bond market emerges from the shadows

By Josh Noble

Financial Times October 23, 2013

Since the days of Marco Polo, China has been stuck with the label of the world's largest untapped market.

At roughly $4tn, China's domestic bond market is the world's fourth largest, and far larger than the Shanghai equity market's $2.4tn. It is also growing about 30% a year.

Yet for global investors, Chinese credit has been almost entirely off limits, with opportunities limited to relatively small offshore markets – whether in US dollars or renminbi – where a small number of mainland companies have chosen to borrow. But change is afoot as financial reforms crack open the door to domestic Chinese bonds.

'As the market opens up, it's going to become one of the most important capital markets in the world,' says Geoff Lunt, Asian fixed-income product specialist at HSBC asset management.

Singapore on Tuesday joined London and Hong Kong as financial centres where investors can apply for quotas under China's renminbi qualified foreign institutional investor scheme. Holders of RQFII licences can use renminbi that they hold offshore to invest directly in domestic Chinese assets, from bonds to stocks to money market funds.

The recent expansion of RQFII – totalling Rmb400bn ($65bn) but of which just Rmb130bn has been allocated – is the latest step in Beijing's broad, long-term goal of improving access to China's domestic financial markets. A sister programme denominated in US dollars has also been expanded to attract more foreign investment.

HSBC, which in July became the first big international bank to get an RQFII licence, says it plans to use its licence to launch funds targeting China's domestic bond market. Central banks are also getting in on the act as they look to diversify their holdings away from the US dollar. In April, the Reserve Bank of Australia said it planned to invest about 5% of its reserves in Chinese government debt.

'Liquidity is better onshore, and the yield pickup is also higher. That's why a lot of central banks have got their own quotas to place funds onshore', says Jack Chang, chief executive of ICBC Asia asset management. His company, whose clients include central banks and sovereign wealth funds, plans to make its first investment in onshore fixed income later this month.

However, few are expecting the swift demise of the offshore – or 'dim sum' – bond market, which is subject to international legal and regulatory standards and offers much simpler tax and repatriation rules for those seeking to exit investments.

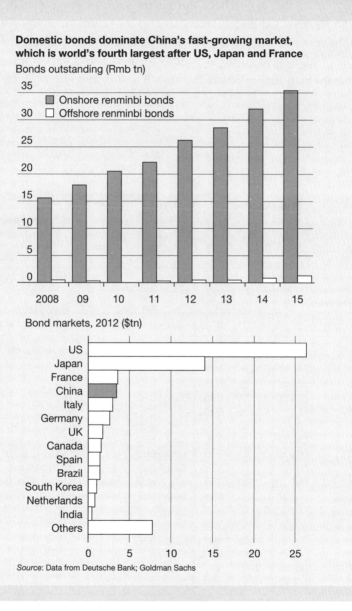

Domestic bonds dominate China's fast-growing market, which is world's fourth largest after US, Japan and France

Bonds outstanding (Rmb tn)

- ■ Onshore renminbi bonds
- □ Offshore renminbi bonds

Bond markets, 2012 ($tn)

Source: Data from Deutsche Bank; Goldman Sachs

Source: Noble, J. (2013) China bond market emerges from the shadows, *Financial Times*, 23 October.

Emerging markets

Less well-developed economy governments may issue bonds in their domestic currency or in the major hard currencies such as the dollar or the euro. Table 3.5 shows a sample of government bonds from emerging countries for which the coupons and principal will be paid in dollars or euros (there are also a couple of high-yield corporate bonds for Bertin and Kazkommerts). Credit ratings from Standard & Poor's, 'S', Moody's, 'M', and Fitch, 'F', are discussed

Table 3.5 High yield and emerging market bonds

Jun 16	Red date	Coupon	Ratings			Bid price	Bid yield	Day's chge yield	Mth's chge yield	Spread vs US
			S*	M*	F*					
High Yield US$										
Bertin	10/16	10.25	BB	Ba3	0	114.79	3.48	0.13	−0.72	2.82
High Yield Euro										
Kazkommerts Int	02/17	6.88	B	Caa1	B	99.88	6.91	0.03	−0.47	6.86
Emerging US$										
Bulgaria	01/15	8.25	BBB−	Baa2	BBB−	104.00	1.21	−0.03	0.37	1.14
Peru	02/15	9.88	BBB+	Baa2	BBB+	105.59	0.95	0.41	−0.01	0.88
Brazil	03/15	7.88	BBB−	Baa2	BBB	104.76	1.18	0.03	0.05	1.07
Mexico	09/16	11.38	BBB+	A3	BBB+	123.27	0.86	−0.05	−0.10	0.39
Philippines	01/19	9.88	BBB	Baa3	BBB−	132.51	2.34	0.00	−0.02	0.65
Brazil	01/20	12.75	BBB−	Baa2	BBB	150.12	2.94	−	−0.35	1.23
Colombia	02/20	11.75	BBB	Baa3	BBB	144.23	3.18	−0.01	0.02	1.48
Russia	03/30	7.50	BBB−	Baa1	BBB	115.25	4.32	0.16	−0.21	2.63
Mexico	08/31	8.30	BBB+	A3	BBB+	143.20	4.62	0.00	0.06	2.02
Indonesia	02/37	6.63	BB+	Baa3	BBB−	113.25	5.59	−	0.10	2.11
Emerging Euro										
Brazil	02/15	7.38	BBB−	Baa2	BBB	103.89	1.10	0.10	0.08	1.08
Poland	02/16	3.63	A−	A2	A−	105.63	0.15	−0.18	−0.34	0.12
Turkey	03/16	5.00	NR	Baa3	BBB−	105.40	1.74	0.05	0.16	1.71
Mexico	02/20	5.50	BBB+	A3	BBB+	121.02	1.59	0.04	−0.12	1.03

US$ denominated bonds NY closer; all other London close. * S − Standard & Poor's, M − Moody's, F − Fitch.
Source: Thomson Reuters

in Chapter 5. Note the additional yield that must be offered on these bonds ('Spread vs US') compared with what the US government has to pay despite the currency of coupons and principal both being US dollars. This is due to the extra risk of default.

Frequently, these bonds are issued under UK or US law to reassure lenders that should default occur there will be greater protection than under the issuer's law. The benefit of this was shown in the case of Greece's default in 2012 – the majority of its sovereign debt was issued under local law and those holders were forced to accept 74% losses in a 'bond exchange' (meaning they swapped the original bonds for lower-value ones). The minority holding the few governed under English law were repaid at par. Mind you, it is not always that easy. Take the case of Argentina's bonds, issued under US law. They defaulted in 2001. Following a deal with most of the bond holders (they got about 35 cents on the dollar) the country refused to pay anything to those who did not agree to the reduction (24% of the holders). The 'holdouts' (mostly hedge funds) fought in US courts for years and won a number of judgments – an Argentine ship was seized in Ghana at one point; the president is reluctant to fly abroad in her plane in case it is seized – which in 2014 resulted in a ruling that they should receive full payment including interest – see Article 3.6.

Article 3.6

Argentina row triggers interest in defaulted debt

By Elaine Moore

Financial Times July 2, 2014

1984 was not a good year for North Korea. That was the year western banks declared Pyongyang in default on debt it had sold in the previous decade, sealing off a possible avenue of funding for the reclusive state.

Yet the defaulted loan did not disappear. Instead, it was repackaged a decade later by French bank BNP into Swiss franc and Deutsche mark denominated debt and has been traded ever since.

North Korea's defaulted debt exists in a sort of twilight state, paying no interest but invested in by those who believe that the country cannot remain severed from the wider world forever. No payout on the loans is in sight, but prices on the securitised loan certificates have moved between 60 cents on the dollar to less than 10 cents over the years, depending on news from the country and indications about the future of sanctions.

Now the battle between Argentina and investors who hold the country's defaulted bonds has reawakened interest in markets such as those North Korean certificates, part of a small and illiquid world of hyper-exotic distressed debt.

If the 'hold out' hedge fund investors receive the money that New York judge Thomas Griesa says is due to them, they could stand to profit not only from the discount at which they purchased the bonds but on unpaid interest due since the default.

So-called past due interest can be the source of spectacular gains to investors patient enough to wait for it.

When Iraq defaulted on sovereign bonds in the 1980s, borrowed in part to fund a war with Iran, the unpaid interest spanned over two decades before the country restructured its debt in 2006. Vietnam repaid past interest on loans that had traded at less than 5 cents on the dollar in the 1990s when it rejoined capital markets and Liberian debt, which also traded at less than 5 cents in the 1990s, was settled at close to six times that when it was restructured.

The prospect of harvesting these sort of returns is why some investors will consider buying non-performing debt from the tiny island of Nauru in the South Pacific, currently trading at 5 cents on the dollar, or debt issued by Sudan before civil war split the country north to south.

Exotic frontier debt is in vogue right now. Debut sovereign bonds issued by Rwanda and Kenya have attracted unexpected levels of interest from investors keen for yield. That has caused concern in some quarters.

'There is an increasing lack of awareness about the illiquidity and implicit risk taken by investors as they move down the curve looking for yield in this zero interest world,' says Sam Vecht at BlackRock Frontiers investment trust.

But others say that long-term investment in defaulted sovereign debt is not necessarily the one-sided risk it might sound. The prospect of low-cost funding has also put pressure on countries such as Argentina to resolve outstanding debts if they are to tap global capital markets.

'There is a big difference between a country and a corporation defaulting because the country won't disappear,' says Christopher Wyke, emerging market debt product manager at Schroders.

One of the markets long considered ripe for turnaround is Cuba, which defaulted on its debt in 1986. This year prices in the secondary market for the discounted debt rose from 6 cents on the dollar to 9 cents. Experts say unpaid due interest could far exceed the sums demanded by investors in Argentinian debt.

'Opportunities [in distressed debt] will usually arise from a credit event such as the lifting of an embargo,' says Julian Adams, chief executive of investment fund Adelante. 'But this market is shrinking as countries embrace capital markets and must sort out their older debts.'

Sovereign foreign currency defaults

Country	Selective default date	Time in selective default
Russia	Jan 27 1999	22 months
Pakistan	Jan 29 1999	11 months
Indonesia, first default	Mar 30 1999	One day
Indonesia, second default	Apr 17 2000	Six months
Argentina	Nov 6 2001	54 months
Indonesia, third default	Apr 23 2002	Four months
Paraguay	Feb 13 2003	18 months
Uruguay	May 16 2003	One month
Grenada, first default	Dec 30 2004	11 months
Venezuela	Jan 18 2005	One month
Dominican Republic	Feb 1 2005	Five months
Belize, first default	Dec 7 2006	Three months
Seychelles*	Aug 7 2008	–
Ecuador	Dec 15 2008	Six months
Jamaica, first default	Jan 14 2010	One month
Belize, second default	Aug 21 2012	Seven months
Grenada, second default	Oct 8 2012	One week
Greece, first default	Feb 27 2012	Three months
Greece, second default	Dec 5 2012	Two weeks
Jamaica, second default	Feb 12 2013	22 days
Grenada, third default	Mar 12 2013	–
Cyprus	Jun 28 2013	Five days

* The rating on Seychelles was withdrawn while it was still in default

Source: Data from Thomson Reuters Datastream

Source: Moore, E. (2014) Argentina row triggers interest in defaulted debt, *Financial Times*, 2 July.
© The Financial Times Limited 2014. All Rights Reserved.

It is going to be much harder for holdouts to force governments to pay up in future – see Article 3.7.

Article 3.7

New framework for sovereign defaults

By Elaine Moore

Financial Times August 28, 2014

A group representing more than 400 of the world's largest banks, investors and debt issuers has agreed a plan for dealing with financially stricken countries and their creditors, in a bid to prevent a repeat of the wrangling that has pushed Argentina into default.

After months of talks convened by the US Treasury in the wake of Greece's restructuring, global debt experts will on Friday unveil a new framework that could transform the relationship between critically indebted nations and lenders.

Lawsuits filed by creditors against defaulting governments have doubled over the last decade and the changes come at a time when levels of sovereign debt have risen to record highs around the world in the wake of the financial crisis.

The fallout from recent defaults reignited calls for an international bankruptcy court, but market participants and Washington authorities favour a voluntary response rather than new statutory mechanisms.

The International Capital Market Association, whose members include banks, investors and debt issuers, has created fresh clauses for inclusion in sovereign debt contracts that will give countries the option to bind all investors to decisions agreed by the majority.

The new approach will make it difficult for small holdout investors to undermine restructuring deals by giving countries the option to employ a single vote across all bonds, with a 75% voting threshold, if they restructure their debt. This will hinder the chances of so-called 'vulture' investors from buying up blocking stakes.

Alternatively governments can choose to take votes on each bond, or votes on individual bonds and a second vote across all debt. The final option has become a standard clause in eurozone government bonds since 2013 in the wake of the bloc's debt crisis.

When Greece restructured billions of euros of debt in 2012 private investors with more than €6bn of Greek bonds would not accept the deal. Their actions put the country's financial future at risk, say analysts, and set a precedent that threatened to discourage investors from agreeing to future restructuring deals.

A further change to be outlined on Friday is intended to make clear that the common 'pari passu' clause, which hedge fund investors have used to argue for full repayment on Argentine debt, means equal treatments but not equal payments for bond holders.

Around half of all government debt defaults now trigger creditor lawsuits and in countries such as Congo, Ecuador, Iraq, Peru and Poland, small numbers of private investors have refused to take part in government plans to restructure unaffordable debt, holding out for full repayment.

Additional reporting by Robin Harding.

Source: Moore, E. (2014) New framework for sovereign defaults, *Financial Times*, 28 August.

International bond investors tend to be focused on those issued in hard currency, but it must be borne in mind that the vast majority of emerging economy government borrowing is in the domestic market in the local currency, and increasingly international investors are buying in those markets as inflation and government spendthrift habits are tamed and high economic growth with reasonably stable exchange rates is established – see Article 3.8.

Article 3.8

Markets: the road to redemption

By Robin Wigglesworth

Financial Times January 31, 2013

Developing nations have largely tackled their poor exchange rates, high inflation, crushing debt burdens, trade imbalances and budget deficits that helped sink them in the 1980s and 1990s.

One of the most remarkable shifts is the rapid growth of their domestic bond markets. Over the past decade they grew fivefold to about $10tn by late 2011, according to the latest comprehensive data, which is estimated to equal almost one-sixth of the world's total bond stock.

This is a revolutionary development. Throughout modern economic history, most countries that have needed long-term loans have been forced to borrow abroad in one of the world's major currencies, predominantly the US dollar. Although many have had banking sectors or even local bond markets to tap, the domestic lending capacity has often been limited, and the duration of the loans has been exceedingly short.

More than a decade ago, the economists Barry Eichengreen and Ricardo Hausmann named the emerging markets' inability to borrow abroad in their local currency as 'original sin'. Professor Hausmann: 'It seemed to be a huge, persistent problem that all emerging markets were born with, and had remarkable problems getting rid of'.

Original sin is pernicious. Borrowing in foreign currencies can both trigger and exacerbate financial and economic crises. When a country's debts are denominated in foreign currencies, it forces policy makers to keep exchange rates pegged or heavily managed. If the rate buckles, the authorities have to burn through valuable reserves and raise interest rates to protect the value of the local currency – even in the midst of a recession if necessary.

Almost inevitably, the peg breaks, the local currency tumbles, the foreign currency-denominated debt burden becomes too great and a destructive government default ensues.

Spurred by these crises, emerging market policy makers have spent the past decade getting their finances in order. Crucially, they have nurtured and developed domestic bond markets denominated in local currencies.

'We saw with our own eyes how hard [the Asian financial crisis in 1998] hit our neighbours, and how harshly the IMF treated them – far worse than it is treating the eurozone,' Cesar Purisima, the Philippine finance minister, told the Financial Times. 'We learnt lessons from that.'

The changes across emerging markets are eye-catching. The domestic Mexican peso bond market, for example, exploded from about $28bn in US dollar terms in 1996 to $445bn in late 2011. South Korea's bond market surged fivefold to $1.1tn over the same period, while Poland's zloty market grew sevenfold to $203bn.

It has been a gradual process. Local institutional investor bases have often had to be started from scratch through reforms that encourage domestic pension and insurance industries to take root. Above all, inflation – the nemesis of bond investors but a perennial problem in emerging markets – had to be tamed.

'When I started trading, emerging markets were the wild west,' recalls Sergio Trigo Paz, head of emerging market debt at BlackRock. 'Local markets were considered no-man's land, even domestically, due to hyperinflation.'

Kenneth Rogoff and Carmen Reinhart have shown that the share of domestic debt to total government debts in emerging markets declined gradually from a peak of about 80% in the 1950s to a low of about 40% in the early 1990s. But by 2010 the percentage had climbed sharply back to more than 60%. In fact, experts now say domestic debt levels could return to those highs of the 1950s.

'There were very large local bond markets before, but high inflation pretty much wiped them out,' says Mr Rogoff, an economics professor at Harvard. 'Things are changing. Developing countries have been very keen to rebalance their borrowing away from foreign markets.'

The financial crisis reinforced this trend. Domestic bond sales now account for the vast majority of government borrowing in the developing world, perhaps as much as 90% of it in 2012.

International investors have become increasingly infatuated by the economic prospects for the developing world and have piled into local bond markets in recent years. From less than $150bn in March 2009, foreign holdings of local currency emerging market bonds climbed to well over $500bn last year.

The rating agencies have also cheered the rise of local bond markets and have rewarded developing countries with better grades. 'One of the key reasons for the improvement in emerging market resilience and robustness – and the increase in their ratings – is the changing make-up of their debt,' says David Riley, head of sovereign ratings at Fitch Ratings.

Although positive, more vibrant local bond markets do not completely inoculate countries from crises. Deep local markets can even act as a temptation for governments to borrow excessively. Once they do, many countries have in the past found it easier simply to inflate the debts away – throttling local bond markets in the process. Some have simply defaulted. For example, Russia's short-term debt market allowed it to delay its inevitable default in 1998, but exacerbated the ensuing chaos.

Local bond markets are also of little help if a country has a current account deficit. Countries that import more than they export need foreign currency inflows to make up the difference, whether through borrowing or overseas investment. Even governments with healthy budget surpluses can run into trouble if the current account is negative.

It also remains tricky to sell longer-term bonds locally. While some have managed to lengthen the 'duration' of their markets, even some of the more advanced emerging economies struggle to sell bonds with a maturity longer than 10 years.

'Original sin is receding for some countries, but mostly for the advanced ones,' says Marie Cavanaugh, managing director and member of the sovereign ratings committee at Standard & Poor's. 'Poorer, less developed emerging economies are often still very dependent on foreign capital.'

Of the almost $10tn worth of locally denominated debts tallied by BofA, almost two-thirds are in Brazil, China and South Korea. Many smaller countries have found it harder to nurture local markets.

In fact, the IMF has started to become concerned that the current eagerness of investors to lend to emerging economies could lead some of these smaller states to forget the hard-learnt lessons of the past and borrow too much in dollars.

Countries such as Zambia and Mongolia have been identified as being at particular risk of reviving the bane of original sin. Mongolia late last year sold a $1.5bn bond – equal to a fifth of its annual economic output in a single offering.

Some fund managers also fret that emerging market companies could become future sources of instability, after selling record amounts of dollar-denominated corporate bonds in recent years.

Professors Hausmann and Eichengreen agree that original sin is a less pressing problem than in the past, but argue that improvements are the result of a drastic curtailment of dollar borrowing – not a rise in international investor participation on local bond markets. Indeed, these days some countries have imposed barriers to keep foreign investors out of their markets, rather than enticing them in. Capital inflows can cause currencies to appreciate, making a country less competitive. Foreign investors are often more fickle than local ones, and sharp outflows can unsettle local markets.

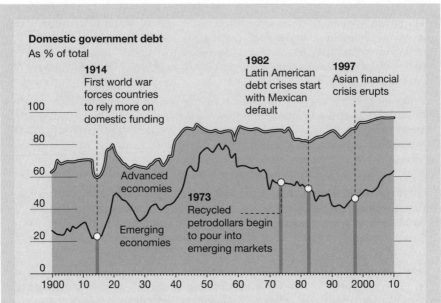

Domestic government debt
As % of total

1914
First world war
forces countries
to rely more on
domestic funding

1982
Latin American
debt crises start
with Mexican
default

1997
Asian financial
crisis erupts

Advanced
economies

1973
Recycled
petrodollars begin
to pour into
emerging markets

Emerging
economies

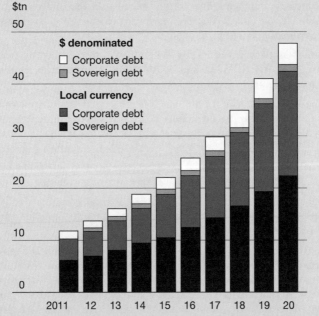

Global emerging markets debt projections
$tn

$ denominated
☐ Corporate debt
▨ Sovereign debt

Local currency
▨ Corporate debt
■ Sovereign debt

Sources: Data from C Reinhart and K Rogoff, 'The Forgotten History of Domestic Debt,' NBER, 2010;
Ashmore Group.

Nonetheless, the rise of domestic bond markets has proved a tremendously positive development not just for emerging economies but also for the wider international financial system. Rather than being sources of instability – as was often the case in the past – many emerging markets are now self-funding carthorses for the global economy.

The progress of the past decade is already striking. As long as policy makers do not forget the lessons of past crises, local bond markets are likely to continue to gain in size, vibrancy and importance, experts say.

 Source: Wigglesworth, R. (2013) Markets: the road to redemption, *Financial Times*, 31 January.
© The Financial Times Limited 2013. All Rights Reserved.

Africa has underdeveloped local bond markets, but even here many of its countries are now welcomed in the international dollar-denominated market – see Article 3.9.

Article 3.9

Sub-Saharan bond rush spreads east to Kenya and Tanzania

By Javier Blas in London and Katrina Manson

Financial Times September 3, 2013

Ever since Ghana became the first sub-Saharan African country to issue a sovereign bond in 2007, the trend to tap capital markets has been confined to the west and south of the continent. Now, east Africa is joining.

Kenya and Tanzania are close to debuts in the US dollar-denominated sovereign bond market, with notes worth up to $2.5bn – joining a string of other African countries that have already raised a record $6.2bn in international debt this year, three times as much as in 2011, according to data provider Dealogic.

Until now, only Rwanda has tapped the debt market from east Africa. But the arrival of Kenya and Tanzania is set to put the region firmly on the radar of international investors – barely a decade after the region benefited from billions of dollars in debt relief.

'East Africa is the second fastest growing region in the world, only behind developing Asia,' says Ragnar Gudmundsson, head of the International Monetary Fund in Kenya. 'That is why investors are attracted to the region.'

David Cowan, Africa economist at Citigroup, adds that east African nations would also benefit from investors' interest in diversifying their exposure from countries such as Nigeria, Ghana and Gabon. 'There is strong appetite to diversify from the west African sovereign bond story, which is mostly linked to oil,' he says.

The JPMorgan Nexgem Africa index, which tracks the bond market in the region, is yielding 7.3%, up from a low-point in January of 5.3%. Still, interest rates for sovereign issuers in sub-Saharan Africa remain well below the most recent peak of 14% set during the global financial crisis in 2008.

Zambia's debut last year marked the top for the sub-Saharan market, raising $750m at a yield of 5.6%. But since then other countries have paid higher yields: Ghana paid an interest rate of 7.85% in June, and Nigeria paid 6.6%.

Mohammed Hanif, head of Insparo Asset Management, which manages a $160m emerging markets fixed-income fund that holds Nigerian and Zambian sovereign debt among others, says investor appetite for African debt is so strong the company will launch an Africa-only fixed-income fund later this year.

'There is a clear lack of tradeable African debt around,' he says.

But he warns that many investors attracted by 'a bit of euphoria in the market' but who are not familiar with Africa are easily wrong footed. Insparo did not join in the rush for Rwanda's debut $400m bond, which launched earlier this year and has already fallen significantly. He says Rwanda's small, aid-dependent economy is at too early a stage of development to warrant a bond. Still, Mr Hanif says Kenya and Tanzania instead present 'great stories' with more mature economies that offer 'sustainable growth' and Insparo expects to participate in both bonds.

In Dar es Salaam, the commercial capital of Tanzania, William Mgimwa, finance minister, put the example of a private placement the country launched earlier this year as a sign of the interest that investors have in east Africa.

'In March this year I was online requesting [offers] for investors. I was looking for $500m but it was oversubscribed to $2.5bn,' he says, adding: 'We already have very good investors who are actually waiting for [the bond] opportunity.'

Maiden sovereign bond issuances

Country	Date issued	Amount	Yield at issue
Gabon	Dec 6 2007	$1,000m	8.25%
Ghana	Sep 27 2007	$750m	8.5%
Kenya	Q4 2013	$1,500m	n.a.
Namibia	Oct 27 2011	$500m	5.84%
Nigeria	Jan 21 2011	$500m	7.13%
Rwanda	Apr 2013	$400m	6.63%
Senegal	Dec 15 2009	$200m	9.47%
Seychelles	Sep 27 2006	$200m	9.47%
Tanzania	Q4 2013	$1,000m	n.a.
Zambia	Sep 13 2012	$750m	5.63%

➡

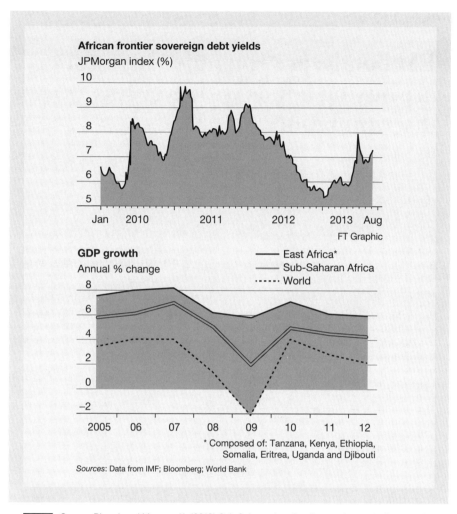

African frontier sovereign debt yields
JPMorgan index (%)

FT Graphic

GDP growth
Annual % change

— East Africa*
— Sub-Saharan Africa
······ World

* Composed of: Tanzana, Kenya, Ethiopia,
Somalia, Eritrea, Uganda and Djibouti

Sources: Data from IMF; Bloomberg; World Bank

FT

Source: Blas, J. and Manson, K. (2013) Sub-Saharan bond rush spreads east to Kenya and
Tanzania, *Financial Times*, 3 September.
© The Financial Times Limited 2013. All Rights Reserved.

Clearly, many emerging markets are for the bravest of investors, but it can pay
off if you buy at high yields and then the generality of investors become less
afraid, start buying, pushing up the bond price and lowering yields, as they did
with Irish and Belarusian debt following their crises. But there is brave and
there is foolhardy – see Article 3.10.

Article 3.10

EM bonds: are you nuts? Investors are buying bonds with ever less discrimination

Lex column

Financial Times June 11, 2014

On Tuesday a transnational group of terrorists seized Iraq's second-largest city, Mosul. The army did not resist. Abandoned equipment and millions of dollars left in Mosul's banks are now at the disposal of the Islamic State of Iraq and the Levant.

But never mind that. Would you like to take the government's side for a yield of 6.7%? That is where risk is being priced in Iraq's US dollar bond due in 2028. This would be *after* the market had digested ill tidings from Mosul.

Not so sure of the risk-reward there? Investors may prefer to buy into the stability of the regime of President Abdel Fattah el-Sisi, with Egyptian hard-currency bonds that mature in a quarter of a century. These yield just below 7%. How about Belarus? There is a 6.5% yield on bonds due in 2018. Trust that no revolution in Minsk disrupts cash flows before then.

The point here is not simply that some dodgy sovereigns are being priced with low yields. Risk assets are being bid up generally, even as US Treasury yields have fallen so far in 2014. Foreign-currency EM bonds are still cheaper overall than high-yield

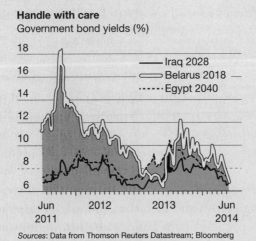

Handle with care
Government bond yields (%)

——— Iraq 2028
⊂⊃ Belarus 2018 —
······ Egypt 2040

Jun 2011   2012   2013   Jun 2014

Sources: Data from Thomson Reuters Datastream; Bloomberg

developed-market credit. Even so, investors are beginning to buy these bonds with ever less discrimination.

A brave investor may also argue that fundamentals favour the Iraqi bond. The country sells lots of oil. But 6.7%? EM bond risks may not seem so high when risk has become favoured everywhere. That is not the same as riskless.

Source: Lex column (2014) EM bonds: are you nuts?, *Financial Times*, 11 June.
© The Financial Times Limited 2014. All Rights Reserved.

Local authority/municipal/quasi-state/ agency bonds

Local authority, municipal, quasi-state and agency bonds are issued by governments and organisations at a sub-national level, such as a county, city or state. They pay a rate of interest and are repayable on a specific future date, similar in fact to Treasury bonds. They are sometimes called **semi-sovereigns** or **sub-sovereigns**. They are an important means of raising money to finance developments, buildings or expansion by the local authority or agency. They are riskier than government bonds (the issuers cannot print their own money as governments might) as from time to time cities, counties, etc. do go bust and fail to pay their debts. However, many issuers, particularly in Europe and the US, obtain **bond insurance** from a private insurance group with a top credit rating, guaranteeing that the bond will be serviced on time. This can boost an issue's credit rating, as its rating will then be based on the insurer's credit rating, which reduces the interest rate the sub-sovereigns pay.

In the UK, local authority bonds or quasi-state bonds are out of favour at the moment, although Transport for London issued a 25-year bond in 2006, and in 2012–2013 raised £1.6 billion with four bond issues with maturities ranging from 5 to 33 years. There has been talk of issuing a 'Brummie' bond (by Birmingham City Council), but this has yet to be finalised. In July 2013 the city of Leeds raised more than £100 million with an oversubscribed bond issued to finance a social housing project.

US municipals

Municipal bonds ('**munis**', pronounced *mew-knees*) are issued by state and local government departments and special districts. Much of the infrastructure

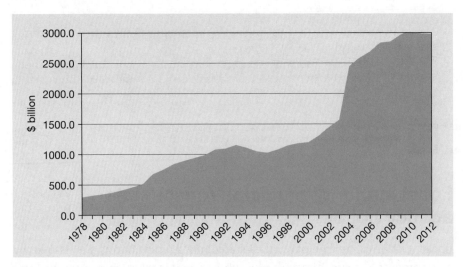

Figure 3.9 State and local government debt in the US over time

Source: Data from Financial Accounts of the United States, June 2013

in the US has been and still is financed by municipal bonds, the first of which was issued in 1812. These bonds have proved to be a valuable source of finance for local communities.

The US muni market is enormous, with a total in outstanding bonds of over $3 trillion in 2012 – see Figure 3.9. Special districts are independent government bodies managed by a board and they provide some type of service to a particular area, e.g. airports, ports, roads, bridges, public transport, parking facilities, fire services, libraries, parks, cemeteries, hospitals, nursing homes, conservation, sewerage, waste disposal, stadiums, water, electricity and gas. They tend to be issued in minimal denominations of $5,000.

General-obligation bonds offer the bond holder a priority claim on the general (usually tax) revenue of the issuer in the event of a default, whereas a holder of a **revenue bond** receives interest and principal repayment from the revenues of a particular project, e.g. the income from a toll bridge.

Some municipal bond issuers have made bad investment decisions and have gone bust, notably those issued by Orange County, California, in 1994, where the county treasurer lost more than $1.5 billion; by Jefferson County, Alabama, in 2011, which went bankrupt owing $4.2 billion; and by the city of Detroit, Michigan, the former hub of the US motor industry, which in 2013 went down owing $18 billion. Investors who bought bonds where the issuer has gone bankrupt face losing some or all of their investment. Despite these few well-publicised defaults, overwhelmingly municipal bonds provide a valuable service to their communities and their investors with very few problems.

Investors in US municipal bonds issued by state and local governments are usually exempt from federal income tax on the interest they receive. In many states the income is exempt from state taxes. Because of these concessions they usually trade at lower yields to maturity than US government bonds. The investor groups dominating the municipal securities market are households (some investing via mutual funds), commercial banks and some insurance companies able to benefit the most from the tax concessions. Municipal bonds are less liquid than federal government bonds in the secondary market, so investors may have greater difficulty selling in some of the smaller issues and the dealer spreads (bid-ask) can be wide.

Some municipals outside of America

In Japan, the Japan Finance Organization for Municipalities (JFM) established in 2008, issues long-term bonds. Most of these are domestic bonds but some are international issues. The amount outstanding in 2014 was about ¥22 trillion (US$220 billion), which provided loans to finance local projects.

The German Länder (federal states) are also large issuers, with more than €350 billion of bonds outstanding in 2014, about the same as the Netherlands. There are also quasi-state organisations issuing bonds in Europe. In France, Société Nationale des Chemins de Fer Français (SNCF, the state-owned French railway operator), and in Germany, Deutsche Bahn (DB, the state-owned German railway company), are just some of the institutions that have issued bonds. Sweden and Finland both run schemes where local communities join together to issue bonds to raise finance. By keeping the schemes local, the risk is reduced so that the bonds receive higher credit ratings. Article 3.11 discusses some local authority bonds.

Article 3.11

Local authorities turn to capital markets

By Elaine Moore

Financial Times September 30, 2014

Public sector debt is piling ever higher, driven by the lure of low borrowing costs and strong investor demand.

Borrowers ranging from supranational organisations like the World Bank to individual towns and states are issuing record amounts of debt.

In theory, the sudden rise in debt issued by public sector organisations in the wake of the financial crisis should fall back as the economy recovers. But so far, that has not happened.

Last year, supranationals such as the World Bank, European Stability Mechanism and others issued $267bn – a record level of debt. Local authorities are also borrowing more than ever – issuing $7.2bn in bonds so far this year compared with $3.7bn by the same point last year.

Collectively, quasi-government borrowers make an unwieldy group. At one end of the scale are enormous organisations created by multiple governments in response to political or economic crisis.

At the other end are sub-government authorities with the ability to borrow on capital markets to fund local projects.

Between the two are government-sponsored banks such as Germany's KfW and AFD in France, which fund programmes with specific economic or social functions. These agencies borrowed slightly less last year than in 2012, but still issued a sum of debt that exceeded borrowing in 2010.

All tend to boast similar credit ratings to the governments that back them, and offer a slight bump in yields to investors.

The Belgian sub-sovereign Flemish Community, for example, offers about 40 basis points more than the equivalent Belgian five-year bond, according to Rabobank.

'Traditionally you get at least a few basis points over sovereign debt yields,' says Matthew Cairns, strategist at Rabobank. However, he points out that the investor base for public debt has broadened from conservative central banks to global banks under the direction of new regulation. This, combined with the fall in governments, afforded the highest, triple-A credit rating, and the drop in debt issued by US agencies – such as Fannie Mae and Freddie Mac – is pushing up order books.

'The yield makes the sector attractive, but now there is more demand than paper available and yields are falling. We don't know how far that can go,' says Mr Cairns.

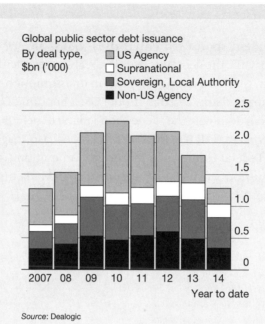

Global public sector debt issuance

By deal type, $bn ('000)

☐ US Agency
☐ Supranational
■ Sovereign, Local Authority
■ Non-US Agency

Source: Dealogic

Investor appetite for public sector debt has become intense, says George Richardson, head of capital markets at the World Bank Treasury.

In the UK, local authorities are hoping to kick start a market in municipal bonds to take advantage of low global borrowing rates by creating central agencies.

The UK's Local Government Association has said that creating an agency able to issue debt on behalf of councils could save them more than £1bn in borrowing costs.

More than £4.5m has so far been raised to create the Local Capital Finance Company, and the organisers say they hope to raise the first bond by March or April 2015.

Bankers say the success of municipal bond agencies in Nordic countries, Switzerland, Italy and now France, bodes well.

In Sweden, Kommuninvest raises sums that standalone councils would not be able to do, something UK councils will be aware of. Launched in the late 1980s, by the end of last year Kommuninvest's total lending had reached $28bn.

And in the US, the vast municipal bond market, which reached $3.7tn by the end of last year, is an established source of saving for households.

Source: Moore, E. (2014) Local authorities turn to capital markets, *Financial Times*, 30 September.

Agencies

Agencies (government-sponsored enterprises, GSEs) are set up to fulfil a public purpose and while the debt they issue is not always explicitly guaranteed by the government, there is a strong implication or assumption that the state will step in to make good any shortfall. In the US, a handful of organisations (quasi-governmental) dominate the agency bond market, including the Federal Home Loan Bank System (FHLBS), the Federal National Mortgage Association (Fannie Mae), the Federal Home Loan Mortgage Corporation (Freddie Mac),[2] Tennessee Valley Authority (TVA) and the Student Loan Marketing Association (Sallie Mae).

---

[2] Fannie Mae and Freddie Mac were taken over by the US government in 2008 to save them from failure after the mortgage crisis.

CHAPTER 4
CORPORATE BONDS

Most companies at some time need to borrow large sums of money to finance their operations, and it is vital that they try to do so to their best advantage, e.g. at the lowest cost, with an optimum mix in terms of maturity dates and with an acceptable pattern of cash outflows.

If a company finds that it needs extra debt capital to operate successfully, one of the ways it can source the capital is by issuing corporate bonds. These bonds are simply IOUs issued by the company and bought by investors who, in return for lending the company their money, receive interest payments (usually) and payment of the principal amount at a set time. In general, corporate bonds offer a higher rate of return than reputable government bonds but as you might expect, this comes with a greater degree of risk of failure to pay what was agreed. Having said that, because many governments are less reputable than some companies within the country, corporate borrowing can be at lower rates of return than that of their governments. Corporate bonds are generally issued with a coupon (usually taxable) paying a set amount annually or semi-annually, and their yield is calculated in the same way as government bonds. Most corporate bonds are medium to long dated and are rarely more than 20 years.

Corporate bonds can be a very useful way for companies to raise money without issuing equity, which brings the possibility of losing a degree of control over the company, or accepting the constraints imposed by bank lenders. Issuance depends on investors and corporate managers having confidence in the economy and in the prospects for the specific company as well as the interest rate level. Investor appetite for corporate bonds ebbs and flows, as does managerial confidence in the benefits of additional debt. Sometimes, as in August 2013, there is great economic uncertainty and a considerable drop in the amount being issued – see Article 4.1.

Article 4.1

Global corporate bond issuance at lowest level in five years

By Ralph Atkins

Financial Times August 25, 2013

Global corporate bond issuance has this month fallen to the lowest level in five years as market turmoil triggered by rising US Treasury yields persuades companies worldwide to shelve funding plans.

Just $61bn in investment grade corporate debt has been raised so far in August. In August last year, more than $121bn in new corporate debt was issued.

The slowdown follows the US Federal Reserve's announcement that it would slow the pace of its asset purchases, or 'quantitative easing', from as early as next month.

Ben Bernanke, Fed chairman, first hinted at his QE 'tapering' plans on May 22. Since then the yield on 10-year US Treasuries has risen to more than 2.9%, compared with a low of 1.61% at the start of May. Higher bond yields, which move inversely to prices, have left investors nursing losses on the value of their portfolios.

'What has been worrying people has been the speed and abruptness of moves. It has made people more nervous,' said Bryan Pascoe, global head of debt capital markets at HSBC.

In the first months of this year, corporate bond issuance was running at a rapid pace as companies took advantage of historically low interest rates. A high water mark was reached in April when Apple, the US maker of the iPhone, sold bonds worth $17bn. But since May, weekly data show global corporate debt issuance tumbling. The steepest decline has been in emerging markets, where bond and equity markets have seen sharp price falls in recent weeks as investors have withdrawn capital.

However, bankers pointed out that US corporate bond issuance had remained relatively strong, with debt markets buoyed by investment flows returning from emerging markets. They also attributed the slowdown in Europe to a return to a more normal summer lull – after several years in which companies have felt compelled to issue whenever conditions were relatively favourable. Companies that have issued bonds this month have included Viacom, Royal Dutch Shell and China's Wuhan Iron & Steel Group.

Some 'corporate bonds' are in fact issued by business enterprises owned by a government. Also, the biggest issuers are banks and other financials rather than non-financial commercial corporations. An important sub-set of corporate bonds are the **utilities**, including telecommunication companies, water, electricity and gas suppliers. Because these are often regulated by a government agency they may have a different risk/return profile to bonds from standard **industrials** (manufacturers and service companies).

Trading of bonds

While the government bond markets in developed economies are very liquid, with single government bond issues raising billions and with thousands of investors trading in the market, by contrast corporate bond market activity can be very low. Companies may raise merely millions of pounds/dollars in an issue, and most investors buy and hold to maturity rather than trade in and out. Some companies issue bonds on a regular basis, every few months or years, each with its own coupon and terms, thus there might be a dozen bonds for one company and tens of thousands of different corporate issues in the secondary market place. The wide range reduces the market depth for any one issue. This means that an investor might not be able to buy or sell particular bonds because there is none being traded – see Article 4.2.

Article 4.2

Battle is on to make bonds more transparent

By Stephen Foley

Financial Times May 1, 2013

A retail investor who gets her hands on an Apple bond can sleep pretty soundly. Not only can she be pretty sure the iPhone maker will be good for the interest payments. If she decides, at some point in the future, to sell the bond, she can be pretty sure there will be a ready buyer there to take it off her hands at the prevailing market price.

Would that this could be said for all bonds.

The scale of Apple's $17bn debt offering means there ought to always be lots of bonds changing hands, and it will be easy to keep tabs on the price at which they are trading. They join an elite group of liquid corporate bonds. Most issues are not so easy to buy and sell.

In fact, of the 30,000 investment-grade corporate bonds trading in the US alone, only 20 trade more than ten times a day, according to MarketAxess. The proportion of the market that turns over in a year has slipped below 75%. The situation in municipal bonds, issued by state and local governments, is even worse.

And that means it is not so easy for a bond investor to be sure of the price she will have to pay if she puts in an order, or end up receiving if she tells her broker to sell.

US corporate bond market grows in size . . .

Amounts outstanding

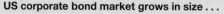

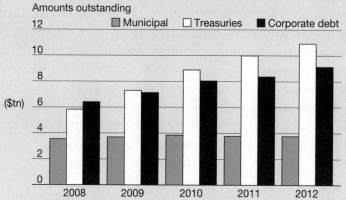

. . . but secondary market trading of IG debt sinks

Investment grade corporate debt, 12-month rolling turnover

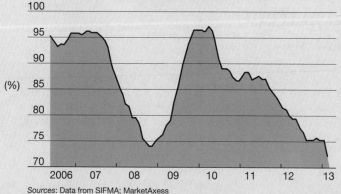

Sources: Data from SIFMA; MarketAxess

At an industry forum earlier this month, the independent financial adviser Ric Edelman went as far as to claim investors were, in effect, being 'lied to . . . We understand why that happens, that no deceit is intended, but they are shocked to discover what they thought was $105 was in fact $98 and don't know that until they have sold. We have huge education and disclosure problems within the industry.'

The issue is getting scrutinised by regulators in the US and Europe like never before. Technological advances bring the tantalising prospect of more liquidity and there is already more transparency on price, at least after bonds have traded.

But the US Securities and Exchange Commission for one is sceptical that the benefits are flowing through to retail investors. They fear that the opacity of the market allows big dealers to take advantage by taking big mark-ups on trades.

The agency is considering demanding more transparency in corporate and municipal bond trading, although it has to weigh concerns that new rules could be detrimental to some big players in the market.

As for investors being able to see a price for their specific bond before they trade, that is a harder problem to crack. Traditionally, there has been no substitute to brokers calling round the trading desks of Wall Street to ask what a specific lot of bonds will fetch.

Some corporate bonds are sufficiently liquid to trade on the London Stock Exchange and other exchanges in Europe, Asia or the Americas and may also be traded on **electronic communication networks** (**ECNs**), which facilitate trading outside stock exchanges, but the vast majority of trading occurs in the **over-the-counter** market directly between an investor and a bond dealer. Bond dealers stand ready to quote bid and offer prices depending on whether the investor wants to buy or sell. Fund managers, or brokers acting for investors, will have to contact a number of these dealers by telephone to get quote prices. The bid–offer spreads are generally higher than for equities – even large company bonds can have a spread of 15%, but most are less than this.

There have been attempts to shift a large volume of trading on to computer-based systems – see Article 4.3. These electronic trading venues allow investors to input their desired buy or sell offer prices and amounts. Such an offer may be fulfilled by the computer matching up with other clients (or the bank) on the other side of the trade (**crossing trade**). The competition, transparency and efficiency brought by the electronic systems will, it is hoped, reduce transaction costs. Many such platforms are now operating but they still account for only 1% of trades. Investors are irritated by the splitting of such trades between numerous venues, mostly run by an investment bank with its own agenda (**single-dealer systems**) and would prefer to see one dominant platform (**multi-dealer platform**) emerge, run in a way that would benefit them. Concern has been expressed that platform providers are using data from the trading venue to inform their own team of traders and market makers – this knowledge might be used against investors. Market makers in the OTC market appear to be somewhat reluctant to shift from one-to-one trades with high spreads allowing them to pocket the difference between bid and offer prices to a computer system doing cheaper automatic trades – turkeys not voting for Christmas, I guess.

Article 4.3

Electronic trading to muscle in on corporate debt

By Michael Mackenzie, Dan McCrum and Tracy Alloway

Financial Times April 3, 2013

Computers rule on trading desks – except in the corporate bond market, one of the last bastions of telephone based transactions between investors and Wall Street dealers. But that may be about to change.

A recent surge in buying and selling of Dell's corporate bonds, triggered by the news of a leveraged buyout of the company, suggests electronic trading systems are set to muscle into this corner of the bond market.

While advocates of electronic trading are highlighting the shift in behaviour, some say the $9tn US corporate bond market is not designed for a seamless transition to computerised interactions, the way equities and foreign exchange trade.

'Human judgment is what we're paid for in this business,' says Bonnie Baha, global credit portfolio manager for DoubleLine. With many small debt issues, prices on a screen for thinly traded securities would quickly become stale, she adds.

But for all the attachment to long standing and cosy relationships between sales staff at dealers and investors, changing conditions are leading the way to greater adoption of electronic trading.

Since the financial crisis, higher capital costs and regulatory scrutiny have forced Wall Street banks to sharply reduce their presence in the corporate bond market. With banks holding a smaller 'inventory' of bonds, it is harder for so-called 'buyside' investors to buy and sell large amounts of debt.

Coming forward to fill this gap are electronic trading platforms such as MarketAxess, Bonds.com, BondDesk, and TradingScreen. While attracting growing volumes, for the most part, trading on these platforms involves so-called 'odd lots' or small trades of older bond issues.

At least, that was the case until trading activity in Dell bonds on several platforms surged earlier this year. For one electronic platform, Bonds.com, the heightened activity in Dell bonds that helped its daily market share jump fivefold to around 10% was a watershed and points to a future solution. 'It shows the model works, really well, or one like it could,' says Thomas Thees, chief executive at Bonds.com.

He says the industry needs to reach a consensus around one trading venue. The dilemma for the industry is that an already fragmented bond market, comprised of thousands of individual bond issues, requires a common solution, not an ecosystem of competing electronic trading platforms. As a host of venues and initiatives by dealers are fighting for leadership, investors have yet to throw their weight behind one of them.

But at some point the investor community needs to take the lead. 'The buyside has to be very engaged and involved with getting out in front of the liquidity issue, rather than sitting back and waiting for a solution,' says Chris Rice, global head of trading at State Street Global Advisors. 'We need to take control of our destiny and start supporting emerging bond trading venues.'

Some dealers say efforts to build electronic corporate bond trading platforms have had to start slowly. Electronic trading can help banks reduce costs in their bond-trading businesses, by automating trades and eliminating expensive staff, but the trade-off is greater price transparency and potentially smaller profits per trade. Banks are reluctant to give up their profitable 'high-touch' dealing in the bonds before they absolutely have to, some dealers say privately. Still, many banks have been experimenting with their own platforms, including Goldman Sachs, Morgan Stanley and UBS.

For many large bond investors, the use of single dealer platforms is limited, given that the dealer selects the bonds being transacted and can also gain an insight into what investors are doing.

Source: Mackenzie, M., McCrum, D. and Alloway, T. (2013) Electronic trading to muscle in on corporate debt, *Financial Times*, 3 April.

Because most corporate bond market trading is a private matter between the dealer and its customer in the OTC market it is difficult to obtain prices of recent trades; they are not shown in the *Financial Times*, for example. Some websites provide prices and other details on a few dozen corporate bonds, for example www.fixedincomeinvestor.co.uk, www.hl.co.uk, www.selftrade.co.uk, http://finra-markets.morningstar.com/BondCenter/Default.jsp.

Corporate bonds are generally the province of investing institutions, such as pension and insurance funds, with private investors tending not to hold them, mainly due to the large amounts of cash involved – the minimum denomination for bonds to be listed on a European stock market under EU Directives without a prospectus is €100,000 (or its equivalent in another currency at time of issue). The par value on one bond, at, say, £100,000, €100,000 or $100,000, is said to have minimum **lot** or **piece**. By keeping the denomination above these sizes, thus putting off retail investors, the issuer is exempt from the requirement for high levels of disclosure and ongoing financial reporting (e.g. exempt from yearly and half-yearly reports) because they are issuing to professional investing organisations.

Having said that the main bond market is a wholesale one, I need to add that there is another regulated market in London. In 2010 the London Stock Exchange (LSE, www.londonstockexchange.com) launched the **Order Book for Retail Bonds (ORB)**, which offers retail investors the opportunity to trade a number of gilts, corporate bonds and international bonds, where lots are often £100 or £1,000, with a typical initial minimum investment of £2,000, and the costs of trading are relatively low.

Corporates are able to issue bonds on ORB in sizes smaller (from only £25 million) than on the wholesale markets, where issues are usually £250 million plus. Issuers must apply and be accepted by both (1) the United Kingdom Listing Authority (UKLA), part of the financial services industry regulator, the Financial Conduct Authority (FCA), and (2) the LSE. Trading is facilitated by competing market makers advertising bid and offer prices on the LSE system during the trading day, 8am to 4.30pm. Retail investors can buy through a stockbroker, wealth manager or other regulated intermediary. Since 2010, companies on ORB have raised more than £4 billion with 42 new issues. Table 4.1 presents some of the issues, showing the amounts raised.

Table 4.1 Some bonds available to retail investors on the London Stock Exchange's
Order Book for Retail Bonds market

Issuer	Market	Date Listed	Issue Size
Ladbrokes Group Finance plc	ORB	17-Jun-14	£100m
Paragon Group of Companies plc	ORB	30-Jan-14	£125m
Premier Oil plc	ORB	11-Dec-13	£150m
A2D Funding plc	ORB	21-Oct-13	£150m
Bruntwood Investments plc	ORB	25-Jul-13	£50m
Helical Bar plc	ORB	25-Jun-13	£80m
International Personal Finance plc	ORB	08-May-13	£101.5m
Provident Financial plc	ORB	27-Mar-13	£65m
Paragon Group of Companies plc	ORB	05-Mar-13	£60m
EnQuest plc	ORB	15-Feb-13	£155m
Alpha Plus Holdings plc	ORB	19-Dec-12	£48.5m
Unite Group plc	ORB	12-Dec-12	£90m
Tullett Prebon plc	ORB	11-Dec-12	£80m
St. Modwen Properties plc	ORB	08-Nov-12	£80m
London Stock Exchange Group plc	ORB	05-Nov-12	£300m
Workspace Group plc	ORB	10-Oct-12	£57.5m
Beazley plc	ORB	25-Sep-12	£75m
Intermediate Capital Group	ORB	20-Sep-12	£80m
CLS Holdings	ORB	12-Sep-12	£65m
ICAP	ORB	31-Jul-12	£125m
Primary Health Properties plc	ORB	24-Jul-12	£75m
Severn Trent plc	ORB	11-Jul-12	£75m
Tesco Personal Finance plc	ORB	23-May-12	£200m
HSBC	ORB	02-May-12	£196m
Provident Financial	ORB	02-Apr-12	£120m
Places for People	ORB	31-Jan-12	£40m
Intermediate Capital Group plc	ORB	22-Dec-11	£35m
Tesco Personal Finance plc	ORB	16-Dec-11	£60m
Royal Bank of Scotland	ORB	07-Nov-11	£20m
National Grid	ORB	06-Oct-11	£285.5m

Figures 4.1 to 4.5 show the secondary bond price movements for some well-known companies.

Figure 4.1 Secondary bond price movements: Aviva

Source: Data from www.fixedincomeinvestor.co.uk

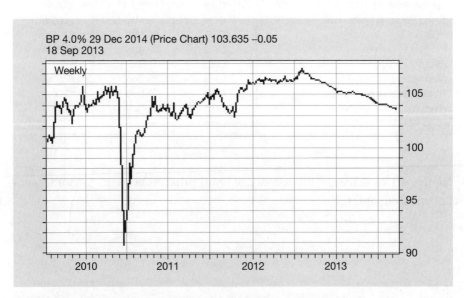

Figure 4.2 Secondary bond price movements: BP

Source: Data from www.fixedincomeinvestor.co.uk

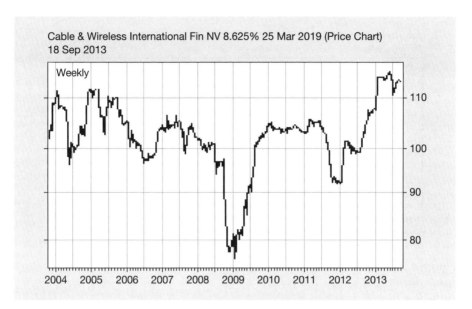

Figure 4.3 Secondary bond price movements: Cable & Wireless

Source: Data from www.fixedincomeinvestor.co.uk

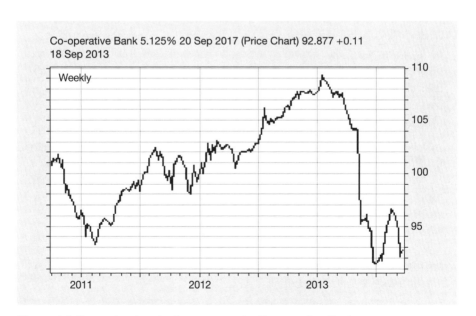

Figure 4.4 Secondary bond price movements: Co-operative Bank

Source: Data from www.fixedincomeinvestor.co.uk

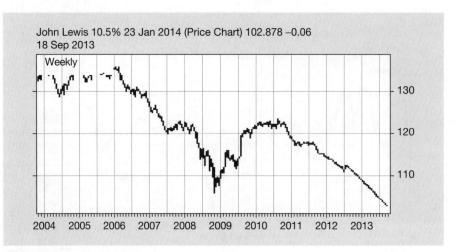

Figure 4.5 Secondary bond price movements: John Lewis

Source: Data from www.fixedincomeinvestor.co.uk

Case study

Tesco Bank ('Personal Finance') bond

We now look at a bond issue on ORB in more detail: Tesco Bank's 8.5-year 5% Sterling Fixed Rate Bond issued in May 2012 and due to be redeemed at £100 on 21 November 2020. However, it may be redeemed (at 100% of face value), purchased or cancelled by Tesco Bank before then. This may happen if the tax rules change to make Tesco Bank pay more, or in the case of default. Interest is paid on 21 May and 21 November each year.

When first issued the minimum purchase was a mere £2,000 and the issue price was 100% of the face value. Barclays Bank and Investec Bank both helped with the sale of the bonds in the primary market. They were **book-runners** (organisers of the issue) who received in fees 0.75% of the amount raised (0.75% of £200 million, i.e. £1.5 million), of which two-thirds was passed on to eight **distributors**, stockbrokers who sold the bonds to investors. Barclays Bank and Investec Bank subsequently acted as market makers in the secondary market. Many free financial websites display information about the bond and the trading prices in the secondary market – an example is shown in Figure 4.6, taken from www.ADVFN.com. Trades are settled after two business days (T+2).

Figure 4.7 shows the price movements of Tesco Bank's bond during its first two years.

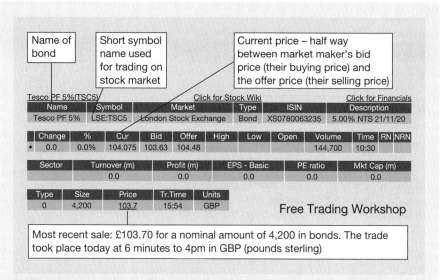

Figure 4.6 Trading details of Tesco Bank's bond on ADVFN

Source: advfn.com

Figure 4.7 Price chart of Tesco Bank 5% sterling 2020 bond

Source: advfn.com

Not all the bonds issued in ORB are borrowing with the same level of safety because they may not have the backup from the strongest part of a group of companies under the same ownership – see Article 4.4.

Article 4.4

Concerns mount over UK retail bond issues

By Steve Johnson

Financial Times August 18, 2013

By most measures, the London Stock Exchange's order book for retail bonds has been a runaway success.

Since its launch in 2010, the electronic hub has hosted 38 corporate bond issues and raised £3.4bn from yield-hungry small investors, who have been able to snap up the bulk of these issues in denominations of just £100. As yet, not one of these retail bonds has defaulted and most are trading above par.

The development filled an embarrassing hole in the UK's capital market landscape; whereas countries such as Germany, France, Italy and Spain have long had flourishing retail bond markets, UK companies' historic unwillingness to issue paper in denominations of less than £50,000 had long stymied a similar market in London.

'In terms of the development of the market, it has been a very good thing,' says Kate Ball-Dodd at law firm Mayer Brown. 'It has allowed access to a type of investment that was difficult for retail investors to access before because of the very high denominations.'

However, some investment industry professionals are raising concerns about the nature of some of these bond issues. One concern is that retail investors may be unwittingly assuming more risk than traditional institutional bond buyers.

National Grid and Severn Trent have issued retail bonds backed by cash flows from their holding companies, rather than the regulated operating companies that stand behind many of their bonds aimed at institutions.

The key difference is that the regulated entities are barred by the regulator from taking on too much debt, reducing the risk to lenders.

'[A retail bond] might have a good name on the tin but the debt may be issued by an overseas subsidiary,' says Jason Hollands, managing director of Bestinvest. 'You need to know where you sit in the capital structure of the overall business if the company runs into trouble.'

Tesco Personal Finance, the banking subsidiary of the retailer, has issued three retail bonds. [Have] all the buyers understood that the debt is issued by a subsidiary, not the parent company?

Retail and institutional bonds have been issued by the same entity, but with the retail version paying a lower coupon. For instance, Provident Financial, a subprime lender, simultaneously issued a retail bond with a 7% coupon and an institutional one paying 8% last year.

Mini bonds

There is another class of bonds targeted at retail investors, but these do not have a secondary market. They have been dubbed **mini-bonds** (**mini-retail** or **self-issued bonds**) and are issued in very small amounts by small companies – see Article 4.5 for some examples. With these bonds lenders are committed for the full term (usually 3–5 years), to a small, usually non-stock market-quoted firm, with less open accounting than quoted firms. The marketing and information material has not been vetted by the FCA. The covenants placed on the bond to reduce lender risk tend to be much lighter than those of normal bonds. The interest rates offered on the bonds described in Article 4.5 are greater than those on ORB due to the additional liquidity and default risk. They also suffer from not being eligible for inclusion in retail investors' tax shelters such as self-invested personal pensions and not being covered by the regulators' Financial Services Compensation Scheme should something go wrong.

Article 4.5

'Crowdfunding' muscles in on the bond market

By Thomas Hale

Financial Times June 24, 2014

'Crowdfunding' is coming for the bond market. Two UK restaurant chains have raised fixed-income debt in the past week through Crowdcube, a crowdfunding platform with 75,000 registered users.

Chilango, a Mexican restaurant chain, is looking to raise up to £3m through its crowdfunded retail bond – the 'first in the world' of its kind.

The 5-year bond, which yields 8%, also included a free weekly burrito for those willing to invest over £10,000.

Just days later, River Cottage, a restaurant chain founded by Hugh Fearnley-Whittingstall, the celebrity chef, also crowdfunded a £1m bond.

So-called 'mini-bonds', a type of retail security used by smaller, high-growth companies, have grown in popularity in the past few years. Research by Capita Registrars suggests that the market for mini-bonds could rise to £8bn by the end of 2017.

➡

But this market is 'archaic' and ripe for disruption, said Luke Lang, one of Crowdcube's founders. Rather than paying fees, which it says usually total more than £100,000, Crowdcube charges companies 5% of the total raised once the target has been met.

'We're trying to cut out some of the fat from the City of London,' said Mr Lang. 'With mini-bonds, fees from financial advisers, lawyers, compliance and marketing companies can rack up pretty quickly.'

While attracting high-yield investors, the bonds have also drawn scrutiny. Critics point out that there is no secondary market, and the bonds are unsecured – meaning that investors rank behind secured investors in the case of a default.

'Some of the conventions of the institutional market have been thrown out the window, but those conventions are there for a reason,' said James Tomlins, a high-yield bond portfolio manager at M&G.

He added that the products represent a 'new area of capital' and that the use of the word bond may be inappropriate. 'You've got linguistic arbitrage here,' he said. 'You've got equity-like downside with bond-like upside.'

Previously, companies such as Crowdcube have targeted equity investors looking to benefit from the profit potential of small but fast-growing companies. In issuing bonds, crowdfunding companies hope to diversify their investment offerings and attract companies with the cash flow available to service fixed income debt.

While the average size of an equity issuance on Crowdcube is £200,000, retail bonds are all expected to raise at least £1m. The company says it is currently in talks with companies – including 'household name brands' – over future bond issuances, some of which may reach a price of up to £15m.

 Source: Hale, T. (2014) 'Crowdfunding' muscles in on the bond market, *Financial Times*, 24 June.
© The Financial Times Limited 2014. All Rights Reserved.

Infinite variation

Corporate bonds come in an infinite variety of forms in many different currencies and maturities, with the most common currencies being the US dollar and the euro.

Straight (plain vanilla or bullet) bonds

These are straightforward bonds and the most commonly issued, with regular (usually semi-annual or annual) fixed coupons and a specified redemption date. If the entire issue matures on a single date they are often called **term bonds**.

Floating-rate notes (FRNs)

A major market has developed over the past three decades called the **floating-rate note** (**FRN**, also called **variable-rate note** (**VRN**)) market. Two factors have led to the rapid growth in FRN usage. First, the oscillating and unpredictable inflation of the 1970s and 1980s caused many investors to make large real-term losses on fixed-rate bonds as the interest rate fell below the rate of inflation. Lenders became reluctant to lend at fixed rates on a long-term basis. This reluctance led to FRNs being cheaper for the issuer because it did not need to offer an interest premium to compensate the investor for being locked into a fixed rate. Second, a number of corporations, especially financial institutions, hold assets which give a return that varies with the short-term interest rate level (for example, banks have loans assets) and so they had a preference for a similar floating-rate liability.

FRNs pay an interest rate that is linked to a benchmark rate – such as the Libor. The issuer will pay, say, 70 basis points (0.7 of a percentage point) over the 'reference index' of Libor. The coupon might be set for the first six months at the time of issue, after which it is adjusted every six months, so if Libor was 3%, the FRN would pay 3.7% for that particular six months. The most common reference rates are three-month or six-month Libor. Interest rates may be linked to a variety of other benchmark rates, such as the Fed Funds rate, municipal and mortgage interest rate indexes, a particular money market rate or the rate of inflation. The interest rate may be fixed daily, weekly, monthly, etc.

In 2013 concern about rises in interest rates led to an upsurge in the number of FRNs being issued – see Article 4.6.

Article 4.6

Floating rate bond issuance jumps in Europe

By Christopher Thompson and Ralph Atkins

Financial Times August 29, 2013

European companies have switched to issuing debt at variable interest rates as investors fret about higher global borrowing costs.

The proportion of European corporate bonds issued in August as 'floating rate notes' has more than doubled month-on-month to nearly a fifth of overall issuance.

Overall European companies have issued $25bn of floating rate bonds for the year to date, the highest total since $42.4bn achieved in 2007 over the same period.

Global issuance has spiked to $96bn from $52bn last year.

The rise in US Treasury yields has led to a marked slowdown in overall corporate bond issuance recently as companies ponder the implications of longer-term higher costs.

The switch to floating rate notes is part of the same trend.

'Companies are simply tapping into the market which is hottest with investors, given the widespread worry about rising rates,' said Matt King, at Citigroup.

'If rates were to rise, it would be a negative for those companies concerned . . . but bank loans they had previously would have been floating-rate, and many issuers traditionally swap fixed-rate bond issuance back into floating, so the impact should be no worse than it would have been anyway.'

Shrinking bank lending has pushed many companies to seek more funding from the public bond markets as European companies move towards a more US-style market based model of corporate finance.

European non-financial corporate issuance rose nearly 20% in the first half of this year to $333bn as companies took advantage of historically low interest rates.

As longer term borrowing costs rise, Europe's banks are also turning to bonds with floating interest rates.

While their issuance dipped to $3.2bn in June it rose to $6.2bn in July and stands at $6.7bn so far this month, according to Dealogic.

That followed comments by Ben Bernanke, chairman of the US Federal Reserve, about the prospect of tapering the Fed's asset purchasing programme known as quantitative easing.

Global financial institutions' floating rate bond issuance has risen to $182.4bn so far this year from $127.4bn over the same period in 2012.

For banks, which lend at variable interest rates, the issuing of floating rate bonds allows them to better match assets and liabilities.

FRNs may come with additional features such as a **floor**, which means that the coupon can fall but there is a minimum beyond which it cannot go, and **caps**, which permit a rise in the coupon with the underlying benchmark only up to a point, there is a maximum. If there is both a floor and a cap the bond is said to be a **collared FRN**.

FRNs will trade at par value on each of the coupon **reset days**. But if interest rates rise between reset days they will trade slightly below par because investors can now obtain the higher rates on alternative bonds and so are less willing to hold the FRNs unless the price falls commensurately. If rates fall then FRNs will trade at slightly above par until the next reset day.

Coupons linked to other variables

Bonds issued in the last few years have linked the interest rates or principal payments to a wide variety of economic events, such as a rise in the price of silver, exchange rate movements, stock market indices, the price of oil, gold, copper – even to the occurrence of an earthquake. These bonds were generally designed to let companies adjust their interest payments to manageable levels in the event of the firm being adversely affected by the changing of some economic variable. For example, a copper mining company, with its interest payments linked to the price of copper, would pay lower interest on its finance if the copper price were to fall. Sampdoria, the Italian football club, issued a €3.5 million bond that paid a higher rate of return if the club won promotion to the Serie A division. If it stayed in Serie B it paid 2.5%. If it moved to Serie A the interest rate was 7%. If it found itself in the top four clubs the coupon would rise to 14%.

Callable bonds

The issuer retains the right but not the obligation to redeem these bonds before maturity at a set price which is usually a little more than the par price, say $1,050 instead of $1,000 (the difference is the **call premium**). In return for this privilege, the bond will pay a higher coupon. If interest rates fall, it would be advantageous for the company to call in its bonds, redeem them and issue new replacement bonds with a lower coupon, thus reducing their cost of borrowing.

European-style callables have a single call date determined at issuance. If the issuer does not call the bonds on that date they become non-callable bonds for the remainder of their term. **American-style callable bonds** are continuously callable, at any time after the first call date, until the redemption date. **Bermudan-style callables** have multiple discrete call dates when the bond can be redeemed in whole or in part. Call provisions generally allow for the first five or ten years of the bond's life to be excepted, when the call does not apply (**deferred callable bonds**), which gives some protection to investors. This **lockout period** (up to the first call date) has been as short as three months. **Freely callable bonds**, meanwhile, do not offer the investor any protection against a call because the issuer can call them any time.

For investors the attraction of a higher coupon rate on callable bonds is somewhat offset by the risk that, should interest rates fall, the value of a callable bond may also fall or at least fail to rise due to the threat of being called at a low price relative to a similar non-callable bond, contrary to the behaviour of normal bonds where value rises if interest rates fall. This is called **price compression** risk. Callable bonds also suffer from reinvestment risk – see page 133.

Irredeemable (perpetual) bonds

These bonds have no fixed redemption date but ostensibly pay their coupon indefinitely. Many of these bonds have been issued by banks, but non-financial companies also issue perpetual bonds which serve as permanent capital, with some characteristics similar to equity but with the added advantage that in raising money this way there is no dilution of existing shareholders' percentage share of the company votes – see Article 4.7.

Article 4.7

Trafigura raises $500m with perpetual bond

By Javier Blas in London and Jack Farchy

Financial Times April 10, 2013

Trafigura, one of the world's largest commodities trading houses, has launched its first perpetual bond, tapping the public capital market.

The trading house raised $500m with its bond, up from an initial target of $300m. The note, which was five times subscribed, will yield a 7.65% coupon.

Trafigura is the world's second-largest independent metals trader after Glencore, and the third-largest oil trader behind Vitol and Glencore.

The bond issue is the latest sign that the traditionally employee-owned commodity trading industry is opening up to new sources of capital, as European banks scale back their lending activities in the sector just as traders need more credit.

Louis Dreyfus Commodities, one of the world's top food commodities traders, last September tapped the public capital markets for the first time in its 160-year history, raising $350m in a perpetual bond.

The perpetual bond, which international accounting rules count as equity, will strengthen the balance sheet of Trafigura without diluting existing shareholders. Claude Dauphin, chief executive and one of the founders of the group, owns less than 20% while more than 500 senior employees control the rest.

'We want to get the long-term liquidity while maintaining our credit standing,' Pierre Lorinet, Trafigura chief financial officer, said in an interview. '[The perpetual bond] provides us with long-term money [with an] equity treatment.'

The bond will be listed on the Singapore Exchange, forcing Trafigura to release publicly semi-annual accounts for the first time. Until now the company has only released financial information to a small group of investors and bankers.

The new sources of financing in the Swiss commodities industry are partly driven by a change in the business model of the trading houses.

Companies have moved away from their traditional role as middleman – selling and buying commodities in a business of large volumes but razor-thin margins – increasingly to become vertically integrated groups, with interest spanning production, logistics, trading and processing.

The new areas, such as investing in oil refineries, require long-term capital that the trading houses in the past did not need. Some trading houses have not opened their equity to outsiders, but are seeking bond investors.

 Source: Blas, J. and Farchy, J. (2013) Trafigura raises $500m with perpetual bond, *Financial Times*, 10 April.

Despite their name and the characteristic of irredeemability at the insistence of the holders, they are often callable (usually after the first five years), thus the issuer can redeem them. They therefore pay a higher rate of interest to compensate investors for the extra risks: (a) that the amount invested will never be repaid and (b) that if the bonds are called the investor may not be able to reinvest at a similar rate of interest.

Puttable bonds

The holder has the right but not the obligation to demand early redemption of the bonds on a set date or dates. The benefit to purchasers is that if interest rates rise, they can cash in their bonds and reinvest in another investment offering a higher rate of interest. The disadvantage is a slightly lower rate of return in the first place.

Deep discounted bonds

Bonds that are sold at well below the par value are called **deep discounted bonds,** the most extreme form of which is the zero coupon bond. They are sold at a large discount to the nominal value and the investor makes a capital gain by holding the bond instead of receiving coupons. These bonds are particularly useful for firms with low cash flows in the near term, for example firms engaged in a major property development that will not mature for many years.

Bearer bond and registered bond

With **bearer bonds** the coupons are traditionally attached to the paper bond held by the investor. When it is time for a coupon the investor presents to the issuer the relevant coupon section – the coupon bond is **clipped**. Information on the holder is not kept on a database – useful for avoiding the prying eyes of governments. Bearer bond holders are vulnerable to theft, as possession of the bond is all that is required to receive money from the issuer. Today many 'bearer' bonds exist only as electronic entries rather than paper (see Chapter 7), but anonymity from government remains. With **registered bonds**, the holder's identity is recorded by the issuer and coupon payments are sent in the post or electronically transferred to the bank account of the registered owner.

During its life, a registered bond is usually held in a **dematerialised form,** that is ownership, trading and settlement are merely a computerised **book-entry**. The largest organisations that run global electronic clearing systems are Euroclear and Clearstream. Settlement (when the money for a trade is transferred) for corporate bonds is generally either two or three days after the deal is struck.

Debentures and loan stocks

In the UK and many other countries the most secure type of bond is called a **debenture** (it is different for the US – see page 135). Debentures are usually secured by either a fixed or a floating charge against the firm's assets. A **fixed charge** means that specific assets (e.g. buildings, machinery) are used as security, which, in the event of default, can be sold at the insistence of the debenture bond holders and the proceeds used to repay them. Debentures secured on property may be referred to as **mortgage debentures**.

Bonds secured through a fixed charge often have legal provisions in the debt agreement that allow the issuer to dispose of a proportion of the property or plant (such as a crane or fleet of cars) used as collateral, but when they do so they must make provision for the redemption of a proportion of the fixed-charge bonds. These are known as **release of property** clauses. The usual rule is that these bonds are retired at par value, but some agreements allow a redemption price other than par.

A **floating charge** means that the debt is secured by a general charge on all the assets of the corporation, or a class of the firm's assets such as inventory or receivables (debtors). In this case the company has a high degree of freedom to use its assets as it wishes, such as sell them or rent them out, until it commits a default which 'crystallises' the floating charge, i.e. the floating charge is converted to a *fixed charge* over the assets which it covers at that time. If this happens an **administrative receiver** or **administrator** will be appointed with powers to manage the business, to either pay the debt through income generation, or dispose of the assets followed by distribution of the proceeds to creditors, or sell the entire business as a going concern.

Even though floating-charge debenture holders can force a **liquidation**, fixed-charge debenture holders rank above floating-charge debenture holders in the payout after insolvency. Floating-charge holders rank behind **preferential creditors** who are given priority by statue, such as the tax authorities and employees owed wages.

Similar collateral charges to the floating charge are the **floating lien** in the US and a few other places, and the **commercial pledge** in many European countries.

The terms bond, debenture and **loan stock** are often used loosely and interchangeably, and the dividing line between debentures and loan stock is a fuzzy one. As a general rule debentures are secured with collateral and loan stock is unsecured, but there are examples that do not fit this classification. If liquidation occurs, the unsecured loan stock holders rank beneath the debenture holders.

However, in the US and some other countries the definitions are somewhat different and this can be confusing. Here a debenture is a long-term *unsecured* bond and so the holders become general creditors who can only claim assets not otherwise pledged. In the US the secured form of bond is referred to as a **mortgage bond** and unsecured shorter-dated issues (less than ten years) are called **notes**. US **subordinated debentures**, as well as being unsecured, are further back in the queue for a cash distribution in the event of the company failing to pay its debts than both mortgage bonds/debentures and regular US-style debentures. They carry higher interest rates to compensate and are often classified as junk bonds (see Chapters 5 and 6).

Trust deeds and covenants

Bond investors may be willing to accept a lower rate of interest if they can be reassured that their money will not be exposed to a high risk. Reassurance is conveyed by placing risk-reducing restrictions on the firm. A **trust deed** (or **bond indenture**) sets out the terms of the contract between bond holders and the company. A **trustee** (if one is appointed) ensures compliance with the contract throughout the life of the bond and has the power to appoint an administrative receiver to liquidate the firm's assets if necessary. If a trustee is not appointed the usual practice is to give each holder an independently exercisable right to take legal action against a delinquent borrower.

The loan agreement will contain a number of **affirmative covenants**. These usually include the requirements to supply regular financial statements and make interest and principal payments. The deed may also state the fees due to the lenders and details of what procedures should be followed in the event of a technical default, for example non-payment of interest. The issuer may also have the right to 'call' the bond and/or the lenders to insist on selling back to the issuer. The trust deed also states what, if anything, is **'backing'** the bond in the form of collateral acting as security.

In addition to these basic covenants are the **negative (restrictive) covenants**. These limit the actions and the rights of the borrower until the debt has been repaid in full. Some examples are:

● *Limits on further debt issuance.* If lenders provide finance to a firm they do so on certain assumptions concerning the riskiness of the capital structure. They will want to ensure that the loan does not become more risky due to the firm taking on a much greater debt burden relative to its equity base, so they limit the amount and type of further debt issues – particularly debt that has a higher (**senior**) ranking for interest payments or for a liquidation payment. **Subordinated debt (junior debt)** – with a low ranking on liquidation – is more likely to be acceptable. A **negative pledge** is the term used to describe a clause that prohibits the issue of more senior debt requiring the pledge of assets, thus jeopardising the existing bonds.

- *Limits on the dividend level.* Lenders are opposed to money brought into the firm by borrowing at one end and then being taken away by shareholders in dividend payments at the other. An excessive withdrawal of shareholders' funds may unbalance the financial structure and weaken future cash flows required to pay bond holders.

- *Limits on the disposal of assets.* The retention of certain assets, for example property and land, may be essential to reduce the lenders' risk. **Disposal of assets covenants** often allows a cumulative total of up to, say, 30% of the gross assets of the firms, but no more.

- *Financial ratios.* A typical covenant here concerns the interest cover, for example: 'The annual profit should remain four times as great as the overall annual interest charge.' Other restrictions might be placed on **working capital ratio** levels (the extent to which current assets exceed current liabilities) and the **debt to net assets ratio** (a **gearing ratio covenant**) may require that the total borrowing of the firm may not exceed a stated percentage of net worth (share capital and reserves) of, say, 100%.

- *Cross default covenant.* The trustee has permission to put all loans into default if the borrower defaults on a single loan.

While negative covenants cannot ensure completely risk-free lending they can influence the behaviour of the managerial team so as to reduce the risk of default. They can also provide the management team with an early warning signal to take action. The lender's risk can be further reduced by obtaining guarantees from third parties (for example, **guaranteed loan stock**). The guarantor is typically the parent company of the issuer.

The trustee, responsible to bond holders, will inform them if the firm has failed to fulfil its obligation under the trust deed and may initiate legal action against the firm. If the firm has to go through a reorganisation of its finances, administration or liquidation, the trustee will continue to act on behalf of the bond holders.

Other professional help

Once the bond is in issue, the issuer will need administrative support to carry out key tasks throughout its life. A **paying agent's** main function is to receive money from the issuer to then pay coupons and redemption amounts. When no trustee has been appointed, instead of a paying agent there will be a **fiscal**

agent to undertake the paying agent's role. The fiscal agent is appointed by and is the representative of the issuer, in contrast to the trustee's role as the representative of the lenders. Nevertheless, the fiscal agent must not act in a harmful way toward the bond holders. As well as payments it performs a number of administrative tasks such as sending information on the bond/issuer to the holders.

A **registrar** or **transfer agent** keeps a record of bond ownership and notes all changes of ownership. A **listing agent** is required only if the bond is listed on a stock exchange such as in London or Luxembourg. The listing agent keeps the stock exchange informed and ensures required documents are delivered to the exchange. In the UK the listing agent must be authorised to act in that capacity by the FCA.

Repayments

The principal on most bonds is paid entirely at maturity. However, some bonds, e.g. callable bonds, can be repaid before the final redemption date. Another alternative is for the company to issue bonds with a range of dates for redemption; so a bond dated 2024–2027 would allow a company the flexibility to repay a part of the principal over the course of four years. This may help prevent 'a crisis at maturity' by avoiding a large cash outflow at a singular redemption. A range of dates is also useful if machinery subject to depreciation, e.g. a ship, is used as collateral because the amount owed declines as the asset backing declines in value. When there are many maturity dates the bonds are referred to as **serial bonds**.

Another way of redeeming bonds is for the issuing firm to buy outstanding bonds by offering the holder a sum higher than or equal to the amount originally paid. A firm is also able to purchase bonds on the open market.

Sinking fund

The most trusted corporates are able to sell bonds without the need to be specific about how the debt will be repaid – the implication is that they will be redeemed using general income flowing from operations or by the issue of more bonds or bank borrowing. Borrowers with lower credit ratings may need to state specific provisions for principal repayment to reduce investor anxiety about the safety of their money.

One way of paying for redemption is to set up a **sinking fund**, overseen by a trustee, which receives regular sums from the firm that will be sufficient, with added interest, to redeem the bonds at maturity or to periodically retire a proportion, thus reducing its debt burden over time. Bonds may be purchased in the market at market prices, at the issue price, at a stated call price in the sinking fund provision or at face value, depending on the original agreement. The indenture/trust deed may allow freedom for the issuer to arbitrarily retire the bonds or to do so only on fixed dates.

Bonds might be selected randomly through a lottery for early redemption. The alternative is the pro rata method with which all bond holders are treated equally, thus they all might be required to retire 10% of their holdings if the issuer decides to reduce the bonds outstanding by 10%.

Because a bond with a sinking fund provision is less risky for the investor, as there is money being set aside, there is a push down on the rate of return offered. However, offsetting this for the investor are the negative effects of not knowing when or how many bonds will be retired.

Some risks for investors

Corporate bond investors are subject to many types of risk.

Default risk (credit risk)

This is the likelihood that the issuer cannot/will not pay one or more coupons in a timely manner or pay the principal sum of the debt at maturity. Bonds are usually higher ranked than equity for payments if a company is in difficulty, but there is always the risk of failure to make agreed payments. This risk depends on creditworthiness, which in turn depends on competitive strength, competence and integrity of the managers, financial structure (e.g. debt levels) and the bond's ranking in the pecking order for repayment in the event of the firm running into difficulty (seniority of the debt).

Event risk

Some adverse event may occur which devalues the bond, e.g. a natural disaster wipes out company profits and damages the ability of the company to pay its obligations. Or an issuer is merged with another firm and the debt burden increases significantly, causing a credit downgrade and lower bond prices.

Sometimes a **poison put** provision (**change of control clause**) in the trust deed/indenture protects bond holders because this allows them to sell their bonds back to the borrower when there is a merger/takeover – see Article 4.8. LBO means **leveraged buyout**, when high levels of debt relative to the equity in the company are used to purchase a business.

Article 4.8

LBOs and bonds: animal antidote
Change of control clauses may offer only limited protection to investors

Lex column

Financial Times February 26, 2013

Leveraged buyouts that load up companies with new debt to pay existing share-holders are bondholder poison. Investors are left with securities in a riskier company, falling prices and ratings downgrades. After being caught off guard during the buyout boom of 2005–07, investors demanded some protection. Some 22% of US investment grade corporate bonds by market capitalisation, 25% by the number of bonds, now include something called a change of control clause, reckons JPMorgan, versus less than 4% in 2006.

Change of control clauses enable bondholders to put their bonds back to the company if there is a change of majority control and that results in the bonds being downgraded to junk. Most, but not all of the bonds that do not have them are from issuers not considered to be LBO targets – banks and companies with market caps exceeding $20bn–$30bn.

Most of the change of control provisions would have the company buy the bonds back at 101 cents on the dollar. But that is cold comfort for investors that bought bonds at big premiums. Plunging interest rates in recent years have driven the prices of many investment grade bonds sharply higher. The average dollar price for the Barclays index tracking them is 112, for example. While change of control provisions can mitigate bondholders' LBO risk, the extreme market conditions of the past few years mean they are no antidote for potential losses if the animals do get restless again.

Interest rate risk (market risk)

The prices of fixed-rate bonds tend to fluctuate according to the current rate of interest. If interest rates rise, the price of the bonds will fall and selling them at the new price could result in a loss. Put provisions may build in some protection for fixed-rate bonds, by placing a floor on the price falls because the holder can insist that the company pay a certain minimum. Of course, floating-rate bonds have more protection against interest rate movements if their coupons are linked to an interest benchmark. Interest rate risk was a hot topic of conversation in 2014. Even the UK regulator warned investors to consider the consequences – see Article 4.9. Also note the hint at liquidity risk, discussed below.

Article 4.9

Watchdog sounds alarm over corporate bond funds

By Emma Dunkley

Financial Times July 29, 2014

Investors buying funds that hold corporate bonds risk losing a significant amount of capital if interest rates rise and will find it hard to sell out if market sentiment plunges, the City watchdog has warned.

The Financial Conduct Authority issued the alert as bond funds continue to attract large sums from individual investors seeking a steady income.

Corporate bond funds invest at least 80% of assets in 'investment grade' companies, which have a low risk of defaulting on interest and capital repayments.

However, current and prospective investors are being urged to consider other risks if market conditions change or interest rates rise, which the Bank of England has signalled could happen in the months ahead.

Analysts at Barclays said the confluence of positive economic developments was 'bad news' for bonds because it increased the likelihood of a rate rise. 'Interest rate increases will put downward pressure on the prices of fixed-income securities, leading to mark-to-market losses for bond portfolios,' they said.

The FCA is now warning about the effect of a rate rise on bonds, which could leave many investors nursing losses and spark a rush for the exit.

'Interest rate movements have an impact on corporate bond and fund unit prices,' the watchdog said. 'So, for example, as interest rates rise, bond prices fall. This is the key difference to deposit accounts, where the capital value is constant.'

> Although fund managers aim to ensure investors can buy or sell their fund hold-
> ings on any day, there is concern they would be unable to sell enough bonds to meet
> redemption requests in a tough market environment, leaving investors stranded.

Source: Dunkley, E. (2014) Watchdog sounds alarm over corporate bond funds, *Financial
Times*, 29 July.
© The Financial Times Limited 2014. All Rights Reserved.

Liquidity risk (marketability risk)

If there is no active secondary market in the bonds it might not be possible
to sell them prior to maturity. Other markets have some liquidity but do not
qualify for highly liquid status, that is, the bond cannot be sold at a predictable
price with low transaction costs. The no- or low-liquidity bonds are likely to
carry higher interest rates – a **liquidity risk premium (LRP)** – to compensate
for the difficulty of selling quickly without moving the price. Bonds of larger
companies issuing in hundreds of millions or billions are generally the most
liquid.

Inflation risk (purchasing power risk)

This is where the purchasing power of money invested in the bond is eroded
despite coupon and principal flows. This could leave a diminished positive real
return or produce a negative real return, resulting in lower purchasing power
than the investor had to start with. Inflation risk may also refer to the ensuing
difficulty of selling an investment devalued through inflation.

Many companies have issued inflation-linked corporate bonds/notes (inflation-
indexed or corporate inflation protected) paying coupons and principal which
rise with inflation in a similar fashion to inflation-linked Treasuries (see
Chapter 2). With some of these bonds the coupons are paid semi-annually.
Others may pay interest monthly. Of course, the interest rate is usually higher
than for government bonds due to the additional default risk. For example, in
2013 water company Severn Trent issued around £100 million worth of RPI-linked
bonds in a ten-year sterling bond, offering a 1.3% annual coupon and a repayment of capital. Both the coupon and the principal will in line with the retail
prices index. Investors were allowed to subscribe for as little as £2,000. This
followed National Grid's ten-year RPI-linked issue, which raised £282 million
from private investors, and Tesco Bank's offer of £60 million of eight-year bonds.

Reinvestment risk

This is the risk arising from the need to reinvest money received from a bond investment. For example, some issuers retain the right to redeem bonds at their insistence; bonds thus called may then leave investors struggling to find a replacement investment offering a similar rate of interest. Another example: coupons received are likely to be reinvested in other bonds, but the rate of return then available may be lower than when the bond was first issued.

Call risk

There are three downsides for the lender when a bond agreement allows the issuer to buy them back from the holder before the normal redemption date:

1 Uncertainty regarding the cash flow from the investment because it is not known whether a call will be enacted.

2 Calls are likely to be exercised if interest rates fall, thus the investor faces reinvestment risk, i.e. buying other bonds at a lower yield.

3 A call provision will limit the capital appreciation potential of the bond because the price may not rise much above the price at which it could be called.

Supply risk

A company may issue further bonds of the same type, which could result in an over-supply in the market and the price falling.

Tax risk

A government might change its tax policy to the detriment of corporate bond holders.

Sector risk

Investors become unwilling to buy bonds in a certain sector (e.g. those issued by banks) regardless of the merits of an individual borrower, thus bond prices fall even for sound issuers.

Foreign exchange (currency) risk

Bonds denominated in a foreign currency have an uncertain value in the home currency if exchange rates vary.

Political risk

Bond values may be adversely affected by civil unrest, nationalisation of assets, inflation, government interference in markets, coups or dictatorships.

Company health risk

Corporate bond prices are often more closely linked to the health of the issuer than movements of interest rates within the economy than is the case for government bonds. Thus when general interest rates rise, a corporate bond's price may not go down as much as a reputable government bond of similar maturity because of the company's strong operating performance and/or improving credit standing. Offsetting this benefit for a bond on a lower credit rating is that its price movements will be even more influenced by the company's health in terms of cash generation, financial structure and economic standing. Deterioration in health can cause price falls to add hundreds of basis points to the rate of return on current bonds and those it might need to issue in the future.

The issue process

Investment banks lie at the heart of the primary corporate bond market, with the expertise, contacts and reputation to advise on corporate finance and to organise the selling of bonds into the market. If the issue is relatively small a single bank will handle it, but larger issues are more likely to be underwritten by a syndicate of investment banks, especially if the bonds are sold in a number of countries. Each syndicate member bank will be allocated a proportion of the issue to sell.

The process might begin with competing banks offering their services to the corporate. They will indicate the price/yield at which they think the bonds can be sold together with the size of their fees. The issuer will consider these factors along with the bank's reputation and standing. The bank that wins the **mandate** for the issue will be termed the **lead underwriter**, **lead manager** or

book-runner. The lead underwriter will then usually team up with a number of other banks to simultaneously offer the bonds to the market. This **syndicate** often comprises banks from many countries. A **co-lead manager(s)** might be appointed to help sell the bonds in particular countries, where the lead manager does not have large client bases.

The usual method is the **fixed-price re-offer**. The investment bank syndicate agrees a fixed price and a fixed commission. It also agrees the quantity each member is to take to offer to the market at the agreed price. In this way the lead manager avoids the problem of some syndicate members selling the bonds at a low price in the grey market just to shift the bonds ('dumping'). The **grey market** is the buying and selling of bonds before they have officially arrived on the market – they are traded on investors' anticipation of their allocation. The obligation to stick to a fixed price means that the lead manager does not have to step in to support the price by buying back the bonds. After the first settlement date in the secondary market the restriction on syndicate members' selling prices is lifted.

In a **bought deal** the issuer is offered a package: a fixed price for a fixed quantity bought by the lead manager or managing group (not a syndicate). The issuer then has a few hours to decide whether to accept. If accepted the lead manager then either buys the whole issue to distribute to other investors or sells portions to other banks for distribution to investors – **placement** of the bonds. In anticipation of issuer acceptance many of the bonds will usually have been pre-placed with institutional investors (pension funds, insurance companies, etc.) before the bid was made. Obviously, bought deals are conducted by lead managers with large capital bases and with high placement ability; they might be left holding ('wearing') the bonds if they cannot find buyers, thus tying up capital and damaging their reputation for accurately assessing market demand, pricing and marketing bonds.

Most corporate bonds are **underwritten** by an investment bank(s) on a **firm commitment basis**, meaning that the issuer is guaranteed a certain amount from the sale. However, some are **best-efforts offerings** where the bank(s) does not guarantee a firm price to the issuer, merely agreeing to act as a placing or distribution agent. A fee will be paid for this service. The downside of best-efforts issues is that investors are aware that the investment bank(s) has not committed any of its own funds and so they are usually unwilling to pay a price as high as they might with a firm fixed-price commitment from the lead underwriter.

The lead manager (often in cooperation with other syndicate members) will help the issuer prepare the **prospectus** to be presented to potential investors, detailing the issue and explaining the company and its finances. It will also deal with the legal issues and other documentation, using either an in-house legal team or an external one.

Fees as a percentage of funds raised for underwriting (agreeing to buy those not sold to the public) and selling bonds tend to be greater for longer maturities and for those lower down the credit rating scale, but smaller for large issues given the economies of scale. Fees will rise if the issue is more **exotic** (unusual and/or complex) rather than straight vanilla, but are typically in the range 0.25–0.75% of the par value. The issuer will also have to factor in their own time and that of their accountants, legal advisers, etc.

When pricing a bond the lead manager often focuses on a benchmark bond currently trading in the market with the same maturity as the new issue and uses that as a reference. The new bond might be priced as so-many basis points of spread over or under the benchmark.

Private placements

In **private placements** an investment bank(s) uses its contacts to find financial institutions willing to purchase the whole issue between them, usually no more than ten in the group. This allows the issuing company to develop a closer relationship with a tight-knit group of investors, first gaining understanding of the business and later communicating progress, perhaps opening the possibility of raising more at a later date. Private placings also avoid the cost of obtaining and maintaining a credit rating for publicly traded bonds and the costs of additional disclosure.

In the US, where this market is very strong, privately placed bonds are **unregistered** with the Securities and Exchange Commission, with minimal disclosure required, and so can be resold only to large, financially sophisticated investors; they are therefore not available to retail investors. Most privately placed bonds are **144a securities**, meaning that they are exempt from SEC registration under Section 144a of the 1990 Securities Law. Private placement costs much less than a **public offering** because the issuer does not have to comply with generally accepted accounting principles and because marketing to only a handful of investing institutions is cheaper. A detailed prospectus does not need to be prepared; instead a much simpler **private placement memorandum** is sent to prospective investors.

Privately placed bonds tend to be illiquid and so are generally bought by institutions willing to buy and hold without going to the secondary market; interest rates tend to be higher to compensate for the illiquidity and because most of the issuers are less well known than for publicly placed bonds – the bonds are generally not 'investment grade', i.e. with credit ratings under BBB–. Europeans are trying to grow a strong local private placement market – see Article 4.10.

Article 4.10

Thirst for funds lifts appeal of private placements

By Andrew Bolger

Financial Times June 24, 2014

Britvic is an official supplier to Wimbledon, where its Robinsons Squash has helped quench the thirst of many tennis players since the invention of Lemon Barley Water in 1935.

This quintessentially British company has found inventive ways of quenching its funding needs, including in recent years £650m in private placements, a market that was developed by US insurers as a way to make strong returns from long-term investment in companies.

Insurers and pension funds – including some from Europe – achieve this by issuing securities that are not sold through a public offering but instead directly to chosen investors.

Now leading European investors and finance trade bodies that admire this US funding model are trying to develop a similar pan-European placement market.

'The development of the market should stimulate further growth, enabling more companies to access the capital markets in Europe and provide investors with a new investment opportunity,' says Calum Macphail, head of private placements at M&G Investments, which has invested €5.6bn in private placements since 1997.

The private placement market for European issuers has grown in recent years, especially in France and the UK, which had an estimated combined volume of €8bn in 2013.

Private placements typically provide fixed-rate financing of between three and 15 years, most commonly for seven to 10 years. Mr Macphail says pension funds are attracted to the characteristics of private placements – strong, stable cash flows and covenant protections similar to a loan.

'In addition to diversification and stronger documentation compared to public bonds, investors benefit from an illiquidity premium when investing in medium or long-term assets which provide regular income, giving a pension fund more bang for their buck,' he says.

The International Capital Market Association is co-ordinating the work of the pan-European Private Placement Working Group that aims to establish a guide to best market practice, principles and standardised documentation. The working group will build on a Charter for Euro Private Placements, a French initiative.

The European private placement market is smaller than its $50bn US equivalent, which issued €12.4bn to European companies, and Germany's Schuldschein market, which issued €8.5bn to European companies last year.

The Schuldschein is a fixed- or floating-rate loan instrument, ranging in size from €10m to €500m. The market is used primarily, but not exclusively, by investment-grade companies.

Source: Bolger, A. (2014) Thirst for funds lifts appeal of private placements, *Financial Times*, 24 June.
© The Financial Times Limited 2014. All Rights Reserved.

Despite the progress made in Europe, even today European companies often choose to issue privately placed bonds on the other side of the Atlantic where there is a well-established clientele, infrastructure, regulation and procedures – see Article 4.11.

Article 4.11

Midsized issuers welcome funding scheme

By Andrew Bolger

Financial Times February 16, 2015

An ambitious framework for a European private placement market has been published that aims to widen access to finance by midsized companies.

For many years, lots of midsized European businesses have accessed the US private placement market, which allows insurers to provide long-term finance to companies that wish to avoid the expense and scrutiny of issuing publicly listed bonds.

But a working group led by the International Capital Market Association has launched a voluntary guide for common market standards and best practices which it says are essential for the development of a pan-European market.

'The guide will be a big help in communicating with and within midsized corporates about an alternative source of finance,' says Colin Tyler, chief executive of the Association of Corporate Treasurers. 'For potential midsized issuers that have not used private placements before, it will give confidence that there are clear paths to issuing – it is not venturing into Wild West territory.'

Private placements are medium- to long-term senior debt obligations – in bond or loan format – issued privately by companies to a small group of investors. The private placement market typically provides fixed-rate financing of between three and 15 years, most commonly for seven to 10 years.

With private placement deals providing longer maturities than many bank loans, this helps to release companies from the burden of refinancing bank debt every couple of years.

Calum Macphail, head of private placements at M&G Investments, one of the largest European investors in private placements, says the guide provides companies interested in exploring this market an understanding of the process, who was involved and information potential investors would require.

'As the financing landscape changes as banks de-lever, natural sources of longer-term finance, namely pension funds and institutional investors, are filling this gap,' he says. 'Pension funds are attracted to the characteristics of private placements – strong, stable cash flows and covenant protections similar to a loan.'

In addition to diversification and stronger documentation compared with public bonds, he says investors will also benefit from an illiquidity premium which could provide an enhanced yield as well as regular income over the medium to long term.

The popularity of private placements has accelerated since the onset of the financial crisis, with markets in countries such as France and Germany providing borrowers with a local solution.

ICMA, which represents institutions across the international capital markets, says demand for private placements is set to increase as the EU's approximately 200,000 midsized companies look to diversify their sources of funding away from the traditional bank loan market, and view private placements both as an alternative and as an intermediate step towards the listed bond markets.

The guide builds on existing practices and documents used in the European bond and loan markets, especially a charter developed by the Euro PP Working Group, a French financial industry initiative. It is expected costs will be lowered by promoting the use of recently standardised documentation.

Daniel Godfrey, chief executive of the Investment Association, says common market standards for European private placement transactions will remove a significant barrier to the development of the private placement market in the UK and Europe.

'Our members are major investors in UK businesses and, having worked closely with members and government on the proposed withholding tax exemption for privately placed debt in the UK, in December 2014, we were able to announce that five institutions intend to make investments of around £9bn in private placements and other direct lending to UK companies,' he said.

The French and German domestic private placement markets issued approximately €15bn of debt in 2013 in addition to a further $15.3bn raised by European companies in the $60bn US private placement market.

Standard & Poor's estimates €2.7tn of debt will need to be refinanced by midsized companies between now and 2018, at a time when banks continue to retreat from long term lending markets.

As well as trade bodies, the pan-European private placement initiative has received strong support from government officials in the UK and France, as it is closely aligned with the European Commission's goal of bringing about a capital markets union, on which a green paper is expected this week.

Welcoming the guide, Fabio Panetta, deputy governor of the Bank of Italy, said: 'It is a useful tool for developing a European private placement market for corporate debt and, consequently, for broadening and diversifying sources of funding to the European economy.'

Source: Bolger, A. (2015) Midsized issuers welcome funding scheme, *Financial Times*, 16 February.

Timetable for an issue

The timetable for a bond issue can range from a few days to several months; it is longer for more complex issues, those in numerous jurisdictions, when it is the first bond for this issuer, and when the bonds are to be listed on a stock exchange. Here are the basics of the process (except for a bought deal or private placement):

● *Pre-launch and launch.* The lead manager appoints the trustee or fiscal agent, the principal paying agent, the other members of the syndicate, and prepares the prospectus and other documents. The lead manager or co-lead managers will discuss with the issuer and potential investors the specifications, such as size of issue, coupon and price. As discussion progresses these will be 'firmed up'. A book-building public promotion period might span two weeks ('pre-selling the bonds'). Within that, a roadshow and a series of conference calls might take four days with, say, 10 to 100 attendees per meeting in different cities across the country.

- *Announcement day*. It is only on the announcement day that the issue is formally announced (a press notification is usual), including the decision on the maturity and coupon rate or range of coupon rates. The lead manager formally invites the prospective syndicate members to participate, telling them the timetable and their obligations. On the **pricing day**, the price of the bond relative to par (say £99.85 if the par is £100) is agreed by the borrower and the syndicate group.

- *Offering day/signing day*. The bonds are formally offered the day after the pricing day. The borrower and managing group sign the agreement on the specifications. The size of the allotments to syndicate members is announced by the lead manager. Signing usually occurs between two days and one week before closing and can take place at a meeting or, more frequently these days, by fax or email.

- *Closing*. The trust deed or fiscal agency agreement are signed, the bond is created and investors pay for the bonds they have purchased.

- *Listing*.For listed bonds the relevant documentation must be delivered to the listing authority (e.g. in Britain it is the UKLA, part of the FCA) and the stock exchange.

Auction issue

In an **auction issue** the cost of management fees is bypassed because the issuer goes to investors directly asking for price and quantity bids for prospective bonds with specified maturity and coupon. The disadvantage is that the expertise of the lead manager and others in the syndicate is forgone with regard to market knowledge, contacts, reputation, etc. Thus auction issues are for high-quality, well-known borrowers only.

United States of America

The US has the largest corporate bond market in the world. The **Financial Industry Regulatory Authority** (**FINRA**) supervises all aspects of bond trading and its participants. FINRA (www.finra.org) lists over 40,000 corporate bonds, with details of each bond (coupon, maturity, etc.) and, if it has one, its credit rating. To take an example: the Ford Motor Co has about 190 bonds listed, with maturities ranging up to 2097 and coupon rates varying from

0.571% to 12%. About two-thirds of Ford's bonds have the same credit rating, Baa3 from Moody's and BBB– from Standard & Poor's and Fitch, and recent sales prices vary from $41 to $202.375.

Disney has 26 bonds listed, including its famous Sleeping Beauty bond, a 100-year bond issued in 1993 paying a coupon of 7.55% on par (the yield to redemption was 4.071% at the time of writing). This bond is continuously callable and of the initial offering of $300 million, $99 million has been redeemed. It is rated single-A. According to Morningstar, the investment research centre, the Ford Motor Co had $7.7 billion of outstanding bonds and Walt Disney had $13.3 billion in 2014, illustrating how important the bond markets are for funding their operations.

Publicly traded US corporate bonds usually carry a minimum denomination of $1,000. Those paying coupons usually do so every six months. More than 7,000 corporate bonds are listed on the NYSE (more than on any other exchange in the US), but the bulk of trading is in the off-exchange OTC market. Data from the **Securities Industry and Financial Markets Association (SIFMA)**, a trade association for financial enterprises, shows the increase in corporate debt from 1980 to the present, with a total outstanding in 2014 of $9.8 trillion (see Figure 4.8) and daily trading in these bonds averaging over $20 billion.

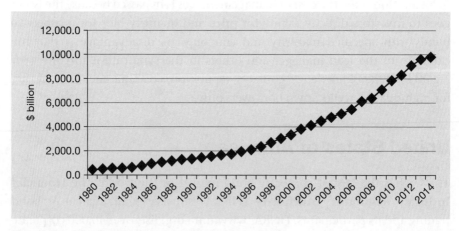

Figure 4.8 US corporate debt outstanding from 1980

Source: Data from www.sifma.org

Many non-US companies issue US\$ bonds in both the public debt market and the private placement market because they are more attractive to investors than bonds issued in a not-so-strong currency. Increasingly, with globalisation corporate bonds are issued all over the world, so a UK company might issue bonds in Japan denominated in yen or dollars because it is transacting business there.

Asia

Bond issuance in China is booming as corporates tap the markets rather than automatically source borrowed funds from banks. The big issuers are the state-owned enterprises, ranging from the oil company Sinopec to China National Nuclear. But there are many private companies tapping into markets offering good interest rates. Alongside the greater issuance has been the growth in secondary market trading with institutions and retail investors enthusiastic about adding fixed-income securities to their portfolios in what is now a reasonably liquid market. China is beginning to realise the importance of overseas investment in its domestic markets, and has paved the way for renminbi-qualified foreign institutional investors (RQFIIs) to invest their foreign-held renminbi in Chinese corporate (and government) bonds.

Domestic pension funds and other institutions in many Asian countries are keen to obtain assets denominated in their own currencies and so welcome further growth of their corporate bond markets – see Article 4.12. Pension funds are particularly interested in bonds of a longer maturity providing a better match to their pension liabilities than short-maturity issues. From the companies' perspective, they benefit from the stability that comes with locking in fixed-rate money for a decade or more.

Article 4.12

Asian credit markets expand at a record pace

By Chris Flood

Financial Times July 27, 2014

Asian credit markets are expanding at a record pace, attracting growing numbers of both international and local institutional investors. New corporate issuance is expected to rise to near $150bn this year, from $120bn in 2013. Yields on offer appear generous compared with other fixed income markets. Bond-buying programmes by leading central banks have squeezed yields and spreads elsewhere to historically low levels.

David Bessey at Pramerica Fixed Income says the large scale of Asian corporate bond issuance has meant that the tightening in credit spreads has lagged behind developed markets, providing relative value opportunities for managers running global and multi-sector funds.

Raja Mukherji at Pimco, the world's largest bond house, adds that many US and global investors remain underinvested in Asia and want to add exposure.

'Local investors, especially insurance companies, pension funds and sovereign wealth funds, are increasingly participating in new issues,' he says.

Rajeev De Mello at Schroders agrees. He has seen strong interest from US investors in investment-grade credit across Asia, with clients showing a stronger appetite for risk than in previous years.

Mr De Mello adds that Asian local-currency bonds provide a distinct yield advantage over US Treasuries, pointing out there is better value in those markets where interest rates have already increased, such as China, India and Indonesia.

But he cautions that some other Asian credit markets now look 'frothy'. Indeed, yields are described as low in export-orientated Asian countries such as Taiwan, South Korea and Thailand, although there are selective pockets of value elsewhere for tactical investors.

Robert Stewart at JPMorgan Asset Management says: 'Indonesia is attracting a lot of interest from global fixed income investors anticipating that Joko Widodo will pursue a reform agenda after his recent election as president.'

In India, Mr Bessey says Pramerica hopes that the new Modi government will pursue a more orthodox fiscal approach than its predecessors. The Modi government has a 'unique mandate' after winning a large election majority, adds Mr De Mello. He says India's central bank has also appointed a 'very credible' governor,

Raghuram Rajan, who is determined to bring inflation down to sustainable levels, an important commitment for building confidence among bond investors.

However, Indonesia and India play less influential roles in Asian credit markets than China. The Chinese corporate bond market is now the world's largest. Non-financial debt is expected to grow from around $14.2tn at the end of 2013 to $20tn over the next four years, according to Aberdeen Asset Management.

But Aberdeen warns that a third of Chinese debt is sourced from the informal shadow banking sector while signs of stress continue in the country's property markets.

But the sense is clients in Asia see China's credit markets as 'an exciting area' as Beijing gradually liberalises capital flows. Mr Stewart says: 'We are also starting to see interest from other (non-Asian) international investors in onshore Chinese corporate bonds, which look relatively attractive in the current low-yield environment.'

Source: Flood, C. (2014) Asian credit markets expand at record pace, *Financial Times*, 27 July.

Bond indices

A bond index provides information, such as price movements and returns over a period for a particular category of bond, e.g. an average for 100 or so corporate bonds denominated in euros or a few dozen inflation-linked bonds across the world. Among other uses they allow investors to compare their bond portfolio performance against a benchmark. The main indices are managed by Markit (the iBoxx indices) and FTSE. Leading investment banks supply bid and ask (offer) prices through the trading day to these organisations, which then compile the indices.

In Table 4.2, an example of the bond indices table from the *Financial Times*, the first column shows whether the bonds are denominated in sterling, dollars or euros, the second column shows the number of bonds included in the index. The final column does not indicate the yield to maturity but the return to an investor who bought one year ago, including capital gains and losses, if they sold now. These index suppliers produce many more indices than those shown in Table 4.2 – see www.markit.com and www.ftse.co.uk for the other indices and much more analytical data, such as average yield and duration.

Table 4.2 Bond indices in the *Financial Times*

			BOND INDICES				
		Index	Day's change	Month's change	Year change	Return 1 month	Return 1 year
Markit iBoxx Jul 8							
Overall (£)	1093	260.40	0.48	0.13	3.94	0.22	4.22
Overall ($)	3262	218.50	0.14	−0.49	3.47	−0.49	3.47
Overall (€)	2276	208.90	0.09	0.15	6.21	0.63	7.78
Global Inflation-Lkd†	97	256.03	0.13	−0.60	6.14	0.85	10.43
Gilts (£)	33	258.11	0.51	0.15	3.62	0.25	2.94
Corporates (£)	703	274.03	0.40	0.07	4.80	0.09	7.94
Corporates ($)†	2111	246.21	0.20	−0.47	5.10	−0.47	5.10
Corporates (€)	1196	206.45	0.09	0.17	5.05	0.53	6.81
Treasuries ($)†	156	208.25	0.13	−0.54	2.75	−0.54	2.75
Eurozone Sov (€)	261	210.02	0.08	0.13	7.10	0.64	8.70
ABF Pan-Asia unhedged	541	179.44	0.08	0.31	4.92	0.93	4.69
FTSE Jul 8							
Sterling Corporate (£)	66	108.63	0.45	−0.05	1.54	0.35	6.72
Euro Corporate (€)	304	109.28	0.12	0.39	3.08	0.64	6.59
Euro Emerging Mkts (€)	7	96.09	0.13	0.14	2.70	0.50	7.83
Eurozone Gov't Bond	260	109.94	0.07	0.24	5.58	0.50	9.18

Source: Data from www.ft.com http://markets.ft.com/RESEARCH/markets/DataArchiveFetchReport?Category=BR&Type=BOND&Date=07/08/2014

CHAPTER 5
CREDIT RATINGS
FOR BONDS

Time was when a country's financial credibility was measured by the amount of gold in its vaults. Modern life has overtaken precious metal's capacity to underpin the credit standing of countries, or that of companies or individuals. Nowadays we often rely on some independent outside body to be an 'impartial' judge of each borrower's standing, and so the credit rating industry was established.

As we have already seen, the standing or creditworthiness of a country or company is crucial as it affects the rate of interest that will be applied to its securities. The assessment of its standing is made by credit rating agencies (CRAs), which, after a thorough investigation, issue a rating that is generally accepted worldwide as a reasonably accurate evaluation of the issuer's relative ability to avoid default, and the likely payout should default occur.

Borrowers pay to have their bonds rated by the CRAs. Standard & Poor's, Moody's and Fitch Ratings are the three most important credit rating companies, but there are also many less well-known CRAs in North America (e.g. Kroll Bond Rating Agency, DBRS and Morningstar) and in other countries, including Dagong from China.

Standard & Poor's was founded in 1860 by Henry Varnum Poor to give information about US railroad companies, but did not assign ratings to corporate bonds until 1922. Moody's was established in 1900 by John Moody to give statistics on US bonds and shares, providing its first credit rating in 1909. Fitch was founded in 1913 by John Knowles Fitch to provide financial statistics to help the US investment industry and began rating in 1924. Dagong is a relative newcomer, founded in 1994.

The As, Bs and Cs

When investing in bonds, the larger banks, fund managers and corporates often conduct their own credit analysis of individual bond issues, but the majority of the huge volume of bond investments are made using CRA ratings for guidance. The top part of Table 5.1 shows the ratings regarded as **investment grade** (**prime grade**). This is important because many institutional investors are permitted to invest only in investment-grade securities. The difference in bond yield between the different grades can be as little as 30 basis points, but this can rise dramatically at times of financial trauma, e.g. in early 2009.

The ratings that CRAs give to countries, **sovereign ratings**, can vary – see Table 5.2. A **notch** is a one-stage move on the rating scale, e.g. moving from A– to BBB+. The UK lost its AAA rating with some of the CRAs in 2013, due to concern about future financial stability. S&P downgraded the US to AA+ in 2011 after the prolonged political wranglings over the US government debt level, and the Chinese agency, Dagong, caused controversy by downgrading the US rating by several notches, from AAA to A–, in 2013 when the US government could not agree on its financial policy (again, arguments in Congress over the debt ceiling) and came dangerously close to being unable to meet the payments due on its bonds. The Chinese are concerned about the US debt burden as they are the biggest holders of US Treasury securities, at $1.3 trillion:

> For a long time the U.S. government maintains its solvency by repaying its old debts through raising new debts, which constantly aggravates the vulnerability of the federal government's solvency. Hence the government is still approaching the verge of default crisis, a situation that cannot be substantially alleviated in the foreseeable future.
>
> Dagong Global (http://en.dagongcredit.com)

Table 5.1 Credit rating systems for long-term debt (more than one year)

Moody's	S&P	Fitch		Dagong	
Investment grade					
Aaa	AAA	AAA	Highest quality, minimal credit risk	AAA	Highest credit quality
Aa1	AA+	AA+	High grade, high quality, very low credit risk	AA+ AA AA−	Very high credit quality
Aa2	AA	AA			
Aa3	AA−	AA−			
A1	A+	A+	Upper medium grade, low credit risk	A+ A A−	High credit quality
A2	A	A			
A3	A−	A−			
Baa1	BBB+	BBB+	Lower medium grade, moderate credit risk, possessing certain speculative characteristics	BBB+ BBB BBB−	Medium credit quality
Baa2	BBB	BBB			
Baa3	BBB−	BBB−			
Non-investment grade (speculative grade)					
Ba1	BB+	BB+	Speculative elements, subject to significant credit risk	BB+ BB BB−	Low–medium credit quality
Ba2	BB	BB			
Ba3	BB−	BB−			
B1	B+	B+	Speculative, high credit risk	B+ B B−	Relatively low credit quality
B2	B	B			
B3	B−	B−			
Caa	CCC+		Poor standing, very high credit risk	CCC	Low credit quality
Ca	CCC	CCC	Highly speculative, likely, in the near future, to default with some prospect of principal and coupon recovery	CC	Very low credit quality
C	CCC−		Typically in default with little prospect for recovery of principal or interest	C	Lowest credit quality
	D	D	In default. These trade on the assumed recovery rate following default		

Source: Data from Rating agencies

Table 5.2 Sovereign ratings

	Dagong	S&P	Moody's	Fitch
Australia	AAA	AAA	Aaa	AAA
Belgium	A+	AA	Aa3	AA
Brazil	A–	BBB+	Baa2	BBB
Canada	AA+	AAA	Aaa	AAA
China	AA+	AA–	Aa3	A+
Egypt	B–	B–	Caa1	B–
Finland	AAA	AAA	Aaa	AAA
France	A+	AA	Aa1	AA+
Germany	AA+	AAA	Aaa	AAA
Greece	CC	B–	Caa3	B
Hong Kong	AAA	AAA	Aa1	AA+
India	BBB	BBB–	Baa3	BBB–
Ireland	BBB	A–	Baa1	BBB+
Italy	BBB–	BBB	Baa2	BBB+
Japan	A	AA–	Aa3	A+
Luxembourg	AAA	AAA	Aaa	AAA
Mexico	BBB	A	A3	BBB+
Netherlands	AA+	AA+	Aaa	AAA
New Zealand	AA+	AA+	Aaa	AA
Norway	AAA	AAA	Aaa	AAA
Portugal	BB	BB	Ba1	BB+
Russia	A	BBB	Baa1	BBB
Singapore	AAA	AAA	Aaa	AAA
South Africa	A–	BBB+	Baa1	BBB
South Korea	AA–	AA–	Aa3	AA–
Spain	BBB+	BBB	Baa3	BBB+
Sweden	AAA	AAA	Aaa	AAA
Switzerland	AAA	AAA	Aaa	AAA
UK	A+	AAA	Aa1	AA+
USA	A–	AA+	Aaa	AAA

Source: Data from CRAs' websites

When the rating agencies disagree we have a **split rating** – as you can see, this occurs quite often. The rating and re-rating of bonds is followed with great interest by borrowers and lenders and can give rise to some heated argument. Italians were very upset in 2014 when S&P was accused of taking insufficient account of the country's qualities – see Article 5.1.

Article 5.1

Italy accuses S&P of not getting 'la dolce vita'

By Stephen Foley and Guy Dinmore

Financial Times February 4, 2014

If financial analysts had spent more time admiring a Michelangelo fresco or reading Dante instead of poring over spreadsheets, they might not have touched off the inferno that engulfed the Italian sovereign debt market, Italy's state auditor is claiming.

Standard & Poor's revealed on Tuesday it had been notified by Corte dei Conti that credit rating agencies may have acted illegally and opened themselves up to damages of €234bn, in part by failing to consider Italy's rich cultural history when downgrading the country.

The potentially gigantic claim, which S&P dismissed as 'frivolous and without merit', relates to the string of downgrades the rating agency issued on Italian debt when the eurozone crisis intensified in 2011.

Notifying S&P that it was considering legal action, the Corte dei Conti wrote: 'S&P never in its ratings pointed out Italy's history, art or landscape which, as universally recognised, are the basis of its economic strength.'

An official in Italy confirmed the judicial inquiry into S&P and its smaller peers, Moody's and Fitch.

Previous reports have indicated the auditor is considering whether 'reckless' rating agency reports on Italy's public debt contributed to a worsening of the sovereign debt crisis, forcing the governments of Silvio Berlusconi and then Mario Monti to take emergency measures.

While it remains uncertain that the claim will be brought, the auditor's dramatic threat – and the size of damages it has suggested – reflects anger in European political circles at the role played by rating agencies in the market turmoil that threatened the eurozone.

The prospect of sovereign downgrades caused waves of selling of government debt from countries such as Italy and Spain, raising their borrowing costs and further damaging their public finances.

A spokesman for Moody's also said the allegations were without merit.

Fitch said it would co-operate with the probe. 'As we understand the prosecutor's concerns, we believe Fitch at all times acted appropriately and in full compliance with the law.'

The rating agencies are constantly reviewing countries to detect reasons for thinking that default risk has improved or deteriorated. As Article 5.2 shows, in the years following the financial crisis there were some dramatic changes, with Europe declining and developing countries prospering.

Article 5.2

Turning point for European debt ratings

By Ralph Atkins and Keith Fray

Financial Times March 31, 2014

The financial crises of the past seven years drove sweeping changes in the global credit ratings map. The US and European governments were downgraded. Emerging markets rose.

The story of the past 12 months has been more complex. The rating performance of developing economies has been at best mixed. But signs are appearing that Europe has reached a possible turning point.

'What we have tried to emphasise is how much divergence there is in terms of exposure to the turning tide in global capital,' says Moritz Kraemer, chief sovereign ratings officer at Standard & Poor's. 'It is really country-specific policy actions that are likely to overshadow rating actions, rather than global factors.'

Credit ratings guide investors' decision making by indicating the likelihood of defaults.

Top performers compared with a year ago in terms of rating upgrades are Mexico and the Philippines. Near the bottom, unsurprisingly, is Ukraine, which has come close to financial collapse.

By weighting countries according to the size of their outstanding debt, the FT's analysis also shows the changing size of bond markets by credit rating category. Downgrades in the past year have thrown the Netherlands out of the shrinking club of economies rated triple A by all three agencies.

But, overall, average credit ratings in the developed world stabilised in the past year, although with significant country-by-country variations.

With Europe still reeling from its debt crisis and recession, France and Italy were downgraded. But Spain and Greece headed in the opposite direction, and there are signs that the 18-country eurozone trend is no longer downwards. Rating 'outlooks' – which indicate possible future actions – have been switched from negative to stable by at least one agency for six eurozone countries, including Germany and Portugal.

'At the beginning of last year, we had two-thirds of the eurozone on negative outlook. Now it's just one-third,' says James McCormack, at Fitch. 'If you'd known

➡

before the crisis that a third would be on negative outlook, you would have right-fully thought that was pretty bad, but it has stabilised. Relative to where we were, things have certainly improved.'

Any turnround in European credit ratings will be slow, however. Mr Kraemer at S&P points out that when Sweden and Finland lost their triple A status in the early 1990s, it was a decade before it was regained.

Similarly, France and the UK are unlikely to see a quick return to triple A status, warns Mr McCormack. 'We have suggested that debt ratios need to come down in a more meaningful way – there has to be a track record of fiscal adjustment.'

Ratings in emerging markets over the past year have improved in Asia, central and eastern Europe and the Caribbean. But African, Middle East and Latin American

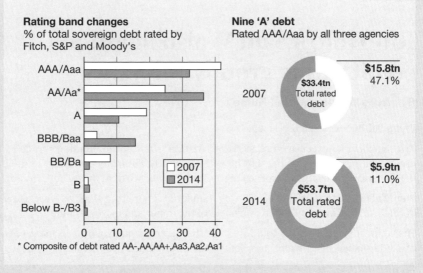

Average rating changes by region, 2007–14 – countries weighted by size of government debt – modified from FT chart

Developed Europe	DOWN 2.4 notches
Eurozone	DOWN 2.9 notches
Caribbean	DOWN 0.1 notches
All developed markets	DOWN 0.8 notches
Africa	DOWN 1.1 notches
M East and N Africa	DOWN 2.6 notches
CIS	DOWN 1.4 notches
Latin America	UP 1.9 notches
Central and E Europe	UP 0.8 notches
Developing Asia	UP 1.4 notches
All emerging markets	UP 1 notch

Rating band changes
% of total sovereign debt rated by Fitch, S&P and Moody's

AAA/Aaa
AA/Aa*
A
BBB/Baa
BB/Ba
B
Below B-/B3

0 10 20 30 40

☐ 2007
■ 2014

* Composite of debt rated AA-,AA,AA+,Aa3,Aa2,Aa1

Nine 'A' debt
Rated AAA/Aaa by all three agencies

2007
$33.4tn Total rated debt
$15.8tn
47.1%

2014
$53.7tn Total rated debt
$5.9tn
11.0%

countries have seen downgrades on average. Brazil was downgraded by S&P last week.

As well as country-specific factors, the future performance of emerging markets could depend on China's prospects. 'China has generated a lot of economic activity, which has driven a lot of trade and improved the fiscal position of a lot of countries in, say, Latin America,' says Mr Oosterveld (head of sovereign ratings] at Moody's. 'Things look very different if you assume, in a downside scenario, China is going to grow by 4% a year rather than 8%.'

But changes in the global ratings map do not necessarily reflect what happens on the ground. Economists at UniCredit argued that the subjective part of rating decisions often blurred their predictive powers. 'History is littered with countries being over- and underrated by the rating agencies, with – at times – dramatic consequences,' they wrote. 'The biggest casualty was the eurozone periphery, which was downgraded far too heavily during the 2009–11 sovereign debt crisis.'

Source: Atkins, R. and Fray, K. (2014) Turning point for European debt ratings, *Financial Times*, 31 March.
© The Financial Times Limited 2014. All Rights Reserved.

While corporate borrowers' credit ratings are generally of great concern to them, because those with lower ratings tend to have higher costs, some companies are fairly sanguine, particularly if they regard the CRAs as using unreasonable methods and they can persuade finance providers of their point of view – see Article 5.3 for the example of Rio Tinto.

Article 5.3

Rio Tinto's Sam Walsh questions credit rating groups' relevance

By James Wilson and Neil Hume

Financial Times December 11, 2013

Rio Tinto's chief executive has signalled that he is not afraid of a downgrade by credit rating agencies, saying that he will not run the company according to their demands, in spite of possible consequences for borrowing costs at the indebted miner.

Sam Walsh said that agencies including Standard & Poor's and Moody's were using yardsticks that were of limited relevance to the miner and its shareholders.

His comments came as Rio told investors that it would make a priority next year of paying down debt, which has soared after misguided acquisitions and heavy investment.

Mr Walsh acknowledged that he no longer saw Rio's single-A rating, given by Standard & Poor's and Moody's, as sacrosanct.

'You have got to be very careful that you manage the business and that Standard & Poor's or Moody's or what-have-you don't end up running the business [by] default,' said Mr Walsh.

'I believe we have done all the things we need to retain an A-rating. But I am not about to be driven by a rating which takes into account things that we and our shareholders don't take into account.'

The Anglo-Australian miner expects to end the year with $19bn of net debt, down from $22bn in midyear but the same level as at the start of 2013. Its gross debt stood at $29.5bn at midyear.

Credit rating agencies' judgments have been increasingly called into question since the financial crisis, when they were viewed as having given overly reassuring ratings to many of the complex debt instruments that were at the heart of the crisis.

Rio has long been focused on maintaining its single-A credit rating. S&P put the rating on 'negative' outlook in February, citing risks that its debt, including costs for pensions or for mines at the end of their lives, could rise.

He acknowledged Rio's rating was 'clearly an issue' for its borrowing costs. 'It is not totally irrelevant but you cannot be driven by what others think you should be doing,' he said.

 Source: Wilson, J. and Hume, N. (2013) Rio Tinto's Sam Walsh questions credit rating groups' relevance, *Financial Times*, 11 December.

How rating judgements are formed

The **rating** given to securities depends on the likelihood of payments of interest and/or capital not being paid (default) and in some cases on the extent to which the lender is protected in the event of a default by the loan contract, the **recoverability of debt**. Rating agencies say that they do not in the strictest sense give an opinion on the likelihood of default, but merely evaluate *relative* creditworthiness or *relative* likelihood of default, and because rating scales are relative, default rates for a rating grade fluctuate over time. Thus, a group of middle-rated bonds is expected to be consistent in having a lower rate of default than a group of lower-rated bonds, but they will not, year-after year, have a default rate of, say, 2.5% per year. With regard to the recovery rate ('loss given default') element, much will depend on the extent of **credit enhancements** such as collateral backing, strength of covenants and priority ranking relative to other debt.

The agencies consider a wide range of quantitative and qualitative factors in determining the rating for a bond. The quantitative factors include the ratio of company assets to liabilities, cash flow generation and the amount of debt outstanding. Ratios such as the number of times profits exceed interest are likely to be considered, together with the extent to which shareholder funds in the business are greater than total debt. Also considered are funding diversity, profitability and liquidity of assets.

The qualitative factors include competitive position, quality of management, vulnerability to the economic cycle, dependence on one or a few products or customers, and geographic diversity – see Article 5.4 for a qualitative discussion of Microsoft's and Apple's relative default risk.

Article 5.4

Microsoft beats Apple in the credit ratings league

By Michael Mackenzie and Vivianne Rodrigues

Financial Times May 1, 2013

It is a long standing rivalry and on one score, Microsoft still trumps Apple – when it comes to the rating of their respective debt securities. While Apple effortlessly sold a record $17bn in debt that attracted $52bn in demand from investors on Tuesday, the paper comes with a Double A plus rating, one notch below the gold standard of Triple A.

In contrast, Microsoft is rated Triple A by both Moody's and Standard & Poor's. Fitch, which has not yet rated Apple, assigns a Double A plus rating to Microsoft.

This comes in spite of Apple having an enormous gross cash pile of $145bn, and enjoying solid sales for its very popular products. While that would suggest Apple should qualify for a top rating, it has been awarded a slightly lower rating due to its hefty reliance on sales to consumers. The rating agencies deem this market to be more volatile than sales to corporate customers.

In turn, the Triple A club has a very select membership of just four US companies, ADP, Johnson & Johnson, ExxonMobil and Microsoft. What links these companies, say analysts, is their strong leadership in their respective sectors.

'Generally, Microsoft has a recurring fee business, while Apple is more of a consumer products company,' says Jack Ablin at Harris Private Bank.

Gerald Granovsky at Moody's says: 'Microsoft's ratings reflect our confidence in the company's revenue stream and also the fact their customers have very little

➡

option but to buy Microsoft products. The consumer profile for the companies is slightly different.'

He adds: 'Apple's credit profile is tied to the company's ability to keep up with innovations and maintain its unique corporate culture. The rapid rise and fall of new products demonstrates these sectors are particularly prone to transformational changes that could lead to shifts in market leadership.'

Fitch said the company would likely fall in the high single 'A' rating category, based on the inherent business risk of consumer-centric hardware companies.

'Consumer product companies such as Sony, Nokia, and Motorola Mobility have proven the risks related to ever-changing consumer tastes, low switching costs, and a highly competitive environment,' said James Rizzo at Fitch. 'Each has historically had a dominant market position and strong financial metrics, only to falter over a relatively short period of time.'

'Apple's better diversification and the stickiness of its iTunes ecosystem clearly make it a stronger credit that would likely be at the highest end of the 'A' category,' said Mr Rizzo.

While there is a one notch difference in ratings between Apple and Microsoft, investors appear less discerning based on the pricing of recent bond issues by both companies. Apple's blockbuster bond issue priced very close to where Microsoft's much smaller $1.95bn offering of five-, 10-, and 30-year debt was sold last week.

While Microsoft sold $1bn of 10-year debt at 70 basis points over Treasury yields, Apple's $5.5bn issue arrived at 75 bps over benchmark government debt. There was a difference of 10 basis points in pricing between their 30-year bonds.

 Source: Mackenzie, M. and Rodrigues, V. (2013) Microsoft beats Apple in the credit ratings league, *Financial Times*, 1 May.
© The Financial Times Limited 2013. All Rights Reserved.

A checklist for a rating assessment might include:

- breakdown of sales by geography and product lines – degree of diversification is of particular interest
- market position of main goods and services produced, pointing out competitive advantages
- life-cycle position of main goods and services: are they old, tired or in decline?
- costs
- sources of inputs: any competitive advantages or weaknesses there, e.g. reliant on one supplier for a key input
- intellectual property ownership (trademark, copyright, advantage given by government or regulatory concession/licence)

- any restriction on price charged, e.g. under competition authority rules or other regulators
- excessive dependence on one/few customers
- thought-through strategy or changed by whim at short notice
- vulnerability to technological change
- main drivers of profits and cash flow
- managers' track record
- delivery on past plans
- risk management processes
- plans for further cash raising, equity or bonds; how receptive might the markets be; will the changes unbalance the capital structure, creating risk?
- how sensible the dividend policy is
- any worries over the legal structure of the group, such as subsidiaries in overseas companies borrowing, government controls on moving money across borders
- contingent liabilities, e.g. pensions, legal liabilities, environmental
- strength of bank relationships
- derivative risk exposure.

The sovereign issuer might be asked for the following:

- national economic and financial data
- government budget forecasts
- independent reports on the country, e.g. from the International Monetary Fund
- economic strategy, e.g. fiscal policy, monetary policy, planned privatisations, microeconomic reforms, exchange rate policy
- political trends and risks
- general government debt burden
- government debt owed to foreigners (external debt)
- taxation powers
- strength of political institutions and trends
- contingent liabilities
- private sector external debt (owing to foreigners) burden.

As well as specific bond ratings the CRAs provide **issuer ratings** to firms and other organisations, which are assessments of the creditworthiness of the whole entity. The vast majority of ratings, however, apply to a particular security issue by the firm. Ratings on some securities may have a higher rating than the issuing company as a whole because the specific security is secured on a very reliable asset.

Obtaining a rating can be expensive, of the order of 0.05% of the amount raised with a minimum of $80,000, but for some companies the benefit of being able to borrow at lower interest rates due to the rating can be worth ten times as much as the fees paid for it. For other companies the equation does not work out that way and they choose not to obtain one – see Article 5.5.

If a bond does not have a rating, it could simply mean that the borrower has chosen not to pay for one, rather than implying anything untoward or sinister. Indeed, some bonds are sold on a **name recognition** basis, that is, the issuer has such a good reputation with lenders accepting that their financial standing is such that there is a very low likelihood of default and they do not require a formal credit rating. However, 'unrated' is often used to mean poorer default risk.

Article 5.5

'Dash for trash' lifts unrated debt sales

By Andrew Bolger and Robin Wigglesworth

Financial Times May 19, 2014

Now it is the turn of the tiddlers. Even companies too small to be graded by the leading rating agencies – or that choose not to – are benefiting from voracious investor appetite for European corporate bonds.

Mahle, a German car parts maker, SEA, an Italian airport operator, and Bureau Veritas, a France-based inspection and certifying company, are among those to have recently issued unrated bonds.

These bring the total volume of unrated corporate bonds issued in Europe this year to more than $20bn, and open up the prospect of yet another record year for grade-less company debt. Last year there were $58bn worth of unrated corporate bond sales.

Other prominent unrated deals so far this year include Sodexo, the French caterer, which borrowed $1.1bn in January, ProSiebenSat, the German broadcaster, which borrowed $828m in April, and CGG, an Irish support services group, which raised $750m in March.

However, unrated bond issues remain relatively rare, given many investors are limited to buying certain grades, and most prefer the transparency that a rating confers. They have accounted for about 10% of the European corporate bond market in recent years.

Unrated bonds also tend to be smaller and less liquid than rated debt. Half such bonds issued over the past three years were for less than $250m. The companies therefore have to pay lenders a premium to the yields at which they would normally expect to issue.

But Rupert Lewis, a debt syndicate banker at BNP Paribas, says that the extra cost of issuing unrated debt has come down over the last couple of years from approximately 100 basis points to 50bp – or potentially less, depending on the company.

'It's a horses for courses market,' he says. 'They tend to be companies that don't issue that often and therefore don't want to go through the workload and costs of getting and maintaining a credit rating for infrequent borrowing. Without a rating they don't go in indices, so a large amount of investors cannot buy, but despite that the cost has definitely come down.'

Jean-Marc Mercier, global head of debt syndicate at HSBC, says: 'A lot of companies don't want to take on the cost, work and management time involved with obtaining a rating – particularly family-controlled companies.'

However, unrated bonds have also been issued by large companies such as SAP, the German software group, which has borrowed several billions of euros via such bonds. Household names that have used the market and subsequently acquired ratings include the Dutch brewer Heineken and Thomas Cook, the UK travel group.

The rating agency Fitch says some household names have been able to take advantage of their higher profiles among retail investors to issue unrated bonds. These include Skanska, the Swedish engineering group; Finnair in Finland; Air France-KLM; and Sixt, the German-based car rental group.

Mike Dunning at Fitch says: 'UK companies can also access the US private placement market to raise funds on an unrated basis – which is easier than going through the full bond rating process.'

The agency says that a sizeable proportion of the larger issues of unrated bonds display credit profiles that could be classified as investment, or near-investment grade. This is in spite of a significant level of opportunistic issuance by smaller, non-eurozone domiciled corporates.

'The European institutional bond market is generally receptive to the first, opportunistic, unrated bond from a new issuer, but increasingly looks for a rating if repeat visits, particularly for smaller issuers, are contemplated,' says Tom Chruszcz, an analyst with Fitch.

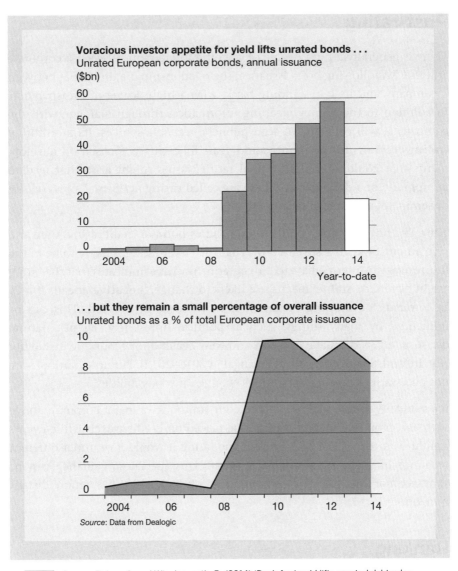

Voracious investor appetite for yield lifts unrated bonds . . .
Unrated European corporate bonds, annual issuance ($bn)

. . . but they remain a small percentage of overall issuance
Unrated bonds as a % of total European corporate issuance

Source: Data from Dealogic

A rating decision generally takes a few weeks and is made by a rating committee assessing the evidence, rather than by an individual. The committee notifies the issuer of the rating and the rationale behind it.

The agencies are also available to carry out credit analysis as a service to lenders. They thus produce **unsolicited company analysis and credit ratings** without necessarily gaining the cooperation of the issuing company (or country).

Post-rating

There is generally a high degree of ongoing interaction between a corporate and its CRA following bond issuance; the relationship is akin to that between a company and its longstanding bank, with a high degree of transparency. In addition to the agency gleaning information through dialogue with the company it will continue to scan publicly available sources. Its monitoring (**ratings review**) in the months and years following is focused on developments that could alter the original rating. Issues might arise that lead to an **upgrade** or a **downgrade**. These are called **rating actions**. A press release disseminates a change of rating.

The CRAs not only give countries/companies/bonds a credit rating, they also give **an outlook**, an assessment of what the credit rating is likely to be in the future over the intermediate to longer term: '**positive**' indicates that the rating might be raised, '**stable**' means not likely to change, '**negative**' means it may be lowered, '**developing**' means it may be raised or lowered. This can be influenced by many things, such as political unrest (e.g. Egypt), natural disasters (e.g. earthquake in Japan and New Zealand) or economic instability (e.g. Ireland, Spain, Greece and Portugal in 2010–2012). But note, outlooks are not necessarily a precursor to ratings changes, just possibilities.

If a company announces or is expected to announce a major corporate move such as a proposed merger it might be placed on **credit watch** while events unfold. Sometimes the CRA assesses the rating it would give under different scenarios likely to stem from the event. This special surveillance can be short-term or long-term focused, unlike an outlook which has a more distant horizon.

Ranking

In the event of financial failure of a company (liquidation/bankruptcy), the ranking ('priority') order for bonds is:

1 Senior secured debt holders will be paid first. An example of this would be a mortgage loan secured on the mortgaged asset.

2 Senior unsecured debt is paid next, if any money is left. This is debt consisting of loans which are not secured on an asset(s), but it is stated in the trust deed that they will be near the front of the queue for payouts of annual

coupons and of proceeds from liquidation. After this group has been paid the subordinated bond holders may receive nothing.

3 Senior subordinated debt – high-yield or junk bonds, secured or unsecured.

4 Subordinated debt is the last type of debt to be paid out after all other creditors.

The situation becomes more complicated when group companies are forced into liquidation. For example, it is possible for senior debt issued by the holding company to be subordinated to debt issued by a subsidiary (senior or junior) if the subsidiary's lenders have legal access to assets of the subsidiary.

The variety of insolvency regimes across Europe, with different rules on bond priorities following insolvency, is thought to have inhibited bond market growth relative to that in the single system across the US – see Article 5.6.

Article 5.6

Europe looks for common default process

By Andrew Bolger

Financial Times August 11, 2014

European companies have been able to access a flood of high-yield loans and bonds over the past few years – so far with remarkably few defaults, thanks partly to low interest rates.

But rating agencies and lawyers warn that investors may not appreciate the complexity of the different European insolvency procedures they may have to deal with, when the market returns to more normal conditions.

Moody's says the default rate among high-yield issuers was 2.2% in the second quarter, down from 3.4% at the same stage last year. It expects the global high-yield default rate to finish this year at 2% – well below the historical average of 4.7% since 1983.

'The benign default rate outlook is supported by robust liquidity which has continued for quite some time,' says the rating agency. 'Lowly rated companies have been able to access the capital markets and refinance their debt with issuer friendly terms, which will probably keep the default rates low into the first half of next year.'

However, no one expects the present benign conditions to last once interest rates start to increase.

Michael Dakin, a partner at the law firm Clifford Chance, likens the recent sell-off of high-yield bonds to 'blowing the froth off the cappuccino'. But he predicts a 'flood' of selling when the currently 'ludicrously low' level of company defaults moves back closer to its historic average.

One potential problem is that US investors are used to dealing with corporate re-organisations conducted under the Chapter 11 procedure, which applies in all states, and is subject to the US bankruptcy code, providing for valuations of the debtor's assets and ranking of competing claims.

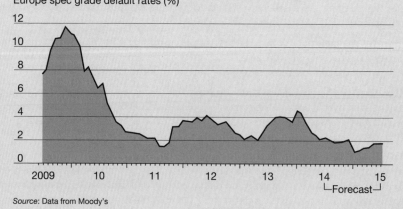

Companies that defaulted in Europe over past year . . .
Non-financial corporate defaults in EMEA

Company	Country	Industry	Date	Defaulted amount ($m)
Songa	Norway	Energy	Dec 20 2013	660
ATU	Germany	Retail	Dec 9 2013	620
Invitel	Netherlands	Telecom	Jul 15 2013	457
Codere	Spain	Gaming	Sep 16 2013	300
Cognor	Poland	Metals & mining	Nov 29 2013	164
Travelport	US	Technology services	Mar 4 2014	135
PagesJaunes	France	Media publishing	Apr 11 2014	28
Schoeller Arca	Netherlands	Packaging	Aug 22 2013	21
Ideal Standard	Belgium	Consumer products	Mar 24 2014	–
Total				**2385**

. . . but default rates are forecast to stay low
Europe spec grade default rates (%)

Source: Data from Moody's

'In Europe, there is no common process, law or statutory timetable equivalent to Chapter 11,' says Philip Hertz, joint leader of the restructuring and insolvency group at Clifford Chance.

'While high-yield products may have originated in the US, a European high-yield transaction, with a European issuer and a primarily European business, is a European deal in restructuring terms. If that deal falters, its restructuring will be largely driven by European considerations.'

But there are moves afoot to develop a more consistent regime across Europe. Continental European companies such as the German building materials group Monier, Italian directories publisher Seat Pagine Gialle and Spanish retailer Cortefiel, shifted jurisdiction to the UK to access more creditor-friendly, court-sanctioned schemes of arrangement, despite reforms in their own jurisdictions.

Many UK companies have used such schemes to restructure not only their liabilities governed by English law, but also non-English law liabilities.

Source: Bolger, A. (2014) Europe looks for common default process, *Financial Times*, 11 August.
© The Financial Times Limited 2014. All Rights Reserved.

Bond ratings in the *Financial Times*

The *Financial Times* shows credit ratings daily in the tables titled 'Bonds – Global Investment Grade' and 'Bonds – High Yield & Emerging Market', together with yields to redemption ('bid yield' – based on the bid price offered by market makers) and other details – see Tables 5.3 and 5.4. These give the reader some idea of current market conditions and the redemption yield demanded for bonds of different maturities, currencies and risk. The ratings shown are for August 2014 and will not necessarily be applicable in future weeks because the creditworthiness and the default risk of a specific debt issue can change significantly in a short period. A key measure in the bond markets is the '**spread**', which is the number of basis points a bond is yielding above a benchmark rate, usually the government bond yield to maturity for that currency and period to redemption.

Bond credit ratings are available direct from rating agency websites, www.standardandpoors.com, www.moodys.com, and www.fitchratings.com.

Note the higher variation in the price, yield and spread of the high-yield bonds, compared with investment-grade bonds.

Table 5.3 Global investment-grade bonds, 7 August 2014

Aug 7	Red date	Coupon	Ratings			Bid price	Bid yield	Day's chge yield	Mth's chge yield	Spread vs Govts
			S*	M*	F*					
US $										
BNP Paribas	06/15	4.80	BBB+	Baa2	A	103.28	0.98	0.03	-1.13	0.89
GE Capital	01/16	5.00	AA+	A1	0	106.09	0.64	-0.02	-0.08	0.55
Erste Euro Lux	02/16	5.00	A-	0	0	104.24	2.11	-0.03	-0.17	1.65
Credit Suisse USA	03/16	5.38	A	A1	A	107.24	0.89	–	-0.05	0.28
SPI E&G Aust	09/16	5.75	A-	A3	A-	107.50	2.07	-0.04	-0.08	1.63
Abu Dhabi Nt En	10/17	6.17	A-	A3	0	113.54	1.79	0.01	-0.05	0.73
Swire Pacific	04/18	6.25	A-	A3	A-	114.04	2.26	-0.07	-0.06	1.38
ASNA	11/18	6.95	A-	Baa2	A	119.10	2.19	-0.06	-0.18	0.58
Codelco	01/19	7.50	AA-	A1	A+	121.29	2.40	-0.16	-0.17	0.79
Bell South	10/31	6.88	A-	WR	A	123.05	4.88	-0.04	-0.17	2.45
GE Capital	01/39	6.88	AA+	A1	0	134.85	4.51	-0.02	-0.15	1.26
Goldman Sachs	02/33	6.13	A-	Baa1	A	120.02	4.52	-0.04	-0.15	2.09
Euro										
JPMorgan Chase	01/15	5.25	A	A3	A+	102.21	0.04	-0.52	-0.49	0.01
Hutchison Fin 06	09/16	4.63	A-	A3	A-	108.16	0.71	-0.07	-0.12	0.71
Hypo Alpe Bk	10/16	4.25	0	Caa1	0	92.01	8.33	0.02	2.01	8.32
GE Cap Euro Fdg	01/18	5.38	AA+	A1	0	116.03	0.64	-0.04	-0.09	0.60
UniCredit	01/20	4.38	BBB	Baa2	BBB+	113.61	1.74	0.01	0.05	1.43
ENEL	05/24	5.25	BBB	Baa2	BBB+	126.60	2.19	-0.10	-0.13	1.27
Yen										
Deutsche Bahn Fin	12/14	1.65	AA	Aa1	AA	100.21	0.95	0.01	0.18	0.92
Nomura Sec S 3	03/18	2.28	0	0	0	104.49	1.00	-0.04	-0.05	0.92
£ Sterling										
Slough Estates	09/15	6.25	NR	0	A-	104.82	1.90	-0.02	-0.07	1.11
ASIF III	12/18	5.00	A+	A2	A+	110.20	2.48	0.00	-0.17	0.79

US $ denominated bonds NY close; all other London close. S* – Standard & Poor's, M* – Moody's, F* – Fitch.

Source: Thomson Reuters

Table 5.4 High-yield and emerging market bonds, 7 August 2014

Aug 7	Red date	Coupon	Ratings S*	M*	F*	Bid price	Bid yield	Day's chge yield	Mth's chge yield	Spread vs US
High Yield US$										
Bertin	10/16	10.25	BB	Ba3	0	113.06	3.85	0.03	0.14	3.26
High Yield Euro										
Kazkommerts Int	02/17	6.88	B	Caa1	B	100.75	6.52	0.17	-0.38	6.52
Emerging US$										
Bulgaria	01/15	8.25	BBB-	Baa2	BBB-	102.75	1.72	0.68	0.39	1.68
Peru	02/15	9.88	BBB+	A3	BBB+	104.31	0.92	0.00	-0.37	0.87
Brazil	03/15	7.88	BBB-	Baa2	BBB	103.78	1.20	-0.03	-0.10	1.16
Mexico	09/16	11.38	BBB+	A3	BBB+	121.25	1.12	–	0.27	0.66
Philippines	01/19	9.88	BBB	Baa3	BBB-	131.48	2.34	-0.05	-0.04	0.72
Brazil	01/20	12.75	BBB-	Baa2	BBB	148.20	3.05	0.17	0.12	1.41
Colombia	02/20	11.75	BBB	Baa2	BBB	143.64	3.11	0.03	0.06	1.51
Russia	03/30	7.50	BBB-	Baa1	BBB	111.50	4.98	0.25	0.72	3.35
Mexico	08/31	8.30	BBB+	A3	BBB+	147.38	4.33	-0.03	-0.13	1.91
Indonesia	02/37	6.63	BB+	Baa3	BBB-	112.88	5.61	0.19	-0.15	2.37
Emerging Euro										
Brazil	02/15	7.38	BBB-	Baa2	BBB	103.05	0.95	-0.25	0.06	0.92
Poland	02/16	3.63	A-	A2	A-	104.73	0.40	-0.01	0.11	0.40
Turkey	03/16	5.00	NR	Baa3	BBB-	105.50	1.39	0.04	-0.11	1.38
Mexico	02/20	5.50	BBB+	A3	BBB+	120.85	1.53	0.02	-0.04	1.14

US $ denominated bonds NY close; all other London close. S* – Standard & Poor's, M* – Moody's, F* – Fitch.

Source: Thomson Reuters

Crisis of confidence

CRAs advance the argument that their ratings are mere opinions and are thus protected under free speech laws. They have no contract with the investing institutions, nor do they have a fiduciary duty to them, so say the agencies. Thus they can publish an opinion without being liable for mistakes or misleading statements.

But a lot of weight is placed on bond ratings by financial institutions and investors who rely on them for investment decisions. They can feel aggrieved if a bond rating fails to live up to expectations. It has been suggested that during the run-up to the financial crisis of 2008 the CRAs gave unduly high ratings to bonds that were shaky. Many have called into question the CRAs' judgement when it became apparent that many bonds rated 'A' and above were, in fact, worthless. Just before Lehman Brothers went into bankruptcy, its credit rating was A, and Bear Stearns was downgraded from AA to A shortly before the company became insolvent. It would seem that the CRAs seriously underestimated the risks undertaken by these and many other companies. In particular, the CRAs have been criticised for not spotting the dangers in a number of bonds which gained their income from thousands of US mortgages, and several lawsuits were launched, with the CRAs being accused of causing financial loss through their perceived as inaccurate ratings.

There have been some serious legal challenges to the CRAs' claim that an 'opinion' should not lead to claims of carelessness or negligence if their judgement turns out to be wrong. Article 5.7 shows the state of the law in Australia, which will probably have an impact on other jurisdictions: CRAs have a duty of care to investors, not just their paymasters, the issuers.

Article 5.7

S&P loses Australia appeal over misleading investors

By Jamie Smyth and Sam Fleming

Financial Times June 6, 2014

Standard & Poor's has lost its appeal against a landmark court ruling in Australia, which found the credit rating agency misled investors by giving AAA ratings to toxic financial products that lost almost all their value.

The ruling by the Federal Court of Australia in a case that also involved ABN Amro, which is now owned by Royal Bank of Scotland, paves the way for similar court actions elsewhere from investors who lost billions of dollars during the financial crisis.

John Ahern, a partner at law firm Jones Day, said the judgment augured ill for rating agencies. 'The position that the court took is logically the conclusion that courts in other jurisdictions could arrive at, given [there is] a good deal of similarity in the principles of negligence – at least in common law jurisdictions.'

S&P originally lost the Australian case in November 2012, when the court issued a scathing ruling that the rating agency was 'misleading' and 'deceptive' when it awarded a AAA credit rating to a complex debt instrument.

The judgment was the first time a court found a credit-rating agency liable for losses incurred by investors on financial products, which it had erroneously awarded a gilt-edged credit rating. It also said that rating agencies have a duty of care to investors.

The court found that the notes were sold to local councils in Australia on the basis that the AAA rating was based on reasonable grounds, and as the result of an exercise in reasonable care and skill, while neither was true.

'S&P also knew them not to be true when they were made,' concluded the original ruling.

Local councils lost tens of millions of dollars on the collateralised debt instruments when the financial crisis struck.

ABN AMRO, which created the toxic products, and Local Government Financial Services, which sold them to councils, also engaged in misleading and deceptive conduct, according to the original court judgment.

The dismissal of the appeal by Judge Peter Jacobson is a setback for S&P, which is fighting multiple legal actions in the US and Europe related to claims it issued misleading credit ratings before the 2008 financial crisis.

Regulators around the world have tried to keep closer tabs on the CRAs in recent years. The European Union set up a new regulator, the **European Securities and Markets Authority**, in part to scrutinise the CRAs' conduct. The Federal Reserve and the Securities and Exchange Commission in the US tightened regulation, e.g. by prohibiting the agencies from also advising the issuers (for a fee) on how to structure a bond issue to obtain a favourable rating. The fear was that the CRAs would lower standards in order to generate business for their consultancy wing. In addition, the agency's fee negotiator (for the rating exercise) has to be someone who is not involved in the rating assessment. Also, more disclosure on how ratings are determined, and disclosure of historical ratings performance, are required. One of the tools regulators are employing is the encouragement of rival CRAs to criticise and give alternative unsolicited opinions on ratings – see Article 5.8. Structured bonds, discussed in the article, have special individualised features to attract particular investors, usually with derivative features, e.g. an option to gain from a rise in the stock market, or bonds whose value derives from a collection of loans or other bonds (for more on securitisation see Chapters 15 and 16).

Article 5.8

Doubts raised over rating agency reform

By Tracy Alloway and Christopher Thompson

Financial Times June 11, 2014

On a Friday night in New York City, the block around the Westin Hotel near Times Square heaves with activity. Throngs of tourists head for dinner at Sardi's, or to the St James Theatre for an evening showing of the musical 'Bullets over Broadway'.

On Wall Street, bullets of a very different sort are flying. And, here too, the Westin is in the thick of the action.

Fitch, one of three big rating agencies, this week criticised credit ratings given by its competitors to a securitisation containing a loan secured by the Westin – the latest instance of agencies sparring with each other over so-called structured finance deals.

Such deals bundle together a wide variety of loans into bonds that can be sold to large fund managers who use the evaluations of credit rating agencies to help inform their investment decisions.

Typically, these opinions are paid for by the financial firms that create the deals. But, since the financial crisis, regulators have encouraged credit rating agencies to give 'unsolicited' opinions on deals that they are not hired to evaluate, as part of an effort to avoid the 'ratings shopping' that proliferated before 2008.

However, as the rating agencies trade public barbs amid a resurgence of certain types of structured products, questions are being raised as to whether these unsolicited opinions actually have much effect on investors' thinking. And are the banks that securitise loans simply taking their deals to the agencies likely to give them the highest ratings?

'You're seeing them [the agencies] having to be vocal because there's no other visible ramification for their competitors being wrong,' says Gene Phillips at PF2, a structured finance consulting firm.

'A preferable alternative is a system which says you can rate whatever you like wherever you like but you will lose business as a result of being wrong. Unfortunately that's not happening. People aren't choosing or aren't able to choose based on quality or ratings performance.'

In the aftermath of the crisis, when subprime mortgage securitisations turned out to be anything but the pristine investments that their triple-A credit ratings implied, regulators rushed to reform the agencies hired to evaluate such securities.

At the top of their list was encouraging the agencies to be more vocal about their competitors' ratings by publishing their own unsolicited opinions. To do so, they created a special website for issuers to share deal data, so that competing agencies could evaluate securitised products they were not formally hired to rate.

The idea was to help expose spurious ratings and encourage smaller agencies that might help challenge the dominance of 'the big three' – Fitch Ratings, Moody's and Standard & Poor's.

Fitch's criticism of Wells Fargo Commercial Mortgage Trust 2014-Tish, which includes a $210m loan secured by the Westin Hotel, is the most recent example of a rating agency publishing an unsolicited commentary. 'Fitch believes a number of recently issued large loan transactions have debt levels that are inconsistent with the ratings assigned,' the agency's analysts wrote in the commentary.

Larger credit rating agencies, in particular Fitch, have been among the most prolific when it comes to issuing unsolicited opinions. Smaller groups such as Kroll and Morningstar have not published any unsolicited ratings or commentaries, according to their respective spokespeople.

'We believe that [publishing unsolicited commentaries] will enhance our credibility with investors and they will encourage issuers to use Fitch more frequently,' says Kevin Duignan, global head of securitisation and covered bonds at Fitch. 'We think that's healthy.'

But, while the competition between rating agencies to issue unsolicited opinions has heated up, it appears to have had little impact on the behaviour of investors or issuers, say market participants. 'They [the rating agencies] have been sidelined by US regulation so they could be just fighting each other in a shrinking market. I would expect some laundry cleaning in public,' said a securitisation banker.

Indeed, there are rumblings of a return of ratings shopping – the pre-crisis practice where issuers would sound out rating agencies for their initial feedback on a deal, and then hire the agency that offered the best possible designation.

When Moody's criticised a residential mortgage-backed security in 2011, for instance, the company that created the deal simply decided to use Fitch's ratings instead. 'The sponsor disagreed with Moody's preliminary assessment of the risks attributable to the mortgage loans,' the prospectus for the deal read.

Fitch says it was asked to provide initial feedback on the CMBS backed by the Westin loan and determined that it would have rated the safest slice of the deal AA, and would not have rated some of the riskier pieces of the deal at all. S&P and Morningstar rated the top slice of the deal triple-A. Says Mr Duignan: 'Unsolicited commentaries may not be the best solution but they are a far better solution than remaining silent.'

A major debate is whether the investing institutions rather than the borrowers should pay for ratings. After all, they would be the beneficiaries of a more robust examination of the likelihood of default without the, supposed, tainting of the potential conflict of interest arising from the examinee paying – a case of he who pays the piper calling the tune, it is alleged. The CRAs retort that they live and die by their reputations; they cannot be seen to be anything less than objective and impartial. Also, with lenders paying, they might decide not to publicise the rating they pay for; lack of public information could result in distortion of trading in the market or duplication of rating assessments. Egan-Jones is an example of a CRA paid by bond investors, but remains a minnow, with 95–97% of ratings conducted by S&P, Moody's or Fitch. Despite this dominance, new rating agencies are springing up to challenge the big three – see Article 5.9.

Article 5.9

Scope Ratings aims to shake up hegemony

By Patrick Jenkins

Financial Times April 15, 2013

A new pan-European rating agency is expanding from modest German roots with an ambition to challenge established names such as Standard & Poor's and Moody's.

Scope Ratings, a family-owned company based in Berlin, will on Tuesday open a London office, with a focus on banks.

The London operation will be headed by Sam Theodore, formerly head of European bank ratings at Moody's and more recently a regulator first with the UK's Financial Services Authority and latterly with the European Banking Authority.

The move comes in the same week that another German ratings initiative, by a non-profit arm of the Bertelsmann media group, got under way. On Monday, the Financial Times reported that the Bertelsmann Foundation's International Non-profit Credit Rating Agency (Incra) had initiated its coverage of US government debt with a AA+ rating.

The established Big Three of the ratings world have been widely criticised for failing to spot the warning signs that led to the financial crisis and for being slow in reforming their methodologies to reflect the post-crisis world.

Scope believes its fresh start in rating the banking industry will allow it to take a less formulaic approach. Mr Theodore and his team will incorporate more qualitative analysis of business models and relations with regulators alongside regulator-style stress-testing of loan portfolios and capital strength.

The agency has no plans to move into sovereign ratings and sees its pan-European role as sharply focused on banks for the time being. It has ambitions to rate 50 to 60 mostly large European lenders over the next 18 months.

A third German ratings initiative – from the consultancy Roland Berger – remains in the planning stage, though company insiders said the project was progressing.

Source: Jenkins, P. (2013) Scope Ratings aims to shake up hegemony, *Financial Times*, 15 April.

Bond default rates

Table 5.5 and Figure 5.1 show research from Fitch, detailing the proportion of corporate finance bonds that have defaulted one, two, three, four, five and ten years after issue over the period 1990–2013. Notice the large differences in

Table 5.5 Global corporate finance defaults 1990–2013

Rating	1-year	2-year	3-year	4-year	5-year	10-year
AAA	0	0	0	0	0	0
AA+	0	0	0	0	0	0
AA	0	0	0.11	0.28	0.46	0.36
AA–	0.06	0.06	0.06	0.07	0.07	0.21
A+	0	0.1	0.2	0.27	0.4	0.89
A	0.06	0.25	0.45	0.69	0.94	2.05
A–	0.17	0.31	0.46	0.57	0.74	2.53
BBB+	0.13	0.28	0.51	0.82	1.16	2.39
BBB	0.09	0.64	1.29	1.97	2.58	4.79
BBB–	0.39	1.14	1.89	2.66	3.6	7.54
BB+	0.92	2.62	4.17	5.71	7.13	10.15
BB	0.79	2.84	4.55	6.36	7.69	13.78
BB–	1.59	2.6	4.08	5.08	6.01	9.19
B+	1.01	3.65	6.08	7.83	9.04	10.12
B	2.28	5.11	8.2	11.52	14.24	13.97
B–	2.63	4.92	6.16	7.42	9.19	10.19
CCC to C	23.51	31.48	34.96	37.01	39.58	39.54
Investment grade	0.11	0.35	0.61	0.88	1.17	2.27
Speculative grade	2.88	5.33	7.38	9.16	10.7	13.38
All corporate finance	0.73	1.43	2.04	2.59	3.07	4.07

Source: Data from Fitch – Credit Market Research Report
www.fitchratings.com/web_content/nrsro/nav/NRSRO_Exhibit-1.pdf

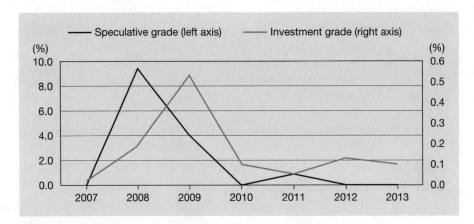

Figure 5.1 Global corporate finance issuer default rates

Source: Data from Fitch – Credit Market Research Report www.fitchratings.com/web_content/nrsro/nav/
NRSRO_Exhibit-1.pdf

default rates between the ratings. After five years only 0.46% of AA bonds had defaulted, whereas 14.24% of B bonds had defaulted.

When examining data on default rates it is important to appreciate that default is a wide-ranging term and could refer to any number of events, from a missed payment to liquidation. For some of these events all is lost from the investor's perspective. For other events a very high percentage, if not all, of the interest and principal is recovered. Hickman (1958)[1] observed that defaulted publicly held and traded bonds tended to sell for about 40 cents on the dollar. This average recovery rate rule of thumb seems to have held over time – in approximate terms – with senior secured bank loans returning roughly 60% and subordinated bonds less than 30%. But the average disguises a wide variety, with many defaulted bonds offering nothing and others giving a recovery of 80% or more.

---

[1] Hickman, W.B. (1958) 'Corporate bond quality and investor experience', National Bureau of Economic Research, 14, Princeton.

CHAPTER 6
HIGH-YIELD AND HYBRID BONDS

High-yield (junk) bonds

High-yield bonds are debt instruments offering a high return with a high risk. Credit ratings of less than Baa3 or BBB– are non-investment and are often labelled as 'junk'. They may be either unsecured or secured but rank behind senior loans and bonds. This type of debt generally offers interest rates 2–9 percentage points more than that on senior debt and frequently gives the lenders some right to a share in equity values should the firm perform well. This kind of finance ranks for payment below straight debt but above equity – it is thus described alternatively as **subordinated**, **intermediate** or **low grade**. With the prevalence of continued low interest rates investors have been seeking securities that pay higher returns and this demand has fuelled the increase in the issuance of junk bonds – see Article 6.1.

Article 6.1

Triple C bond sales hit record high

By Vivianne Rodrigues

Financial Times November 15, 2013

Global borrowers with weaker credit quality are taking advantage of investors' relentless search for higher yields to sell a record amount of bonds so far in 2013.

Intelsat, the world's largest satellite-services company, the US casino owner Caesars Entertainment and the luxury chain Neiman Marcus have been among the low-rated borrowers to have sold a combined $38.1bn debt this year, according to Dealogic. That amount surpassed the previous record of $37bn for the whole of 2012.

Bonds with the lowest possible credit ratings have soared in popularity with investors, who have been diverted from top tier government and corporate debt where central banks are suppressing interest rates.

Heavy buying has pushed down the average yield on triple C rated bonds to 7.75% from 9.80% a year ago, significantly cutting the compensation that investors receive for the higher risk of default.

Michael Collins, a senior investment officer for Prudential Fixed Income, said the risk-return equation involving very low rated bonds is now 'asymmetric'.

'Investors are not being fully compensated for holding some of these bonds.'

The demand for yield has become the big driver of investor behaviour as they downplay high valuations for junk bonds.

The gamble for investors is that as long as the Fed keeps on trying to suppress interest rates, and as long as corporate default rates – currently 2.3% per year – remain below historical norms, the prospect of losses is limited.

But the risks are twofold: a general rise in rates could cause investors to abandon risky overpriced assets, while weaker economic growth or falling lending standards could cause a spike in defaults.

'Easy money has pushed investors to take more and more risk,' said Sabur Moini, a high-yield bond portfolio manager at Payden & Rygel.

'A severe downturn in the US economy and a freeze in the high-yield market is a potential big risk. But investors can make the argument that, from a perspective on margins and cash flow, the average company is healthier now than it was five years ago.'

Total returns on this tier of the junk bond market have been higher than nearly all fixed-income asset classes this year and now stand at 11.6%, according to Barclays data.

That compares with returns of 5.9% on junk bonds as a whole and a negative return of 2.2% on investment grade corporate debt.

While top tier corporate bonds are rated on the basis of an investor being repaid their principle with interest, the assumption behind junk debt is that the company could at some point default on its obligations.

 Source: Rodrigues, V. (2013) Triple C bond sales hit record high, *Financial Times*, 15 November.
© The Financial Times Limited 2013. All Rights Reserved.

One of the major attractions of this form of finance for the investor is that it often comes with equity **warrants** or **share options** attached, which can be used to obtain shares in the firm – this is known as an **equity kicker**. These may be triggered by an event taking place, such as the firm joining the stock market. They give the right but not the obligation to buy shares at a fixed price in the future. If this is at, say, £1 per share and the firm performs well, resulting in the share rising to, say, £5, the warrant or option holders can make high returns.

Bonds with high-risk and high-return characteristics may well have started as apparently safe investments but have now become more risky (**fallen angels**) – see Article 6.2 for an example – or they may be bonds issued specifically to provide higher-risk financial instruments for investors who are looking for a higher return and are willing to accept the accompanying higher risk (**original-issue high-yield bonds**). This latter type began its rise to prominence in the US in the 1980s and is now a market with more than $130 billion issued per year. The rise of the US junk bond market meant that no business was safe from the threat of takeover, however large – see Box 6.1 on Michael Milken.

Article 6.2

Moody's cuts Sony rating to junk

By Jennifer Thompson

Financial Times January 27, 2014

Moody's Investors Service has cut the credit rating of Sony to junk status saying that the Japanese group's profitability is likely to remain 'weak and volatile' until the turnround of its television and personal computer businesses translates into better earnings.

The credit rating agency on Monday downgraded Sony to Ba1, one level below investment grade, from Baa3. Moody's said the majority of the group's consumer electronics businesses, such as televisions, digital cameras and personal computers, faced loss of technology leadership and increasing competition.

Fitch Ratings downgraded the credit rating of Sony to junk in 2012. Standard & Poor's rates Sony's credit at BBB, or two notches above junk.

Like other Japanese electronics companies Sony is battling rivals Apple in the US and South Korea's Samsung, particularly in smartphone sales.

But unlike its peers Sharp and Panasonic, which lean more towards household electronics, Sony faces a second dilemma: its focus on entertainment devices, such as radios, digital cameras and televisions, mean that the success of one of its divisions often comes at the expense of the other as smartphones become more sophisticated.

'The primary reason [for the downgrade] is intense competition and the shrinkage in demand, the result in turn of cannibalisation caused by the rapid penetration of smartphones,' Moody's said in a statement.

Box 6.1

The junk bond wizard: Michael Milken

While studying at Wharton Business School in the 1970s Michael Milken came to the belief that the gap in interest rates between safe bonds and high-yield bonds was excessive, given the relative risks. This created an opportunity for financial institutions to make an acceptable return from junk bonds, given their risk level.

At the investment banking firm Drexel Burnham Lambert, Milken was able to persuade a large body of institutional investors to supply finance to the junk bond market as well as provide a service to corporations wishing to grow through the use of junk bonds. Small firms were able to raise billions of dollars to take over large US corporations. Many of these issuers of junk bonds had debt ratios of 90% and above – for every $1 of share capital, $9 was borrowed. These gearing levels concerned many in the financial markets. It was thought that companies were pushing their luck too far and indeed many did collapse under the weight of their debt.

The market was dealt a particularly severe blow when Michael Milken was convicted, sent to jail and ordered to pay $600 million in fines. Drexel was also convicted, paid $650 million in fines and filed for bankruptcy in 1990.

The junk bond market was in a sorry state in the early 1990s, with high levels of default and few new issues. However, it did not take long for the market to recover.

Issuers of high-yield bonds

High-yield bond finance is sometimes used when bank or senior bond borrowing limits are reached and the firm cannot or will not issue more equity. Junk bonds provide cheaper finance (in terms of required return) to the company than would be available on the equity market and they allow the owners of a business to raise large sums of money without sacrificing control because bonds do not carry votes, whereas new equity usually assigns votes over key company matters, so selling shares to outsiders would mean lower percentage control over the company for existing shareholders.

Senior lenders to a firm (e.g. banks and bond holders) usually impose limits on the senior debt to equity ratio. However, subordinated debt might be acceptable to senior bond holders and equity holders alike. Thus, junk bonds are a form of finance that permits the firm to move beyond what is normally considered an acceptable debt:equity ratio (financial gearing, leverage levels). This might be useful for rapid company expansion.

High-yield bonds have been employed by firms 'gearing themselves up' to finance merger activity by raising cash to pay for the target's shares. They are also useful for **leveraged recapitalisations**. For instance, a firm might have run into trouble, defaulted and its assets are now under the control of a group of creditors, including bankers and bond holders. One way to allow the business to continue would be to persuade the creditors to accept alternative financial securities in place of their debt securities to bring the leverage to a reasonable level. They might be prepared to accept a mixture of shares and high-yield bonds. The bonds permit the holders to receive high interest rates in recognition of the riskiness of the firm, and they open up the possibility of an exceptionally high return from warrants or share options should the firm get back to a growth path. The alternative for the lenders may be a return of only a few pence in the pound from the immediate liquidation of the firm's assets.

Junk bond borrowing usually leads to high debt levels, resulting in a high fixed-cost imposition on the firm. This can be a dangerous way of financing expansion and therefore the use of these types of finance has been criticised. Yet some commentators have praised the way in which high gearing and large annual interest payments have focused the minds of managers and engendered extraordinary performance. Also, without this finance, many takeovers, buyouts and financial restructurings could not take place.

Market price movements

Investment-grade bond prices and returns tend to move in line with government bond interest rates, influenced mainly by perceptions of future inflation rather than the risk of default. Junk bond prices (and their yields), meanwhile, are much more related to the prospects for the company's trading fundamentals because the company needs to thrive if it is to cope with the high debt and raised interest levels, and to cause the equity kicker to have some value. Thus the factors that affect equity valuation also impact on junk bond valuations.[1]

---

[1] For equity valuation you could consult Arnold, G. (2014) *The Financial Times Guide to Investing*, 3rd edition, or, for more depth, the university textbook, Arnold, G. (2013) *Corporate Financial Management*, 5th edition.

As a result high-yield bonds are, in general, far more volatile than investment-grade bonds, going up and down depending on expectations concerning the company's survival, strength and profitability. In 2009, for example, investors were very risk averse, requiring yields of more than 20% for a typical euro high-yield bond; in 2014 they lent 'high-yield' for less than a 5% return per year, perceiving company business risk to be relatively low, lured by low recent default rates and factoring in low inflation expectations.

Comparing US and European high-yield bond markets

Historically, high-yield bonds have been much more popular in the US than in Europe, but as the recovery from the financial crises takes hold, high-yield bonds have grown in popularity in Europe (see Article 6.3) and now the annual amounts raised are about the same, both more than €100 billion or $130 billion. For Europe this is rapid growth for a market that started only in 1997 when the first high-yield bond denominated in a European currency was issued: Geberit, a Swiss/UK manufacturer, raised DM157.5 million by selling ten-year bonds offering an interest rate 423 basis points higher than on a ten-year German government bond.

Article 6.3

European junk bonds hit a sweet spot

By Andrew Bolger

Financial Times October 31, 2013

Record issuance levels and a wall of money rushing into Europe's high-yield bond market suggests 'junk' is the place to be. Will it last?

More than $46bn of euro-denominated high-yield bonds – also labelled 'sub investment grade' or 'junk' – have already been issued this year. This is 50% more than in the whole of 2012, and almost double the amount issued by the same stage last year, according to Dealogic.

Christine Johnson, London-based head of fixed income at Old Mutual's corporate bond fund, says 'Europe is in a sweet spot, growth is flat, or only gradually recovering, so there is a "lower for longer" feeling about interest rates. Where is the place in the world where you least expect interest rates to rise? It has got to be Europe.'

The high-yield market is also being driven by more fundamental shifts, such as the need for European corporates to tap the bond markets for finance as capital-constrained banks shrink their balance sheets by refusing to renew loans to traditional customers.

Fraser Lundie, of Hermes Credit's global high-yield bond fund, says 33% of European high-yield bonds have come over the past year from companies that were first-time issuers, whereas in the US the comparable figure was 5%.

'It shows you where the US market is, and where the European market is going,' he says.

Mitch Reznick, at Hermes Credit, says that the size of the European high-yield sector has trebled since 2008. The sector has also been boosted by 'fallen angels' – companies that have slipped below investment grade – and a recent influx of small companies.

Moody's, the rating agency, says there has also been a flurry of small companies issuing high-yield bonds for the first time, with six companies, each with core annual earnings (earnings before interest, tax, depreciation and amortisation) of less than $50m, raising a total of about $2bn.

Moody's adds: 'It is encouraging to see the success of these small companies in issuing bonds at the bottom of the ratings spectrum. However, it remains to be seen if this is a temporary consequence of investors' search for yield, that will diminish as interest rates rise.'

Increasingly, corporates are borrowing more, for longer and cheaper, which can often mean poor value for the bond investor on the other side of that trade.

Paul Smith, corporate bond fund manager at Premier Asset Management, believes that 'For corporate issuers this can be an opportunity to lock in fixed-rate, long-term capital before rates start to rise . . . which can often mean poor value for the bond investor on the other side of that trade, although defaults will remain low for the near-term.'

Ms Johnson sees potential dangers in bonds rated BB or Ba1 – the top end of the high-yield market.

'BB looks overbought, since it has been backed by investors who are not really high-yield people, and could exit quickly. But single B and CCC bonds still offer 9% yields. You've got to do your homework, but selectively there are still good opportunities.'

At Hermes, Mr Lundie argues that any shift in sentiment that spooks investors in BB-rated bonds will also hit lower-rated issues. Part of his strategy is to focus on bonds that have been issued in the past 12 months and now trade below face value.

He says: 'High-yield bonds usually offer change-of-control put options that allow investors to redeem at more than face value. This "optionality" further improves the potential for returns from investing in bonds below face value.'

Covenant light and payment-in-kind notes

These are extreme forms of high-yield bonds. **Covenant light** (**cov-lite**, **covenant-lite**) means that the covenants imposed on issuers are less onerous than normal. Issuers can get away with eliminating the restrictiveness of many of the usual covenants because investors are particularly keen to lend. This may be because they are **yield-hungry** due to alternative investments offering low yields relative to the covenant lights. Private equity houses often use such bonds when they are taking over a company through a **leveraged buyout**, that is, buying a company or part of a company using a large amount of debt and little equity in the capital structure.

For bonds higher up the rating ladder the normal covenants are often put in place to provide early warning signs of distress or threats to the collateral backing, for example:

● the property assets of the issuer must remain greater than the debt

● the profits/cash flow must be a minimum multiple of the interest payments

● the piling on of more debt is prohibited

● no/low payouts to shareholders when debt is high.

If these are breached the lenders can request cash or a debt restructuring, where they gain a powerful negotiating position. Covenant light legal structures eliminate many of these safeguards. A further erosion of the lender's position is the shrinkage of the call protection: while there is typically a six-year non-call period on standard bonds, this can be reduced to three years or less on covenant light bonds. Critics point out that the absence of key covenants makes them dangerous for the lenders – the lack of meaningful covenants results in prudence going out of the window – see Article 6.4.

Companies have also increasingly been making use of payment in kind (PIK) toggle notes where payments due to lenders can, at the option of the issuer, be rolled over into a further debt; lenders can be paid with more debt (more PIK toggle notes or other payments in kind such as equity) rather than cash. The interest paid in additional notes is set at a higher rate than the cash interest rate. During boom times for bonds when lenders are searching for higher yield, which usually happens following a period of subdued default levels, these instruments become a popular way for companies to finance leveraged buyouts. This exuberance was present in the run-up to the 2008 crisis and again in

Article 6.4

Loan terms eased in search for yield

By Anne-Sylvaine Chassany

Financial Times March 23, 2014

Ceva Santé Animale, a veterinary drug producer based in France's Saint-Émilion wine region, is tapping into increasingly generous credit markets.

A group of banks including Goldman Sachs and Nomura have agreed to lend nearly €1bn to the private equity-backed company without requesting the typical creditor protections attached to highly indebted borrowers. It is one of the largest 'covenant light' financings arranged for a European company this year.

The loan package, which the banks are marketing on both sides of the Atlantic, highlights the way that credit markets have become more accommodating of European companies, as institutional investors snap up riskier debt securities and abandon protective clauses in their hunt for yields.

European private equity-backed companies have mostly tapped US investors for loans rather than their region's investors, who have historically demonstrated a greater resistance to 'cov-lite' loans.

But volumes are also picking up in the region. Nearly €8bn in euro-denominated loans of this type were issued last year. Dollar-denominated covenant light loans to US and European companies reached a record $260bn in 2013, or 57% of the total volume, and 69% more than in 2007.

'Covenants are being dropped, lenders' arranging fees are going down, interest margins are going down, the amount of debt you can borrow is going up – it's a great time to be a borrower,' says William Allen, a partner at Marlborough, London-based debt adviser. 'There simply isn't enough paper to satisfy investors' demand and European investors wanting to invest in European loans are having to accept increasingly loose terms.'

Ceva's financing, which will comprise a euro tranche and a dollar tranche, has features that became common at the peak of the credit bubble in 2007. The company, which has taken the unusual step of issuing a new financing before starting a competitive process to sell a stake, will not have to comply with debt-to-earning ratios every quarter during the entire seven-year maturity of the loan.

It will not have to pay down any principal amount before the very end, and will be able to roll over interest payments into debt instead of paying them for about a quarter of the package (in a so-called 'payment in kind' debt). 'It's a dream for Ceva,' a person close to the deal said.

It's not a dream for the debt holders, however, according to Jon Moulton, the British veteran private equity executive. 'Cov-lites are pretty dangerous pieces of paper for those who advance the loan.'

Ceva's creditors will not be able to request a debt restructuring or a cash injection from the company's shareholders in case its creditworthiness deteriorates. This is despite the fact that Ceva's total debt will equal up to 7.5 times its earnings before interest, tax, depreciation and amortisation, a level reminiscent of the leveraged buyout boom.

Buoyant credit markets are also translating into higher amounts of debt in LBOs, which have increased in Europe and in the US to near the 2007 all time highs of six times ebitda on average, according to S&P.

While the Bank of England and the European Central Bank have not yet raised the alarm, they are starting to take an interest in the matter, in the wake of the US regulators, including the Federal Reserve, being concerned about 'deteriorating underwriting practices'.

'Private equity is its own worst enemy when it comes to leverage,' said Neil MacDougall, managing partner of Silverfleet, a London-based private equity group. 'As an industry, we'll just use it to maximise prices.'

2013–2014 when investment-grade debt gave very low interest rates. PIKs can give yields in double figures, but that 'yield' may be in the form of more bonds – see Article 6.5.

Article 6.5

Pre-crisis debt products make comeback

By Vivianne Rodrigues and Tracy Alloway

Financial Times October 22, 2013

Risky lending practices that were a hallmark of the boom years before the financial crisis are staging a comeback in the US as companies take advantage of investor hunger for higher returns.

The issuance of payment-in-kind toggle notes, which give a company the option to pay lenders with more debt rather than cash in times of squeezed finances has surged in recent months.

The esoteric debt structures last gained prominence during the leveraged buyout boom that defined the 2006–2007 credit bubble, and their return has raised concerns that markets could once again be overheating.

PIK note issuance has taken off in the past month, with deals from luxury retailer Neiman Marcus, drive-through burger joint Checkers & Rally's, and Ancestry.com, pushing the amount sold so far this year to $9.2bn, according to S&P LCD [Leveraged Commentary and Data]. That is the highest volume since 2008, when $13.4bn worth of PIK notes were sold.

A wave of junk-rated borrowers, including Michaels Stores, the chain of arts and crafts shops, and CommScope, a maker of communications cable equipment, have also included PIK structures as part of new bond deals earlier this year.

PIK-toggles were widely criticised for fuelling the bubble in cheap credit before the crisis. About 32% of the companies that issued PIK bonds during the bubble era defaulted at some point from 2008 to mid-2013, according to Moody's, although the rating agency says the outlook for today's issuers is less bleak.

'PIK structures are back,' said Lenny Ajzenman, senior vice-president at Moody's.

'It has become easier for companies to issue such notes given lower borrowing costs and use the proceeds to fund dividend payments to shareholders. And with the low yields in debt markets, investors are snapping up all these notes.'

Bankers say the intense demand for higher-yielding bonds and loans has made selling such assets much easier in recent years.

 Source: Rodrigues, V. and Alloway, T. (2013) Pre-crisis debt products make comeback, *Financial Times*, 22 October.
© The Financial Times Limited 2013. All Rights Reserved.

PIKs relieve the company of making cash payments, but regularly add to the amount of debt, which can then become excessive and cause problems, as it did for the fashion company New Look – see Article 6.6.

Article 6.6

New Look launches £800m bond to grasp debt nettle

By Duncan Robinson and Anne-Sylvaine Chassany

Financial Times April 26, 2013

New Look has launched an £800m bond offering to repay part of a loan that rolls up interest as extra debt and was blamed for scuppering the fashion retailer's aborted initial public offering in 2010.

The cash raised will be used to pay off half of the £746m in payment-in-kind notes that accounted for the bulk of the private equity-owned retailer's £1.1bn net debt.

The remaining PIK notes were due to mature in 2015, but will now not do so until 2018, giving vital breathing space to new chief executive Anders Kristiansen, who took over the business late last year.

New Look, owned by private equity groups Apax and Permira, will pay a coupon of 12% on the new payment-in-kind notes, compared to 9% plus Libor the retailer had paid previously.

'People were expecting the keys to be handed over to the payment-in-kind holders in 2015,' said one person familiar with the situation. The £425m left over from the bond will – along with some of the group's cash – refinance the retailer's remaining senior debt.

The move comes three years after New Look scrapped a planned £650m IPO as potential investors raised questions about the low-cost fashion retailer's debt. Annual interest costs on the debt, which came to slightly more than £100m in 2012, have since hindered the group's profitability.

New Look, founded in 1969, has more than 1,000 stores globally. In 2012, it had revenues of £1.5bn and adjusted earnings before interest, tax, depreciation and amortisation of £198m. Late last year, New Look was forced to beat off suggestions that it was close to going into administration and wrote to suppliers to reassure them of its financial strength.

Hybrid securities

Convertible bonds

Convertible bonds (or **convertible loan stocks**, or **converts**, or **CBs**), like other hybrids, combine a debt security element and an equity element. Convertible bonds carry a rate of interest in the same way as ordinary bonds, but they also give the holder the right to exchange the bonds at some stage in the future into ordinary shares according to some prearranged formula.[2] The owner of these bonds is not obliged to exercise this right of conversion and so the bonds may continue until redemption as an interest-bearing instrument.

---

[2] Alternatively they may be convertible into preference (preferred) shares.

They are not particularly popular in the UK, but in the US and some other parts of the world they form a significant percentage of securities, and issuance has risen as investors seek the better returns that may come from the link to equity – see Article 6.7.

Article 6.7

Rate rise fears spark boom in convertible bonds

By Michael Stothard and Arash Massoudi

Financial Times July 19, 2013

Demand for convertible bonds is expanding sharply as fears of rising rates have hit prices in traditional debt markets, while at the same time equity markets are bouncing to record highs.

The convertible bond acts as a powerful weapon for investors looking to get the potential upside of the equity markets while staying within the more cautious realm of fixed income.

A convertible bond is essentially a low yielding corporate debt issue with an attached equity option. If the share price of the company rises past a fixed point, the investor benefits. If it falls, the investor still has the yield from the debt.

These features – in a market where shares have been rising but bonds falling in recent months – have bolstered demand, with a record-breaking net inflow into convertible bond funds of \$4.8bn in the past six months, according to EPFR.

This follows three-and-a-half years of outflows from the asset class, and the net figure is 36 times larger than the previous record half-year inflow back in 2009. The boom reflects investors' bets that improving economic conditions will be good for equities, while pushing interest rates up from near-zero levels and putting pressure on the price of regular bonds.

Traditional hedge funds, which dominated the market with very leveraged bets before the financial crisis, have been edging back into the game. BlueMountain Capital Management, a \$13bn hedge fund, launched a convertibles desk last year.

The big managers have been buying as well. 'It has been a great year for the asset class,' says Leonard Vinville, manager of the M&G Global Convertibles Fund, whose assets under management have grown 50% this year.

'People want to have exposure to equities, but they also want a degree of protection on the downside if equities fall or if the wider markets start to see a lot more volatility.'

Those bets have paid off, at least compared with pure fixed-income investments. Convertible bonds have returned 12.8% this year, compared with 3.2% for high yield and a loss of 3% for investment grade debt.

The strong demand has prompted companies to take advantage of the instruments as a source of cheap and flexible financing. Companies around the world raised $48bn in the first half of the year.

And it is not just the traditional unrated companies in the technology or bio-technology sector – which struggle to get normal bond market funding – that are

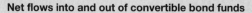

Net flows into and out of convertible bond funds
Six-month figures ($bn)

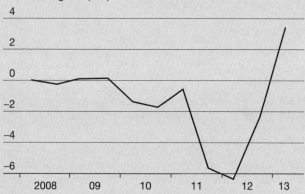

Global convertible bond issuance
Value ($bn)

Sources: Data from EPFR; Dealogic

borrowing. ArcelorMittal, the world's largest steelmaker, raised $2.2bn through a convertible bond while Volkswagen raised $1.6bn.

Terms for many of these deals have been attractive for issuers. Online travel company Priceline.com was able to raise nearly $1bn in seven-year debt in May with a coupon of just 35 basis points, alongside an option premium of 66%.

'Given the ultra-low pricing issuers can get on convertible bonds right now, lots of blue-chip companies are looking to tap the market as well as smaller ones,' says Klaus Hessberger of JPMorgan.

The greatest danger looming for investors in convertible bonds is really share prices going down substantially. Many convertible bonds trade in close alignment to equity, and so can be hit in a downturn more than regular fixed income.

'The option element does mitigate the risk, but convertible bonds will typically fall when equity markets fall,' says Mark Wright, a fund manager at Miton Group. 'That is our biggest worry.'

Source: Stothard, M. and Massoudi, A. (2013) Rate rise fears spark boom in convertible bonds, *Financial Times*, 19 July.
© The Financial Times Limited 2013. All Rights Reserved.

The **conversion price** can vary from as little as 10% to over 65% greater than the share price at the date of the bond issuance. So, if a £100 bond offered the right to convert to 40 ordinary shares, the conversion price would be £2.50 (that is £100 ÷ 40), which, if the market price of the shares is £2.20, would be a **conversion premium** of 30p divided by £2.20, which equals 13.6%. The right to convert may be for a specific date or several specific dates over, say, a four-year period, or any time between two dates. The company may have the option to redeem the bonds before maturity.

Case study

Ford Motor Co

The Ford Motor Co issued 30-year convertible bonds in 2006, raising $4.5 billion. The bonds were sold at a premium of 25% above the share price at the time of $7.36. That is, the conversion price was at $9.20 per share. The bonds will mature in 2036 if they have not been converted before this and were issued at a par value of $1,000. The coupon was set at 4.25%. They are non-callable for the first ten years. From this information we can calculate the **conversion ratio**:

$$\text{Conversion ratio} = \frac{\text{Nominal par value of bond}}{\text{Conversion price}} = \frac{\$1,000}{\$9.20} = 108.6957 \text{ shares}$$

Each bond carries the right to convert to 108.6957 shares, which is equivalent to paying $9.20 for each share at the $1,000 par value of the bond.

In November 2010 Ford, desperate to reduce its corporate debt and try to regain a better credit rating (move up to investment grade), after having had its commercial paper downgraded in 2005, persuaded holders of $1.9 billion of convertibles (this issue together with some other convertibles due for redemption in 2016) to swap debt for shares in the company. Ford gave the holders of the 2036 convertibles 108.6957 shares plus a cash payment equal to $190 for every $1,000 in principal amount, along with accrued and unpaid interest.

Box 6.2

Technical terms for convertibles

Conversion ratio

This gives the number of ordinary shares into which a convertible bond may be converted:

$$\text{Conversion ratio} = \frac{\text{Nominal (par) value of bond}}{\text{Conversion price}}$$

Conversion price

This gives the price of each ordinary share obtainable by exchanging a convertible bond:

$$\text{Conversion price} = \frac{\text{Nominal (par) value of bond}}{\text{Number of shares into which bond may be converted}}$$

Conversion premium

This gives the difference between the conversion price and the market share price, expressed as a percentage:

$$\text{Conversion premium} = \frac{\text{Conversion price} - \text{Market share price}}{\text{Market share price}} \times 100$$

The length of time to maturity affects the conversion premium: the longer it is, the greater likelihood the share will rise above the conversion price and therefore the more an investor will pay for the option to convert.

Conversion value

This is the value of a convertible bond if it were converted into ordinary shares at the current share price:

Conversion value = Current share price × Conversion ratio

The value of a convertible bond (a type of **equity-linked bond**) could be analysed as a 'debt portion', which depends on the discounted value of the coupons and principal, and an 'equity portion', where the right to convert is an equity option. Generally, the value is strongly influenced by the equity option value, which rises or falls with the market value of ordinary shares, at a lower percentage rate. They can therefore be quite volatile. But convertibles with large conversion premiums trade much like ordinary bonds because the option to convert is not a strong feature in their pricing. They are therefore less volatile and offer higher yields.

A convertible bond has two values forming lower bounds through which it should not fall: (1) it must sell for more than its conversion value, otherwise an arbitrageur could buy bonds and immediately convert them to shares, selling the shares, making a quick low-risk profit; (2) the value as a straight bond (ignoring the conversion option) (see Chapter 13 for such valuations). When the share price is low, the straight bond value is the effective lower bound, with the conversion option having little impact. When the share price is high, the bond's price is overwhelming driven by the conversion value.

To illustrate convertible bond price movements consider the Ford bond selling at $1,000, which can be converted to 108.6957 shares at $9.20 per share when shares are currently trading at $7.36:

1 If you bought shares and then they double to $14.72 you would make 100% return.

2 If, instead, you bought a convertible for $1,000 and shares double your return will be 60% (the convertible rises to 108.6957 × $14.72 = $1,600). The lower return than in (1) is due to you effectively paying $9.20 per share rather than $7.36. In reality, the value of the convertible would be slightly

higher than this because it will tend to trade at a slight premium to its conversion value (it still has the safety feature of the straight debt, and a timing option on the conversion).

3 Conversely, if the share price falls, say, to $5 and you made a pure share investment, you will be down by 32%, that is $2.36/$7.36. The conversion value on the bond falls from $800 to $5 × 108.6957 = $543.4785.

4 However, its price does not go down that low because the minimum price is the greater of its conversion value *or* its value as straight debt. Assuming the value of comparable straight debt is $750 given current yields to redemption in the bond markets, the convertible will fall by a maximum of only 25%. Again, it is very likely to trade at more than this, a premium to its straight value, because the conversion right is still in place, even though conversion has become a more distant prospect. Thus a convertible offers the benefit of a reduced downside risk compared with equity, but also a reduced upside potential because the premium per share is paid.

5 Of course, if the share price is constant but market-determined redemption yields rise, then the value of the convertible will fall, as will its floor, being determined by its value as straight debt.

6 If the credit rating of Ford deteriorates, then the convertible price will fall, as will the straight-debt floor level.

If the share price rises above the conversion price, investors may choose to exercise the option to convert if they anticipate that the share price will at least be maintained and the dividend yield is higher than the convertible bond yield. If the share price rise is seen to be temporary, the investor may wish to hold on to the bond. If the share price remains below the conversion price, the value of the convertible will be the same as a straight bond at maturity.

Advantages for investors of convertibles

1 Investors are able to wait and see how the share price moves before investing in equity. They may take advantage of the upside.

2 In the near term there is greater security for their principal compared with equity investment, and the annual coupon is usually higher than the dividend yield.

3 For companies that do not pay dividends the investor can gain a regular income stream through a convertible and then (possibly) make a capital gain via conversion.

Disadvantages for investors of convertibles

1 The yield on the bond will be less than on a comparable straight bond. If the option value never materialises because the share does not appreciate, the holder may regret choosing a convertible over a vanilla bond.

2 There is a greater risk of default than for ordinary bonds because they are usually subordinated – down the pecking order upon administration and liquidation than most other bonds, but above equity.

3 Interest rate risk (see Chapters 4 and 13) is greater because the fixed interest rate offered is lower than for vanilla bonds; thus an increase in market interest rates causes a greater decline in price in the convertible compared with the non-convertible. This problem may be compounded if general market interest rate rises are accompanied by declines in the equity market reducing the chance of the share price rising above the conversion price and the bond being converted.

4 The bonds might be called by the company to the detriment of the holder, i.e. when the price has risen above the call rate.

5 Disadvantage for share owners: conversion of these bonds into shares may have the effect of diluting the value of individual shares – there is an increase in the number of shares as more are created, but not necessarily any increase in the profits/value of the company.

Advantages to the issuing company of selling convertible bonds

1 *Lower interest than on a similar debenture.* The fact that a firm can ask investors to accept a lower interest rate because the investor values the right to conversion was a valuable feature for many dot.com companies when they were starting out, e.g. Amazon and AOL could pay 5–6% on convertibles – less than half the amount they would have had to pay on vanilla bonds. Great Portland issued a convertible offering a coupon of only 1% – see Article 6.8.

2 *The interest is tax deductible.* Because convertible bonds are a form of debt, the coupon payment can be regarded as a cost of the business and can therefore be used to reduce taxable profit.

3 *Self-liquidating.* When the share price reaches a level at which conversion is worthwhile the bonds will (normally) be exchanged for shares so the company does not have to find cash to pay off the loan principal – it simply issues more shares. This has obvious cash flow benefits. However, the disadvantage is that the other equity holders may experience a reduction in earnings per share and dilution of voting rights.

Article 6.8

Great Portland strikes with convertible bond

By Ed Hammond

Financial Times September 3, 2013

Great Portland Estates has underscored the strength of demand for London property by issuing one of the lowest-paying convertible bonds in UK history.

On Tuesday, the group, which specialises in developing and owning real estate in London's West End, announced the final terms of £150m-worth of five-year unsecured convertible loan notes, and said the annual interest payment, or coupon, for holders would be 1%. This compares with an average coupon of about 5% for bonds issued by European property companies last year.

Great Portland set the initial conversion price – at which the bonds may be converted into equities – at £7.145 per share, representing a premium of 35% to the average market price of its shares during the bookbuilding.

4 *Fewer restrictive covenants.* The directors have greater operating and financial flexibility than they would with a secured debenture. Investors accept that a convertible is a hybrid between debt and equity finance and do not tend to ask for high-level security (they are usually unsecured and subordinated) or strong restrictions on managerial action or insist on strict financial ratio boundaries. Many Silicon Valley companies with little more than a web portal and a brand have used convertibles because of the absence of a need to provide collateral or stick to asset:borrowing ratios.

5 *Underpriced shares.* A company that wishes to raise equity finance over the medium term, but judges that the stock market is temporarily underpricing its shares, may turn to convertible bonds. If the firm does perform as the managers expect and the share price rises, the convertible will be exchanged for equity.

6 *Cheap way to issue shares.* Managers tend to favour convertibles as an inexpensive way to issue 'delayed' equity. Equity is raised at a later date without the high costs of rights issues, etc.

7 *Available finance when straight debt and equity are not available.* Some firms locked out of the equity markets (e.g. because of poor recent performance) and the straight debt markets (because of high levels of indebtedness) may still be able to raise money in the convertible market. Rating agencies treat them as part bond, part equity, usually half-and-half,[3] thus their issue does not impact leverage levels as much as vanilla debt for assessments such as default ratings, making downgrades less likely.

Note that a bond's conversion price will be adjusted for corporate actions such as share splits (say doubling the number of shares by simply giving existing shareholders one extra share for each one currently held), rights issues (shareholders buying more shares from the firm) and stock dividends (shares issued as an alternative to a cash dividend).

Some variations

A variation on the convertible idea is to have rising conversion prices, e.g. £3 in the first three years, £4 for the next five years, and so on. These are known as **step-up convertibles**. Obviously, with these the bond converts to fewer shares over time. Another variation is the **zero coupon convertible bond**, issued at a discount to par value. Going further we can have the zero coupon convertible bond, which is both issued and redeemed at par, i.e. there is no capital gain to make up for the lack of coupons (a **par-priced zero coupon convertible**). Here the investor is expecting the equity value to rise, but has an element of capital protection through the issuer's promise to repay at par. Yet another possibility is a variable-coupon bond, which can be converted into a fixed-interest rate bond – useful if you can judge when interest rates have reached a peak because you can convert and lock in high interest rates.

The bonds sold may give the right to conversion into shares not of the issuers but of another company held by the issuer. Note that the term **exchangeable bond** is probably more appropriate in these cases.

Contingent convertible bonds (cocos)

Cocos are convertible bonds which give the investor the right to convert to equity if a pre-specified 'contingency' occurs, such as the share price exceeding

---

[3] But sub-investment-grade issuers often do not qualify for the 50% equity treatment.

a specified value for a specified amount of time. The coco market really got going in the mid-2000s when a number of, particularly US, companies issued bonds which were convertible into shares only once the share price moved beyond a threshold (set even higher than the strike price for the convertible). This type is known as an **upside contingent bond**.

Also issued were **downside contingent bonds** which convert if a low threshold is breached. This downside idea was extended following the financial crisis. Banks needed to raise more reserve capital (the gap between what they owe and what they own) as a buffer against running into difficulties. Banks tend to run with tiny amounts of equity put into the business by the ultimate risk takers, the shareholders. They might put up, say, 3% of the amount that the bank owes to depositors and other creditors. If it loses more than 3% by, say, making bad loans, then it will owe more than its assets, i.e. be insolvent.

The regulators insisted on a programme of gradual beefing-up of equity buffers. Most banks have done this by selling more shares through, say, a rights issue or by retaining more profit in the business rather than paying dividends. However, some bankers thought they did not want to continue increasing the amount of equity capital in the business and looked for alternatives. The main instrument they adopted was the contingent convertible. Some banks opted for the downside contingent bond, which forces the holder to convert to shares automatically if the equity as a percentage of bank assets falls below a pre-determined level (note: the holder has no choice). This boosts the buffer of capital that will be subject to total loss if the bank has to be liquidated, thus providing greater protection for depositors and other creditors to the bank. In the jargon: it boosted the bank's 'Tier One capital', reducing the odds of it falling below the regulatory amount. (See Arnold, G. (2014) *The Financial Times Guide to Banking* for more on bank solvency buffers.)

Some banks issued another type of bond to help cope with losses. The **total writedown bond** (**sudden death bond, total loss bond** or **wipeout coco**) is written off completely if the contingency occurs. Thus the bank eliminates a portion of its debts and improves its leverage ratios. This is usually triggered by the equity capital buffers falling below a trigger level approved by the country's financial regulator.

Because of the risks involved of losing the income from the original bond, or losing the amount invested entirely, cocos pay a higher rate of return, up to 8% at a time when interest rates in much of the world are less than 1%, and so hold considerable attraction to investors – see Articles 6.9 and 6.10.

Article 6.9

'Sudden death' bank bonds on the increase

By Christopher Thompson and Tracy Alloway

Financial Times August 29, 2013

Some call them 'sudden death' bonds; others talk about 'wipeout' bonds. Both refer to the potential of some cocos, or contingent convertible bonds issued by banks, to turn debt investors' gold into lead. Either way, European banks are issuing them in growing numbers despite mounting criticism that they discriminate against investors.

As regulators encourage banks to hold more capital where investors would take losses if a bank defaults, cocos are seen as a relatively quick fix when it comes to bolstering tier one capital ratios.

Tier one capital, a key regulatory measure of financial health, is considered the safest portion of a bank's capital and traditionally comprises common equity and retained earnings.

There have been two types of coco to date: those which convert into equity when a bank's capital ratio falls below a pre-agreed trigger and those which are written off entirely.

It is the latter that are proving controversial – and increasingly popular.

'The bank doesn't have to default to trigger these cocos . . . the point is they can push losses on to bondholders and provide capital while the bank is still a going concern,' says Jenna Barnard at Henderson.

Such criticism has not deterred the banks, particularly as demand has been buoyed by wealthy Asians who can snap up cocos with borrowed money, bolstering their returns.

Year to date global coco issuance stands at $8.5bn from eight deals, a record number, according to figures from Dealogic, all from European banks.

Keith Skeoch, chief executive of UK life company Standard Life, describes wipeout cocos as 'death-spiral bonds'. However, he says they have a role where 'there is a desperate need, particularly in the banking sector, for the provision of loss absorbing capital'.

Barclays issued a $3bn death spiral coco last November and followed it up with another $1bn issue in April. They yielded 7.6% and 7.7% respectively.

Earlier this month Credit Suisse issued its own $2.5bn wipeout coco, which yielded 6.5%, that followed a $1bn issue from Belgium's KBC with an interest rate of 8%.

The Swiss bank said similar issues would follow, not least as it seeks to lock in historically low interest rates and take advantage of investors' hunger for relatively high-yielding instruments.

It is why even coco critics, such as Ms Barnard, admit the asset class 'will become quite hard to ignore'.

Other banks are choosing to plot a middle path.

Société Générale is preparing what it refers to as a 'write-down, write-up' hybrid bond in which investors would take losses if the bank's tier one capital falls below 5.1%. However, if the bank recovers, bondholders would begin to get their money back.

'It's not exactly a coco but it has a writedown mechanism . . . if the trigger is reached only a proportion will be written down, depending on where the capital ratio of the bank stands,' says Stéphane Landon, Société Générale's head of asset and liability management. 'If the bank gets better this amount can be reinstated and so the bond can be reinstated.'

In the US, a more restrictive definition of regulatory capital effectively prevents US banks from including cocos in their tier one buffers.

US regulators are said to have been scarred by their experience during the financial crisis with other types of hybrid bank instruments combining equity and debt characteristics. Many of these hybrid products failed to absorb bank losses during the financial crisis.

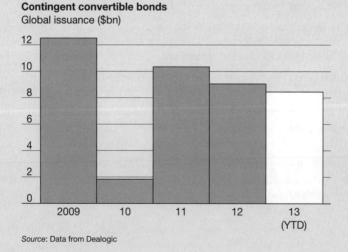

Contingent convertible bonds
Global issuance ($bn)

Source: Data from Dealogic

Article 6.10

Coco sell-off unveils high-yield bargains

By Christopher Thompson

Financial Times August 14, 2014

Is that the sound of the coco bubble going pop? Yield-hungry investors have had their appetites sorely tested over the past few weeks as high-risk, high-return contingent convertible bonds, or cocos, recorded their worst monthly performance to date.

Cocos are hybrid bonds which count towards a bank's capital. Banks can issue cocos up to the value of 1.5% of their risk-weighted assets under incoming Basel III rules.

'Regulatory headwinds and Bank of America Merrill Lynch's ruling that cocos will no longer be eligible for high yield or investment grade indices, has led to a strong sell off in the sector,' says Armin Peter at UBS.

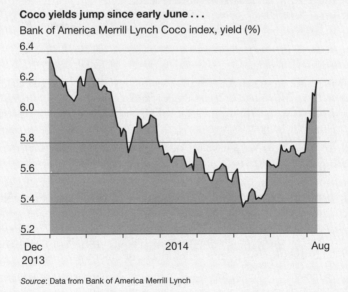

Coco yields jump since early June . . .
Bank of America Merrill Lynch Coco index, yield (%)

Source: Data from Bank of America Merrill Lynch

The UK's Financial Conduct Authority earlier this month announced a ban on retail investors buying cocos, which now constitute a €45bn market according to RBS, albeit one dominated by institutions and hedge funds.

Some see the sell-off as restoring a measure of sobriety to what had become an increasingly frenzied market whose gyrations were exacerbated in part due to fast-money investors selling-out at the first sign of trouble.

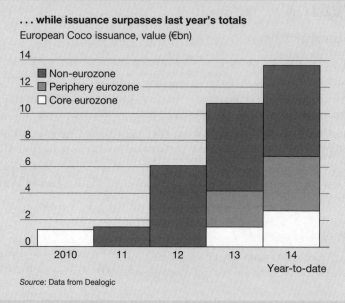

... while issuance surpasses last year's totals
European Coco issuance, value (€bn)

Source: Data from Dealogic

The sell-off comes on the back of frantic coco buying. In May average yields hit a record low of 5.54%, while Deutsche Bank reported about €25bn of orders for its maiden €1.5bn coco, underlining investor willingness to shoulder more risk in their hunt for higher-yielding bank assets.

'When I see cocos at 5.5% I personally don't think I'm getting paid for the risks,' says Jorge Martin Ceron, a portfolio manager at Lombard Odier.

The bond's conversion mechanism – which can allow for coupon cancellations even while the bank is a 'going concern' and potentially paying dividends to shareholders – remains untested. Coco supporters point out that European banks' continued deleveraging and recent capital raising has made the prospect of outright conversion, if not coupon cancellations, increasingly unlikely. But the wider market fall-out highlights the asset's exposure to 'tail-risks', or unforeseen events.

Regulatory incentives remain for banks to tap the coco market, not least because they offer a cheaper way of raising capital than issuing equity. 'For banks, using cocos is still a very cost effective way to fill your capital bucket,' says Mr Weinberger [head of capital markets engineering at Société Générale].

Catastrophe bonds

These are issued by insurance companies. If no major catastrophe, e.g. earthquake in California, occurs they pay coupons and a redemption amount at the end of their lives, usually around three years. If the specified catastrophe does occur before maturity the principal and further coupons are 'forgiven' by the holders: they get no more money from the insurance company. Thus the insurance company has passed on some of the risk – see Article 6.11.

Article 6.11

Cat bond investors show their limits

By Alistair Gray

Financial Times July 1, 2014

The World Bank attracted attention last week when the development institution issued its first ever catastrophe bond, the latest instance of yield-hungry investors leaping into this hottest of asset classes.

Another $5.7bn worth have been issued so far this year, bringing the total outstanding to $22bn. 'There's still lots of money coming in, but people are becoming a little bit more sensitive about the yields,' says James Vickers, of Willis Re International.

It is not hard to see the appeal of catastrophe bonds, which insurers, reinsurers and other institutions issue to minimise losses arising from earthquakes and hurricanes. They are among the very few securities that appear to have genuinely little correlation with broader financial markets.

The returns have also been strong. The bonds have produced annualised returns of 8.4% since 2002. This, however, has pushed typical yields down about 30% over the past 18 months or so, to little more than 5%.

Niklaus Hilti, head of insurance linked strategies at Credit Suisse, says a 'historic' shift has taken place as the catastrophe bond market, once largely the domain of hedge funds and other specialists, has attracted more mainstream investors – from endowment funds to wealthy individuals. Higher prices are an inevitable consequence of a more mature market, he adds. About half of European and US pension funds now have some exposure to the asset class. Although most allocate less than 1% of their total funds under management, even relatively small allocations can have a big impact given the trillions of dollars at their disposal.

Insurance executives question whether such investors properly appreciate the risks they are running in buying the bonds, which incur losses only when especially

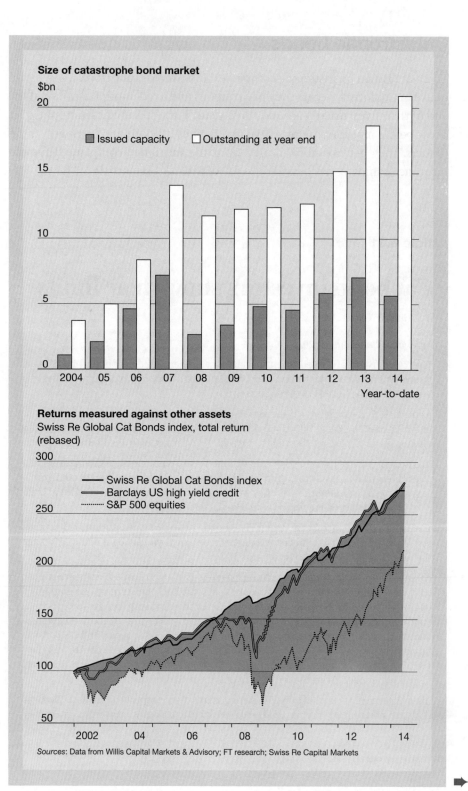

Size of catastrophe bond market

$bn

■ Issued capacity   □ Outstanding at year end

Year-to-date

Returns measured against other assets
Swiss Re Global Cat Bonds index, total return
(rebased)

—— Swiss Re Global Cat Bonds index
—— Barclays US high yield credit
········· S&P 500 equities

Sources: Data from Willis Capital Markets & Advisory; FT research; Swiss Re Capital Markets

costly disasters – those expected to occur less frequently than once in 50 years – strike.

Even Hurricane Sandy, which caused almost $70bn worth of damage when it struck the US east coast in 2012, left the bondholders unscathed. Only about a dozen of the bonds – equating to less than 2% of the sums at risk – have ever incurred any losses.

CHAPTER 7
INTERNATIONAL BONDS

This chapter focuses on ways of raising money by selling bonds outside of the issuer's home currency. This may be done by issuing bonds in another country under the regulatory constraints of that country (foreign bonds) or may be done outside of the jurisdiction of any country, with no interference from national regulators or tax authorities (Eurobonds). It may also be done by setting up an ongoing programme of issuance of a number of medium-term bonds/notes through an arrangement with an investment bank(s) acting as a manager helping the sale of bonds every few weeks in the amounts, currency and type that suit the borrower at that time. Finally, the chapter discusses the principles behind the rapidly growing market in Islamic bonds; still less than 30 years old, this market is now worth well over $230 billion.

International bonds are government (sovereign) or corporate bonds issued in a country or a currency foreign to the investor. The amount outstanding in the international bond markets was over $20 trillion in 2014, in a variety of currency denominations. International bonds fall into two main categories.

- **Foreign bonds** are issued in the domestic currency of the country where the bond is issued by a non-resident, and are usually given a name that relates to the country of the currency of issue, e.g. Samurai bonds are issued in Japan in yen by a non-resident issuer.
- **Eurobonds** are bonds issued outside the jurisdiction of the currency of issue, e.g. a Eurodollar bond is issued outside the US and so the US authorities have no control over this market.

The different types of bonds are outlined in Table 7.1.

The term **global bond** is used where bonds are issued simultaneously in different countries by large companies trading internationally or by sovereign entities. These may be issued and traded in the foreign bond markets of one or more countries, and/or the Eurobond market, and/or in the domestic market of the issuer. Thus, they may be issued and trade in many different currencies.

Table 7.1 The attributes of the different types of bonds

Type of bond	Currency of issue	Nationality of issuer	Place of issue	Primary investors
Domestic bond	Domestic	Domestic	Domestic	Domestic
Foreign bond *Bulldog, Yankee, Panda, etc.*	Domestic	Foreign	Domestic	Domestic
Eurobond	Eurocurrency *Euroyen Eurodollars, Eurosterling, etc.*	Any	International	International

The majority of international bonds are issued in US dollars or euros, with the euro now having overtaken the dollar – of all the international bonds outstanding 45% are denominated in euros and 36% in dollars. Note that most of those denominated in euros are not under the jurisdiction of any eurozone country (they are Eurobonds), with most of their trading taking place in financial centres outside of the continent, such as London. While only 9% of international bonds are issued in sterling, London is the major centre for secondary trading, responsible for more than 70% of Eurobond trades.

Foreign bonds

Foreign bonds are given names relevant to the country where they are issued and regulated, for example in Canada bonds issued by non-Canadian companies denominated in Canadian dollars are known as Maple bonds and the interest and capital payments are in CAD. Other foreign bonds from around the world issued by non-domestic entities in the domestic market include:

Yankee bonds (US), dollar bonds issued in the US by a non-US issuer

Bulldog bonds (UK), sterling bonds issued in the UK by a non-UK issuer

Rembrandt bonds (the Netherlands)

Matador bonds (Spain)

Panda bonds (China)

Kangaroo or Matilda bonds (Australia)

Kiwi bonds (New Zealand).

Many deeply furrowed brows can be seen in financial circles when trying to come up with nicknames for new types of foreign bonds – see Article 7.1.

Article 7.1

The rise of the . . . Masala bond?

By James Crabtree

Financial Times April 10, 2014

The World Bank's move doubling to $2bn its offshore-rupee bond programme today marks a significant moment in the international development of India's currency. But it leaves one big question unanswered: what should these new Indian instruments be called?

Offshore debt naming is not difficult: just pick a food or animal commonly linked to the country in question, and add extra points for alliteration.

China manages both of the above, with 'dim-sum' offshore renminbi bonds and 'panda' bonds for those from non-Chinese entities, such as the Rmb500m ($80m) issuance brought out by Germany's Daimler last month.

Almost every other country follows the same pattern, from tasty baklava bonds in Turkish lira, to lively kangaroo bonds down under.

Yet even when the International Finance Corporation, the World Bank's private sector arm, launched its first $1bn rupee-linked programme last year, an Indian equivalent failed to stick.

India hardly lacks for recognisable food and fauna, while a handful of local media outlets did begin speculating last year. The 'samosa bond' might soon take hold, one said; another floated the rather blander 'tiger bond' as an option.

But the IFC has so far distanced itself from any attempts to attach a cheery moniker to its programmes. Those familiar with the group's thinking say it is being extra-cautious, for fear of riling one of India's famously vocal and prickly lobby groups with its endorsement.

Yet the IFC's new $2bn programme will in time be followed by numerous other offshore rupee issuances as the Indian economy grows in coming decades, leaving the naming issue as something of a conundrum.

And what about [our] favoured option: the masala bond? Unquestionably Indian in flavour, the title could just catch on, says Eswar Prasad, professor at Cornell University and a particular expert on India's gradual capital account liberalisation.

'Masala bonds might well resonate,' he says. 'Certainly foreign investors seem to like their taste so far, even if they are still a bit spicy and exotic, you might say.'

For investors, foreign bonds carry the disadvantage of being subject to currency fluctuation. For example, a £100,000 foreign bond bought by a US investor when the exchange rate was $1.60 to the £ would cost $62,500. Three years later, the bond reaches maturity and the investor receives back the par value of £100,000, but now the exchange rate is $1.85 to the £, so he receives only $54,054 and makes a capital loss.

Another disadvantage for investors is that foreign bonds are traded on foreign markets where investors do not have the same degree of protection as they would in their own domestic market. Political unrest or disputes could cause investors to lose control of their foreign investments as the foreign government could ban all payments on externally raised finance. Not infrequently investors in foreign bonds have found their coupon payments subjected to an extra withholding tax imposed by the country where the bonds are issued.

Nevertheless, institutional investors taking foreign bonds into their portfolios are able to achieve greater diversification and hedge against foreign currency fluctuations. Not all foreign bonds are issued by companies – Article 7.2 discusses the foreign bond issued by the Bulgarian government.

Article 7.2

Bulgaria lines up €3.5bn bond issues as crises ease

By Andrew MacDowall

Financial Times January 29, 2014

After a difficult two years that saw five governments, ongoing street protests and a banking crisis, Bulgaria's politics and economy may be getting back to something approaching normality in 2015.

Blessed with greater stability – but with a significant fiscal deficit and loans to repay – the country plans to raise 6.9bn lev (€3.5bn) from bond issues this year. But investors may still be wary of the risks of a slow-growing country with a recent history of instability.

On January 8, Vladislav Goranov, finance minister, said the government planned to raise the cash from foreign investors in two issues, one in the first half of the year and one in the autumn. He implied that the first issue would be sooner rather than later, pointing to market liquidity.

'We expect good results on yields, meaning Bulgaria gets cheap financing,' Goranov said early this month.

The money raised will be used to help bridge a fiscal deficit that the government expects to come in at 3% of GDP this year. It will also finance the rollover of a €1.5bn loan it used to finance last year's deficit, which was increased by the need to guarantee deposits and recapitalise banks following the collapse of Corporate Commercial Bank (KTB or Corpbank) and a run on another domestic lender.

The loan was syndicated by Citi, HSBC and the Bulgarian units of Société Générale and UniCredit, which will also arrange the first foreign bond issue this year.

The 6.9bn lev bonds will increase Bulgaria's public debt to 28.4% of GDP this year, Reuters reported, from 18% in 2013.

While this is still one of the lowest levels in the European Union, observers have mixed views on Bulgaria's creditworthiness. GDP growth is expected to come in at under 1% this year, according to a recent forecast by the European Bank for Reconstruction and Development, though the Economist Intelligence Unit expects a respectable average of 3% between 2015 and 2019.

'Bulgaria's banking crisis and the chronic political instability which has been plaguing the country of late have taken their toll on the country's creditworthiness,' says Nicholas Spiro of consultancy Spiro Sovereign Strategy. 'Many of Bulgaria's underlying weaknesses have been exposed over the past several months even though the country's low level of public indebtedness sets it apart from some of its more fiscally challenged CEE peers. Growth remains lacklustre and the budget deficit has deteriorated significantly over the past year – albeit from a relatively strong position.'

While quantitative easing from the European Central Bank will provide a liquidity boost that somewhat offsets the US Federal Reserve's monetary tightening, Spiro does not expect this to boost demand for Bulgarian sovereign debt considerably.

'A huge burst of monetary stimulus from one of the world's leading central banks is inevitably positive for emerging-market assets. But Bulgarian yields were already at exceptionally low levels to start with, offering little carry for investors – not least given the mounting risks in the country and the relatively illiquid nature of the market.'

In December, Fitch affirmed Bulgaria's foreign and local currency ratings at investment-grade BBB – and BBB, respectively, with a stable outlook. The agency noted the stabilisation of the banking sector and the government's efforts to reduce its deficit, as well as downside risks from the eurozone and the crisis in Ukraine. However, the same month, Standard & Poor's cut the country's sovereign credit rating to junk.

There are grounds for optimism. A snap election last October brought an unwieldy four-party coalition to power, including two groupings that are themselves awkward alliances of smaller parties. But a pro-reform government source told beyondbrics the administration's progress was a case of 'so far, so good'.

'There are no major cracks in the government, and none in sight,' the person said. 'Some reforms are already under way in health, justice and education, without any sign of social discontent.'

There were also tentatively positive signs on the chaotic and indebted energy sector, with a 'major focus' on improving energy security, while in the banking system, ECB supervision and a move towards the eurozone (the lev is already pegged to the euro in a currency board arrangement) were part of the government's programme.

Still, there is much work to be done – and all with an economy that is both sluggish and vulnerable.

'The governing coalition, although composed of four rather different parties, has already demonstrated that it can deliver,' says Daniel Smilov, programme director at the Centre for Liberal Strategies, a Sofia think-tank. 'Bulgaria's position on the South Stream project and the start of judicial reforms are positive signs. Thus far, the government has handled the banking situation well – what remains to be done is a thorough investigation of responsibility for the Corpbank collapse. As for the energy sector, concrete actions have not been taken yet, and the government has still not announced a detailed plan for tackling the problems.'

Source: MacDowall, A. (2014) Bulgaria lines up 3.5bn bond issues as crises ease, *Financial Times*, 29 January.
© The Financial Times Limited 2014. All Rights Reserved.

Because foreign bonds are regulated by the domestic authority of the country where the bond is issued the rules can be demanding and an encumbrance to companies seeking to act quickly and at low cost. Some regulatory authorities have also been criticised for stifling innovation in the financial markets. The growth of the less restricted Eurobond market, where the bonds are not under the jurisdiction of the country of issue, has put the once dominant foreign bond market in the shade.

Eurobonds

Let's get one misunderstanding out of the way: Eurobonds are not connected with the euro currency. They were in existence decades before Europe thought of creating the euro – the first Eurobond issue was in 1963 on the Luxembourg stock exchange, with the $15 million Eurodollar issue by Autostrade, the Italian motorway company.

The term 'euro' in Eurodollar and Eurobond does not mean European. The name 'Eurodollar' came about when the former Soviet Union transferred dollars from New York to a French bank at the height of the cold war in 1957. The cable address just happened to be EUROBANK and the money transferred became Eurodollars – dollars beyond the reach of US tax and government restrictions. Bonds issued outside of the US in Eurodollars were called **Eurodollar bonds**, but they are often referred to simply as Eurobonds. Eurobonds are issued all over the world – see Article 7.3 for examples.

Article 7.3

Sub-Saharan market: high yields fire appetite for African Eurobonds

By Fiona Rintoul

Financial Times November 3, 2013

Investors have flocked to Eurobonds as an attractive alternative to bonds issued in local currencies such as Nigeria's naira.

In October 2007, Ghana became the first sub-Saharan African country outside South Africa for 30 years to issue a dollar-denominated bond. Its $750m Eurobond, which had an 8.5% coupon rate, was four times oversubscribed and signalled a flurry of successful African Eurobond issues.

Countries such as Gabon, Ivory Coast, Namibia, Nigeria, Senegal, Rwanda and Zambia have all since issued sovereign bonds. Corporate issues have taken place in Nigeria and Ghana, and there has been a government-backed agency issue in Mozambique.

African Eurobonds offer high yields and a way into the African story for fixed-income investors wary of the currency and liquidity risks associated with even higher-yielding local currency bonds.

Antoon de Klerk, portfolio manager for emerging markets fixed income at Investec Asset Management, cites the example of Rwanda, which issued a $400m Eurobond in May with a 6.625% coupon that was nearly nine times oversubscribed.

'Unless you believe Rwandan fundamentals have changed since then, it remains a good investment opportunity,' he says.

Of course, changes to US monetary policy affected the investment. But Mr de Klerk believes the scenario is not as dire as it is sometimes depicted.

'Something people miss a lot is the yield protection, which means you run relatively low interest-rate risk,' he says. 'The yield movements in the US and Rwanda were similar during the sell-off, but after the sell-off the US still only yielded 2.8%, while Rwanda yielded 8.7%.'

According to Vimal Parmar at Burbidge Capital, it is now likely to take place this December or early next year. On the basis of other African Eurobond issues, investors may ask for a higher yield than was expected when the issue was planned. Ghana certainly paid a premium to investors on its second Eurobond issue in July, but Zambia's 15 times-oversubscribed issue in October shows investor appetite for African Eurobonds is still keen.

There have been judders: the Seychelles and Ivory Coast have defaulted on Eurobonds. On the other hand, Eurobonds attract new investors. 'Anything that diversifies funding sources from traditional concessional loans, which haven't got Africa that far, is definitely good,' says Stephen Charangwa, fixed-income portfolio manager at Silk Invest.

In the meantime, Angola, Cameroon, Tanzania and Uganda also plan debut Eurobond issues, as does Ethiopia when it has secured a credit rating.

Source: Rintoul, F. (2013) Sub-Saharan market: high yields fire appetite for African Eurobonds, *Financial Times*, 3 November.
© Andrew Macdowall.

Eurobonds are distinct from euro bonds – euro bonds are bonds denominated in euros and issued in the eurozone countries. Of course, there have been euro-denominated Eurobonds issued outside the jurisdiction of the authorities in the euro area; these are euro-Eurobonds.

Eurobonds can be described as 'external bonds', but the more precise definition of 'bonds sold outside the jurisdiction of the country of the currency in which the bond is denominated' is more descriptive. So, for example, the UK financial regulators have little influence over Eurobonds issued in Luxembourg and denominated in sterling (known as **Eurosterling** bonds), even though the transactions (for example interest and capital payments) are in sterling.

Eurobonds are medium- to long-term instruments with standard maturities of three, five, seven and ten years, but there are also long maturities of 15–30 years driven by pension fund and insurance fund demand for long-dated assets. Because they are issued outside the country of the currency of issue, they are not subject to the rules and regulations imposed on foreign bonds. One such requirement for foreign bonds is to issue a detailed prospectus, which can be expensive. More importantly Eurobonds are not subject to an **interest-withholding tax**. In many countries the majority of domestic and foreign bonds are subject to a withholding tax by which income tax is deducted before the investor receives interest. The fact that Eurobond interest is paid gross without any tax deducted has appeal for investors keen on delaying, avoiding or evading tax. The EU and the US would like to introduce regulations and minimise tax evasion. But the

UK, the world centre for Eurobonds, is sticking to its tax exemption, making it difficult for other jurisdictions to tax this source of income – this stateless money will flow to where it is most advantageous to lenders and borrowers, thus any tax rules in one or a few countries only will be bypassed.

Eurobonds are also bearer bonds, so holders do not have to disclose their identity. All that is required to receive interest and capital is for the holder to have possession of the bond. Originally this meant physically held bonds, but today many bearer bonds are held in a central depository so that trading and post-trade settlement can take place electronically – a paperless system. The clearing organisations (e.g. Euroclear or Clearstream) 'present' the bonds for coupon payment on the appropriate dates. The anonymity from the government authorities makes tax avoidance even easier. In contrast, domestic bonds are usually registered, allowing companies and governments to identify the owners and ensure that taxes are paid.

Despite the absence of official regulation, the **International Capital Market Association (ICMA)**, a self-regulatory body based in Zurich, imposes some restrictions, rules and standardised procedures on Eurobond issue and trading. Securities dealers from dozens of countries accept rules on issues such as standardised methods of calculating bond yields, procedures for settling secondary market transactions and computerised mechanisms for reporting trades in the market.

The development of the Eurobond market

In the 1960s many countries (e.g. the USSR), companies and individuals held surplus dollars outside the US and were reluctant to hold these funds in American banks where they would be subject to US jurisdiction. Also rigorous US tax laws were offputting, as was the tough regulatory environment in the US domestic financial markets, making it more expensive for foreign institutions to borrow dollars in the US. These factors encouraged investors and borrowers alike to undertake transactions in dollars outside the US. London's strength as a financial centre, the UK authorities' more relaxed attitude to business and its position in the global time zones made it a natural leader in the Euro markets.

The market grew modestly through the 1970s and then at a rapid rate in the 1980s. By then the Eurodollar bonds had been joined by bonds denominated in a wide variety of currencies. The market was stimulated not only by the tax and anonymity benefits, which brought a lower cost of finance than for domestic and foreign bonds, but also by the increasing demand from transnational companies and governments needing large sums in alternative currencies and with the potential for innovatory characteristics. The Eurobond market was further boosted by the recycling of dollars from the oil-exporting countries, which generated vast amounts of dollars needing an investment home, and by other countries not wanting to keep dollar assets in the US, e.g. Iran, and by American companies choosing not to send profits to head office because of the high tax rates if they did so. Apple, for example, had more than $150 billion held outside of the US in 2014, while eBay said it faced a tax charge of $3 billion on $9 billion of foreign earnings it was bringing back to the US that it had been storing offshore.

In 1979 less than $20 billion worth of international bonds were issued in a variety of currencies. By the end of 2013 the rate of new issuance had grown to about $900 billion, with a total amount outstanding of about $23,500 billion (these were mostly Eurobonds, but some were foreign bonds) – see Figure 7.1.

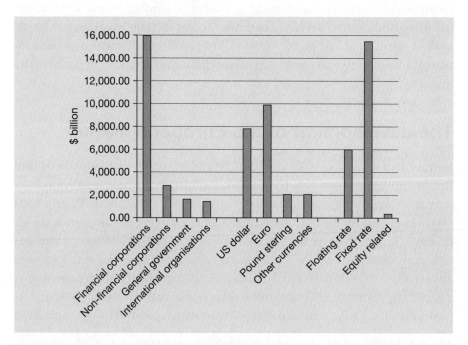

Figure 7.1 International bond and note (including foreign bonds) outstanding, December 2013

Source: Data from BIS Quarterly Review, March 2014 www.bis.org

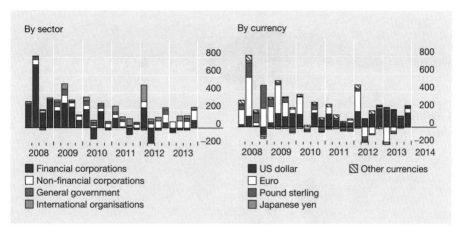

Figure 7.2 Net international debt securities issuance

Non-financial corporations account for a relatively small proportion in most years – see Figure 7.2. The biggest issuers are the banks and other financial institutions. Issues by governments and state agencies in the public sector account for a small fraction of issues. Other issuers are international organisations such as the World Bank, the International Bank for Reconstruction and Development and the European Investment Bank (also referred to as **supranational organisations**).

Even though the majority of Eurobond trading takes place through London, sterling trades are not as important as USD and EUR trades, and what is more, it tends to be large US and other foreign banks located in London that dominate the market. While American issuers are the largest, they account for less than one-seventh of all the issues because the issuing organisations are dispersed all over the world – see Figure 7.3.

Since the financial crisis Eurobonds have become increasingly important for financing European businesses, the growth in the market assisted by reduced appetite in banks for business lending and the ability to sell across the eurozone – see Article 7.4.

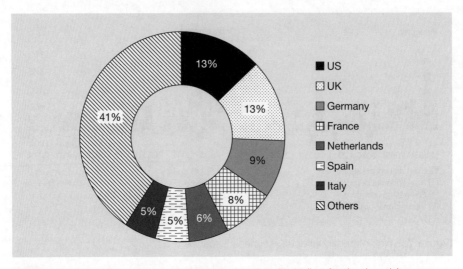

Figure 7.3 Percentage share of international bonds (including foreign bonds) outstanding at the end of 2013, by nationality of issuer

Source: Data from BIS Quarterly Review, March 2014 www.bis.org

Article 7.4

Eurobonds: a change of gear

By Ralph Atkins and Michael Stothard

Financial Times June 30, 2013

The Autostrada del Sole, which joins Italy's north and south and was completed in 1964, was as much part of the country's postwar revitalisation as Fiat 500 cars and film stars wearing Gucci loafers. Behind the company that built the toll road was a deal that transformed global finance.

On July 1, 1963, Autostrade had issued the world's first eurobond. Despite its name, the bond was dollar-denominated and pitched at US currency investors operating across national borders.

'Capital at that time was not so accessible and the company wanted to reduce its reliance on the Italian state,' says Giovanni Castellucci, chief executive of Autostrade.

Exactly 50 years later, European corporate bond markets could be on the verge of another significant shift. Today's bond pioneers believe that weaknesses in the continent's banking system and historically low interest rates will encourage companies to tap capital markets much more for finance and rely increasingly less on bank loans.

Traditional bank ties remain strong, especially in continental Europe. On some measures, emerging economies have experienced a bigger shift towards capital market funding of companies since 2008. But just as the launch of eurobonds kick-started the globalisation of corporate finance, the crises of the past six years could bring Europe's markets closer to the depth and liquidity of those in the US.

'In five to 10 years, I think the European market will look broadly similar to the US market in terms of bank and bond percentages,' says Michael Ridley at JPMorgan.

Eurobonds were created out of necessity – as well as changes in the 1960s in US tax rules that encouraged investors to keep dollars outside the country. But their pioneers consider Autostrade's launch issue as part of a broader shift in capitalism in the decades after the second world war.

The success of eurobonds cemented London's position as Europe's financial capital. In 1999, came the launch of the euro, the continent's boldest experiment yet in economic integration. 'Once the euro came into being, it accelerated hugely the growth of the European corporate bond market,' says Chris Whitman at Deutsche Bank.

The early years of this century saw a wave of issuance as European telecoms companies raised funds to buy 3G licences. 'That was really the first time European markets had been aggressively peppered on a consistent basis by very large corporate deals,' recalls Bryan Pascoe at HSBC.

Cross-border issuance of corporate bonds has become ubiquitous. 'Eurobonds largely replaced domestic markets in Europe – there was no point launching a bond in just one country when you can tap an international investor base at no extra cost,' says Chris O'Malley, whose book *Bonds without borders* will be published next year.

Mr Tuffey [head of investment-grade capital markets and syndicates] from Credit Suisse says: 'The move towards capital markets in Europe has been slower partly due to uncertainty over regulation but also [because of] the huge players out there defending parochialism. German and French banks, for example, have historically lent to local corporates at generous rates.'

Meanwhile, many smaller European companies remain wary of the extra transparency required under today's more stringent rules. 'It will be some time before midsized European companies overcome their disquiet about the regular reporting required by capital markets,' says Paul Watters at Standard & Poor's. 'If you have a relationship with a bank, the detailed information that you provide remains private.'

Data on corporate bond issuance show a move this year towards companies funding themselves more in debt markets and relying less on bank loans. Encouraging the shift will be low interest rates and increased concerns about the stability of banks – which have encouraged companies to pay much more attention to their funding requirements – and it could quickly become firmly established if European economies saw stirrings of a revival in growth.

With government finances under severe pressure and banks continuing to struggle, European policy makers want to promote alternative forms of finance. The European Commission has launched initiatives to encourage capital market development.

Expanding corporate bond markets

Annual corporate bond issuance as a % of each region/country's GDP

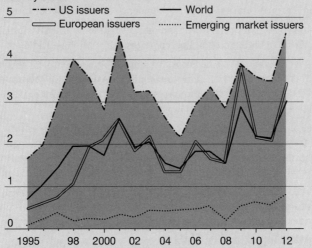

Internationally issued bonds

Global debt capital market issuance, excluding domestic and foreign market types* ($bn)

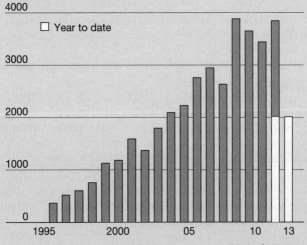

* Total outstanding, Jun 2013 = $19,480bn

Source: Data from Dealogic

Paving the possible way ahead has been the rapid development of corporate bond markets in the world's emerging economies. During the past quarter, emerging-market companies obtained three times as much funding from the bond markets as from bank syndicates, the biggest gap in at least a decade.

Additional reporting by Rachel Sanderson.

 Source: Atkins, R. and Stothard, M. (2013) Eurobonds: a change of gear, *Financial Times*, 30 June.
© The Financial Times Limited 2013. All Rights Reserved.

Types of Eurobonds

The Eurobond market is innovative in producing bonds with all sorts of coupon payment and capital repayment arrangements, for example the currency of the coupon changes half way through the life of the bond, or the interest rate switches from fixed to floating rate at some point. We cannot go into detail here on the rich variety but merely categorise the bonds into broad types.

1 *Straight fixed-rate bond*

The coupon remains the same over the life of the bond. These are usually paid annually, in contrast to domestic bond semi-annual coupons. The redemption of these bonds is usually made with a 'bullet' repayment at maturity.

2 *Equity related*

These take two forms:

a *Bonds with warrants attached*

An equity warrant, for example, would give the right, but not the obligation, to purchase shares. There are also warrants for commodities such as gold or oil, and for the right to buy additional bonds from the same issuer at the same price and yield as the host bond. Warrants are detachable from the host bond and are securities in their own right, unlike convertibles.

b *Convertibles*

The bondholder has the right (but not the obligation) to convert the bond into ordinary shares at a pre-set price (see Chapter 6).

3 *Floating-rate notes (FRNs)*

These have variable coupons reset on a regular basis, usually every three or six months, in relation to a reference rate, such as Libor. The size of the spread over Libor reflects the perceived risk of the issuer. The typical term for a Eurobond FRN is about 5–12 years, but some companies, particularly banks, favour issuing perpetual, or undated, FRNs.

4 *Zero coupon bonds*

These pay no interest but are sold at a discount to face value so that the holder receives a gain in a lump sum at maturity – also called **pure discount bonds**. This is of investor benefit in countries where income is taxed more onerously than capital gains.

5 *Dual-currency bonds*

These bonds pay the coupon in one currency but are redeemed in a different currency. The redemption currency is usually the US dollar and the coupon payments are often made in a currency which offers the issuer the chance of a lower rate of borrowing.

Within these broad categories all kinds of 'bells and whistles' (features) can be attached to the bonds, for example **reverse floaters** – the coupon declines as benchmark interest rate, say Libor, rises – and **capped bonds** – the interest rate cannot rise above a certain level. Many bonds have **call back features** under which the issuer has the right, but not the obligation, to buy the bond back after a period of time has elapsed, say five years, at a price specified when the bond was issued. This might be at the par value but is usually slightly higher. Because there are real disadvantages for investors, bonds with call features offer higher interest rates. Issuers like call features because a significant price rise for the bond implies that current market interest rates are considerably less than the coupon rate on the bond. They can buy back the original bonds and issue new bonds at a lower yield. Also some bonds place tight covenant restrictions on the firm so it is useful to be able to buy them back and issue less restrictive bonds in their place. Finally, exercising the call may permit the corporate to adjust its financial leverage by reducing its debt. A Eurobond may also have a **'put' feature** (see Chapter 4).

Issuance

The majority of Eurobonds (more than 80%) are rated AAA or AA, although some are issued rated below BBB–. Denominations are usually $1,000, $5,000, $10,000, $50,000 or $100,000 (or similar large sums in the currency of issue – known as 1,000, 5,000 or 50,000 lots or pieces). Details of some international bonds are shown in Tables 7.2 and 7.3 taken from FT.com. The issue process leading to this point is described in Chapter 4. Note the large volume of money raised in this market in one week (selected at random).

Table 7.2 New international bond issues, 7 August 2014

Borrower	Amount m.	Coupon %	Price	Maturity	Fees %	Spread bp	Book-runner
US Dollars							
Ecobank Nigeria	200	8.75	99.011	aug 2021		Undiscl	Deutsche Bank/Standard Chartered/Ned
Euros							
Hamburg	300	1	100.747	jun 2021		Undiscl	CMZ/HSH Nord/ LBBW/WGZ/
IBB	75	FRN	100.000	aug 2020	6mE	Undiscl	IBB
Swiss Francs							
Canton Ticino	100	0.625	101.055	maj 2022		Undiscl	Credit Suisse/ BasleKB

Bond issue details are online at ft.com/bondissues. Final terms, non-callable unless stated.
Spreads relate to German govt bonds unless stated.
Source: Thomson Reuters

Eurobonds present significant advantages to their issuers relative to domestic bonds – see Table 7.4, which also lists their drawbacks.

Secondary market

Eurobonds are traded on the secondary market through intermediaries acting as market makers. Some bonds are listed on the London, Dublin, Luxembourg, Channel Islands or other stock exchanges around the world. Listing enables some institutions to invest that would otherwise be prohibited. Despite this, the market is primarily an over-the-counter one. Most deals are conducted using the telephone, computers, telex and fax, but there are a number of electronic platforms. The extent to which electronic platforms will replace telephone dealing is as yet unclear. It is not possible to go to a central source for price information. Most issues rarely trade; those that do are generally private transactions between investor and bond dealer and there is no obligation to inform the public about the deal.

Table 7.3 New international bond issues weekly summary, 15 August 2014

Borrower	Amount m.	Maturity	Coupon %	Price	Launch spread bp	Moodys/S&P Ratings Book-runner
US Dollars						
American Water Capital Corp	200	01-12-2042	4.3	99.589		BofA Merrill/RBC CM/RBS/TD Securities
American Water Capital Corp	300	01-03-2025	3.4	99.857		RBS/BofA Merrill Lynch/RBC CM/TD Securities
Burlington Northern	700	01-09-2024	3.4	99.771		Citi/BofA Merrill Lynch/Goldman Sachs
Burlington Northern	800	01-09-2044	4.55	99.446		Citi/BofA Merrill Lynch/Goldman Sachs
CBS Corp	550	15-08-2044	4.9	98.639		CS/Deutsche Bk/BofAML/RBS/UBS/BNPP/Mizuho/SMBC Nikko
CBS Corp	600	15-08-2019	2.3	99.696		CS/Deutsche Bk/BofAML/RBS/UBS/BNPP/Mizuho/SMBC Nikko
CBS Corp	600	15-08-2024	3.7	99.76		CS/Deutsche Bk/BofAML/RBS/UBS/BNPP/Mizuho/SMBC Nikko
China Constr Bank	750	20-08-2024	4.25	99.577		ANZ/BofAML/CCB International/Citi/DeutscheBank/HSBC/UBS
Consumers Energy	250	31-08-2064	4.35	99.137		Scotia Capital/Barclays/RBCCM/SuntrustRobinsonHumphrey/WFC
Consumers Energy	250	31-08-2024	3.125	99.898		Scotia Capital/Barclays/RBCCM/SuntrustRobinsonHumphrey/WFC
Gulfport Energy Corp	300	01-11-2020	7.75	106		Credit Suisse
Minerva Luxembourg	200	31-01-2023	7.75	100		*Banco BTG Pactual/HSBC/ItauBBA/BofA Merrill Lynch/Santander*
PRICOA Global Funding I	500	18-08-2017	1.35	99.93		*Citi/Credit Suisse/JP Morgan/Wells Fargo*
UBS AG Stamford	1250	14-08-2017	1.375	99.678		UBS Investment Bank
UBS AG Stamford	2500	14-08-2019	2.375	99.836		UBS Investment Bank
World Bank	100	28-08-2019	1.7	100.000		Morgan Stanley
Euros						
Baden Wuerttemburg	300	18-07-2022	1	100.030		DZ/HSH Nord/HSBC/LBBW/Nord/LB/Nordea
BayernLB	100	13-08-2021	1.25	99.970		BLB
BP	300	15-03-2040	2.75	114.015		BAML/CMZ/LBBW/Nord/LB/RBS
HSH Nordbank	125	21-08-2017	FRN	99.927	3mE-59 bps	HSH Nordbank
IBB	100	19-08-2022	FRN	100.000	3mE+12.5 bps	IBB
IBB	50	21-08-2019	FRN	99.950	3mE+8 bps	LBBW
Lower Saxony	500	18-08-2022	1	99.725		CMZ/Nord/LB/BLB/LBBW

	Amount m	Maturity	Coupon %	Price	Spread	Bookrunner
Sterling						
EIB	200	01-02-2019	1.5	98.565		Deutsche Bank/HSBC
Swiss Francs						
Canton de Vaud	250	--/--/2023	2	112.193		ZKB
Credit Suisse	370	18-08-2015	FRN	100.000	3mL+22bps	Credit Suisse
Credit Suisse	155	19-08-2016	FRN	100.000	3mL+27bps	Credit Suisse
Municipality Finance	150	17-09-2024	0.75	101.328		Credit Suisse
Total	800	29-08-2024	1	100.584		UBS
WellsFargo	250	30-09-2020	0.625	100.456		Credit Suisse/UBS
WellsFargo	250	03-09-2024	1.25	100.513		Credit Suisse/UBS
Australian Dollars						
KBN	150	16-07-2025	4.25	100.213		TD/WBC
Province of Ontario	225	22-08-2024	4.25	99.096		TD Securities
Norwegian Krone						
WFS	500	22-08-2017	2	99.727		ANZ/Deutsche Bank
Swedish Krona						
Hemso Fastighets AB	200	26-01-2016	FRN	Undisclosed	3mS+40 bps	Danske/Handelsbanken
Lansforsakringar Bank	200	21-08-2017	FRN	100.000	3mS+37 bps	Swedbank
WFS	500	22-08-2016	0.96	100.000		Handelsbanken

Bond issue details are online at ft.com/bondissues. Final terms, non-callable unless stated. Spreads relate to German govt bonds unless stated.

Source: Thomson Reuters

Table 7.4 Advantages and drawbacks of Eurobonds as a source of finance for corporations

Advantages	Drawbacks
1 Large loans for long periods are available.	1 Only for the largest companies – minimum realistic issue size is about £100m – and only those with good 'name recognition' (widely regarded as creditworthy) or good credit rating.
2 Often cheaper than domestic bonds. The finance provider receives the interest without tax deduction and retains anonymity from the tax authorities and therefore supplies cheaper finance. Economies of scale also reduce costs. Also a wider investor base can be tapped than in the domestic market.	2 Because interest and capital are often paid in a foreign currency there is a risk that exchange rate movements mean more of the home currency is required to buy the foreign currency than was anticipated.
3 Ability to hedge interest rate and exchange rate risk. For example, a Canadian corporation buying assets in Europe (such as a company) may finance the asset by taking on a Eurobond liability in euros, thus reducing variability in net value (in Canadian dollars) when the C$/€ exchange rate moves.	3 The secondary market can be illiquid.
4 The bonds are usually unsecured. The limitations placed on management are less than those for a secured bond.	
5 The lower level of regulation allows greater innovation and tailor-made financial instruments.	
6 Issuance procedures are relatively simple and bonds can be issued with speed, allowing borrowers to take advantage of an opportunity (e.g. raising money for a corporate purchase) in a timely way.	
7 Being outside the control of governments they cannot be frozen in an international dispute.	
8 Enhances the international profile of the borrower.	

Euro medium-term notes and domestic medium-term notes

By issuing a **medium-term note (MTN)** a company promises to pay the holders a certain sum on the maturity date, and in many cases coupon interest in the meantime. These instruments are typically unsecured and may carry floating or fixed interest rates. Medium-term notes have been sold with a maturity of as little as 9 months and as great as 30 years, so the term is a little deceiving, but the period is usually 5–10 years. They can be denominated in the domestic currency of the borrower (MTN) or in a foreign currency outside the control of the authorities of the currency (**Euro MTN**). MTNs normally pay an interest rate above Libor, usually varying between 0.2% and 3% over Libor.

An **MTN programme** stretching over many years can be established with one set of legal documents. Then, numerous notes can be issued under the programme in future years. Such a programme allows greater certainty that the firm will be able to issue an MTN when it needs the finance and allows issuers to bypass the costly and time-consuming documentation associated with each stand-alone note/bond. The programme can allow for bonds of various qualities, maturities, currencies or type of interest (fixed or floating). Over the years the market can be tapped into at short notice in the most suitable form at that time, e.g. US dollars rather than pounds, or redemption in three years rather than in two. It is possible to sell in small amounts, e.g. $5 million, and on a continuous basis, regularly dripping bonds into the market. The banks organising the MTN programme charge a **commitment fee** on any available funds authorised by the programme but not used. Management fees will also be payable to the syndication of banks organising the MTN facility.

The success of an MTN programme depends on the efficiency of the lead manager and the flexibility of the issuer to match market appetite for lending in particular currencies or maturities with the issuer's demands for funds. The annual cost of running an MTN programme, excluding credit rating agency fees, can be around £100,000. The cost of setting up an MTN programme is high compared with the cost of a single bond issue (and more expensive than most bank debt, except for the very best AAA, AA and some A-rated companies). Many companies are prepared to pay this because they believe that the initial expense is outweighed by the flexibility and cost savings that a programme can provide over time.

Vodafone's MTN programme is one of the most varied I have come across. If you download an annual report you will find a list of over two dozen MTNs in issue, with a wide variety of currencies, maturities and coupon payment intervals (see Vodafone's *Notes* to the accounts). It has two MTN programmes: a €30 billion medium-term note (EMTN) programme and what is called a 'US shelf programme'. The US **shelf programme** (**shelf registration** or **shelf offering** or **shelf prospectus**) is one where there is a single prospectus approved by the Securities and Exchange Commission at the outset under which numerous MTNs can be issued in subsequent years. For each issue the borrower must file a short statement pointing out material changes in its business and finances since the shelf prospectus was filed.

Here is a summary of three examples of Vodafone's MTNs:

● Australian dollars (A\$250 million) raised at an interest rate of 6.75% with a semi-annual coupon. Minimum purchase for lenders of A\$100,000.

● €1.25 billion raised as a floating-rate note. Interest is Euribor (variable rate in euros – discussed in Chapter 8) plus 35 basis points. Interest is payable quarterly. Minimum denomination of €50,000.

● £250 million raised with a coupon of 5.625% and due to mature in 2025. Interest is paid annually and the minimum denomination is £50,000.

Islamic bonds (*sukuk*)

From its inception in 1975, when the Islamic Development Bank and the Dubai Islamic Bank (the first commercial Islamic bank) were established to operate in strict accordance with **sharia (shari'ah)** law, Islamic finance has made significant progress worldwide. It is growing much faster than traditional banking and global Islamic investments now exceed \$1 trillion. Most of this is bank based, but some is bond market based (i.e. sukuk).

Sukuk (the plural form of the Arabic word sakk, meaning legal document or certificate, from which the word cheque is derived) are bonds which conform to sharia law, which forbids interest income, or **riba**. However, Islam does encourage entrepreneurial activity and the sharing of risk through equity shares.

There was always a question mark over the ability of modern finance to comply with Islamic sharia law, which not only prohibits the charging or paying of interest but insists that real assets underlie all financial transactions. Money alone should not create a profit and finance should serve the real economy, not just the financial one. Ways have been found to participate in the financial world while still keeping to sharia law, although certain Islamic scholars oppose some of the instruments created.

Whereas conventional bonds are promises to pay interest and principal, sukuk represent part *ownership* of tangible assets, businesses or investments, so the returns are generated by some sort of share of the gain (or loss) made and the risk is shared.

The **Accounting and Auditing Organization for Islamic Financial Institutions (AAOIFI)**, which is based in Bahrain and sets standards for Islamic finance, defines *sukuk* as:

> certificates of equal value representing undivided shares in ownership of tangible assets, usufructs and services or (in the ownership of) the assets of particular projects or special investment activity.

Sukuk are administered through a **special purpose vehicle (SPV)**, a company set up as a separate organisation for a particular purpose, which issues sukuk certificates. These certificates entitle the holder to a rental income or a profit share from the certificate. Sukuk may be issued on existing assets as well as specific assets that may become available at a future date.

Currently, there is some confusion over whether investors can always seize the underlying assets in the event of default on sukuk or whether the assets are merely placed in a sukuk structure to comply with sharia law. Lawyers and bankers say that the latter is the case, with most sukuk being, in reality, unsecured instruments. They differentiate between 'asset-backed' and 'asset-based' sukuk:

● *Asset-backed*: there is a true sale between the originator and the SPV that issues the sukuk, and sukuk holders own the underlying asset and do not have recourse to the originator in the event of a payment shortfall. The value of the assets owned by the SPV, and thence the sukuk holders, may vary over time. The majority of sukuk issues are not asset backed.

● *Asset-based*: these are closer to conventional debt in that they hand investors ownership of the cash flows but not the assets themselves; the sukuk holders have recourse to the originator if there is a payment shortfall.

There is no overarching regulator for Islamic finance but the rulings of the AAOIFI are most widely followed in the Gulf. In Malaysia and other parts of Asia other guidelines are adopted.

At the beginning of 2013 3,875 sukuk had been issued, 223 international and 3,652 domestic, with a total issuance value of $473 billion. The most common types of sukuk are:

- *Bai' Bithaman Ajil* – the issuer sells an asset(s) to investors with the promise that it will buy the asset back at a predetermined price which allows for a profit to the finance provider(s). Payment is on a deferred or instalment basis over a pre-agreed period. The assets generally comprise land, buildings, vehicles and equipment.

- *Ijarah* – one of the most common *sukuk* types, this is a leasing contract, for well-defined assets, in which the lessee can gain benefit from the use of equipment or other asset in return for regular lease payments providing a return to sukuk holders. Some types permit legal title to be passed to the user after the end of the lease, others do not. The ijarah contract is a binding contract which neither party may terminate or alter without the other's consent.

- *Istisna'a* – this is the financing of manufacturing, assembly or construction capacity by arranging money to be transferred from the finance providers prior to production. Payment is made at an agreed price for something that does not yet exist in a lump sum or in instalments. The finance providers may sell the asset once created. It is not necessary that the seller itself is the manufacturer, merely that it causes the manufacture to take place. The item must be described in detail and construction must fit the specifications. Istisna'a is invalid for an existing asset or for natural things such as corn or animals.

- *Mudarabah* – this is for when a partnership between two parties is formed. One party acts as capital provider(s), giving a specific amount of capital to another person, a named entrepreneur, to make use of the capital given for the benefit of the business. Profits are shared according to a pre-arranged ratio. Losses are borne by the finance providers.

- *Murabaha* – this a fixed-income bond for the purchase of an asset such as property or a vehicle, with a fixed rate of profit for the finance providers determined by a fixed profit margin. The asset acts as collateral until the contract is settled. It is similar to rent-to-own arrangements, with sukuk holders as owners and creditors until all required payments are made.

- *Musharakah* – these are for business venture partnerships between two or more people/organisations where money comes from all the partners. A profit and loss sharing contract is made and all partners have a right to share in the management. Profit or losses would be divided according to their contribution.

- *Salam* – this is a sale whereby the seller undertakes to supply some specific goods to the buyer at a future date in exchange for an advanced price fully paid at spot. Salam is used to finance agricultural goods.

- *Wakalah* – the organisation that wants to be financed (e.g. a financial institution) acts as an agent for the finance providers to purchase the sharia-compliant products. An example from the UK's HM Revenue and Customs: 'The investor receives only the agreed ratio against investment. Anything made above that ratio is kept by the financial institution and not given to the investor. *Example:* an investor agrees to invest a sum with the bank for an agreed return (e.g. 5%). The bank pools the investor's funds with the funds of other investors and its own capital and invests in Sharia compliant assets. At the end of a given period (e.g. a month) the bank returns the invested sum to the investor along with the agreed 5%. Any additional revenue that the bank makes on the customer's money is kept by the bank (e.g. if the bank makes 6% then 5% is given to the customer and the additional 1% is kept by the bank). If the bank does not make the agreed percentage return then the investor gets what has been made whilst the bank gets nothing (e.g. if only 4% is achieved then the investor gets the full 4%).' (www.hmrc.gov.uk/manuals/vatfinmanual/vatfin8500.htm)

The first sukuk (a Bai Bithaman Ajil) was issued in 1990 in Malaysia by Shell and denominated in the Malaysian currency, ringgit. International sukuk were introduced in 2001 with the $100 million sovereign ijarah issue by the Central Bank of Bahrain, and the market has grown rapidly since then, albeit with a blip as a result of the 2008 global crisis – see Figures 7.4 and 7.5. It is estimated by the International Islamic Financial Market (IIFM) that there is more than $230 billion ($191 billion of domestic and $45 billion of international) sukuk outstanding, and this figure is expected to increase rapidly.

Malaysia takes the lion's share of the domestic market, with nearly 80% of the world total, and has 12% of the international market. United Arab Emirates dominates the international market with 44%, followed by Saudi Arabia with 13%, and then Malaysia. The UK and Luxembourg are important European

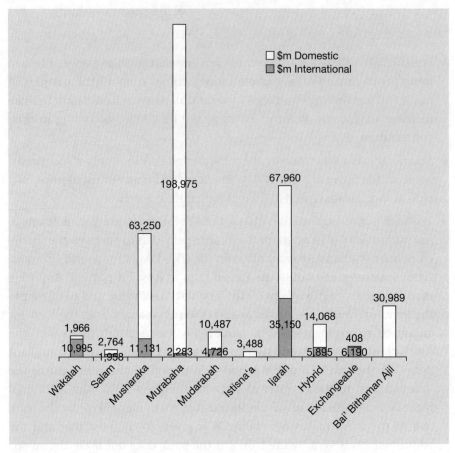

Figure 7.4 International and domestic sukuk issuance, 2001–2013

Source: Data from Islamic International Financial Market, sukuk issuance database

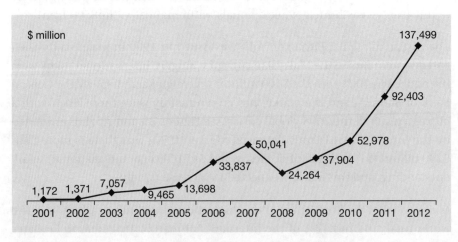

Figure 7.5 Amount of sukuk issued each year from 2001 to 2012

Source: Data from IIFM, sukuk issuance database

centres for Islamic finance. In the UK there are more than 20 banks providing this service and numerous professionals skilled and experienced in its complex details. To April 2015 more than US$38 billion had been raised through 53 issues of sukuk on the London Stock Exchange. See Article 7.5 for a discussion on the competition between financial centres for Islamic finance.

Article 7.5

Islamic finance: by the book

By Robin Wigglesworth

Financial Times May 25, 2014

London wants to be a global centre in the fast-growing industry despite fierce competition.

This spring, a clutch of politicians, civil service mandarins, bankers and overseas dignitaries gathered in the gilded halls of the UK Foreign Office's Lancaster House in west London. Unusually for such a gathering, there was not a glass of wine in sight.

For this was a reception designed to celebrate London's credentials as an aspiring hub for Islamic finance – a niche but fast-growing industry that meshes modern capitalism with Muslim religious principles. The speeches were brief and toasted with glasses of still water and mango juice rather than alcohol from the Foreign Office's cellars. The reception was interrupted briefly for evening prayers in an adjoining room prepared for the occasion.

The UK government last year announced plans to become the first western country to issue an Islamic bond, or sukuk – a security structured to adhere to the Muslim prohibition on interest. For industry insiders, it was further confirmation that Islamic finance had arrived.

'The UK is one of the world's biggest and most established economies, and it is saying Islamic finance is good to go,' says Afaq Khan, head of Saadiq, Standard Chartered's Islamic arm. 'It's a vote of confidence and sends the signal that the UK is open to Islamic finance.'

Some sceptics may blanch at the government rolling the red carpet out for a little-understood industry that adheres to sharia, or Islamic, law. Yet the attractions are obvious. From humble beginnings just a few decades ago, the global Islamic finance industry is expected to hit $2tn this year – extending to banks, mutual funds, insurance, private equity and even some (contentious) hedge funds.

The gambit is part of a wider government strategy to ensure that the City of London continues to enjoy its lucrative but sometimes contentious status as a freewheeling entrepôt for global finance in the 21st century. Bolstering Islamic finance is an important aspect of this, especially if, as the government hopes, it triggers an accompanying wave of investment from appreciative Muslim countries and financiers.

The UK is stepping into a crowded field, however. The biggest Islamic finance markets are Malaysia, Iran and Saudi Arabia. But Iran is in effect cut off from the rest of the industry by international sanctions and different sharia interpretations, leaving the other two centres as the leading powerhouses.

Saudi Arabia and Malaysia have the size and depth to act as regional centres of gravity for the Middle East and Asia, and aspirations to lead the global industry.

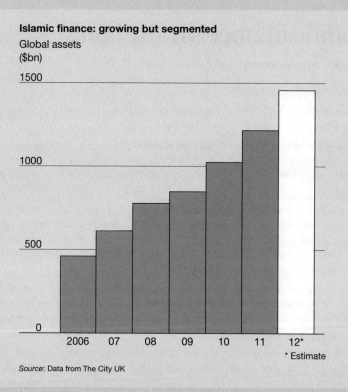

Islamic finance: growing but segmented

Global assets
($bn)

Source: Data from The City UK

Then there are established offshore hubs, led by Bahrain – one of the industry's pioneers – but with ambitious Dubai increasingly asserting itself. Bahrain has a head start, but Dubai has already stolen its crown as the Middle East's financial centre and hopes to become the capital of the emerging 'Islamic economy' as well.

London is the leading western centre but Luxembourg, Hong Kong and South Africa are now competing with the UK to become the first non-Islamic country to issue a sovereign sukuk to make themselves stand out.

Several factors came together to nurture an industry now courted by a host of countries. Growth came quickly after devout Arab merchants established a handful of Islamic banks in the 1970s and 1980s, with many Muslims attracted to the promise of having access to financial services without breaking their religious principles. Malaysia began promoting Islamic finance after setting up its sharia-compliant financial institution in 1983.

Essentially, bankers, lawyers and clerics who are well versed in Islam's financial tenets work together to use one or a combination of permissible concepts in sharia to get around bans on fixed interest rates and pure monetary speculation. They also need to fulfil injunctions for real assets to back transactions and for profit-and-loss sharing investments.

Still, the industry has its detractors. Some Muslim critics feel it is merely a means to give conventional finance a veneer of sharia, following the letter of Islamic law rather than its spirit.

Critics charge that the industry fails in the area that some proponents like to hold up as its prime selling point: Islam's injunction for profit-and-loss sharing equity investments, rather than usurious debt. In practice, however, Islamic finance often deviates little from its conventional counterpart.

Tarek El Diwany, a derivatives trader turned Islamic finance proselyte, is a particularly fierce critic of the modern industry. He argues it has simply copied the institutional framework and products of conventional banking. 'That's not just a failure of vision, it's often completely counter to the objectives of Islamic law,' he says.

Some proponents feel that Islamic finance has occasionally compromised its principles in its efforts to grow. That has led to periodic pushback from the 'sharia scholars', the specialist clerics who act as guardians of the industry's religious foundations.

In 2007 Sheikh Muhammad Taqi Usmani, one of the most distinguished sharia scholars, indicated that some prominent sukuk structures strayed too far from the spirit of Islamic law. Briefly, 'a cold sweat broke out across the industry', recalls Harris Irfan of EIIB-Rasmala, an Islamic investment bank, but standards were quickly tightened and growth was revived.

Many Muslims are simply agnostic on Islamic finance. Despite high hopes, Islamic retail banking has failed to take off in the UK, for example. Even in Egypt, a populous bastion of the Muslim world, the industry has failed to establish firm roots.

Western banks have also largely withdrawn after profitability disappointed. Most damningly, HSBC, which helped spearhead the industry's growth, decided to cut back its sharia-compliant Amanah arm two years ago, ending its retail services everywhere but Malaysia and Saudi Arabia. While it remains active in Islamic investment banking, the diminution of Amanah was a blow to the wider industry.

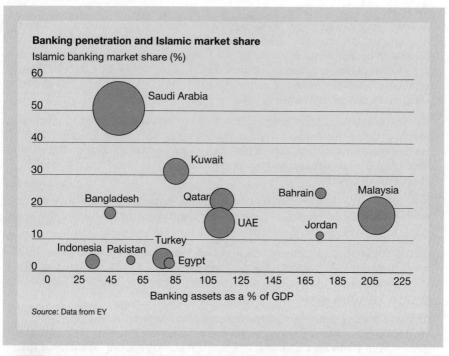

Banking penetration and Islamic market share

Islamic banking market share (%)

Source: Data from EY

As well as Shell, Tesco and Toyota have both issued ringgit sukuk (both musharakah) in Malaysia. In a further development in November 2009, General Electric (GE) became the first large western corporation to expand its investor base into this arena with the issuance of its $500 million ijarah sukuk. The assets underlying this sukuk are GE's interests in aircraft and rental payments from aircraft leasing. The London Shard building was partly financed with sharia-compliant funds. As the importance of Islamic finance grows, it is thought that more European and US companies will enter this market and tap the vast investment resources available. The UK government raised £200 million by issuing a sukuk in 2014, hoping that this would be a catalyst for corporates to follow suit. Being the first western country to do so has helped to reinforce London's position as the dominant western hub for Islamic finance. As well as Islamic banks it already has Islamic insurance, murabaha for commodities, mortgages, car loans and a secondary market for sukuk. Many other countries are expected to issue their first sukuk soon – see Article 7.6.

Article 7.6

South Africa to issue maiden sukuk

By Javier Blas

Financial Times August 28, 2014

South Africa aims to become the world's second non-Muslim country to issue a sukuk, announcing on Thursday plans for at least a $500m sharia compliant sovereign bond to be issued as early as next month.

Britain in June became the first western country to issue an Islamic bond, attracting orders of more than £2bn from global investors for its sale of sharia-compliant debt.

Luxembourg and Hong Kong have also announced plans for a sukuk and international companies in western countries have issued them too.

The move represents a potentially significant boost for the profile of Islamic finance in Africa. Until now, Gambia and Sudan have been the only countries on the continent to issue a sukuk – and they were only for tiny sums. But African countries are keen to issue sukuk in order to attract cash-rich Middle Eastern and Asian investors to finance their large infrastructure programmes.

Africa is home to roughly 400m Muslims, about a quarter of the world's total. But until now a mix of financial, legal and political factors have deterred most countries in the continent from tapping the Islamic market.

West African country Senegal, where the majority of the population is Muslim, earlier this year raised 100bn CFA francs ($208m) via its first sukuk.

The use of Islamic finance on the continent could grow further as several north and sub-Saharan African countries – including Morocco, Nigeria, Tunisia and Kenya – are laying the legal groundwork to be able to issue sukuk.

PART 3
MONEY MARKETS

CHAPTER 8
INTERBANK AND EUROCURRENCY

The interbank market

Originally, the **interbank market** was defined as the market where banks lend to each other, in both the domestic and international markets. This is a rather strict (old-fashioned) definition, and increasingly, as well as banks, this group of lenders includes large industrial and commercial companies, other financial institutions and international organisations. Thus, the interbank market exists so that a bank or other large institution which has no immediate demand for its surplus cash can place the money in the interbank market and earn interest on it. In the opposite scenario, if a bank needs to supply a loan to a customer but does not have the necessary deposit to hand, it can (usually) borrow on the interbank market. A variety of interbank overnight lending rates is published daily in the *FT* – see Table 8.1. We live in very strange times, with negative interest rates in euros (the lender gets back less than it lent!)[1] and zero interest rates in Swiss francs.

There is no secondary trading in the interbank market; the loans are **non-negotiable** – thus a lender for, say, three months cannot sell the right to receive interest and capital from the borrower to another organisation after, say, 15 days. The lender has to wait until the end of the agreed loan period to recover the money. If a bank needs funds, it simply ceases to deposit money with other banks or borrows in the market.

---

[1] Apart from interest rates being very low due to central bank intervention, banks did not want to encourage large deposits from other banks because this would increase the amount they need to retain as equity reserves. See Chapter 16 for more on bank reserve requirements.

Table 8.1 Interbank overnight interest rates, annualised, 4 September 2014

Interbank lender	Latest	Today's change
Budapest: BUBOR	1.28%	−0.09
Canadian: Libor	1.04%	0
Euro: Libor	−0.03%	>−0.01
GBP: Libor	0.47%	>−0.01
Oslo: OIBOR	2.21%	−0.01
Swiss: Libor	0.00%	+0.01
US$: Libor	0.09%	<0.01
Yen: Libor	0.06%	<0.01

Source: Data from FT.com

The loans in this market are not secured with collateral. However, the rate of interest is relatively low because those accepting deposits (borrowers) are respectable and safe banks. The interest rate charged to the safest banks creates the **benchmark** (reference) interest rate, e.g. Libor – explained below. Banks with lower respectability and safety will have to pay more than the benchmark rates set by the safest institutions.

Interest rates

In the financial pages of serious newspapers you will find a bewildering variety of interest rates quoted from all over the world. Following is an explanation of some of the terms in common use.

Libor

Libor or **LIBOR**, the **London InterBank Offered Rate**, is the most commonly used benchmark rate, in particular the three-month Libor rate, which is the interest rate for one bank lending to another (very safe) bank for a fixed three-month period. Obviously these lending deals are private arrangements between the two banks concerned, but we can get a feel for the rates being charged by surveying the leading banks involved in these markets. This is done every trading day. Libor, and other such benchmark interest rates, are crucial to an economy and its citizens, as benchmark rates are used to set rates for loans, mortgages, savings accounts, etc. It is therefore imperative that confidence in the validity of benchmark rates is maintained. A small change in a benchmark rate has the ability to affect millions of financial products, from one person's small hire purchase loan on a washing machine to a corporate's billion dollar loan for expansion. London's historical and current preeminent position in the financial world has seen Libor used as a benchmark interest rate not only in the UK but also in many other countries, where an interest rate might be quoted as Libor plus a few basis points, with universal comprehension of what this means.

Until 2013 the official Libor rates were calculated by Thomson Reuters for the **British Banking Association (BBA)** by asking a panel of 23 UK and international banks at what rates they could borrow money in unsecured loans of various maturities. The size of the panel for a particular currency varied from 7 (e.g. New Zealand dollar) to 18 (e.g. US dollar). For sterling it was (and is) 16. Contributor banks were (and still are) asked to base their Libor submissions on the question:

> **At what rate could you borrow funds, were you to do so by asking for and then accepting interbank offers in a reasonable market size just prior to 11 am?**

The rates from the submitting banks were ranked in order from the highest to the lowest and the average of only the middle two quartiles was taken, i.e. with 16 submitting, the top four and bottom four quoted each day were removed and then the middle eight rates were averaged to calculate Libor. The Libor figures appeared on millions of computer screens around the world each day at midday (now around 11.45am).

For over two decades the BBA produced Libor interest rates for borrowing in ten currencies with a range of 15 maturities from overnight (borrowing for 24 hours) to 12 months quoted for each currency, producing 150 rates each business day, even though many of them might be based on actual loans only occasionally. The rates are expressed as an annual rate even though the loans may be for only one day, a few days or weeks, e.g. if an overnight sterling rate from a contributor bank is given as 2.00000%, this does not indicate that a contributing bank would expect to pay 2% interest on the value of an overnight loan. Instead, it means that it would expect to pay 2% divided by 365.

Following the Libor scandal (see below) it was decided that there was not enough data to keep calculating 150 benchmarks and those rarely used were open to manipulation; for some, such as 9-month sterling, a big bank may do

Table 8.2 Libor rates on 16 April 2014

Libor	EUR	USD	GBP	JPY	CHF
Overnight (1 day)	0.15143	0.09070	0.46375	0.05571	−0.01000
1 week	0.17786	0.12150	0.46656	0.07571	−0.00800
1 month	0.22071	0.15200	0.48531	0.10143	−0.00500
2 months	0.26000	0.19300	0.50531	0.12286	0.00700
3 months	0.29143	0.22635	0.52531	0.13500	0.01600
6 months	0.38771	0.32090	0.62381	0.19107	0.07540
12 months	0.55029	0.54650	0.91063	0.34500	0.19540

Source: Data from www.global-rates.com

50 borrowing deals per year, but nevertheless had to submit a new estimate every day. The less frequently used currencies/maturities have been dropped, resulting in a more manageable 35 rates per day, 7 maturities in 5 currencies.

The data shown in Table 8.2 is for those currencies and maturities that are currently available.

Because the Libor rate is calculated in different currencies, its influence is spread worldwide, and is particularly used in dollar lending outside the US. In all, Libor is used to price around £200 trillion of financial products; for comparison, the output of all UK citizens in one year (GDP) is around £1.5 trillion. Remarkably, about 90% of US commercial and mortgage loans are thought to be linked to the Libor rates, usually 2–3% over Libor.

Libor scandal

The fact that Libor was not necessarily based on actual transactions because there were simply not enough lending transactions in each of the currencies/ maturities every day meant that a bank was asked to 'estimate' or to 'predict accurately' the correct rate for currencies or maturities based on its knowledge of its credit and liquidity risk profile. The inability to base many Libors on recorded loans gave all the leeway needed for unscrupulous bankers to manipulate the reported rate to further their own ends. This led to the now infamous Libor scandal and fines imposed on the banks involved amounting to billions. Up to 20 banks and a number of brokers are involved in investigations in Europe, America and Asia.

There were two main elements to the manipulative behaviour. First, the value of billions of pounds/dollars' worth of derivatives is determined by the level of Libor. If derivative traders could persuade those in their bank (and in some of the other banks) who had responsibility to submit daily Libor rates to change the submission slightly, they could make a fortune on the movements in derivatives. With the huge values involved in derivative trading, a difference of a few pips (one-hundredth of 1%) had the potential to make (or lose) huge amounts of money. From 2005 on (and perhaps earlier) rate submitters were regularly cajoled, bribed and leant on to do the derivative guys a favour – and some senior bankers encouraged this. It was an international game, with many interlocking personal relationships in the very small world of rate submitters and derivatives traders located in the major financial centres.

Within this web, an alternative way of making money illegally using derivatives was for traders to receive advanced word on which direction rates would move. It wasn't just banks; some interdealer brokers, who facilitate derivative trades between banks, also came under investigation for coordinating manipulation.

Second, following the financial crisis of 2007–2008, banks did not want to appear weak. A clear sign of weakness, and therefore seeming to be a higher risk, is for a bank to admit that it has to borrow from other banks at high interest rates. Thus, the rate submitters were leant on to 'lowball' their submissions to make the banks appear healthier than they really were. Admittedly, there was so little confidence in banks generally at that time that actual tangible interbank lending became very thin, if not completely shut down, and so submitters frequently had to fall back on their judgement of what they might have to pay to borrow 'were you to do so'. They were caught out by email records showing that, far from merely using good judgement about what rate the bank might have to pay, they were deliberately underestimating borrowing rates to fool outsiders – they falsified.

An insider's view

In the tight-knit world of interest rate derivatives and Libor submissions, the bankers know each other by first name, regularly phoning, texting, messaging and emailing. They were ridiculed in the press as crass money-obsessed shallow people. Their confidence and bonuses knew no bounds at a time when millions

▶

suffered in a recession created by greedy bankers, an image that was not helped by the email correspondence made public, for example:

- 'Dude, I owe you big time! Come over one day after work and I'm opening a bottle of Bollinger.' In response to a manipulation of USD Libor.
- 'When I write a book about this business your name will be written in golden letters.'
- 'If you keep the 6s [the six-month yen Libor rate] unchanged today . . . I need you to keep it as low as possible . . . if you do that . . . I'll pay you . . . I'm a man of my word.'
- 'It's just amazing how Libor-fixing can make you that much money or lose it if opposite. It's a cartel now in London.'

And from the submitters:

- 'Always happy to help.'
- 'Done . . . for you big boy.'
- 'You know, scratch my back yeah an all.'

In response to a request to submit a lower Libor:

- 'I am going for 90 altho 91 is what I should be posting' [assumption: he is referring to the annualised rate in basis points].

The response from bank leadership was interesting. Here is a quote from *The Economist*:[2]

> **Risibly, Bob Diamond, [Barclays] chief executive, who resigned on July 3rd as a result of the scandal, retorted in a memo to staff that 'on the majority of days, no requests were made at all' to manipulate the rate. This was rather like an adulterer saying that he was faithful on most days.'**

The authorities went on the warpath – see Article 8.1.

---

[2] 'Briefing: The LIBOR scandal.' *The Economist*, 7 July 2012, 25–27.

Article 8.1

Daily fix that spiralled out of control

By Brooke Masters, Caroline Binham and Kara Scannell

Financial Times December 19, 2012

UBS traders and managers on three continents used phone calls, electronic chat rooms and emails to manipulate benchmark interest rates in five currencies on an almost daily basis, according to documents filed by US, UK and Swiss authorities.

The web of activity spanned the globe, taking in traders in Japan and the US, brokers in London and elsewhere and rate submitters based in London and Switzerland.

About 40 UBS employees, traders at five other banks and 11 employees at six inter-dealer brokers were directly involved or aware of efforts to manipulate Interbank lending rates in various currencies, according to the UK Financial Services Authority final notice.

US authorities have charged two former UBS traders, Tom Hayes and Roger Darin, with criminal conspiracy, and Mr Hayes also faces a criminal price-fixing charge in connection with allegations he 'colluded' with another bank to manipulate the yen Libor rate.

The charging and settlement documents include excerpts from myriad emails and chat room messages focused on the daily fixing process for Libor, the collective name for benchmark lending rates set in London for 10 currencies, and Euribor and Tibor, similar rates set in Brussels and Tokyo.

All of the benchmarks rely on averaging daily estimates from panels of banks, so they can in theory be moved if one or more banks deliberately aim high or low.

That was not a problem in Libor's infancy in the mid-1980s when it was used primarily to price corporate and other lending. But the Interbank lending rates became a crucial benchmark for derivatives in the late 1990s, transforming the importance of the daily fixings. A swing of only a few basis points changed from being a rounding error on a loan rate to making the difference between a bonanza trading day and devastating losses.

According to the regulators, that shift also drew the attention of UBS traders, who, according to the Swiss regulator Finma, could triple or even sextuple their annual salaries with bonuses for good results.

The FSA documented more than 2,000 requests to move rates, including more than 800 internal conversations at UBS between traders and rate submitters – nicknamed the 'cash boys' – and more than 1,100 external contacts.

The US Commodity Futures Trading Commission said that it found rate requests focused on yen Libor on 570 of the trading days between 2006 and 2009, or roughly three-quarters of the time.

A US criminal complaint alleges that Mr Hayes, based in Tokyo, used an electronic chat room to tell Mr Darin, who helped submit UBS's Libor estimates, that he had a big derivative riding on the six-month US dollar Libor rate. 'Can we try to keep it on the low side pls?' he wrote in April 2008.

Mr Darin allegedly responded 'I'll submit something low . . . but if u can u should square it up', adding 'the correct 6m is 1.08'. UBS then submitted a rate of 0.98, the criminal complaint said.

The internal contacts were so pervasive that one submitter responded to a January 2007 rate request with 'standing order, sir', the FSA said.

UBS traders also reached out directly to their counterparts at other banks and they sometimes worked in concert.

But the vast majority of external requests, particularly for yen Libor, went through the interdealer brokers. The FSA said four UBS traders based in Tokyo used 11 employees at six brokerages as conduits, asking them to pass on requests for specific rates to traders and more broadly influence the market.

Although brokers do not participate in the rate setting process directly, they were frequently contacted for market information by submitters at some panel banks. So UBS traders also asked the brokers to report false bids and offers – known as 'spoofs' – and asked them to manipulate the rates shown on their trading screens to skew market perceptions, according to the FSA.

The brokers were repaid for their assistance in two ways. In one broker's case, UBS traders would place 'wash trades' – transactions that have no purpose other than to generate fees – with the helpful party. In addition, UBS made corrupt payments of £15,000 per quarter to brokers to reward them for their assistance over a period of at least 18 months.

Source: Masters, B., Binham, C. and Scannell, K. (2012) Daily fix that spiralled out of control, *Financial Times*, 19 December.

The new regime

In 2013 the BBA was stripped of its 'sponsor' role and a new administrator created, **ICE Benchmark Administration Limited (IBA),** part of the US-based Intercontinental Exchange Group. The benchmark administrator is overseen by the Financial Conduct Authority, the financial regulator (formerly the Financial Services Authority) – see Figure 8.1.

ICE began its role on 1 February 2014 and issued its first **ICE Libor** rates on 3 February – see Article 8.2. Note the determination to move away from rates based on theoretical loans to actual lending agreements.

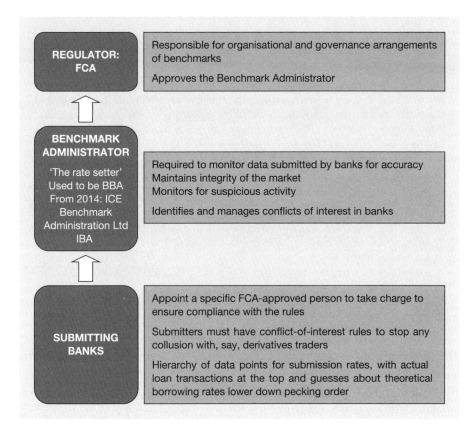

Figure 8.1 The new Libor structure

Article 8.2

Intercontinental Exchange to take over running Libor benchmark

By Philip Stafford

Financial Times January 17, 2014

Intercontinental Exchange will take over the administration of the scandal-tainted Libor benchmark from February 1 after receiving approval from UK regulators on Friday.

The US derivatives exchange has also appointed André Villeneuve, a senior City executive, as chairman of the ICE subsidiary that will collate and monitor the data submitted by banks.

The handover of administration to ICE from the British Bankers' Association will mark the first steps to rehabilitate the benchmark, which has been tarnished after allegations it has been manipulated by banks around the world. More than €2bn has been collected in fines by regulators after a string of financial institutions, including RBS, UBS and Barclays settled charges.

ICE has been in line to run the process since its purchase of NYSE Liffe, the London derivatives exchange, in November. NYSE won the contract to replace the BBA last year. It plans to move calculation of the benchmark away from the theoretical price quotes submitted by banks to a fixing based on real transactions.

However, ICE said there would be no immediate change to the calculation of Libor. The group is currently moving the technology platform from a NYSE-owned system to one overseen by ICE.

Source: Stafford, P. (2014) Intercontinental Exchange to take over running Libor benchmark, *Financial Times*, 17 January.
© The Financial Times Limited 2014. All Rights Reserved.

The IBA continues to administer Libor in much the same way as the BBA, with a panel of banks submitting seven different maturity rates for five currencies: the US dollar (USD), the British pound (GBP), the euro (EUR), the Swiss franc (CHF) and the Japanese yen (JPY). The highest and lowest 25% of submissions are removed and the remainder averaged to give each rate. This trimming of the top and bottom quartiles allows for the exclusion of outliers (potentially freakishly extreme numbers) from the final calculation.

The submitting banks for each currency are shown in Table 8.3. IBA asks the panel banks to inform Thomson Reuters of the rates they might be asked for if they were to borrow using the same question that the BBA employed. The rates are published and distributed by the ICE Benchmark Administration. The www.global-rates.com website, run for IBA, shows Libor rates updated daily at around 6pm (CET) so that those of us without the expensive computer systems showing the 11.45am postings can also see the rates.

The current system tries to place more emphasis on actual market transactions, but frequently this is not possible due to lack of lending that day for that particular maturity and currency, especially problematic in times of market turmoil. Then the IBA allows the submitters to use 'qualitative criteria' and 'expert judgement' to estimate the rate they would be charged should they

Table 8.3 ICE Libor panel banks

Bank	USD	GBP	EUR	CHF	JPY
Bank of America N.A. (London branch)	✳				
Bank of Tokyo-Mitsubishi UFJ Ltd	✳	✳	✳	✳	✳
Barclays Bank plc	✳	✳	✳	✳	✳
BNP Paribas SA (London branch)	✳	✳			
Citibank N.A. (London branch)	✳	✳	✳	✳	
Credit Agricole Corporate & Investment Bank	✳	✳			✳
Crèdit Suisse AG (London branch)	✳		✳	✳	
Deutsche Bank AG (London branch)	✳	✳	✳	✳	✳
HSBC Bank plc	✳	✳	✳	✳	✳
JPMorgan Chase Bank, N.A. (London branch)	✳	✳	✳	✳	✳
Lloyds TSB Bank plc	✳	✳	✳	✳	✳
Mizuho Bank, Ltd		✳	✳		✳
Rabobank Intl CCRB (Cooperatieve Centrale Raiffeisen-Boerenleenbank BA)	✳	✳	✳		
Royal Bank of Canada	✳	✳	✳		
Santander UK plc		✳	✳		
Société Générale (London branch)	✳	✳	✳	✳	✳
Sumitomo Mitsui Banking Corporation Europe Limited	✳				✳
The Norinchukin Bank	✳				✳
The Royal Bank of Scotland plc	✳	✳	✳	✳	✳
UBS AG	✳	✳	✳	✳	✳

Source: Data from www.theice.com/iba/libor

borrow. ICE would like to move to a system that also takes into account interest rates in the commercial paper and certificates of deposits markets – see Article 8.3. There are voices saying that the compromise of allowing estimates alongside actual rates is not going far enough, that all submissions should be on actual deals – see Article 8.4. Other prominent people such as regulators ponder whether it is best to move towards two systems running in parallel, and this is something which the new administrator, ICE Benchmarks Limited, and the FCA will have to resolve.

Article 8.3

Intercontinental Exchange unveils plans for Libor reform

Philip Stafford

Financial Times October 20, 2014

Intercontinental Exchange wants to rehabilitate Libor by proposing that submitting banks include transactions they conduct with central banks as part of their daily calculations.

To toughen the new rate-setting process, ICE proposes establishing a system in which a wide range of data from around the world is used as a basis for submissions. It also wants to force banks to flag up more clearly those submissions which have been supplemented with human judgments.

It added that it wanted banks to anchor rates based on their unsecured wholesale funding deposits, commercial paper and primary issuance certificates of deposit. The approach follows guidelines recommended by the UK-backed Wheatley report in 2012.

Article 8.4

Regulators warn on Libor reform

By Daniel Schäfer

Financial Times July 22, 2014

A powerful umbrella body for global regulators has criticised the administrators of Libor and two other interbank lending rates for failing to show that they have improved the reliability and accuracy of such benchmarks.

The administrators of Britain's Libor and its European and Japanese equivalents Euribor and Tibor have not provided the data and analysis to demonstrate whether they are anchored in real transactions, the International Organisation of Securities Commissions said in a review of its benchmark principles.

Iosco last year introduced those principles after the scandal over widespread manipulation of Libor sparked an intense debate about radical reform of the way such benchmarks are compiled.

Regulators are keen to ensure that benchmarks are rooted in real market transactions rather than just bank submissions which, since the Libor scandal, are seen as susceptible to manipulation.

'None of the administrators has completed an analysis of methodologies to provide a basis for deciding whether the submissions are anchored in that market,' Iosco said.

The group gave administrators until the end of the year to set out concrete steps to address this issue.

Iosco's report comes shortly after Intercontinental Exchange, which took over the administration of Libor this year, began asking banks for internal transaction data and also started testing a new system to collect and validate rates the banks submit.

Major reference interest rates such as Libor, Euribor and Tibor should be 'to the greatest extent possible' based on actual trade data, the Financial Stability Board said in an additional report on Tuesday.

The FSB also called on market participants to investigate the feasibility of developing alternative, fully transaction-data based reference rates.

 Source: Schäfer, D. (2014) Regulators warn on Libor reform, *Financial Times*, 22 July.
© The Financial Times Limited 2014. All Rights Reserved.

Now that Libor is no longer calculated for the Australian dollar (nor NZ or Canadian dollars or Danish and Swedish krona) the Australians have decided to obtain interbank rates from market transactions – see Article 8.5. Bank bills are discussed in Chapter 11.

Article 8.5

Australia to use market prices for Libor

By Neil Hume

Financial Times March 27, 2013

Australia will use prices displayed electronically by brokers and trading venues to set the price of the country's benchmark Interbank borrowing rate.

The Australian Financial Markets Association, which represents 130 Australian and international banks, brokers and fund managers, announced on Wednesday it would disband the panel used to set the bank bill swap rate.

'Building on the advantage of BBSW being based on a traded market, AFMA proposes to bypass the panel requirement by adopting a process to extract these rates directly from trading venues – brokers and electronic markets. This proposal has the support of market participants,' it said in a statement.

The BBSW is the Australian equivalent of the scandal-plagued London InterBank Offered Rate (Libor) and is used to set interest payments on floating rate securities, derivatives and Australian dollar-denominated loans.

The decision to take rates directly from the market, rather than from submissions, comes after two more banks – Citigroup and HSBC – said they would no longer contribute to the BBSW panel. JPMorgan and UBS withdrew earlier this year.

Banks are quitting rate-setting panels around the world because of tougher scrutiny and a rise in compliance costs brought about by the Libor scandal.

Banks which contribute to the process in the UK will be required to corroborate their submissions and appoint a specific person to take charge of compliance with the new rules.

Australia's BBSW rate differs from Libor in that panellists are asked for the actual rates they observe in the market rather than an indicative quote.

Euribor and some other BORs

There are other rates similar to Libor in common use and many of these have also been caught up in the interbank rate-fixing scandal.

Euribor (Euro InterBank Offered Rate)

Euribor or **EURIBOR** is the rate at which euro interbank term deposits are offered by prime banks to other prime banks within the eurozone (not London) for periods of one week to one year. Euribor came into existence in 1999 with the adoption of the euro currency. It does not cover overnight lending – see Eonia below for that. Euribor is calculated as a weighted average of unsecured lending transactions undertaken within the euro area by a panel of 26 banks. They are mostly eurozone nationality banks, but there are some non-eurozone/international banks. The highest and lowest 15% of quotes received are eliminated and the remainder are averaged to three decimal places and published daily around 11am CET. The panel banks are those with the highest volume of business in the eurozone money markets: they have a first-class credit standing and high reputation.

There used to be nearer 40 banks contributing to the daily survey of rates, but many found themselves embarrassed and exposed to severe fines and legal action for manipulating Euribor and other rates, so they quit the panel to reduce further risk. Others, even though they had behaved well in the past, feared the risk of rogue employees bringing them down, even if it was a small risk – see Article 8.6.

Article 8.6

UBS joins exodus from Euribor panel

By Daniel Schäfer

Financial Times March 19, 2013

UBS is pulling out of the Euribor rate setting panel, thwarting efforts by European authorities to keep intact the number of banks involved in the fixing process following the global rate manipulation scandal.

The Swiss lender joins the exodus from the panel by banks including Dutch lender Rabobank, Citigroup from the US and Bayerische Landesbank in Germany.

This week, Svenska Handelsbanken will become the latest bank to withdraw from the rate-setting panel according to Euribor-EBF, the organisation that administers the benchmark.

UBS said: 'We have decided to withdraw from the Euribor panel and to focus on our core funding markets Swiss franc and US dollar.'

The Swiss lender added that this was related to a strategy announced last October to drastically cut back the investment bank by exiting most of its fixed income businesses.

UBS is one of three global banks that have paid large fines to US and UK authorities over involvement in the manipulation of Libor, another benchmark interest rate.

The Euribor panel currently consists of 39 banks. Authorities including the European Central Bank have been calling on lenders to continue contributing to the fixings to avoid further damage to the credibility of the benchmark.

Michel Barnier, EU commissioner responsible for the financial sector, said last month he was considering forcing banks to contribute to the rate-setting process.

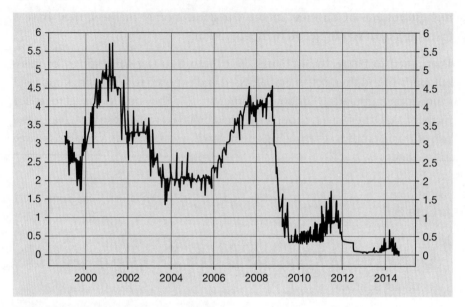

Figure 8.2 Eonia chart since its beginning

Source: European Central Bank www.ecb.europa.euhttp://sdw.ecb.europa.eu/
quickview.do?SERIES_KEY=198.EON.D.EONIA_TO.RATE

Eonia

Eonia or **EONIA (Euro OverNight Index Average)** is the effective overnight
rate for the euro, a 'one-day Euribor'. It is computed as a weighted average of
all overnight unsecured lending transactions in the interbank market initiated
within the European Union and European Free Trade Association (EFTA) countries by the same 26 panel banks as for Euribor. It is calculated by the European
Central Bank. Figure 8.2 and Article 8.7 illustrate the dramatic effect of the
financial crisis and the long recession on Eonia, with policy makers pushing
down interest rates: before 2008 Eonia remained in the range of 2–6%, today it
hovers just above zero.

Article 8.7

Eurozone borrowing costs hit record low

By Christopher Thompson and Elaine Moore

Financial Times August 12, 2014

Benchmark overnight borrowing costs in the eurozone have tumbled to a record low of 0.01% amid worries that Europe's fragile economic recovery is stagnating.

The move follows a package of measures the European Central Bank announced in June to further flood the market with liquidity.

'A low Eonia, along with expectations of further liquidity to come from the ECB, keeps other money market rates low,' said Giuseppe Maraffino at Barclays. The ECB said it would begin charging banks for parking their funds.

But data released last week showed Italy has now slipped back into recession, while manufacturing figures in Germany were below expectations, fuelling hopes among some investors that the ECB will do even more to calm febrile markets.

'Given the clear weakening of European economic activity in the past few weeks there is hope that the ECB will have to do even more, such as buying asset-backed securities or other purchases that would inject further liquidity into the system,' said Vincent Chaigneau at Société Générale.

Yields for two-year German Bunds are now below zero, meaning investors in effect are paying for the security they receive in short-term German government debt.

This decline has been matched by a fall in yields on Berlin's benchmark 10-year debt, which are fast approaching 1%.

'There has been a flight to quality but it has not led to the typical rebalancing of portfolios away from risky periphery debt,' said Gianluca Salford, at JPMorgan. 'That's because this is about investors betting that the ECB will not be able to increase interest rates for years to come.'

Tibor, Sibor and Hibor

Many other countries have markets setting rates for lending between domestic banks. **Tibor (Tokyo Interbank Offered Rate)** is the rate at which Japanese banks lend to each other in Japan. In Singapore there is **Sibor** and in Hong Kong there is **Hibor**.

Federal funds rate and prime rate

In the US, the equivalent to very short-term Libor or Eonia is the **Federal funds rate (Fed funds)**. This is the daily effective rate at which depository institutions lend balances to each other overnight, calculated by the Federal Reserve Bank of New York as a volume-weighted average of rates on brokered trades. This is strongly influenced by the US central bank, the Federal Reserve, which sets a target rate and then can influence the Fed funds rate by increasing or lowering the level of cash or near cash reserves the banks have to hold. Banks often need to borrow from other banks to maintain the required minimum level of reserves at the Federal Reserve. The lending banks are happy to lend because they receive a rate of interest and the money is released the next day (usually). This borrowing is unsecured and so is available only to the most creditworthy.

Fed funds interest rate – borrowing in the US – and the overnight US dollar Libor rate – borrowing in the UK – are usually very close to each other because they are near-perfect substitutes. If they were not close then a bank could make a profit borrowing in one overnight market and depositing the money in another. If the US dollar Libor rate is significantly higher, banks needing to borrow will tend to do so in the Fed funds market and the increased demand will push up interest rates here, while the absence of demand will encourage lower rates in the US dollar Libor market. Having said that, they are not perfect substitutes: the Fed funds rate tends to be slightly lower than US dollar Libor because of the greater safety in the US with the Federal Reserve overseeing and backing up the debt market, including deposit insurance. Thus the arbitrage opportunity is really about the risk premium in London over the Fed funds rate, but the risk premium is usually pretty small.

The Federal Reserve created vast amounts of new money by buying about $3 trillion of bonds over the five years to 2014. It funded this by creating bank reserves. Now that banks have plenty of reserves, interbank lending has reduced dramatically. This has distorted the Fed funds rate and interrupted the normal mechanism for adjusting interest rates through central bank intervention (discussed further in Chapter 16). Article 8.8 considers the possibility of using other measures of short-term dollar borrowing as benchmarks.

Article 8.8

Fed explores overhaul of key rate

By Robin Harding

Financial Times July 10, 2014

The US Federal Reserve is exploring an overhaul of the Federal funds rate – a benchmark that underlies almost every financial transaction in the world – as it prepares for an eventual rise in interest rates.

The Fed funds rate is the main measure of overnight US interest rates and is based on the actual rates reported by brokers for overnight loans between US banks.

According to people familiar with the discussions, the Fed could redefine its main target rate so that it takes into account a wider range of loans between banks, making it more stable and reliable.

Concerns have grown about the reliability of the Fed funds rate since the Fed began buying trillions of dollars of assets during three rounds of quantitative easing. US banks now have huge amounts of cash and have stopped borrowing or lending Fed funds, making the market highly illiquid.

With the Fed targeting rates close to zero, the reliability of Fed funds has been less important but when the Fed starts raising rates – something markets expect it to do in the middle of next year – it needs to be sure that it is targeting a real benchmark.

In particular, the Fed is looking at redefining the funds rate to include eurodollar transactions – dollar loans between banks outside the US markets – as well as traditional onshore loans between US banks.

Other closely related rates that it could include are those on transactions for bank commercial paper and wholesale certificates of deposit between banks.

The Fed hinted at a change in the minutes of its June meeting. 'Participants examined possibilities for changing the calculation of the effective Federal funds rate in order to obtain a more robust measure of overnight bank funding rates,' the minutes said.

Ira Jersey, director of interest rate strategy at Credit Suisse in New York, said eurodollars were a very close substitute for Fed funds. 'In general, at nine in the morning New York time, the only difference between a Fed funds transaction and a eurodollar transaction is the back end coding,' he said.

Mr Jersey said he thought including eurodollars would be unlikely to change the Fed funds rate much right now but the effect when interest rates were higher was hard to judge.

The US **prime rate** is the short-term interest rate US banks charge their best corporate customers. An average is taken from the largest US banks – the most well known is the prime rate calculated by *The Wall Street Journal*. In approximate terms it is around 3% more than the Fed funds rate. It is used as a benchmark for other loans, e.g. consumer credit loan interest rates are often set at so-many basis points above the prime rate, as are credit cards, home equity loans and lines of credit and auto loans. Many small business loans are also indexed to the prime rate.

Sonia and Euronia

The **Wholesale Markets Brokers' Association (WMBA)** is a group of financial companies which act as intermediaries (interdealer brokers) in arranging the wholesale money market operations in London. From the transactions they broker, they provide the details for calculating important benchmark interest rates for the overnight sterling and euro markets, Sonia and Euronia, all published daily at 5pm.

Sonia or **SONIA (Sterling Overnight Index Average)** was launched in 1997 and is a weighted average of the actual unsecured sterling overnight rates in deals in London with a size in excess of £25 million brokered by WMBA members. The weighting is by the principal amount of deposits which were taken on that day (between midnight and 4.15pm).

Euronia or **EURONIA (Euro Overnight Index Average)** is the UK equivalent of Eonia, a weighted average of euro interest rates on unsecured overnight euro deposits arranged by WMBA members in London. There is no minimum deal size for Euronia. The weighting is by the principal amount of deposits which were taken on that day (between midnight and 4pm).

Eurocurrency

Eurocurrency has a large part to play in the interbank market as well as other lending/borrowing markets. The terms **Eurocurrency, Eurodollar, Euroyen, Euroswissfrancs**, etc. have nothing to do with the actual euro currency. Their name simply means that the currency is deposited and lent outside the jurisdiction of the country that issued the currency. For example, an Australian company might make a deposit in yen in a German bank; this would be a

Euroyen deposit. An American corporation might pay a Swiss corporation in dollars; these dollars are deposited in a Swiss bank and are Eurodollars.

Today, it is not unusual to find an individual/company holding a dollar account at a UK bank which pays interest in dollars linked to general dollar rates. This money can be lent to firms wishing to borrow in Eurodollars prepared to pay interest and capital repayments in dollars. The point is that both the Euroyen deposit and the Eurodollars are outside the control of their country of origin – regulators have little influence on this market.[3] The market is a wholesale one with the minimum transaction typically $1m or equivalent in other currencies.

Growth of the Eurocurrency markets

Eurocurrency markets came about after World War II during the 1950s and 1960s, when substantial amounts of US dollars were deposited in Europe (mainly in London). Countries outside the US were wary about depositing their dollars in US banks, where they would be subject to stringent US regulations. Regulation Q of the US Banking Act of 1933 prohibited banks from paying interest on commercial demand deposits. Additionally, 'Iron Curtain' countries were worried that their dollars could be seized or frozen for political reasons if they were placed where the rule of the US authorities was in force. Countries earning dollars, especially oil producing countries, looked for banks outside the US where they could deposit their US dollars and earn market rates of interest. US corporations began to expand into Europe, and wanted their funds outside the control of the US authorities. Even after Regulation Q was finally phased out in the 1980s, US banks were still subject to restrictions and controls, so the Eurocurrency market thrived, where dollars could be deposited free from US regulations, although strictly speaking, the term should be **international market**. Nowadays, there is daily **Eurosecurities** business transacted in all of the major financial centres, but the most significant is London. The Bahamas, Cayman Islands and Singapore are also significant Eurocurrency centres.

---

[3] Just to confuse everybody, traders in this market often refer to all types of Eurocurrency, from Eurosterling to Euroyen, as Eurodollars, and do not reserve the term for US dollars.

Eurocurrency and Eurocredit

To add a little precision: **Eurocurrency** is short-term (less than one year) deposits and loans outside the jurisdiction of the country in whose currency the deposit/loan is denominated. These are term ('time') deposits that may be fixed for just one day (overnight) or for a longer period such as three months. Deals for three-month lending, for example, are struck one day and then two business days later the money is actually transferred – the spot delivery. The funds are repaid with interest at maturity three months after the spot value date (a bullet repayment structure).

Eurocredit is used for the market in medium- and long-term loans in the Euromarkets, with lending rates usually linked to (a few basis points above) the Libor rates. Loans greater than six months normally have interest rates that are reset every three or six months depending on the Libor rate then prevailing for, say, three-month lending. So a corporate borrower with a two-year loan that starts off paying three-month Libor plus 150 basis points when three-month Libor is 3% pays 4.5%. This is expressed as an annual rate – the borrower will pay only one-quarter of this for three months. If, at the start of the next three months, the three-month Libor rate has moved to 3.45%, the corporate will pay 4.95% (annual rate) for three months. Interest on deposits of more than one year is likely to be paid on an annual or six-monthly basis.

Benefits of the Eurosecurities markets

Companies large enough to use the Eurosecurities markets are able to put themselves at a competitive advantage *vis-à-vis* smaller firms.

- The finance available in these markets can be at a lower cost in both transaction costs and rates of return offered. There are economies of scale due to the wholesale nature of the market. The absence of withholding tax on interest and anonymity encourage lenders to offer lower rates.
- There are fewer rules and regulations, such as needing to obtain official authorisation to issue or needing to queue to issue, leading to speed, innovation and lower costs.
- There may be the ability to hedge foreign currency movements. For example, if a firm has assets denominated in a foreign currency it can be advantageous to also have liabilities in that same currency to reduce the adverse impact of exchange rate movements.

● The borrowing needs of some firms are simply too large for their domestic markets to supply. To avoid being hampered in expansion plans, large firms can turn to the international market in finance.

The Eurocurrency market allows countries and corporations to lend and borrow funds worldwide, picking the financial institution which is the most suitable regardless of geographic position. While the world economy is thriving, this works well. However, some spectacular problems were highlighted in 2008. For example, Iceland's financial institutions found themselves in trouble after much of their borrowing in the international debt markets suddenly dried up.

The Eurodollar market has become so deep and broad that it now sets interest rates back in the mother country of the dollar. A very large proportion of US domestic commercial loans and commercial paper interest rates are set at a certain number of basis points above US dollar Libor rates determined by banks operating out of London.

CHAPTER 9
TREASURY BILLS AND COMMERCIAL PAPER

Treasury bills

Throughout the world, government agencies issue **Treasury bills** (**T-bills** or **Treasury notes**).[1] They do not pay a coupon; the return investors receive is the difference between the purchase price and the selling/redemption price – they trade at a discount to their face value, and the discount reflects the current rate of interest on similar securities. They are negotiable securities, which means that they can easily be traded in the secondary market and thus easily liquidated to release cash. They can be one of the most risk-free forms of investing (if you are lending to financially stable governments), but pay a lower return for this reason. T-bills form by far the largest part of the money markets and are generally issued at auction through a national government agency.

UK Treasury bills

In the UK Treasury bills were first issued by the Bank of England in the early 1700s, when the UK adopted the concept of money as an amount written on a piece of paper, rather than a piece of metal with intrinsic value. They are now issued at weekly tenders by the Debt Management Office (DMO) with a face value or par value of £100 and are sold with a maturity date of one month (approximately 28 days), three months (approximately 91 days), six months (approximately 182 days) or twelve months (up to 364 days).[2] At each tender, the DMO publishes the type and amount of bills to be offered the following week. Bills are initially sold by competitive tender to **cash management**

---

[1] In Germany and Austria, a Treasury bill is called a Schatzwechsel; in Russia a Gosudarstvennoe Kratkosrochnoe Obyazatelstvo (GKO); and in France and Canada a Bons du Trésor.

[2] In theory 12-month bills can be issued, but to date none has yet been offered for sale.

counterparties (which must be regulated financial institutions) and 28 **primary participants** who can bid on behalf of clients and can also in turn sell on the bills to other investors. Most holders of Treasury bills are financial institutions. Individuals may buy them, but the minimum purchase amount is £500,000; above this bidding is in £50,000 increments. Bids are ranked according to the yield bid, and bills are allotted to those purchasers who submit yields at or below the yield the DMO thinks necessary to fulfil the amount tendered.

Table 9.1 shows the results from the four sales of Treasury bills which took place weekly during March 2014, on the 7th, 14th, 21st and 28th. Note that the issues occurred every few days as the government borrowed more money or simply replaced maturing debt. Table 9.2 shows the *Financial Times* tender results table for the three-month T-bills on 14 and 21 March 2014.

Tenders are held by the DMO on the last business day of each week (i.e. usually on Fridays), for settlement (paid for) on the following business day, usually Monday. The **redemption date** is the day when the face value of the bill (£100) will be paid to the holder. The T-bills issued at tenders mature on the first business day of the week. The **nominal amount** is the total amount of the face value of the bills offered at the tender (not what was actually paid for them).

Table 9.1 DMO Treasury bill tender results, 1 March 2014 to 31 March 2014

Tender date	Issue date	Redemption date	Nominal amount (£m)	Bid to cover ratio	Average yield (%)	Average price (£)
1 month						
07-Mar-14	10-Mar-14	07-Apr-14	2,000	2.21	0.393578	99.969817
14-Mar-14	17-Mar-14	14-Apr-14	2,000	3.30	0.364505	99.972046
21-Mar-14	24-Mar-14	22-Apr-14	2,000	1.85	0.381211	99.969721
28-Mar-14	31-Mar-14	28-Apr-14	2,000	1.62	0.407344	99.968761
3 months						
07-Mar-14	10-Mar-14	09-Jun-14	1,500	2.64	0.363186	99.909534
14-Mar-14	17-Mar-14	16-Jun-14	2,000	3.09	0.379104	99.905573
21-Mar-14	24-Mar-14	23-Jun-14	2,000	1.95	0.390464	99.902746
28-Mar-14	31-Mar-14	30-Jun-14	2,000	1.51	0.421457	99.895035
6 months						
07-Mar-14	10-Mar-14	08-Sep-14	1,500	2.87	0.409168	99.796392
14-Mar-14	17-Mar-14	15-Sep-14	1,500	3.23	0.394030	99.803910
21-Mar-14	24-Mar-14	22-Sep-14	1,500	2.17	0.400866	99.800515
28-Mar-14	31-Mar-14	29-Sep-14	1,500	1.70	0.422876	99.789585

Source: www.dmo.gov.uk

Table 9.2 UK three-month Treasury bill tender results in the *Financial Times*

	Mar 21	Mar 14		Mar 21	Mar 14
Bills in offer	£2000m	£2000m	Lowest accepted yield	0.3300%	0.3400%
Total of application	£3894m	£6170m	Avg. Rate of discount	0.3901%	0.3787%
Total allocated	£2000m	£2000m	Average yield	0.3905%	0.3791%
Highest acpt yield	0.4180%	0.3850%	Offer at next tender	£2000m	£2000m
About allocated	88.10%	75.95%	Highest acpt yield 28 days	0.4170%	0.3650%

Information shown relates to the three month tender.
Source: DMO including details of the month tender, see www.dmo.gov.uk

The **bid to cover ratio** is the ratio of the amount that was actually bid to the amount of T-bills offered; if the number is greater than 1 it shows that there were more bids than the amount on offer. Although extremely rare it is not unknown for an offer to be undersubscribed[3] – it is a sign of lack of confidence in the government's financial situation and/or indigestion in a market faced with an exceptionally high volume of government borrowing.

Treasury bills in March 2014 yielded a rate as low as 0.364505% for one month T-bills, 0.363186% for 3M T-bills and 0.394030% for 6M T-bills (Table 9.1). The **average price** is the average of the price handed over by bidders for bills which will pay the holders of the bills £100 in one month, three months or six months.

Those participants that wish to purchase compete in the weekly tender by placing bids based on the yield they will accept. The bids are gathered and different yield prices accepted. The DMO determines what is the highest accepted yield (and therefore the lowest purchase price) needed to sell the requisite amount of bills and allocates bills to purchasers bidding below this yield. For the three-month 21 March tender some bidders achieved a yield of 0.418% whereas others offered and received merely 0.33%. Purchasers bidding at the accepted yield may not receive the amount for which they bid.

---

[3] This has happened only twice for UK Treasury bills, both times in 2008, with a six-month bill offered for sale in October and a three-month bill offered for sale in May.

An important consideration to take note of when undertaking any calculations associated with T-bills around the world (and other money market securities) is the **day count convention**. For ease of calculation, some countries/markets use a 30-day month and 360-day year, rather than the actual variable days in a month and a 365-day year, or 366 in a leap year. This can get complicated when the repayment date falls on the 31st of a month, and there are various methods for dealing with this. Other markets use the actual number of days until redemption of the instrument and the actual number of days in a year. Great care must always be taken to check which day count convention is being used and to understand terminology, e.g. actual/360, 360/360, actual/actual, actual/365 and so on – it is imperative that an investor knows which convention is being used and how it works. The UK still uses the 365-day year for Treasury securities.

The DMO published results for the tender on the 21 March for the 23 June bill are shown in Table 9.3. From this it can be noted that the bill was over-tendered by a factor of 1.95, i.e. the amount on offer was £2 billion (at face value), there were actual bids offered totalling nearly £4 billion and about 88% of the bidders achieved the highest yield of 0.418%.

During the life of the bill, its value fluctuates daily as it is traded between investors – see Table 9.4, which gives the daily March and April 2014 figures for this particular bill. The yield shown is the (annual) return that a purchaser in the secondary market will achieve between purchase date and maturity date. Note:

Table 9.3 Results of tender on three-month T-bill ISIN code: GB00B7P4VP73

Lowest accepted yield	0.330000
Average yield	0.390464
Highest accepted yield	0.418000 (About 88.10% allotted)
Average rate of discount (%)	0.390084
Average price per £100 nominal (£)	99.902746
Amount tendered for (£)	3,894,400,000.00
Amount on offer (£)	2,000,000,000.00
Bid to cover ratio	1.95
Amount allocated (£)	2,000,000,000.00

Source: www.dmo.gov.uk

Table 9.4 Daily trading prices for Treasury bill GB00B7P4VP73, 21 March to 16 April 2014

ISIN code	Redemption date	Close of business date	Price (£)	Yield (%)
GB00B7P4VP73	23-Jun-14	21-Mar-14	99.903464	0.388
GB00B7P4VP73	23-Jun-14	24-Mar-14	99.905141	0.385
GB00B7P4VP73	23-Jun-14	25-Mar-14	99.906352	0.384
GB00B7P4VP73	23-Jun-14	26-Mar-14	99.907558	0.384
GB00B7P4VP73	23-Jun-14	27-Mar-14	99.908762	0.383
GB00B7P4VP73	23-Jun-14	28-Mar-14	99.911712	0.384
GB00B7P4VP73	23-Jun-14	31-Mar-14	99.913389	0.381
GB00B7P4VP73	23-Jun-14	01-Apr-14	99.914615	0.380
GB00B7P4VP73	23-Jun-14	02-Apr-14	99.915802	0.380
GB00B7P4VP73	23-Jun-14	03-Apr-14	99.916987	0.379
GB00B7P4VP73	23-Jun-14	04-Apr-14	99.919921	0.380
GB00B7P4VP73	23-Jun-14	07-Apr-14	99.921688	0.376
GB00B7P4VP73	23-Jun-14	08-Apr-14	99.922855	0.376
GB00B7P4VP73	23-Jun-14	09-Apr-14	99.924018	0.375
GB00B7P4VP73	23-Jun-14	10-Apr-14	99.925176	0.374
GB00B7P4VP73	23-Jun-14	11-Apr-14	99.926169	0.385
GB00B7P4VP73	23-Jun-14	14-Apr-14	99.929775	0.372
GB00B7P4VP73	23-Jun-14	15-Apr-14	99.930889	0.371
GB00B7P4VP73	23-Jun-14	16-Apr-14	99.932055	0.370

Source: www.dmo.gov.uk

the price gravitates towards par value as the day of maturity draws nearer because on redemption day, 23 June 2014, the holder will receive the face value of £100.

Emerging market Treasury bills

Many emerging market[4] economies are now able to issue Treasury bills in their own currencies, while some others concentrate issuance in one of the major

---

[4]   Not yet fully developed economies.

currencies of the world, especially the US dollar. By borrowing in the US dollar or another international currency the lenders can borrow at lower interest rates because international lenders are less fearful of a decline in the local currency, but the downside is that when the country has to redeem the T-bills, it faces the risk that the dollar has risen against the local currency and so more local currency than initially thought needs to be paid out to lenders. This problem has caused financial crises in a number of countries over the years, e.g. Mexico in 1995, Russia in 1998 and Brazil in 1999.

US Treasury bills

US Treasury bills are sold by Treasury Direct (www.treasurydirect.gov), which is part of the US Department of the Treasury. They range in maturity from a few days to 52 weeks, with 4-week (28 days), 13-week (91 days) and 26-week (182 days) bills being the most common. They are sold at a discount to par value by auction every week, except for the 52-week bills which are auctioned every 4 weeks. The buyers include securities' houses, banks, institutional investors and private investors. The bidders can bid for the bills in two ways (they have to choose one route or the other at the outset):

- *Competitive*. This is where potential buyers specify the minimum discount rate or yield they are willing to accept. No single bidder may bid for more than 35% of the total on offer. These bids may be:

  a Accepted in the full amount the bidder wanted if the discount rate they specified is less than the discount rate set by the auction. This threshold rate is determined by the Treasury, which, when all the bids are gathered in, sets the level of discount that will shift the bill quantity required. Competitive bids are accepted in ascending order until the quantity reaches the amount offered.

  b Accepted only partially (the bidder does not receive the full amount of bills bid for) if their bid is the same as the cut-off level that sells the amount of bills the government is trying to sell in that auction.

  c Rejected if the bidder stated a level of discount that is higher than that set at the auction.

- *Non-competitive*. The buyer agrees to accept the rate or yield which is set at the auction, in other words, the price set by other investors. The offer to buy can be submitted via the internet. With a non-competitive bid buyers

Table 9.5 US Treasury bills auctioned March 2014

CUSIP	Security term	Auction date	Issue date	Maturity date	Price per $100	Average/ median discount rate	Bid to cover ratio
912796DE6	13-week	03/31/14	04/03/14	07/03/14	99.988625	0.04%	4.83
912796DX4	26-week	03/31/14	04/03/15	10/02/14	99.967139	0.06%	5.18
912796CJ6	4-week	03/25/14	03/27/14	04/24/14	99.996500	0.04%	4.65
912796BP3	13-week	03/24/14	03/27/14	06/26/14	99.987361	0.04%	4.61
912796DW6	26-week	03/24/14	03/27/14	09/25/14	99.962083	0.07%	5.05
912796CH0	4-week	03/18/14	03/20/14	04/17/14	99.995333	0.06%	4.27
912796DD8	13-week	03/17/14	03/20/14	06/19/14	99.987361	0.05%	4.42
912796CB3	26-week	03/17/14	03/20/14	09/18/14	99.959556	0.08%	4.86
912796CG2	4-week	03/11/14	03/13/14	04/10/14	99.995722	0.05%	4.11
912796DC0	13-week	03/10/14	03/13/14	06/12/14	99.987361	0.05%	4.76
912796DV8	26-week	03/10/14	03/13/14	09/11/14	99.959556	0.08%	4.97
912796BA6	4-week	03/04/14	03/06/14	04/03/14	99.996500	0.04%	3.93
912796DP1	52-week	03/04/14	03/06/14	03/05/15	99.878667	0.12%	4.85
912796DA4	13-week	03/03/14	03/06/14	06/05/14	99.987361	0.04%	5.02
912796DS5	26-week	03/03/14	03/06/14	09/04/14	99.959556	0.08%	4.46

Source: www.treasurydirect.gov

are guaranteed to receive the full amount of bills they wanted up to a maximum of $5 million. This is a good method for individual investors who are not expert security traders and therefore can avoid calculating bill discount rates.

All bidders, competitive and non-competitive, receive the same discount rate, and therefore the same yield, as the highest accepted bid and so pay the same amount for their bills (contrasting with UK bills, where bidders pay the amount at which they tendered).

Individuals may bid and the minimum purchase is a lowly $100, unlike in the UK where the minimum bid is £500,000 and individuals may not bid themselves but hold UK Treasury bills only through one of the approved bidders. Table 9.5 gives the results of US T-bill auctions held during March 2014. US T-bill interest is calculated on an actual/360 annual basis.

Commercial paper

Commercial paper (CP) is an unsecured short-term instrument of debt, issued primarily by corporations, banks and other financial institutions to help meet the financing requirements of their accounts receivable (debtors), inventories (stock) and other short-term cash needs, but can also be issued by municipalities. The issue and purchase of commercial paper is one means by which the largest commercial organisations can avoid paying a bank intermediary a middleman fee for linking borrower and lender, e.g. corporations can avoid taking out loans from a bank and go direct to the financial market lenders.

Called 'paper' because originally the promissory note was written on a piece of paper, CP is now more usually dealt with electronically, but is still a promise to pay the holder the designated sum on the designated date. Buyers include money market funds, investment firms, mutual funds, insurance companies, pension funds, governments and banks. Also corporations with temporary surpluses of cash are able to put that money to use by lending it directly to other commercial firms at a higher effective rate of interest than they might have received by depositing the funds in a bank. Investors in CP often buy it from dealers, which are usually banks. Settlement (actual transfer) is normally the same day as the deal is struck (known as T+0).

One of the advantages of CP is its flexibility in terms of maturity. While it has an average maturity of about 40 days, with the normal range being from 30 to 90 days, it can be 270 days in the US and up to a year in some other countries. Normally CP is issued at a discount rather than the borrower being required to pay interest – thus the face value (amount paid on redemption) will be higher than the amount paid for the paper at issuance.[5] The discount, and the yield gained by the lender, tends to be higher than that for T-bills because there is a greater risk of default and because there is less liquidity in the secondary market.

This source of finance is in general available only to the most respected corporations with the highest credit ratings given the absence (usually) of assets pledged to be used to pay the obligation should the borrower fail to do so by other means. Most commercial paper is issued and traded among institutions in denominations of $100,000 or more, but some is issued in smaller denominations.

---

[5] A small amount of commercial paper is issued with interest payments, but this is rare.

Large and frequent borrowers may pay issuance costs of merely one or two basis points. Some companies, such as General Electric, are such frequent issuers of CP that they employ in-house teams to do the selling – **direct placement**. Other issuers ask dealers (usually employed by investment banks) to either buy the issue with the expectation of selling it on (**firm commitment underwriting**) or use 'their best endeavours' to find lenders. These two methods are **dealer-directed** offers.

Short-term debt credit ratings

The main buyers, such as money market funds, are often restricted to having the bulk of their portfolios invested in those issues regarded as carrying a low risk of short-term vulnerability to default. Commercial paper is often rated by the credit rating agencies, which focus on the possibility of the issuer running out of cash over the life of the paper, say 30 days, rather than the solvency of the business in the long run. Moody's has a very simple scale, with P-1, P-2 and P-3 all being investment grade and anything else being Not Prime – see Table 9.6.

With Standard & Poor's, A-3 is on the cusp of investment to non-investment grade – see Table 9.7. Fitch has F1+, F1, F2 and F3 as investment grade and B, C and D for speculative grade.

Demand is very limited for lower-rated issues. Even moving from Prime-1 to Prime-2 means much greater difficulty in finding lenders – see Article 9.1.

Table 9.6 Moody's short-term debt credit ratings

Global Short-Term Rating Scale	
P-1	Issuers (or supporting institutions) rated Prime-1 have a superior ability to repay short-term debt obligations.
P-2	Issuers (or supporting institutions) rated Prime-2 have a strong ability to repay short-term debt obligations.
P-3	Issuers (or supporting institutions) rated Prime-3 have an acceptable ability to repay short-term obligations.
NP	Issuers (or supporting institutions) rated Not Prime do not fall within any of the Prime rating categories.

Source: www.moodys.com/researchdocumentcontentpage.aspx?docid=PBC_79004

Table 9.7 Standard & Poor's short-term debt credit ratings

Short-Term Issue Credit Ratings	
Category	**Definition**
A-1	A short-term obligation rated 'A-1' is rated in the highest category by Standard & Poor's. The obligor's capacity to meet its financial commitment on the obligation is strong. Within this category, certain obligations are designated with a plus sign (+). This indicates that the obligor's capacity to meet its financial commitment on these obligations is extremely strong.
A-2	A short-term obligation rated 'A-2' is somewhat more susceptible to the adverse effects of changes in circumstances and economic conditions than obligations in higher rating categories. However, the obligor's capacity to meet its financial commitment on the obligation is satisfactory.
A-3	A short-term obligation rated 'A-3' exhibits adequate protection parameters. However, adverse economic conditions or changing circumstances are more likely to lead to a weakened capacity of the obligor to meet its financial commitment on the obligation.
B	A short-term obligation rated 'B' is regarded as vulnerable and has significant speculative characteristics. The obligor currently has the capacity to meet its financial commitments; however, it faces major ongoing uncertainties which could lead to the obligor's inadequate capacity to meet its financial commitments.
C	A short-term obligation rated 'C' is currently vulnerable to nonpayment and is dependent upon favorable business, financial, and economic conditions for the obligor to meet its financial commitment on the obligation.
D	A short-term obligation rated 'D' is in payment default. The 'D' rating category is used when payments on an obligation are not made on the date due, unless Standard & Poor's believes that such payments will be made within any stated grace period. However, any stated grace period longer than five business days will be treated as five business days. The 'D' rating also will be used upon the filing of a bankruptcy petition or the taking of a similar action if payments on an obligation are jeopardized.

Source: www.standardandpoors.com/spf/general/
RatingsDirect_Commentary_979212_06_22_2012_12_42_54.pdf

In some countries using credit rating agencies to rate CP is rare, with investors buying paper on the basis of the strength of the name of the organisation issuing it – only the largest, most well known and trusted can issue in these places.

The secondary market in CP is weak or non-existent – while dealers might be found who will buy CP from a lender, it is not easy to complete such deals and can be costly. One way of investing in it while retaining liquidity is to invest

Article 9.1

ADP: commercial success

The Lex team

Financial Times April 21, 2014

Credit ratings matter. But not always the ones that get the most attention. Fortunately ADP, the payroll processing mainstay, knows the difference. In early April, after it announced a spin-off of its Dealer Services business – a unit that provides software to motor sellers – ADP lost its rarefied AAA rating. Perhaps that stung. But the spin-off still looks like a canny move for shareholders. And just as important, ADP managed to keep its top-tier commercial paper rating that is central to its business model.

Since ADP is an intermediary that makes payroll for employees and withholds taxes for the government on behalf of its client companies, it happens to maintain a large cash portfolio or 'float'. That float totalled $28bn at the end of the last quarter. It chooses to invest that money in medium-term bonds that generate interest income that flows straight to earnings. But with the cash tied up in these investments, it relies on commercial paper – short-term debt that matures in less than a year and these days costs about 0.2% – to fund working capital.

Commercial paper is typically available to companies of investment grade quality. However, during the credit crisis of 2008 even borrowers who had the A-2/P-2 rating, the second-highest CP ranking, were locked out of that market.

The ADP Dealer Services business constitutes only about 15% of ADP's current revenue and has been estimated to be worth $5bn (ADP's current market cap is $37bn). With its debt capacity, the motor business will send back $700m in cash to ADP that will be used to buy back shares. And so ADP will remain a massive business, but only focused on payroll and other human resource functions such as benefits and recruiting management. With its formidable size, its CP rating of A-1/P-1 went untouched. The perfect outcome, if you happened to notice.

via a money market fund: the fund buys a range of CP issues (and other instruments) and so, while it is committed to hold each CP to maturity, because it is well diversified, with many securities maturing every day, it is able to pay out to money market fund investors when they demand it. The Federal Reserve Board posts the current rates being paid on US commercial paper by non-financial and financial firms on its website – see Table 9.8.

Table 9.8 US Federal Reserve Federal funds rate and examples of commercial paper rates in August 2014, per cent annualised

Instruments	2014 Aug 25	2014 Aug 26	2014 Aug 27	2014 Aug 28	2014 Aug 29	Week ending		2014 Aug
						Aug 29	Aug 22	
Federal funds (effective)	0.09	0.09	0.09	0.09	0.07	0.09	0.09	0.09
Commercial paper								
Non-financial								
1-month	0.08	0.07	0.07	0.07	0.06	0.07	0.10	0.08
2-month	0.09	0.10	0.09	0.10	0.09	0.09	0.10	0.09
3-month	0.11	0.12	0.11	0.12	0.11	0.11	0.11	0.11
Financial								
1-month	0.09	0.07	0.07	0.08	0.07	0.08	0.09	0.09
2-month	0.12	0.11	0.12	0.11	0.12	0.12	0.12	0.11
3-month	0.13	0.13	0.14	0.13	0.13	0.13	0.13	0.13

Source: Data from www.federalreserve.gov/releases/h15/current/

Note issuance facility (NIF)

Note issuance facilities (variously known as revolving underwriting facilities, RUFs, note purchase facilities, commercial paper programmes and Euronote facilities) were developed as services to large corporations wanting to borrow by selling commercial paper or medium-term notes into the financial markets. The largest corporations often expect to be selling a series of different CPs or MTNs issues over 5–7 years. Instead of handling each individual issue themselves as the need arises they can go to an **arranging bank(s)** at the outset, which will, at various points over the, say, five years, approach a panel of other banks to ask them to purchase the debt as it becomes needed. The loan obligation can be in a currency that suits the borrower at the time. The borrower can also select the length of life of the paper (say, 14 days or 105 days) and whether it pays fixed or floating interest rates.

If there is a time when it is difficult to sell the paper to the banks then the borrower can turn to those banks that have signed up to be underwriters of the facility to buy the issue, or, depending on the deal, borrow from the bank or banks in the syndicate. Underwriters take a fee for these guarantees. Most of the time they do not have to do anything, but occasionally, often when the market is troubled, they have to step in.

Some people draw a distinction between an NIF and an RUF: with an RUF the underwriting banks agree to provide loans should the CP/MTN issue fail, but under an NIF they could either lend or purchase the outstanding CP or notes. However, these definitions do not seem to be rigidly applied.

By allowing borrowers the choice at each point of borrowing of either drawing a loan from the bank(s) at an agreed spread over Libor or selling CP/MTN through banks, the borrower gets the best of both worlds: a bank loan (committed bank facility) fallback, or access to the financial markets in corporate debt instruments. Which is chosen depends on interest rates at the time. One-off fees are payable for arrangement and annual fees for bank participation (actual lending) and commitment (standing ready to lend).

An insider's view

Opus plc agrees a £300 million NIF with a bank for six years. This lead bank asks other banks to join the syndicate. Opus obtains a credit rating for commercial paper that it might issue. Opus can repay funds drawn down under the NIF at will, without penalty. Opus decides it would like to borrow £150 million starting in eight days for a six-month period. It tells the lead bank that it would like either to take a six-month loan at the rate stated in the NIF loan agreement, which is Libor + 95bp, or to issue CP to a predetermined syndicate of banks and dealers at the rate currently being offered by that dealer group. Currently, six-month Libor is 1.4%, thus the loan will cost 2.35% (annual rate) for six months. The lead bank comes back with the CP interest rate of 2.56%, so Opus decides to exercise its right under the NIF to borrow the £150 million from the banks. For the remaining five and a half years Opus will have the right to repay and then take out fresh loans or issue fresh CPs as the need arises.

Really well-known creditworthy issuers can opt to avoid the cost of maintaining the backstop option of access to these loans (arrangement and participation fees) and simply rely on their ability to periodically attract lenders in the CP market under the NIF framework, but they still pay for **swinglines** and **backup**. That is, to obtain a credit rating CP issuers must have unused credit lines from banks to provide liquidity in the event of an interruption to the CP market preventing rolling over (the issue of new CP as old ones mature). Swinglines are bank commitments to provide same-day credit facilities to cover a few days of the CP maturities. Backup lines, sometimes uncommitted, are available for the longer maturities. There is a variety of liquidity backups that can be acceptable for this purpose, including cash and securities, but most CP issuers rely on credit lines from banks.

US commercial paper (USCP)

The largest commercial paper market in the world, by far, is the US, distantly followed by Japan, Canada, France, the UK and other developed economies. According to US law, because its maturity is less than 270 days, commercial paper does not have to be registered with the Securities and Exchange Commission, the main US financial regulator, and therefore is not subject to the time-consuming and costly process required by US federal regulations. Figure 9.1 gives data for USCP from 1992. The amount of CP outstanding peaked in 2006 at nearly $2 trillion, of which half was asset-backed CP, before succumbing to the world-wide recession and loss of confidence and falling to around $1 trillion.

Now about one-third is **asset-backed commercial paper (ABCP)**, i.e. com-mercial paper secured on the collateral of assets – for example, the issuer has the right to receive monthly interest from mortgage payers, credit card holders, vehicle loans or some other regular income and uses the cash flow from these assets to pay the commercial paper when it becomes due and to provide collateral. The issuers of ABCP are usually special entities/companies set up by a bank. These, special purpose vehicles (SPVs) or **structured investment vehicles (SIVs)** or **conduits,** buy the assets (rights to mortgage interest, etc.) after rais-ing money from issuing commercial paper. Thus they are 'bankruptcy remote' from the parent company that supplied the assets – if they go bust the parent bank can still survive. Also they are perceived as less risky for the investors because of the security of the assigned assets, so if the parent goes bust the lenders still have the collateral (right to mortgage income, etc.) in the conduit.

At least that was the theory, but many conduits and their parent banks disap-peared or nearly blew up in 2008 when they could not roll over the ABCP as they were accustomed to doing. When the financial crisis occurred many of these cash flows dried up, causing major problems for both issuers and holders of CP. Rolling over CP became difficult, confidence in this market plummeted and com-panies found it nearly impossible to obtain the CP funding on which they relied.

The commercial paper market can be very influential in corporate life. For example, in 2005, Standard & Poor's downgraded the commercial paper

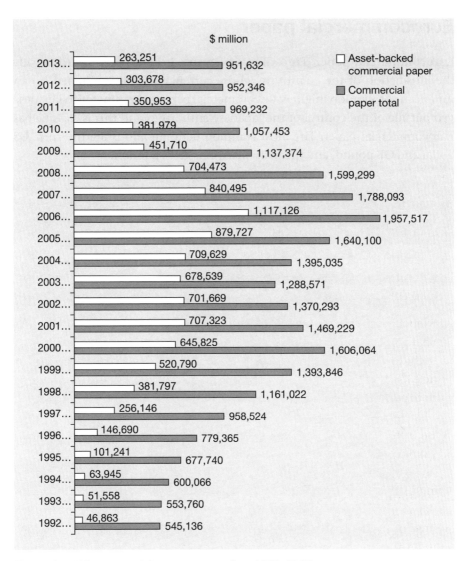

Figure 9.1 US commercial paper outstanding, 1992–2013

Source: Data from www.federalreserve.gov

of Ford and General Motors, making their commercial paper unattractive to investors, leading to an increase in the cost of financing to these companies and reducing the global confidence in both the companies and their products. This contributed to their financial crisis in 2009, when General Motors was forced into bankruptcy.

Eurocommercial paper

Eurocommercial paper (Euro-CP) is paper that is issued and placed outside the jurisdiction of the country in whose currency it is denominated. So an American corporation might issue commercial paper denominated in Japanese yen outside of the control of the Japanese authorities and this is classified as Eurocommercial paper. The most common denominations are the euro, US dollar and GB pound, and the main place of issue is London.

CHAPTER 10
REPURCHASE AGREEMENTS AND CERTIFICATES OF DEPOSIT

Repurchase agreements (repos)

A repo is a way of borrowing large amounts of money for a short time using a sale and repurchase agreement in which securities are sold for cash at an agreed price with a promise to buy them back, or identical ones, at a specified (higher) price at a future date. The interest on the agreement is the difference between the initial sale price and the agreed buy-back.

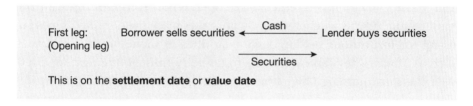

One, or a few days, later:

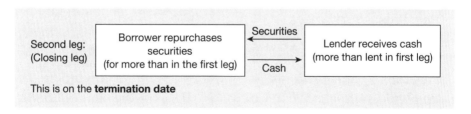

Because the agreements provide collateral backup for the lender, most often in the form of government-backed securities such as Treasury bills, the interest rate is lower than on a typical unsecured loan from a bank. If the borrower defaults on its obligations to buy back on maturity the lender can hold on to or sell the securities they bought in the first leg of the repo. In the absence of such a default if a coupon is payable on bonds during the term of the repo the original owner receives it, maintaining the same economic exposure to the security as though the economic ownership had not been sold. Thus, despite legal title to the securities being transferred, economic benefits and market risk are retained, so if the price of the security falls in the market it is the original owner who suffers the capital loss.

Repos have the advantage that they can be tailor-made to suit circumstances – the maturity can be any number of days and the amount fully variable, whereas many other forms of lending via financial securities tend to be for specific amounts and periods of time.

Repos are used very regularly by banks and other financial institutions to borrow large amounts of money from each other. Secured lending, such as repo lending, increased in volume following the financial crisis as more banks, etc. became reluctant to participate in unsecured lending, deeming it too risky. Companies do use the repo markets, but much less frequently than the banks do. This market is also manipulated by central banks to manage their monetary policy and maintain stability in their economy (see Chapter 16).

The term for repos is usually between 1 and 14 days, but can be up to a year, and occasionally there is no end date, an **open repo**. **Overnight repos** are the most common type, where the repurchase takes place the next day. Repos are useful for institutions holding large quantities of money market securities such as T-bills. They can gain access to liquidity through the repo for a few days while maintaining a high level of inventory in short-term securities.

Example 10.1

Repurchase agreement

A high street bank has the need to borrow £26 million for 14 days. It agrees to sell a portfolio of its financial assets, in this case government bonds, to a lender for £26 million. An agreement is drawn up (a repo) by which the bank agrees to repurchase the portfolio 14 days later for £26,005,285.48. The extra amount of £5,285.48 represents the repo rate of interest (an annual rate of 0.53%) on £26 million over 14 days.[1] The sterling market day count basis is actual/365.

---

[1] The formula for this calculation can be found in Chapter 14.

A **reverse repo (RRP)** is the lender's side of the transaction, an agreement in which securities are *purchased* with a promise to *sell them back* at an agreed price at a future date. Traders may do this to gain interest. Alternatively, it could be to cover another market transaction. For example, a trading house may need to obtain some Treasury bills or bonds temporarily because it has shorted them – sold them before buying – and needs to find a supply to meet its obligations, so it places a reverse repo order to get an inflow of the securities now. In a transaction, the terms repo and reverse repo are used according to which party initiated the transaction, i.e. if a seller initiates the transaction, it is a repo; if the transaction is initiated by a buyer, it is a reverse repo.

Example 10.2

Reverse repo

A bank has £45 million of spare cash for one day. A reverse repo agreement is drawn up, by which the bank agrees to buy £45 million of government securities from a borrower and sell them back the next day for £45,000,517.81. The extra amount of £517.81 represents overnight interest on £45 million at an annual rate of 0.42%.[2]

Repo deals are usually individually negotiated between the two parties (**bilateral repos**) and are therefore designed to suit the length of time of borrowing and the amount for each of them, thus there is usually little need for redemption before the agreed date. However, if circumstances change and the lender needs the money quickly it might be possible to arrange an off-setting reverse repo transaction.

Traditionally banks formed the largest group of borrowers in the repo markets, but now, as Article 10.1 makes clear, hedge funds, property funds and mutual funds have overtaken them.

---

[2] The formula for this calculation can be found in Chapter 14.

Article 10.1

Big investors replace banks in $4.2tn repo market

By Tracy Alloway

Financial Times May 29, 2014

Big investors, including hedge funds, mutual funds and real estate trusts, are replacing banks as the biggest users of the overnight funding market that played a key role in the financial crisis.

The repo market, in which borrowers pledge securities as collateral against very short-term loans, was once a popular method for banks to source cheap financing. But the strategy proved destabilising in 2008, when lenders in the repo market lost confidence in mortgage-backed collateral and pulled back on funding.

Since 2008, the repo market has been shrinking as banks have shifted to longer-term financing in response to new regulatory capital rules and other post-crisis pressures. What remains of the $4.2tn market is increasingly being taken up by non-bank entities such as real estate investment trusts (Reits), mutual funds and hedge funds, turning to repo to boost returns during an era of low rates. By using more borrowed money, or leverage, they can take larger positions, but they are also taking a bet that markets will remain stable.

The growing use of repo has been particularly marked among Reits, which have overtaken banks and broker-dealers as the largest borrowers in the market. To purchase long-term mortgage assets, Reits have increased their repo borrowings to $281bn, up from $90.4bn in 2009.

Closed-end funds, which invest in assets ranging from corporate bonds to municipal debt, also have increased their borrowing in the repo market, from $2.74bn at the end of 2007 to almost $8bn now, according to Fitch Ratings data.

Industry participants say there is ample anecdotal evidence that other types of big investors are lending out more of their assets to generate greater returns.

'It's becoming more of a popular strategy,' said one repo specialist at a large bank. 'It's an opportunity to enhance yield and hit the return hurdles that investors are looking for.'

Closed-end funds have historically used leverage to help increase their returns. 'In the low interest rate environment, repo is very attractive,' said Yuriy Layvand, who analyses closed-end funds at Fitch. 'They're taking that money and investing it further out in the yield curve in fixed income assets.'

Additional reporting by Michael Mackenzie.

Generals, specifics and specials

Repos may be backed by **general collateral (GC repos)** where the securities are fungible and acceptable to the cash lender; the lender of funds is willing to accept any of a variety of Treasury and other related securities as collateral, as long as it is of the required credit quality. An alternative is **specific repos**, where the collateral is a specified security.

Special collateral repos, 'specials', are used extensively in the financial markets. Here the lender designates a particular security as the *only* acceptable collateral. Dealers and others lend money on special collateral repos in order to borrow specific securities needed to deliver against short sales. Superficially, this sounds the same as a specific repo. The key difference is that a special has a repo interest rate that is lower than the GC repo rate. Also there is exceptional specific demand in the cash market for those particular bonds trading 'on special'. Clearly, not all repo rates with a precisely defined agreed security are below the GC repo rate. Such issues could be called 'specifics' but should not be called 'specials'.

To be clear: specials are often used to cover short sales where a dealer sells securities it does not own but still needs to deliver. It then must obtain the designated securities through a repo – a **stock-driven transaction**. It might be so keen to obtain the securities that it will hand over cash for them, expecting little extra cash on the second leg in the repo. The interest rate on a special collateral RP is commonly called a **specials rate**.

From the perspective of the institution that happens to be holding the designated securities, it can gain from temporarily selling them through a repo. This may make sense even if it has no need to borrow money at that time. For example, if the specials rate is 1% per annum, money could be borrowed at this rate using the securities as collateral. This money can then be lent out in the GC repo market. If the interest rate here is 1.4% then a profit can be achieved on the interest rate difference.

There are times when the supply of particular securities is limited. Then the specials rate for the security may be significantly below the general collateral rate. When interest rates are very low, as in 2014 in the eurozone, the repo interest can be negative: the cash transferred in the second leg is less than that in the first.

Benchmarks

In the UK a benchmark for interest charged on repos with a maturity one day later is arrived at daily by the WMBA by consulting a group of interdealer brokers on the rates being charged in the market place with lenders and borrowers who use brokers to transact. The rate is called **RONIA** or **Ronia**, the **Repurchase Overnight Index Average**. This overnight funding rate is the weighted average rate to four decimal places of all secured sterling overnight cash transactions brokered in London by contributing WMBA member firms between midnight and 4.15pm with all counterparties regardless of deal size. The weighting is according to the principal amount of deposits which were taken on that day. The gilts bought and repurchased for these deals are delivered via the settlement system called CREST. The borrowing member has gilts on its account to the required value delivered automatically to the CREST account of the money lender. Some advocates believe that Ronia has the potential to take over from the interbank rate in providing the 'risk-free' interest benchmark – after all, it has collateral backup whereas Libor does not, and it is based on actual transactions.

For euro-denominated repos in the eurozone we have benchmarks calculated daily by the interdealer broker **ICAP BrokerTec** and fixed-income electronic trading platform **MTS**. Together they produce the **RepoFunds Rate** indices based on trades executed through their electronic platforms. These are for one-day repos using government bonds. The main benchmark combines the repos issued in all the eurozone countries, but there are also repo benchmarks for individual German, French and Italian repos using their government bonds and bills as collateral. RepoFunds Rate indices are reported on an actual/360 day count convention and are published at 18:35 UK/19:35 CET via Bloomberg and Reuters. They can also be seen at www.repofundsrate.com – see Table 10.1,

Table 10.1 Euro overnight repo rates, 8 September 2014

	Value (%)	Index Vol (€m)	Initial Vol (€m)
RFR Euro	−0.028	167789	219635
RFR France	−0.045	27942	38162
RFR Germany	−0.059	48231	67208
RFR Italy	0.01	58149	70637

Source: www.repofundsrate.com/overview.htm#

showing average repo rates combining general collateral and specific collateral trades. Note that average interest rates are below zero for three indices. In other words, for a proportion of these deals market participants are willing to pay interest on money *they* lend. The market makers and other dealers are using the repo market to borrow bonds that are in strong demand in the cash market (and therefore sometimes scarce) in order to fulfil delivery commitments on sales of those bonds in the cash market.

The **STOXX® GC Pooling index** is a benchmark for secured euro lending transactions and binding quotations that take place on the **Eurex Repo GC Pooling Market**. These range from overnight to 12-month terms. Eurex Repo also organises a **Swiss Franc Repo Market** for financial institutions to borrow and lend in the interbank repo market. A wide range of high-quality fixed-income securities apart from government bonds and bills is accepted by the market participants with terms from intraday up to 12 months.

In America, the Depository Trust and Clearing Corporation **DTCC GCF Repo Indices** track the average daily interest rate paid for the most-traded repo contracts for the sale and repurchase of (1) US Treasury bills, (2) federal agency securities and (3) mortgage-backed securities (MBS) issued by Fannie Mae and Freddie Mac. Table 10.2 shows the extraordinarily low rates on 9 September 2014 – less than 0.1% per annum. Figure 10.1 tracks how US repo rates changed over a year – the lowest line is for the strongest collateral, Treasury bonds and bills, the middle line is for federal agency securities and the highest line is for mortgage-backed securities. Figure 10.2 displays the amount borrowed: billions every day. The interest on dollar repos is based on actual number of days of the deal divided into a 360-day year.

In the US, the Federal Reserve of New York section known as **The Desk** uses repos and reverse repos for monetary policy, adding or draining reserves of

Table 10.2 US repo rates as reported by the Depository Trust and Clearing Corporation for 9 September 2014

Security	Latest	1-week	52-week		Par value (billions USD)
			High	Low	
Agency	0.076	0.094	0.261	0.020	15.780
MBS	0.082	0.104	0.286	0.019	68.796
Treasury	0.067	0.099	0.255	0.010	89.796

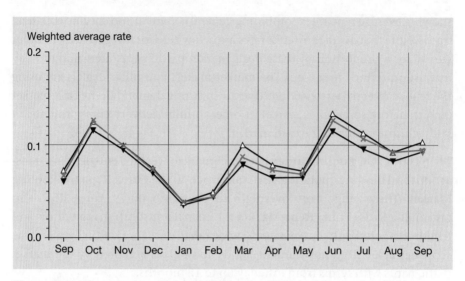

Figure 10.1 US repo rates of interest, September 2013 to 9 September 2014 as measured by the DTCC GCF Repo Index®

Source: www.dtcc.com/charts/dtcc-gcf-repo-index.aspx

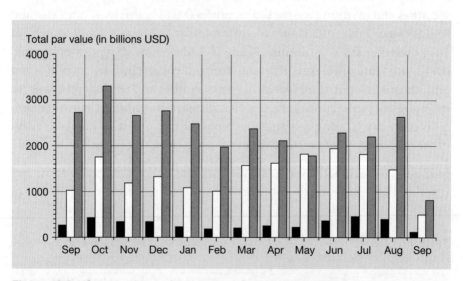

Figure 10.2 US repo volume of transactions September 2013 to 9 September 2014. The first column is agency securities, the second is mortgage-backed securities and the third Treasury

Source: www.dtcc.com/charts/dtcc-gcf-repo-index.aspx

cash to and from the banking system. Repos and reverse repos are arranged by auction among the 21 primary dealers and the 49 reverse repo counterparties approved by the Fed, all of them respected banking/broking institutions. Both primary dealers and reverse repo counterparties must have substantial assets. In 2014 the Fed embarked on greater intervention in the repo market so that it could influence short-term interest rates as the economic recovery took hold – see Article 10.2.

Article 10.2

New York Federal Reserve takes on key role in repo market

By Tracy Alloway and Michael Mackenzie

Financial Times June 19, 2014

The Federal Reserve Bank of New York has emerged as the single largest player in an important segment of the short-term lending market that was at the epicentre of the financial crisis.

The Fed's decision to quadruple its trading with government money market funds in the repurchase or 'repo market' is a sign that the central bank is now engaging more directly with the shadow banking system at the expense of large Wall Street banks.

Historically, the repo market was where big banks pawned out their securities such as Treasury bonds to lenders including money market funds, insurers and mutual funds, in exchange for short-term financing. Now the Fed is stepping in to trade as well as it prepares to end its current near-zero interest rate policy.

Armed with a balance sheet of $4.3tn of bonds purchased during quantitative easing, the Fed is using what it calls its reverse repo programme, or RRP, to trade with money funds at a time when tough new regulatory standards have made such borrowing less attractive for the banks.

Rather than lending to the banks, money market funds have sharply boosted their dealings with the US central bank.

Between September 2013 and the end of May, government money market funds increased their use of repo trades with the New York Fed by $65bn to a total of $87bn, while decreasing their repo holdings with dealer-banks by $38bn, according to a study by Fitch Ratings.

The growing presence of the Fed in repo is a signal that it is testing new ways to control short-term interest rates once it starts tightening monetary policy.

When official short-term rates are eventually pushed higher, the Fed plans to use the RRP to drain cash from the financial system via short-term loans of Treasuries from its huge balance sheet.

Robert Grossman, managing director at Fitch, said the change in the Fed's presence in the repo market had been dramatic and that the central bank could use RRP to significantly escalate its role.

 Source: Alloway, T. and Mackenzie, M. (2014) New York Federal Reserve takes on key role in repo market, *Financial Times*, 19 June.
© The Financial Times Limited 2014. All Rights Reserved.

Haircuts

Although the securities bought and sold are considered relatively safe collateral for the lender of the cash, there is always the danger that the price of the bills, etc. might fluctuate during the period of the agreement to the detriment of the buyer who is committed to a pre-agreed selling price. The buyer might also be exposed to illiquidity risk and counterparty risk related to the securities bought. Therefore it is common practice to impose a **haircut** on the collateral, where the seller receives the amount of cash secured on the collateral less a margin (over-collateralisation). If the haircut were 2%, the seller of a £200 million repo would receive £196,000,000 cash in return for £200 million worth of securities. The repo interest is only applied to the lesser amount.

Another way of looking at this is that if a bank wanted to own £200 million of gilts it would only be necessary to find £4 million of cash. The other £196 million could be borrowed in the repo market by using the £200 million of gilts as security.

Haircuts on Treasuries are relatively low; if the collateral used is mortgage-backed bonds or corporate bonds, the haircut will be a larger percentage. Haircuts rose even for Treasuries in many countries during the financial crisis as doubt crept in about government default risk. Haircuts are lower for high-quality counterparties, e.g. a central bank supplying collateral in a repo. They are also lower for overnight repos than longer-term ones due to the lower securities price fluctuation risk, and for securities trading in highly liquid markets. Longer-term bonds are more volatile than short-term bonds or bills and so if they are used as collateral a large haircut will be required, as it will if a non-standard legal agreement is used for the repo.

Article 10.3 discusses some new rules on minimum haircuts. If the market value of the collateral drops by a larger amount or percentage than an agreed threshold during the term, the lender might be entitled to **variation margin**. This is a call for extra cash or collateral to be handed over.

Article 10.3

Terms laid down for taming shadow bank risk

Sam Fleming and Tracy Alloway

Financial Times October 14, 2014

Global regulators have taken a landmark step towards taming risk in a key segment of the shadow banking system, outlining tougher rules on collateral for short-term lending which will affect both banks and non-bank players.

Shadow banks have emerged as a key regulatory concern as risk migrates out of the traditional banking sector into more thinly policed reaches of the financial markets.

Shadow banks can include a broad array of institutions engaged in bank-like activities, among them hedge funds, private equity groups and money market funds.

The Financial Stability Board, an umbrella group of regulators, on Monday night published a framework imposing minimum requirements on the collateral needed when such firms borrow money from banks through short-term loans secured by stocks or bonds.

The global standards are intended to stop excessive lending, and so avoid a repeat of the reckless behaviour that helped precipitate the financial crisis of 2008. They also take aim at a key segment of the shadow banking world, known as the repurchase, or 'repo', market.

This emerged as a prime area of weakness during the crisis and regulators are said to be concerned about the potential impact that a 'fire sale' of assets used as collateral for loans could have on the wider financial system.

Crucially, the FSB's minimum floors for repo transactions are higher than initial proposals made in August last year, following calls for tough standards from US regulators.

In a significant step, the FSB said it would also consult on applying the standards to deals struck between non-banks, rather than simply limiting them to repo transactions undertaken between banks and non-banks.

However, the FSB rules would still fail to capture transactions that use government bonds as collateral, focusing instead on private debt and stocks, amid anxiety from some governments about the potential impact on sovereign debt markets.

➡

The FSB now wants a minimum 1.5% 'haircut' for corporate bonds with a maturity of between one and five years, up from 1% before, and a 6% haircut for equities, instead of 4% previously. The latter would mean that a borrower would have to post $106 of equity collateral for a $100 loan.

The FSB also set out non-numerical standards aimed at tackling the risk that haircuts get whittled away in benign market conditions. Mark Carney, chairman of the FSB and Bank of England governor, said the rules marked a 'big step forward' in the global shadow banking agenda.

Daniel Tarullo, chairman of the FSB Standing Committee on Supervisory and Regulatory Co-operation, added: 'Securities financing transactions such as repos are important funding tools for a wide range of market participants, including non-bank financial firms.

'The implementation of the numerical haircut floors on securities financing transactions will reduce the build-up of excessive leverage and liquidity risk by non-banks during peaks in the credit and economic cycle.'

The FSB stressed that market participants should continue to set higher haircuts than the official requirements where prudent. The FSB said firms had expected only a 'minimal' impact on market volume from its proposals.

The FSB added that the haircut floors could in future be raised and lowered as part of efforts to lean against fluctuations in the financial cycle, but that this would require further work.

The repo market has already been under pressure from new rules that make it more expensive for banks to broker the transactions or undertake their own repo borrowing. While many in the market concede that runs in the repo market were a prime cause of Lehman Brothers' collapse in 2008, they also warn that limiting the repo market could affect liquidity in a long list of financial assets.

Source: Fleming, S. and Alloway, T. (2014) Terms laid down for taming shadow bank risk, *Financial Times*, 14 October.
© The Financial Times Limited 2014. All Rights Reserved.

Tri-party repo

Many repo markets are based on bilateral deals between borrower and lender. But a common form in the US is the **tri-party repo (TPR)**, where an intermediary, a custodian, acts for both seller and purchaser and undertakes all administrative tasks. There are two custodian banks, Bank of New York Mellon and JPMorgan, which help to administer a repo agreement between two parties. Lenders place money with the custodian bank, which in turn lends it through a repo to another institution. Such a model functions well when liquid assets such as Treasuries are being used, as this type of collateral can easily be sold.

During the credit boom, which peaked in the first half of 2007, the type of collateral being pledged for cash in repo transactions steadily migrated away from Treasuries and towards other assets such as private label mortgages, corporate bonds and equities. This reflected the drive by investors to boost their returns, gaining higher interest when lending against poorer quality collateral. Tri-party was very popular with investment banks as it allowed them to finance their balance sheets with short-term funding. However, as soon as market sentiment turned negative on lower-quality or more complex assets, investors that had funded these repo agreements began to pull their money out. That sparked a run on the investment banks. The vulnerabilities of this system were highlighted with the near-failure of Bear Stearns six months before Lehman's demise. Article 10.4 illustrates the concerns of US authorities about the TPR market.

Article 10.4

Repo 'fire sale' risk worries regulators

By Michael Mackenzie and Tracy Alloway

Financial Times October 2, 2013

The prospect of financial assets being dumped in a 'fire sale' has re-emerged as a substantial risk in a crucial $2tn funding market used by US banks, despite changes since the financial crisis to reduce risk.

The tri-party repo market, where banks loan out their securities in exchange for short-term loans from investors, has been one of the key areas of financial reform after playing a major role in the 2008 collapse of Lehman Brothers.

Banks use the market to pledge their assets as security, or collateral, in exchange for short-term loans from lenders that include money market funds, insurers and mutual funds. In 2008, much of that financing was suddenly pulled away after the value of mortgage-related collateral underpinning the loans was called into doubt.

Fire sales, where assets are sold in a manner that can sharply depress prices and thereby pressure other investors into selling their assets, were a hallmark of the financial crisis.

While much of the market has been strengthened, regulators including Bill Dudley, president of the Federal Reserve Bank of New York, say that a run on repo collateral remains a risk. The issue is likely to dominate a New York Fed conference on Friday.

'This is a process that's providing credit from one part of the market to another,' said Martin Hansen, senior director at Fitch Ratings. 'But the issue is that at one end of this chain of credit you have risk averse, short-term lenders. If they have concerns, then that can create ripple effects along the rest of the chain and beyond.'

Fitch estimates that the use of interest rate-sensitive securities such as US Treasuries and other US government-backed securities as collateral in the tri-party repo market fell $187bn between May and July, after the Fed began talking about winding down its emergency economic support. That suggests sell-offs in the repo market remain an issue more than five years after the crisis.

'The risk is that once a dealer [bank] goes under, money funds have to liquidate the securities they hold and a money fund may not have the expertise to liquidate large amounts of securities,' said Scott Skyrm, a former repo broker.

The New York Fed has overseen reform of the tri-party repo market in recent years, with a heavy focus on the role played by the two custodian banks that incur daily counterparty risk, JPMorgan Chase and Bank of New York Mellon.

While dependence on so-called 'intraday credit' from the two banks, along with poor liquidity and credit risk management practices by the banks, has largely been addressed, the spectre of fire sales remains an issue for regulators.

Regulators also point to a lack of data concerning the bilateral repo market, which operates in a similar way but without custodians. Estimates of the market's size vary from about $3tn to $5tn, and a report from the Office of Financial Research this week warned of 'data gaps' in securities lending and repo markets.

Friday's meeting organised by the New York Fed will bring together academics, market participants and other regulators. Speakers are expected to discuss ways of setting up 'a process for orderly liquidation' of repo collateral.

Whereas in the UK, US and many other developed countries repo rates are currently low, typically between 0% and 1%, in other parts of the world the rate can be considerably higher. The rates reflect the risk element, anticipated current and future degree of inflation, and the credit rating in each country – see Figure 10.3.

The sell/buy-back

Some countries, such as Italy, never developed, or were slow to develop, the legal frameworks, IT systems and settlement systems for repo transactions. The

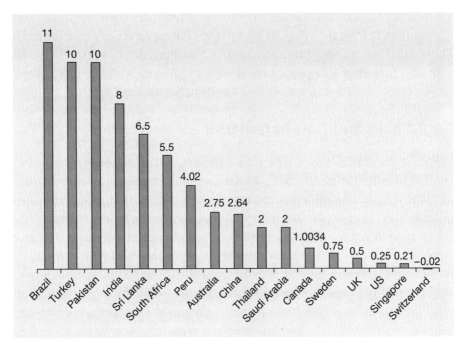

Figure 10.3 Overnight repo rates, per cent (annualised), 2013/2014

Source: Data from national banks and other sources

sell/buy-back was created instead, which is very similar to a repo but involves an outright cash sale of bonds, and a *separate* agreement to buy back the bonds at a forward date. Coupon payments during the term are paid first to the buyer and only given to the original owner on termination.

Certificates of deposit (CDs)

Certificates of deposit are issued by banks when funds are deposited with them by other banks, corporations, individuals or investment companies. The certificates state that a deposit has been made (a **time deposit**) and that at the maturity date the bank will pay a sum higher than that originally deposited, i.e. they are issued at face value and at maturity the holder receives the face amount plus interest. The maturities can be any length of time, with a minimum of one week, and are typically between one to four months. But they can be issued with a maturity date of five years or longer. For those lasting less than one year the interest is generally payable on maturity. However, some short-term CDs also occasionally pay variable interest rates, e.g. the interest on a 6-month CD changes every 30 days depending on interbank interest rates. Those dated for over one year have interest paid annually, or sometimes semi-annually; they may also pay a variable rate of interest, with the rate altered, say, each year, based on the rates on a benchmark rate, e.g. Libor.

Negotiable and non-negotiable

CDs can be negotiable, that is, permitted to be traded in a secondary market to another investor before the maturity date, although many negotiable CDs are not all that liquid, with few potential buyers interested in trading. CDs can also be designated non-negotiable, meaning they have to be held to maturity by the original investor – there is a penalty on withdrawal of cash from the bank before the maturity date. The advantage of negotiable CDs is that although they cannot be redeemed before maturity at the issuing bank without a penalty, the original depositor can achieve liquidity while the bank issuing the certificate has a deposit held with it until the maturity date. The rate of interest paid on negotiable CDs is lower than a fixed deposit because of the attraction of liquidity. A company with surplus funds can put it into a CD knowing that if its situation changes and it needs extra cash, it can sell the negotiable CD. The tradable value of the CD rises as the remaining length of its maturity reduces.

United Kingdom and United States of America

At the centre of the secondary market is a network of brokers and dealers in CDs, striking deals over the telephone or on the internet. CDs are normally issued in lots ranging from £100,000 to £500,000 in the UK. Most sterling CDs are held by other banks operating in the UK, building societies and other money market players. Individual/personal holdings are negligible. For sterling CDs the interest is calculated on an actual/365 days basis.

Lot sizes are generally $100,000 to $1,000,000 in the US for the main wholesale market, with similar sized lots in the eurozone, Japan and other countries. In the US, however, CDs are frequently bought by retail investors in denominations that can go as low as $100. Individuals generally buy non-negotiable CDs because the minimum denomination for a negotiable CD is $100,000 (also termed a **jumbo CD**). Most retail-focused CDs are guaranteed by the Federal Deposit Insurance Corporation (FDIC) for up to $250,000 per depositor, meaning that if the issuing bank does not redeem them this government-sponsored agency will. For US CDs the interest is calculated on an actual/360 basis, with the interest generally paid at maturity.

Quotations

CDs are quoted in the trading markets on a yield to maturity basis. So, if a deposit of £100,000 is made and a CD is handed over which states that after one-quarter of the year the holder will receive £100,500, the yield to maturity is £500 divided by £100,000 multiplied by 4 to annualise it. Thus the annual rate of interest is 2%. (See Chapter 14 for more on CD calculations.)

Many CDs issued today lack a paper certificate, which, given that 'certificate' is in the title, seems a little oxymoronic. These 'dematerialised' CDs are held as electronic book entries only. Euroclear operates a book entry system in London. Here CDs are issued and transferred using **Delivery Versus Payment (DVP)**, meaning that the electronic transfer of ownership in the secondary market is at the same time as payment.

Eurocurrency CDs

As well as domestic currency CDs there are **Eurocurrency certificates of deposit, Euro-CDs**, outside the jurisdiction of the authorities of the currency of denomination. Standard **Eurocurrency deposits** (not CDs) have fixed maturities – say seven days – and you cannot get at that money until the seven days have passed. By issuing Eurodollar CDs banks are able to offer an advantage if those CDs are negotiable, by allowing depositors to sell the CDs to other investors before maturity. Those issued by a bank with a high credit standing are likely to have greater liquidity. Eurodollar CDs tend to offer higher yields than CDs issued in dollars in the US because the American-based CDs have the backing of the Federal Reserve regulatory environment for banks, making them safer for investors.

CHAPTER 11
BILLS OF EXCHANGE AND BANKER'S ACCEPTANCES

Bills of exchange and **banker's acceptances** are instruments that are particularly useful in helping to oil the wheels of international commerce. They enable corporations to obtain credit from suppliers or raise money, and also to trade with foreign corporations at low risk of financial inconvenience or loss. An illustration of the risk problem is provided in the following example.

Example 11.1

The international trade problem

Tractors UK has found a firm in South Africa that wishes to buy £12 million worth of its tractors. Tractors UK cannot simply send its tractors to South Africa in the hope that the payment will be sent, nor can the South African firm send £12 million in the hope that the tractors will be sent. The two companies do not know each other well enough to trust that the transaction will be carried out correctly on each side. The solution is to use a bill of exchange or a banker's acceptance, which will provide a legally enforceable promise of payment of £12 million to Tractors UK, which can send the tractors off to South Africa, knowing with a high degree of certainty that payment will be made.

Bills of exchange

Bills of exchange have been used to smooth the progress of overseas trade for a long time. Known to have been used by the Babylonians, Egyptians, Greeks and Romans, the bill of exchange appeared in its present form during the

13th century among the Lombards of northern Italy who engaged in widespread foreign trading. These instruments became particularly useful in the burgeoning international trade of the 19th and 20th centuries.

The seller of goods to be exported to a buyer in another country frequently grants the customer a number of months in which to pay. The seller will draw up a bill of exchange (also called a **trade bill**). This is a legal document showing the indebtedness of the buyer. The exporter also obtains a **bill of lading** from the carrier to show that the goods have been appropriately despatched. The airline, shipping firm or other carrier signs the bill of lading and sends it to the exporter or its bank, confirming that the goods have been received by the carrier, that the carrier accepts responsibility to deliver the goods to the importer, and showing evidence of ownership of the goods, insurance certificates and commercial invoices. Then the relevant documents are sent to the importer or its bank.

At this point the bill of exchange may be forwarded to and **accepted** by the customer, which means that the customer signs a promise to pay the stated amount and currency on the due date (a **time draft**). The due date is usually 90 days later, but 30-, 60- or 180-day bills of exchange are not uncommon. However, note that some bills of exchange are **sight drafts ('documents against payment' drafts)**, payable on demand immediately.

More usual is for the bill first to be sent to the exporter's bank, which, in turn, sends the draft and the documents to a bank in the importer's country with which the exporter's bank has an ongoing relationship. This **correspondent bank** will be instructed to get the draft signed, that is, accepted, by the importer, or to receive payment in the case of a sight draft. Then the correspondent bank will hand over the bill of lading documents permitting the importer to claim the goods. With payment on a sight draft the correspondent bank will transfer the funds received from the importer to the exporter's bank, which will credit the exporter's account. Fees will be charged for facilitating these transactions. With time bills the exporter will receive a promise to pay in, say, 90 days.

The banks have reduced the risk for the exporter by ensuring that the goods are not released to the importer until money or a promise is in place. Also, for the time draft, there is a legal acknowledgement that a debt exists, facilitating easier access to the legal systems in the event of non-payment.

As well as the benefit of a potential credit period before paying on a time draft, risk for the importer is reduced because payment will be made only if the goods are present and correct with all the documentation.

Trading time drafts

With a time draft the bill is returned to the exporter who can either hold it until maturity or sell it at a discount. Many bills of exchange are traded in an active secondary market. The purchaser (discounter) in this market pays a lower amount than the sum to be received at maturity from the customer. The difference represents the discounter's interest payment. For example, the customer might have signed the bill promising to pay £300,000 in 90 days. The bill is sold immediately by the exporter to a discount house or bank for £297,000. After 90 days the discounter will realise a profit of £3,000 on a £297,000 asset. Through this arrangement the customer has the goods on 90 days credit terms, and the supplier has made a sale and immediately receives cash from the discount house amounting to 99% of the total due. The discounter, if it can borrow at less than 1% over 90 days, turns a healthy profit. The sequence of events is shown in Figure 11.1.

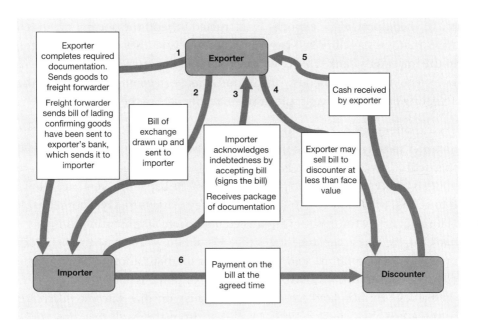

Figure 11.1 Bill of exchange sequence

Despite the simplification of Figure 11.1, many bills of exchange do not remain in the hands of the discounter until maturity but are traded a number of times before then.

Bills of exchange are normally used only for large transactions (> £100,000). The effective interest rate charged by the discounter is usually a competitive 150–400 basis points over interbank lending rates (e.g. Libor). The holder of the bill usually has recourse to both of the commercial companies: if the customer does not pay then the seller will be called upon to make good the debt. This overhanging credit risk for the exporter can sometimes be transferred (to, say, a bank) by buying credit insurance. If the bill is guaranteed by another bank or the importer has a very high credit standing it may not carry recourse rights for the holder to force the exporter to pay.

Banker's acceptances

A banker's acceptance, also known as an **acceptance credit**, is a time draft, which is a document stating the signatory will pay an amount at a future date, say in 90 days. Say, for example, that an importer buys goods from an exporter with an agreement to pay in three months. Instead of sending the bill to the importer, the exporter is instructed to send the document, which states that the signatory will pay a sum of money, at a set date in the future, to the importer's bank. This is 'accepted' by the importer's bank rather than by a customer. Simultaneously the importer makes a commitment to pay the accepting bank the relevant sum at the maturity date of the bill.

The exporter does not have to wait three months to receive cash despite the importer's bank not paying out for 90 days. This is because it is possible to sell this right to investors in the discount market long before the three months are up. This bank commitment to pay the holder of the banker's acceptance allows it to be sold with more credibility in the money markets to, say, another bank (a discounter) by the exporter after receiving it from an importing company's bank. So, say, the acceptance states that €1 million will be paid to the holder on 1 August. It could be sold to an investor (perhaps another bank) in the discount market for €980,000 on 15 June. The importer is obliged to reimburse the bank €1 million (and pay fees) on 1 August; on that date the purchaser of the acceptance credit collects €1 million from the bank that signed the acceptance, making a €20,000 return over six weeks.

While banker's acceptances are similar to bills of exchange between a seller and a buyer, they have the advantage that the organisation promising to pay is a reputable bank representing a lower credit risk to any subsequent discounter, thus they normally attract finer discount rates than bills of exchange. The holder of the instrument has two guarantors: the importer and the bank. It also has the collateral of the goods underlying the trade.

Not all banker's acceptances relate to overseas trade. Many are simply a way of raising money for a firm. The company in need of finance may ask its bank to create a banker's acceptance and hand it over. Then the company can sell it in the discount market at a time when it needs to raise some cash. They are very useful for companies expanding into new markets where their name is not known and therefore their creditworthiness is also unknown; they can take advantage of the superior creditworthiness of the bank issuing the acceptance, which guarantees that payment will be made.

There are three costs involved:

1 The bank charges **acceptance commission** for adding its name to the acceptance.
2 The difference between the face value of the acceptance and the discount price, which is the effective interest rate.
3 Dealers take a small cut as they connect firms that want to sell with companies that wish to invest in banker's acceptances.

These costs are relatively low compared with overdraft costs. However, this facility is available only in hundreds of thousands of pounds, euros, etc. and then only to the most creditworthy of companies. Figure 11.2 summarises the acceptance credit sequence for an export deal.

1 Banker's acceptance drafted and sent by an exporting company (or its bank) demanding payment for goods sent to an importer's bank. Importer makes arrangements with its bank to help it. Acceptance commission paid to the bank by importer.
2 The bank accepts the promise to pay a sum at a stated future date.
3 The banker's acceptance may be sold by the exporter at a discount.
4 The discounter pays cash for the banker's acceptance.
5 The bank pays the final holder of the banker's acceptance the due sum.
6 The importer pays to the bank the banker's acceptance due sum.

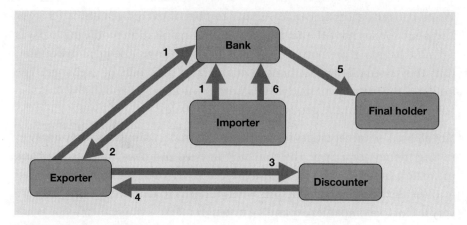

Figure 11.2 Banker's acceptance sequence – for an export deal

Example 11.2

The use of a banker's acceptance

A Dutch company buys €3.5 million of goods from a firm in Japan; it promises to pay for the goods in 60 days' time. The Dutch company asks its bank to accept the banker's acceptance. Once the bank has stamped 'accepted' on the document, it becomes a negotiable (sellable) instrument. The exporter receives the banker's acceptance. After 15 days, the Japanese company decides it needs some extra short-term finance and sells the acceptance at a discount of 0.60%, receiving €3,479,000. The exporter has been paid by banker's acceptance immediately the goods have been despatched. It can also shield itself from the risk of exchange rates shifting over the next 60 days by discounting the acceptance immediately, receiving euros and then converting these to yen. And, of course, the exporter is not exposed to the credit risk of the importer because it has the guarantee from the importer's bank.

Case study

HSBC Canada's banker's acceptance service

HSBC Canada advertises banker's acceptances (BAs) as a good way of raising money for businesses. Here is a page from its website:

Banker's acceptances (BAs)

Available in Canadian and US dollars, banker's acceptances (BAs) are an excellent alternative to traditional short-term borrowing or commercial paper.

BAs may provide your business with a lower cost borrowing alternative

- A BA is an unconditional non-interest bearing note that is issued by a borrowing company
- On acceptance of the BA, HSBC assumes an irrevocable liability for the borrower's debt
- BAs are typically more negotiable and reduce your borrowing costs

BAs are typically issued:

- At a discount to face value
- In bearer form
- With flexible maturity dates to a maximum of 1 year
- From 30 to 90 days

Source: HSBC Canada website www.hsbc.ca/1/2/business/business-banking/finance/bankers-acceptance

Money market interest rates in the *Financial Times*

The *Financial Times* publishes a table each day showing many of the money market interest rates – see Table 11.1 for the 12 September 2014 rates. The FT shows a lot more information at http://markets.ft.com/research/Markets/Bonds. The UK three-month Treasury bill rate of interest is not shown in this table, but it is shown at the bottom of the front page of the *FT* every day. It was 0.56% (annualised rate) for 12 September 2014.

Most of the rates shown have already been described, but the 'SDR int rate' needs some explanation. **Special Drawing Rights (SDRs)** are a composite currency created in 1969 by the **IMF** to act as an international reserve currency to supplement IMF member countries' official reserves. Weak IMF members can sell SDRs to financially strong members, effectively borrowing money from them via the IMF. The SDR rate of interest is decided weekly and is a weighted

Table 11.1 Market interest rates for 12 September 2014, all annualised rates

Sep 12	Over night	Change Day	Change Week	Change Month	One month	Three month	Six month	One year
US$ Libor*	0.09060	0.000	0.000	0.001	0.15360	0.23410	0.33090	0.58220
Euro Libor*	−0.05929	−0.042	−0.033	−0.054	0.00071	0.05000	0.14000	0.29929
£ Libor*	0.47500	–	0.003	0.004	0.50438	0.56025	0.69875	1.04744
Swiss Fr Libor*	−0.00600	−0.002	–	−0.009	−0.00400	0.00500	0.05140	0.15500
Yen Libor*	0.04571	−0.001	−0.009	−0.009	0.08357	0.11786	0.17071	0.32071
Canada Libor*	–	–	–	–	–	–	–	–
Euro Euribor	–	–	–	–	0.01	0.08	0.19	0.35
Sterling CDs	–	–	–	–	0.55	0.77	0.75	1.10
US$ CDs	–	–	–	–	0.00	0.11	0.17	0.42
Euro CDs	–	–	–	–	−0.10	−0.05	0.06	0.23
US o'night repo	0.08	0.010	−0.060	−0.020				
Fed Funds eff	0.09	–	–					
US 3m Bills	0.02	−0.005	−0.010	−0.015				
SDR int rate	0.05	–	−0.020	−0.030				
EONIA	−0.024	−0.036	−0.018	−0.043				
EURONIA	−0.0362	0.046	0.002	0.005				
RONIA	0.4904	−0.013	0.027	0.036				
SONIA	0.4316	0.003	0.002	0.006				
LA7 Day Notice	0.35%–0.30%							
	Over night	One Week	One month		Three months	Six months	One year	
Interbank £	We are no longer able to provide these figures.							

* Libor rates come from ICE (see www.theice.com) and are fixed at 11am UK time. Other data sources: US$, Euro & CDs: dealers; SDR int rate: IMF; EONIA: ECB; EURONIA, RONIA & SONIA: WMBA. LA7 days notice: Tradition (UK).

Source: Data from *Financial Times* http://markets.ft.com/RESEARCH/markets/DataArchiveFetchReport?Category=BR&Type=MNY&Date=09/12/2014

average of the rate charged on money market securities in the currencies that make up the SDR basket. This currency basket is currently based on four key international currencies: the euro, the Japanese yen, pound sterling and the US dollar. There are 188 members of the IMF and on joining each member is allocated a quota of SDRs according to its relative position in the global economy.

The *FT* also publishes in the 'Companies and Markets' section a table showing US, eurozone, UK, Japanese and Swiss official interest rates – see Table 11.2. These are the rates strongly influenced by central bank policy makers, such as the US Federal Reserve trying to manage monetary conditions (more on this in Chapter 16).

Table 11.2 Official interest rates

Sep 12	Rate	Current	Since	Last	Mth ago	Year ago
US	Fed Funds	0.00–0.25	16-12-2008	1.00	0.00–0.25	0.00–0.25
US	Prime	3.25	16-12-2008	4.00	3.25	3.25
US	Discount	0.75	18-02-2010	0.50	0.75	0.75
Euro	Repo	0.05	04-09-2014	0.15	0.25	0.75
UK	Repo	0.50	05-03-2009	1.00	0.50	0.50
Japan	O'night Call	0.00–0.10	05-10-2010	0.10	0.00–0.10	0.00–0.10
Switzerland	Libor target	0.00–0.25	03-08-2011	0.00–0.75	0.00–0.25	0.00–0.25

Source: Thomson Reuters

Comparing interest rates

Despite money market instruments having maturities of less than one year (mostly), it can be seen from the *FT* table in Table 11.1 that they can have remarkably different interest rates depending on the length of time to maturity. For example, on 12 September 2014 a sterling interbank loan for one month cost 0.50438% (annualised) whereas a loan of similar default risk, but lasting for one year, cost more than double that, at 1.04744% for the year. From Table 11.2 we can also see that repo rates can change significantly over time, for example the European Central Bank targeted overnight repo rates at 0.75% in early 2013, which was reduced to 0.5% in May 2013 and fell to a tenth of that level (0.05%) in September 2014.

Figures 11.3 and 11.4 show comparative interest rates from the UK and the US over a 30-year period. A number of observations can be made about the interest rate on different money market instruments:

● Generally, investors require extra return for longer lending periods because of the extra risk involved, so overnight rates will normally be less than rates on longer-term instruments (although this is not always the case). Notice in Figure 11.4 US six-month T-bill rates are slightly higher than those for three-month T-bill lending.

● The creditworthiness of the borrowing institution has a strong influence on the rate of interest charged. The rate offered by reputable national

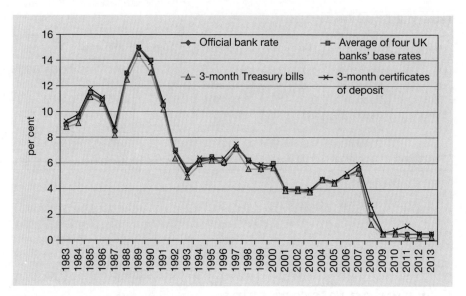

Figure 11.3 UK average interest rates 1983–2013, % annualised rate

Source: Data from www.bankofengland.co.uk

governments will usually be lower than the rate offered by a corporation wishing to raise cash by issuing commercial paper, or by a bank issuing certificates of deposit (see the higher rates on three-month CDs than on three-month Treasuries in both Figures 11.3 and 11.4). However, there are some governments that are required by the financial markets to pay higher interest rates than many corporates – e.g. Greece, Portugal and Ireland in 2011 paid more than many banks in the years following the financial crisis.

● When expectations about future inflation rise, interest rates rise accordingly, which leads to a decrease in the market price of money market instruments. Conversely, when inflation expectations are lowered, interest rates fall and the market price of the instruments rises. Thus we see that interest rates across the board tend to rise and fall together over time. The high rates of interest offered in the 1980s largely reflect the high inflation of the time.

● Supply and demand – for example, if banks need to borrow large sums of money quickly, they will sell more shorter-term instruments. This will have the effect of increasing market supply of these instruments and therefore pushing down their price, which in turn will increase the rate of interest, the yield to maturity.

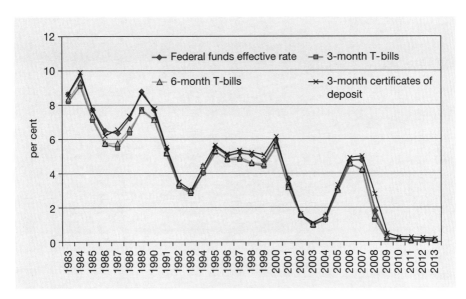

Figure 11.4 US average interest rates 1983–2013, % annualised rate

Source: Data from www.federalreserve.gov

- Money market interest rates with similar terms to maturity stay close together and move up or down with quite a high degree of correlation over time. These rates are all low risk and all short term, thus there is a reasonable amount of substitutability between them for potential lenders. So if interest rates in, say, the CD market fell abnormally below that in, say, the commercial paper market, those banks needing to attract deposits might have difficulty doing so because potential lenders will put more money in the CP market. The banks will have to raise CD interest rates to attract deposits while the commercial paper borrowers will find they can lower rates – thus some degree of convergence takes place.

- Short-term interest rates can be lowered by central banks intervening in the markets when they judge that the economy is in need of a boost. You can see this sort of action in the figures in the years after the shock of the dot.com bust at the turn of the millennium and following the financial crisis of 2007–2008.

PART 4
VALUING BONDS AND MONEY MARKET INSTRUMENTS

CHAPTER 12
FINANCIAL CONCEPTS AND MATHEMATICS

The time value of money

When people undertake to set aside money for investment something has to be given up now. For instance, if someone buys bonds in a firm or lends via commercial paper there is a sacrifice of present consumption. One of the incentives to save is the possibility of gaining a higher level of future consumption. Therefore, it is apparent that compensation is required to induce people to make a consumption sacrifice. Compensation will be required for at least three things:

- *Impatience to consume.* Individuals generally prefer to have £1 today than £1 in five years' time. To put this formally: the utility of £1 now is greater than £1 received five years hence. Individuals are predisposed towards **impatience to consume**, thus they need an appropriate reward to begin the saving process. The rate of exchange between certain future consumption and certain current consumption is the **pure rate of interest** – this occurs even in a world of no inflation and no risk. If you lived in such a world you might be willing to sacrifice £100 of consumption now if you were compensated with £102 to be received in one year. This would mean a pure rate of interest of 2%.

- *Inflation.* The price of time (or the interest rate needed to compensate for impatience to consume) exists even when there is no inflation, simply because people generally prefer consumption now to consumption later. If there is inflation then the providers of finance will have to be compensated for that loss in purchasing power as well as for time.

- *Risk.* The promise of the receipt of a sum of money some years hence generally carries with it an element of risk; the payout may not take place or the amount may be less than expected. **Risk** simply means that the future return has a variety of possible values.

Thus, the issuer of a security, whether it be a share, a bond or a certificate of deposit, must be prepared to compensate the investor for impatience to consume, inflation and risk involved, otherwise no one will be willing to buy the security. A further factor (which, to a large extent, could be seen as a form of risk) is that once the lender has committed the funds to a borrower for a set period of time they have to face the problem that at some point they may need the funds. With some investments there are ways of releasing the money – converting the instrument to cash – quickly, at low transaction cost and with certainty over the amount that would be released – either by insisting that the borrower repays on request or from selling the right to receive interest, etc. to another investor in a market – high liquidity and therefore low liquidity risk. If lenders/investors do not have access to easy and quick liquidity (high liquidity risk) then they are likely to demand an additional return in compensation.

If Mrs Ann Investor is considering a €1,000 one-year investment she will require compensation for three elements of time value. First, a return of 2% is required for the pure time value of money. Second, inflation is anticipated to be 3% over the year. At time zero (t_0) €1,000 buys one basket of goods and services. To buy the same basket of goods and services at time t_1 (one year later) €1,030 is needed. To compensate the investor for impatience to consume and inflation the investment needs to generate a return of 5.06%, that is:

$$(1 + 0.02)(1 + 0.03) - 1 = 0.0506 = 5.06\%$$

The figure of 5.06% may be regarded here as the **risk-free return (RFR)**, the interest rate that is sufficient to induce investment assuming no uncertainty about cash flows. Investors tend to view lending to highly reputable governments through the purchase of bills as the nearest they are going to get to risk-free investing because these institutions have an almost unlimited ability to raise income from taxes or to create money with minimal likelihood of default. This applies only if the country has a reputation for good financial management – Greece had a troublesome 2011–15; between 2011 and 2014 bonds from Spain, Portugal and Ireland were also thought to be risky investments. When investors doubt the soundness of government finances, this has the effect of pushing up the interest rates governments have to pay to allow for the risk of default (non-payment) way beyond the normal RFR accorded a reputable eurozone government, such as Germany.

The RFR forms the bedrock for time value of money calculations as the pure time value and the expected inflation rate affect all investments equally. Whether the investment is in property, bonds, shares or a factory, if expected inflation rises from 3% to 5% then the investor's required return on all investments will increase by 2%.

However, different investment categories carry different degrees of uncertainty about the outcome of the investment. For instance, an investment on the Russian stock market, with its high volatility, may be regarded as more risky than the purchase of a bond in Unilever, with its steady growth prospects. Investors require different **risk premiums** on top of the RFR to reflect the perceived level of extra risk. Thus:

Required return (Time value of money) = RFR + risk premium

In the case of Mrs Ann Investor, the risk premium pushes up the total return required to, say, 10%, thus giving full compensation for all three elements of the time value of money.

The interest rates quoted in the financial markets are (theoretically) sufficiently high to compensate for all three elements – whether investors sometimes over- or under-price bonds, etc. and thus yields are pushed irrationally low or high is a different matter.

Leaving the idea of irrationality to one side, a ten-year loan to a reputable government (such as the purchase of a bond) currently paying 5% will be offering some of this as compensation for time preference and a little for risk, but the majority of that interest is likely to be compensation for future inflation. The same elements apply to the cost of capital for a business; when it issues financial securities, the returns offered include a large element of inflation and risk compensation.

The **nominal rate of interest** is the rate quoted by lenders and includes the inflation element. The **real rate of interest** removes inflation.

Real rate of interest = Nominal rate of interest − Inflation

Mathematical tools for finance

The purpose of this section is to explain essential mathematical skills that will enhance understanding of finance. The author has no love of mathematics for its own sake and so only those techniques of direct relevance to the subject matter of this book are covered.

When there are time delays between receipts and payments of financial sums we need to make use of the concepts of simple and compound interest.

Simple interest

Interest is paid only on the original principal. No interest is paid on the accumulated interest payments.

Example 12.1

Suppose that a sum of £10 is deposited in a bank account that pays 12% per annum. At the end of year 1 the investor has £11.20 in the account. That is:

$$F = P(1 + i)$$

$$11.20 = 10(1 + 0.12)$$

where F = Future value (or terminal value), P = Present value, i = Interest rate.

The initial sum, called the principal, is multiplied by the interest rate to give the annual return. At the end of five years:

$$F = P(1 + in)$$

where n = number of years. Thus,

$$F = 10(1 + (0.12 \times 5)) = 16$$

Note from the example that the 12% return is a constant amount each year. Interest is not earned on the interest already accumulated from previous years.

Compound interest

The more usual situation in the real world is for interest to be paid on the sum that accumulates – whether or not that sum comes from the principal or from the interest received in previous periods.

Example 12.2

An investment of £10 is made at an interest rate of 12% with the interest being compounded. In one year the capital will grow by 12% to £11.20. In the second year the capital will grow by 12%, but this time the growth will be on the accumulated value of £11.20 and thus will amount to an extra £1.34. At the end of two years:

$F = P(1 + i)(1 + i)$

$F = 11.20(1 + i)$

$F = 11.20(1 + 0.12)$

$F = 12.544$

Alternatively,

$F = P(1 + i)^2$

$F = 10(1 + 0.12)^2$

$F = 12.544$

Over five years the result is:

$F = P(1 + i)^n = £10(1 + 0.12)^5 = £17.62$

While these calculations are not overly difficult, they can become cumbersome and time consuming, requiring the use of a calculator and accurate pressing of buttons. It is common practice to use tables for the solution. Table 12.1 shows an extract from Appendix I to this chapter, which gives the future value of £1 invested at a number of different interest rates and for alternative numbers of years.

This gives the results we have worked out above. From the second row of the table in Table 12.1 we can read that £1 invested for two years at 12% amounts to £1.2544. Thus, the investment of £10 provides a future capital sum 1.2544 times the original amount:

£10 × 1.2544 = £12.544

and from the fifth row, the investment of £10 after five years provides a future capital sum 1.7623 times the original amount:

£10 × 1.7623 = £17.623

Table 12.1 The future value of £1

Year	Interest rate (per cent per annum)				
	1	2	5	12	15
1	1.0100	1.0200	1.0500	1.1200	1.1500
2	1.0201	1.0404	1.1025	1.2544	1.3225
3	1.0303	1.0612	1.1576	1.4049	1.5209
4	1.0406	1.0824	1.2155	1.5735	1.7490
5	1.0510	1.1041	1.2763	1.7623	2.0114

The interest on the accumulated interest over five years is therefore the difference between the total arising from simple interest and that from compound interest:

£17.62 – £16.00 = £1.62

Present values

There are many occasions when you are given the future sums and need to find out what those future sums are worth in present-value terms today. For example, you wish to know how much you would have to put aside today that will accumulate, with compounded interest, to a defined sum in the future; or you are given the choice between receiving £200 in five years or £100 now and wish to know which is the better option, given anticipated interest rates; or a bond gives a return of £1 million in three years for an outlay of £800,000 now and you need to establish whether this is the best use of the £800,000. By means of a discount calculation, a sum of money to be received in the future is given a monetary value today.

Example 12.3

If we anticipate the receipt of £17.62 in five years' time we can determine its present value. Rearrangement of the compound interest formula, and assuming a discount (interest) rate of 12%, gives:

$$P = \frac{F}{(1+i)^n} \text{ or } P = F \times \frac{1}{(1+i)^n}$$

$$P = \frac{£17.62}{(1+0.12)^5} = £10$$

Table 12.2 The present value of £1

		\multicolumn{6}{c}{Interest/discount rate (per cent per annum)}
		1	**5**	**10**	**12**	**15**	**17**
Periods	1	0.9901	0.9524	0.9091	0.8929	0.8696	0.8547
	2	0.9803	0.9070	0.8264	0.7972	0.7561	0.7305
	3	0.9706	0.8638	0.7513	0.7118	0.6575	0.6244
	4	0.9610	0.8227	0.6830	0.6355	0.5718	0.5337
	5	0.9515	0.7835	0.6209	0.5674	0.4972	0.4561
	20	0.8195	0.3769	0.1486	0.1037	0.0611	0.0433

Alternatively, as before, we can use discount tables – see Appendix II, which gives the present value of £1, an extract from which is shown in Table 12.2. The factor needed to discount £1 receivable in five years when the discount rate is 12% is 0.5674. This is the $\frac{1}{(1+i)^n}$ element, $\frac{1}{(1+0.12)^5} = 0.5674$.

Therefore the present value of £17.62 is:

$0.5674 \times £17.62 = £10$

Examining the present value of £1 in Table 12.2 you can see that as the discount rate increases, the present value goes down. Also, the further into the future the money is to be received, the less valuable it is in today's terms. Distant cash flows discounted at a high rate have a small present value; for instance, £1,000 receivable in 20 years when the discount rate is 17% has a present value of £43.30 (£1,000 × 0.0433). Viewed from another angle, if you invested £43.30 for 20 years it would accumulate to £1,000 if interest compounds at 17%.

Determining the rate of interest

Sometimes you wish to calculate the rate of return that a project is earning. For instance, a bond may offer to pay you £10,000 in five years if you deposit £8,000 now, when interest rates on similar bonds are offering 6% per annum. In order to make a comparison you need to know the annual rate being offered. Thus, we need to find i in the discounting equation.

To be able to calculate i it is necessary to rearrange the compounding formula.

Since:

$$F = P(1 + i)^n$$

first divide both sides by P:

$$\frac{F}{P} = (1 + i)^n$$

(The Ps on the right side cancel out.)

Second, take the root to the power n of both sides and subtract 1 from each side:

$$i = \sqrt[n]{\frac{F}{P}} - 1 \text{ or } i = \left(\frac{F}{P}\right)^{1/n} - 1$$

Example 12.4

In the case of a five-year investment requiring an outlay of £10 and having a future value of £17.62 the rate of return is:

$$i = \sqrt[5]{\frac{17.62}{10}} - 1 = 0.12, \text{ or } 12\% \text{ or } i = \left(\frac{17.62}{10}\right)^{1/5} - 1 = 0.12, \text{ or } 12\%$$

The rate of interest being offered by the bond mentioned above is:

$$i = \sqrt[5]{\frac{£10,000}{£8,000}} - 1 = 0.04564, \text{ or } 4.564\%$$

so this deal is not competitive with the 6% being offered elsewhere.

A more straightforward alternative is to use the future value table (Appendix I), an extract of which is shown in Table 12.1. In our example, if the return on £10 is £17.62, then the return on £1 worth of investment over five years is:

$$\frac{17.62}{10} = 1.762$$

In the body of the future value table look at the year 5 row for a future value of 1.762.

Read off the interest rate of 12%.

Annuities

In financial calculations, quite often there is not just one payment at the end of a certain number of years, there can be a series of identical payments made over a period of years. For instance:

- bonds usually pay a regular rate of interest
- individuals can buy, from savings plan companies, the right to receive a number of identical payments over a number of years
- a business might invest in a project which, it is estimated, will give regular cash inflows over a period of years
- a typical house mortgage is an annuity.

An annuity is a series of payments or receipts of equal amounts. We are able to calculate the present value of this set of payments.

Example 12.5

For a regular payment of £10 per year for five years, when the interest rate is 12%, we can calculate the present value of the annuity (P) by three methods.

Method 1

$$P = \frac{A}{(1+i)} + \frac{A}{(1+i)^2} + \frac{A}{(1+i)^3} + \frac{A}{(1+i)^4} + \frac{A}{(1+i)^5}$$

where A = the periodic receipt.

$$P = \frac{10}{(1+0.12)} + \frac{10}{(1+0.12)^2} + \frac{10}{(1+0.12)^3} + \frac{10}{(1+0.12)^4} + \frac{10}{(1+0.12)^5} = £36.048$$

Method 2

Using the derived formula:

$$P = \frac{1 - \left[\frac{1}{(1+i)^n}\right]}{i} \times A$$

$$P = \frac{1 - \left[\frac{1}{(1+0.12)^5}\right]}{0.12} \times 10 = 3.6048 \times £10 = £36.048$$

Table 12.3 The present value of an annuity of £1 per annum

Year	Interest rate (per cent per annum)				
	1	5	10	12	15
1	0.9901	0.9524	0.9091	0.8929	0.8696
2	1.9704	1.8594	1.7355	1.6901	1.6257
3	2.9410	2.7232	2.4869	2.4018	2.2832
4	3.9020	3.5460	3.1699	3.0373	2.8550
5	4.8534	4.3295	3.7908	3.6048	3.3522

Method 3

It is useful to understand Methods 1 and 2, but the calculations can be prolonged. Method 3 is recommended, where the relevant figures are looked up using the 'present value of an annuity' table. Table 12.3 is an extract from the more complete annuity table in Appendix III. Here we simply look along the year 5 row and 12% column to find the figure of 3.6048. This is the present value of five future annual receipts of £1. Therefore we multiply by £10:

$$3.6048 \times £10 = £36.048$$

Perpetuities

Some contracts run indefinitely and there is no end to a series of identical payments. Certain government securities do not have an end date; that is, the amount paid when the bond was purchased by the lender will never be repaid, only interest payments are made. For example, the UK government issued consolidated stocks many years ago which may never be redeemed.

Perpetuities are annuities that continue indefinitely. The value of a perpetuity is simply the annual amount received divided by the interest rate when the latter is expressed as a decimal.

$$P = \frac{A}{i}$$

If £10 is to be received as an indefinite annual payment then the present value, at a discount rate of 12%, is:

$$P = \frac{10}{0.12} = £83.33$$

It is very important to note that in order to use this formula we are assuming that the first payment arises 365 days after the time at which we are standing (the present time or time zero).

Discounting semi-annually, monthly and daily

Sometimes financial transactions take place on the basis that interest will be calculated more frequently than once a year. For instance, if a bond paid 12% nominal return per year but credited 6% after half a year, in the second half of the year interest could be earned on the interest credited after the first six months. This will mean that the true annual rate of interest will be greater than 12%. The greater the frequency with which interest is earned, the higher the future value of the investment.

Example 12.6

If you put £10 in a bank account earning 12% per annum then your return after one year is:

$$10(1 + 0.12) = £11.20$$

If the interest is compounded semi-annually (at a nominal annual rate of 12%):

$$10(1 + [0.12/2])(1 + [0.12/2]) = 10(1 + [0.12/2])^2 = £11.236$$

In Example 12.6 the difference between annual compounding and semi-annual compounding is an extra 3.6p. After six months the bank credits the account with 60p in interest so that in the following six months the investor earns 6% on £10.60.

If the interest is compounded quarterly:

$$10(1 + [0.12/4])^4 = £11.255$$

Daily compounding:

$$10(1 + [0.12/365])^{365} = £11.2747$$

Example 12.7

If £10 is deposited in a bank account that compounds interest quarterly and the nominal return per year is 12%, how much will be in the account after eight years?

$$10(1 + [0.12/4])^{4\times8} = £25.75$$

Continuous compounding

If the compounding frequency is taken to the limit we say that there is continuous compounding. When the number of compounding periods approaches infinity the future value is found by $F = Pe^{in}$ where e is the value of the exponential function. This is set as 2.71828 (to five decimal places, as shown on a scientific calculator).[1]

So, the future value of £10 deposited in a bank paying 12% nominal compounded continuously after eight years is:

$$10 \times 2.71828^{0.12 \times 8} = £26.12$$

Converting monthly and daily rates to annual rates

Sometimes you are presented with a monthly or daily rate of interest and wish to know what is its equivalent in terms of annual compound rate (or effective annual rate (EAR)).

If m is the monthly interest or discount rate and i is the annual compound rate, then over 12 months:

$$(1 + m)^{12} = 1 + i$$

So

$$i = (1 + m)^{12} - 1$$

If d is the daily rate:

$$(1 + d)^{365} = 1 + i$$

So

$$i = (1 + d)^{365} - 1$$

Thus, if a credit card company charges 1.5% per month, the annual compound rate, i, is:

$$i = [(1 + 0.015)^{12} - 1] \times 100 = 19.56\%$$

---

[1] The number 'e' is a special number discovered by mathematicians, a mathematical constant. It is the 'natural' exponential because it arises naturally in science and maths, similar to the way *pi* arises naturally in geometry. It is on most calculators.

If you want to find the monthly rate when you are given the annual compound rate:

$$m = (1 + i)^{1/12} - 1 \text{ or } m = \sqrt[12]{(1 + i)} - 1$$

$$m = (1 + 0.1956)^{1/12} - 1 = 0.015 = 1.5\%$$

If you want to find the daily rate when you are given the annual compound rate:

$$d = (1 + i)^{1/365} - 1$$

Or

$$d = \sqrt[365]{(1 + i)} - 1$$

$$d = (1 + 0.1956)^{1/365} - 1 = 0.000489567, \text{ or } 0.04896\%$$

Bond equivalent yield

To compare interest rates, yields are generally converted to annual rates, even for those instruments which mature in only a few days. Money market security yields are converted to an annualised rate called the **bond equivalent yield**.

If you receive £37.92 in interest on a three-month bank deposit (91 days) of £50,000 and want to know what annual rate (the bond equivalent yield, bey) this equates to:

$$\text{bey} = \frac{\text{amount received in interest}}{\text{amount deposited}} \times \frac{\text{days in year}}{\text{days to maturity}} \times 100$$

$$\text{bey} = \frac{£37.92}{£50,000} \times \frac{365}{91} \times 100 = 0.304193\%$$

The bond equivalent yield we have calculated, 0.304193%, is **simple annualised rate of return**. It is not compounded, it is just (roughly) four lots of interest added up (one for each quarter of the year).

An alternative outcome might be that every three months you take your money (principal plus interest) and reinvest in the same deal at the same rate. Thus you can get interest on the accumulated interest as well as on the principal. If you reinvested the principal *and* accumulated interest every three months at this quarterly rate of return for a year you would receive:

$$£50,000 \times \left(1+ \frac{0.00304193}{4}\right)^4 = £50,152.27$$

This **compound annualised rate of return** is calculated by imagining that after the first 91 days the initial investment and the accrued interest, £50,037.92 are invested for a further 91 days, and so on each quarter.

The compound rate of return is slightly more than the simple annualised rate of return of 0.304193%:

$$\left(1+ \frac{0.00304193}{4}\right)^4 -1 = 0.003045402 \textit{ or } 0.3045402\%$$

Note that this is not entirely accurate because there are more than 4×91 days in a year, so if you want to be really precise, a further small adjustment is necessary:

In a 365-day year the number of compounding periods is $365 \div 91 = 4.010989$, thus to be really accurate the compound annualised rate of return is:

$$\left(1+ \frac{0.00304193}{4.010989}\right)^{4.010989} -1 = 0.003045405 \textit{ or } 0.3045405\%$$

Thus, to my mind, there are two bond equivalent yields:

1 Simple annualised bey. This is the one most practitioners and books refer to and it is fine for comparing the rate offered on one money market security with another of the same time to maturity.

2 (What I'll call) compound annualised bey, but many people only use (1).

Appendix I

Future value of £1 at compound interest

$$F = P(1 + i)^n$$

	Interest rate															
Periods (n)	1	2	3	4	5	6	7	8	9	10	11	12	13	14	15	
1	1.0100	1.0200	1.0300	1.0400	1.0500	1.0600	1.0700	1.0800	1.0900	1.1000	1.1100	1.1200	1.1300	1.1400	1.1500	1
2	1.0201	1.0404	1.0609	1.0816	1.1025	1.1236	1.1449	1.1664	1.1881	1.2100	1.2321	1.2544	1.2769	1.2996	1.3225	2
3	1.0303	1.0612	1.0927	1.1249	1.1576	1.1910	1.2250	1.2597	1.2950	1.3310	1.3676	1.4049	1.4429	1.4815	1.5209	3
4	1.0406	1.0824	1.1255	1.1699	1.2155	1.2625	1.3108	1.3605	1.4116	1.4641	1.5181	1.5735	1.6305	1.6890	1.7490	4
5	1.0510	1.1041	1.1593	1.2167	1.2763	1.3382	1.4026	1.4693	1.5386	1.6105	1.6851	1.7623	1.8424	1.9254	2.0114	5
6	1.0615	1.1262	1.1941	1.2653	1.3401	1.4185	1.5007	1.5869	1.6771	1.7716	1.8704	1.9738	2.0820	2.1950	2.3131	6
7	1.0721	1.1487	1.2299	1.3159	1.4071	1.5036	1.6058	1.7138	1.8280	1.9487	2.0762	2.2107	2.3526	2.5023	2.6600	7
8	1.0829	1.1717	1.2668	1.3686	1.4775	1.5938	1.7182	1.8509	1.9926	2.1436	2.3045	2.4760	2.6584	2.8526	3.0590	8
9	1.0937	1.1951	1.3048	1.4233	1.5513	1.6895	1.8385	1.9990	2.1719	2.3579	2.5580	2.7731	3.0040	3.2519	3.5179	9
10	1.1046	1.2190	1.3439	1.4802	1.6289	1.7908	1.9672	2.1589	2.3674	2.5937	2.8394	3.1058	3.3946	3.7072	4.0456	10
11	1.1157	1.2434	1.3842	1.5395	1.7103	1.8983	2.1049	2.3316	2.5804	2.8531	3.1518	3.4785	3.8359	4.2262	4.6524	11
12	1.1268	1.2682	1.4258	1.6010	1.7959	2.0122	2.2522	2.5182	2.8127	3.1384	3.4985	3.8960	4.3345	4.8179	5.3503	12
13	1.1381	1.2936	1.4685	1.6651	1.8856	2.1329	2.4098	2.7196	3.0658	3.4523	3.8833	4.3635	4.8980	5.4924	6.1528	13
14	1.1495	1.3195	1.5126	1.7317	1.9799	2.2609	2.5785	2.9372	3.3417	3.7975	4.3104	4.8871	5.5348	6.2613	7.0757	14
15	1.1610	1.3459	1.5580	1.8009	2.0789	2.3966	2.7590	3.1722	3.6425	4.1772	4.7846	5.4736	6.2543	7.1379	8.1371	15
16	1.1726	1.3728	1.6047	1.8730	2.1829	2.5404	2.9522	3.4259	3.9703	4.5950	5.3109	6.1304	7.0673	8.1372	9.3576	16
17	1.1843	1.4002	1.6528	1.9479	2.2920	2.6928	3.1588	3.7000	4.3276	5.0545	5.8951	6.8660	7.9861	9.2765	10.7613	17
18	1.1961	1.4282	1.7024	2.0258	2.4066	2.8543	3.3799	3.9960	4.7171	5.5599	6.5436	7.6900	9.0243	10.5752	12.3755	18
19	1.2081	1.4568	1.7535	2.1068	2.5270	3.0256	3.6165	4.3157	5.1417	6.1159	7.2633	8.6128	10.1974	12.0557	14.2318	19
20	1.2202	1.4859	1.8061	2.1911	2.6533	3.2071	3.8697	4.6610	5.6044	6.7275	8.0623	9.6463	11.5231	13.7435	16.3665	20
25	1.2824	1.6406	2.0938	2.6658	3.3864	4.2919	5.4274	6.8485	8.6231	10.8347	13.5855	17.0001	21.2305	26.4619	32.9190	25

Periods (n)	16	17	18	19	20	21	22	23	24	25	26	27	28	29	30	
1	1.1600	1.1700	1.1800	1.1900	1.2000	1.2100	1.2200	1.2300	1.2400	1.2500	1.2600	1.2700	1.2800	1.2900	1.3000	1
2	1.3456	1.3689	1.3924	1.4161	1.4400	1.4641	1.4884	1.5129	1.5376	1.5625	1.5876	1.6129	1.6384	1.6641	1.6900	2
3	1.5609	1.6016	1.6430	1.6852	1.7280	1.7716	1.8158	1.8609	1.9066	1.9531	2.0004	2.0484	2.0972	2.1467	2.1970	3
4	1.8106	1.8739	1.9388	2.0053	2.0736	2.1436	2.2153	2.2889	2.3642	2.4414	2.5205	2.6014	2.6844	2.7692	2.8561	4
5	2.1003	2.1924	2.2878	2.3864	2.4883	2.5937	2.7027	2.8153	2.9316	3.0518	3.1758	3.3038	3.4360	3.5723	3.7129	5
6	2.4364	2.5652	2.6996	2.8398	2.9860	3.1384	3.2973	3.4628	3.6352	3.8147	4.0015	4.1959	4.3980	4.6083	4.8268	6
7	2.8262	3.0012	3.1855	3.3793	3.5832	3.7975	4.0227	4.2593	4.5077	4.7684	5.0419	5.3288	5.6295	5.9447	6.2749	7
8	3.2784	3.5115	3.7589	4.0214	4.2998	4.5950	4.9077	5.2389	5.5895	5.9605	6.3528	6.7675	7.2058	7.6686	8.1573	8
9	3.8030	4.1084	4.4355	4.7854	5.1598	5.5599	5.9874	6.4439	6.9310	7.4506	8.0045	8.5948	9.2234	9.8925	10.6045	9
10	4.4114	4.8068	5.2338	5.6947	6.1917	6.7275	7.3046	7.9259	8.5944	9.3132	10.0857	10.9153	11.8059	12.7614	13.7858	10
11	5.1173	5.6240	6.1759	6.7767	7.4301	8.1403	8.9117	9.7489	10.6571	11.6415	12.7080	13.8625	15.1116	16.4622	17.9216	11
12	5.9360	6.5801	7.2876	8.0642	8.9161	9.8497	10.8722	11.9912	13.2148	14.5519	16.0120	17.6053	19.3428	21.2362	23.2981	12
13	6.8858	7.6987	8.5994	9.5964	10.6993	11.9182	13.2641	14.7491	16.3863	18.1899	20.1752	22.3588	24.7588	27.3947	30.2875	13
14	7.9875	9.0075	10.1472	11.4198	12.8392	14.4210	16.1822	18.1414	20.3191	22.7374	25.4207	28.3957	31.6913	35.3391	39.3738	14
15	9.2655	10.5387	11.9737	13.5895	15.4070	17.4494	19.7423	22.3140	25.1956	28.4217	32.0301	36.0625	40.5648	45.5875	51.1859	15
16	10.7480	12.3303	14.1290	16.1715	18.4884	21.1138	24.0856	27.4462	31.2426	35.5271	40.3579	45.7994	51.9230	58.8079	66.5417	16
17	12.4677	14.4265	16.6722	19.2441	22.1861	25.5477	29.3844	33.7588	38.7408	44.4089	50.8510	58.1652	66.4614	75.8621	86.5042	17
18	14.4625	16.8790	19.6733	22.9005	26.6233	30.9127	35.8490	41.5233	48.0386	55.5112	64.0722	73.8698	85.0706	97.8622	112.4554	18
19	16.7765	19.7484	23.2144	27.2516	31.9480	37.4043	43.7358	51.0737	59.5679	69.3889	80.7310	93.8147	108.8904	126.2422	146.1920	19
20	19.4608	23.1056	27.3930	32.4294	38.3376	45.2593	53.3576	62.8206	73.8641	86.7362	101.7211	119.1446	139.3797	162.8524	190.0496	20
25	40.8742	50.6578	62.6686	77.3881	95.3962	117.3909	144.2101	176.8593	216.5420	264.6978	323.0454	393.6344	478.9049	581.7585	705.6410	25

Appendix II

Present value of £1 at compound interest

$$\frac{1}{(1+i)^n}$$

Periods (n)	Interest rate (i)														
	1	2	3	4	5	6	7	8	9	10	11	12	13	14	15
1	0.9901	0.9804	0.9709	0.9615	0.9524	0.9434	0.9346	0.9259	0.9174	0.9091	0.9009	0.8929	0.8850	0.8772	0.8696
2	0.9803	0.9612	0.9426	0.9246	0.9070	0.8900	0.8734	0.8573	0.8417	0.8264	0.8116	0.7972	0.7831	0.7695	0.7561
3	0.9706	0.9423	0.9151	0.8890	0.8638	0.8396	0.8163	0.7938	0.7722	0.7513	0.7312	0.7118	0.6931	0.6750	0.6575
4	0.9610	0.9238	0.8885	0.8548	0.8227	0.7921	0.7629	0.7350	0.7084	0.6830	0.6587	0.6355	0.6133	0.5921	0.5718
5	0.9515	0.9057	0.8626	0.8219	0.7835	0.7473	0.7130	0.6806	0.6499	0.6209	0.5935	0.5674	0.5428	0.5194	0.4972
6	0.9420	0.8880	0.8375	0.7903	0.7462	0.7050	0.6663	0.6302	0.5963	0.5645	0.5346	0.5066	0.4803	0.4556	0.4323
7	0.9327	0.8706	0.8131	0.7599	0.7107	0.6651	0.6227	0.5835	0.5470	0.5132	0.4817	0.4523	0.4251	0.3996	0.3759
8	0.9235	0.8535	0.7894	0.7307	0.6768	0.6274	0.5820	0.5403	0.5019	0.4665	0.4339	0.4039	0.3762	0.3506	0.3269
9	0.9143	0.8368	0.7664	0.7026	0.6446	0.5919	0.5439	0.5002	0.4604	0.4241	0.3909	0.3606	0.3329	0.3075	0.2843
10	0.9053	0.8203	0.7441	0.6756	0.6139	0.5584	0.5083	0.4632	0.4224	0.3855	0.3522	0.3220	0.2946	0.2697	0.2472
11	0.8963	0.8043	0.7224	0.6496	0.5847	0.5268	0.4751	0.4289	0.3875	0.3505	0.3173	0.2875	0.2607	0.2366	0.2149
12	0.8874	0.7885	0.7014	0.6246	0.5568	0.4970	0.4440	0.3971	0.3555	0.3186	0.2858	0.2567	0.2307	0.2076	0.1869
13	0.8787	0.7730	0.6810	0.6006	0.5303	0.4688	0.4150	0.3677	0.3262	0.2897	0.2575	0.2292	0.2042	0.1821	0.1625
14	0.8700	0.7579	0.6611	0.5775	0.5051	0.4423	0.3878	0.3405	0.2992	0.2633	0.2320	0.2046	0.1807	0.1597	0.1413
15	0.8613	0.7430	0.6419	0.5553	0.4810	0.4173	0.3624	0.3152	0.2745	0.2394	0.2090	0.1827	0.1599	0.1401	0.1229
16	0.8528	0.7284	0.6232	0.5339	0.4581	0.3936	0.3387	0.2919	0.2519	0.2176	0.1883	0.1631	0.1415	0.1229	0.1069
17	0.8444	0.7142	0.6050	0.5134	0.4363	0.3714	0.3166	0.2703	0.2311	0.1978	0.1696	0.1456	0.1252	0.1078	0.0929
18	0.8360	0.7002	0.5874	0.4936	0.4155	0.3503	0.2959	0.2502	0.2120	0.1799	0.1528	0.1300	0.1108	0.0946	0.0808
19	0.8277	0.6864	0.5703	0.4746	0.3957	0.3305	0.2765	0.2317	0.1945	0.1635	0.1377	0.1161	0.0981	0.0829	0.0703
20	0.8195	0.6730	0.5537	0.4564	0.3769	0.3118	0.2584	0.2145	0.1784	0.1486	0.1240	0.1037	0.0868	0.0728	0.0611
25	0.7795	0.6095	0.4776	0.3751	0.2953	0.2330	0.1842	0.1460	0.1160	0.0923	0.0736	0.0588	0.0471	0.0378	0.0304
30	0.7419	0.5521	0.4120	0.3083	0.2314	0.1741	0.1314	0.0994	0.0754	0.0573	0.0437	0.0334	0.0256	0.0196	0.0151
35	0.7059	0.5000	0.3554	0.2534	0.1813	0.1301	0.0937	0.0676	0.0490	0.0356	0.0259	0.0189	0.0139	0.0102	0.0075
40	0.6717	0.4529	0.3066	0.2083	0.1420	0.0972	0.0668	0.0460	0.0318	0.0221	0.0154	0.0107	0.0075	0.0053	0.0037
45	0.6391	0.4102	0.2644	0.1712	0.1113	0.0727	0.0476	0.0313	0.0207	0.0137	0.0091	0.0061	0.0041	0.0027	0.0019
50	0.6080	0.3715	0.2281	0.1407	0.0872	0.0543	0.0339	0.0213	0.0134	0.0085	0.0054	0.0035	0.0022	0.0014	0.0009

Periods (n)	16	17	18	19	20	21	22	23	24	25	26	27	28	29	30
1	0.8621	0.8547	0.8475	0.8403	0.8333	0.8264	0.8197	0.8130	0.8065	0.8000	0.7937	0.7874	0.7812	0.7752	0.7692
2	0.7432	0.7305	0.7182	0.7062	0.6944	0.6830	0.6719	0.6610	0.6504	0.6400	0.6299	0.6200	0.6104	0.6009	0.5917
3	0.6407	0.6244	0.6086	0.5934	0.5787	0.5645	0.5507	0.5374	0.5245	0.5120	0.4999	0.4882	0.4768	0.4658	0.4552
4	0.5523	0.5337	0.5158	0.4987	0.4823	0.4665	0.4514	0.4369	0.4230	0.4096	0.3968	0.3844	0.3725	0.3611	0.3501
5	0.4761	0.4561	0.4371	0.4190	0.4019	0.3855	0.3700	0.3552	0.3411	0.3277	0.3149	0.3027	0.2910	0.2799	0.2693
6	0.4104	0.3898	0.3704	0.3521	0.3349	0.3186	0.3033	0.2888	0.2751	0.2621	0.2499	0.2383	0.2274	0.2170	0.2072
7	0.3538	0.3332	0.3139	0.2959	0.2791	0.2633	0.2486	0.2348	0.2218	0.2097	0.1983	0.1877	0.1776	0.1682	0.1594
8	0.3050	0.2848	0.2660	0.2487	0.2326	0.2176	0.2038	0.1909	0.1789	0.1678	0.1574	0.1478	0.1388	0.1304	0.1226
9	0.2630	0.2434	0.2255	0.2090	0.1938	0.1799	0.1670	0.1552	0.1443	0.1342	0.1249	0.1164	0.1084	0.1011	0.0943
10	0.2267	0.2080	0.1911	0.1756	0.1615	0.1486	0.1369	0.1262	0.1164	0.1074	0.0992	0.0916	0.0847	0.0784	0.0725
11	0.1954	0.1778	0.1619	0.1476	0.1346	0.1228	0.1122	0.1026	0.0938	0.0859	0.0787	0.0721	0.0662	0.0607	0.0558
12	0.1685	0.1520	0.1372	0.1240	0.1122	0.1015	0.0920	0.0834	0.0757	0.0687	0.0625	0.0568	0.0517	0.0471	0.0429
13	0.1452	0.1299	0.1163	0.1042	0.0935	0.0839	0.0754	0.0678	0.0610	0.0550	0.0496	0.0447	0.0404	0.0365	0.0330
14	0.1252	0.1110	0.0985	0.0876	0.0779	0.0693	0.0618	0.0551	0.0492	0.0440	0.0393	0.0352	0.0316	0.0283	0.0254
15	0.1079	0.0949	0.0835	0.0736	0.0649	0.0573	0.0507	0.0448	0.0397	0.0352	0.0312	0.0277	0.0247	0.0219	0.0195
16	0.0930	0.0811	0.0708	0.0618	0.0541	0.0474	0.0415	0.0364	0.0320	0.0281	0.0248	0.0218	0.0193	0.0170	0.0150
17	0.0802	0.0693	0.0600	0.0520	0.0451	0.0391	0.0340	0.0296	0.0258	0.0225	0.0197	0.0172	0.0150	0.0132	0.0116
18	0.0691	0.0592	0.0508	0.0437	0.0376	0.0323	0.0279	0.0241	0.0208	0.0180	0.0156	0.0135	0.0118	0.0102	0.0089
19	0.0596	0.0506	0.0431	0.0367	0.0313	0.0267	0.0229	0.0196	0.0168	0.0144	0.0124	0.0107	0.0092	0.0079	0.0068
20	0.0514	0.0433	0.0365	0.0308	0.0261	0.0221	0.0187	0.0159	0.0135	0.0115	0.0098	0.0084	0.0072	0.0061	0.0053
25	0.0245	0.0197	0.0160	0.0129	0.0105	0.0085	0.0069	0.0057	0.0046	0.0038	0.0031	0.0025	0.0021	0.0017	0.0014
30	0.0116	0.0090	0.0070	0.0054	0.0042	0.0033	0.0026	0.0020	0.0016	0.0012	0.0010	0.0008	0.0006	0.0005	0.0004
35	0.0055	0.0041	0.0030	0.0023	0.0017	0.0013	0.0009	0.0007	0.0005	0.0004	0.0003	0.0002	0.0002	0.0001	0.0000
40	0.0026	0.0019	0.0013	0.0010	0.0007	0.0005	0.0004	0.0003	0.0002	0.0001	0.0001	0.0001	0.0001	0.0000	0.0000
45	0.0013	0.0009	0.0006	0.0004	0.0003	0.0002	0.0001	0.0001	0.0001	0.0000	0.0000	0.0000	0.0000	0.0000	0.0000
50	0.0006	0.0004	0.0003	0.0002	0.0001	0.0001	0.0000	0.0000	0.0000	0.0000	0.0000	0.0000	0.0000	0.0000	0.0000

Appendix III
Present value of an annuity of £1 at compound interest

$$P = \frac{1 - \left[\frac{1}{(1+i)^n}\right]}{i} \times A$$

Periods (n)	1	2	3	4	5	6	7	8	9	10	11	12	13	14	15	
1	0.9901	0.9804	0.9709	0.9615	0.9524	0.9434	0.9346	0.9259	0.9174	0.9091	0.9009	0.8929	0.8850	0.8772	0.8696	1
2	1.9704	1.9416	1.9135	1.8861	1.8594	1.8334	1.8080	1.7833	1.7591	1.7355	1.7125	1.6901	1.6681	1.6467	1.6257	2
3	2.9410	2.8839	2.8286	2.7751	2.7232	2.6730	2.6243	2.5771	2.5313	2.4869	2.4437	2.4018	2.3612	2.3216	2.2832	3
4	3.9020	3.8077	3.7171	3.6299	3.5460	3.4651	3.3872	3.3121	3.2397	3.1699	3.1024	3.0373	2.9745	2.9137	2.8550	4
5	4.8534	4.7135	4.5797	4.4518	4.3295	4.2124	4.1002	3.9927	3.8897	3.7908	3.6959	3.6048	3.5172	3.4331	3.3522	5
6	5.7955	5.6014	5.4172	5.2421	5.0757	4.9173	4.7665	4.6229	4.4859	4.3553	4.2305	4.1114	3.9975	3.8887	3.7845	6
7	6.7282	6.4720	6.2303	6.0021	5.7864	5.5824	5.3893	5.2064	5.0330	4.8684	4.7122	4.5638	4.4226	4.2883	4.1604	7
8	7.6517	7.3255	7.0197	6.7327	6.4632	6.2098	5.9713	5.7466	5.5348	5.3349	5.1461	4.9676	4.7988	4.6389	4.4873	8
9	8.5660	8.1622	7.7861	7.4353	7.1078	6.8017	6.5152	6.2469	5.9952	5.7590	5.5370	5.3282	5.1317	4.9464	4.7716	9
10	9.4713	8.9826	8.5302	8.1109	7.7217	7.3601	7.0236	6.7101	6.4177	6.1446	5.8892	5.6502	5.4262	5.2161	5.0188	10
11	10.3676	9.7868	9.2526	8.7605	8.3064	7.8869	7.4987	7.1390	6.8052	6.4951	6.2065	5.9377	5.6869	5.4527	5.2337	11
12	11.2551	10.5753	9.9540	9.3851	8.8633	8.3838	7.9427	7.5361	7.1607	6.8137	6.4924	6.1944	5.9176	5.6603	5.4206	12
13	12.1337	11.3484	10.6350	9.9856	9.3936	8.8527	8.3577	7.9038	7.4869	7.1034	6.7499	6.4235	6.1218	5.8424	5.5831	13
14	13.0037	12.1062	11.2961	10.5631	9.8986	9.2950	8.7455	8.2442	7.7862	7.3667	6.9819	6.6282	6.3025	6.0021	5.7245	14
15	13.8651	12.8493	11.9379	11.1184	10.3797	9.7122	9.1079	8.5595	8.0607	7.6061	7.1909	6.8109	6.4624	6.1422	5.8474	15
16	14.7179	13.5777	12.5611	11.6523	10.8378	10.1059	9.4466	8.8514	8.3126	7.8237	7.3792	6.9740	6.6039	6.2651	5.9542	16
17	15.5623	14.2919	13.1661	12.1657	11.2741	10.4773	9.7632	9.1216	8.5436	8.0216	7.5488	7.1196	6.7291	6.3729	6.0472	17
18	16.3983	14.9920	13.7535	12.6593	11.6896	10.8276	10.0591	9.3719	8.7556	8.2014	7.7016	7.2497	6.8399	6.4674	6.1280	18
19	17.2260	15.6785	14.3238	13.1339	12.0853	11.1581	10.3356	9.6036	8.9501	8.3649	7.8393	7.3658	6.9380	6.5504	6.1982	19
20	18.0456	16.3514	14.8775	13.5903	12.4622	11.4699	10.5940	9.8181	9.1285	8.5136	7.9633	7.4694	7.0248	6.6231	6.2593	20
25	22.0232	19.5235	17.4131	15.6221	14.0939	12.7834	11.6536	10.6748	9.8226	9.0770	8.4217	7.8431	7.3300	6.8729	6.4641	25
30	25.8077	22.3965	19.6004	17.2920	15.3725	13.7648	12.4090	11.2578	10.2737	9.4269	8.6938	8.0552	7.4957	7.0027	6.5660	30
35	29.4086	24.9986	21.4872	18.6646	16.3742	14.4982	12.9477	11.6546	10.5668	9.6442	8.8552	8.1755	7.5856	7.0700	6.6166	35
40	32.8347	27.3555	23.1148	19.7928	17.1591	15.0463	13.3317	11.9246	10.7574	9.7791	8.9511	8.2438	7.6344	7.1050	6.6418	40
45	36.0945	29.4902	24.5187	20.7200	17.7741	15.4558	13.6055	12.1084	10.8812	9.8628	9.0079	8.2825	7.6609	7.1232	6.6543	45
50	39.1961	31.4236	25.7298	21.4822	18.2559	15.7619	13.8007	12.2335	10.9617	9.9148	9.0417	8.3045	7.6752	7.1327	6.6605	50

Interest rate (i)

Periods (n)	16	17	18	19	20	21	22	23	24	25	26	27	28	29	30	
1	0.8621	0.8547	0.8475	0.8403	0.8333	0.8264	0.8197	0.8130	0.8065	0.8000	0.7937	0.7874	0.7812	0.7752	0.7692	1
2	1.6052	1.5852	1.5656	1.5465	1.5278	1.5095	1.4915	1.4740	1.4568	1.4400	1.4235	1.4074	1.3916	1.3761	1.3609	2
3	2.2459	2.2096	2.1743	2.1399	2.1065	2.0739	2.0422	2.0114	1.9813	1.9520	1.9234	1.8956	1.8684	1.8420	1.8161	3
4	2.7982	2.7432	2.6901	2.6386	2.5887	2.5404	2.4936	2.4483	2.4043	2.3616	2.3202	2.2800	2.2410	2.2031	2.1662	4
5	3.2743	3.1993	3.1272	3.0576	2.9906	2.9260	2.8636	2.8035	2.7454	2.6893	2.6351	2.5827	2.5320	2.4830	2.4356	5
6	3.6847	3.5892	3.4976	3.4098	3.3255	3.2446	3.1669	3.0923	3.0205	2.9514	2.8850	2.8210	2.7594	2.7000	2.6427	6
7	4.0386	3.9224	3.8115	3.7057	3.6046	3.5079	3.4155	3.3270	3.2423	3.1611	3.0833	3.0087	2.9370	2.8682	2.8021	7
8	4.3436	4.2072	4.0776	3.9544	3.8372	3.7256	3.6193	3.5179	3.4212	3.3289	3.2407	3.1564	3.0758	2.9986	2.9247	8
9	4.6065	4.4506	4.3030	4.1633	4.0310	3.9054	3.7863	3.6731	3.5655	3.4631	3.3657	3.2728	3.1842	3.0997	3.0190	9
10	4.8332	4.6586	4.4941	4.3389	4.1925	4.0541	3.9232	3.7993	3.6819	3.5705	3.4648	3.3644	3.2689	3.1781	3.0915	10
11	5.0286	4.8364	4.6560	4.4865	4.3271	4.1769	4.0354	3.9018	3.7757	3.6564	3.5435	3.4365	3.3351	3.2388	3.1473	11
12	5.1971	4.9884	4.7932	4.6105	4.4392	4.2784	4.1274	3.9852	3.8514	3.7251	3.6059	3.4933	3.3868	3.2859	3.1903	12
13	5.3423	5.1183	4.9095	4.7147	4.5327	4.3624	4.2028	4.0530	3.9124	3.7801	3.6555	3.5381	3.4272	3.3224	3.2233	13
14	5.4675	5.2293	5.0081	4.8023	4.6106	4.4317	4.2646	4.1082	3.9616	3.8241	3.6949	3.5733	3.4587	3.3507	3.2487	14
15	5.5755	5.3242	5.0916	4.8759	4.6755	4.4890	4.3152	4.1530	4.0013	3.8593	3.7261	3.6010	3.4834	3.3726	3.2682	15
16	5.6685	5.4053	5.1624	4.9377	4.7296	4.5364	4.3567	4.1894	4.0333	3.8874	3.7509	3.6228	3.5026	3.3896	3.2832	16
17	5.7487	5.4746	5.2223	4.9897	4.7746	4.5755	4.3908	4.2190	4.0591	3.9099	3.7705	3.6400	3.5177	3.4028	3.2948	17
18	5.8178	5.5339	5.2732	5.0333	4.8122	4.6079	4.4187	4.2431	4.0799	3.9279	3.7861	3.6536	3.5294	3.4130	3.3037	18
19	5.8775	5.5845	5.3162	5.0700	4.8435	4.6346	4.4415	4.2627	4.0967	3.9424	3.7985	3.6642	3.5386	3.4210	3.3105	19
20	5.9288	5.6278	5.3527	5.1009	4.8696	4.6567	4.4603	4.2786	4.1103	3.9539	3.8083	3.6726	3.5458	3.4271	3.3158	20
25	6.0971	5.7662	5.4669	5.1951	4.9476	4.7213	4.5139	4.3232	4.1474	3.9849	3.8342	3.6943	3.5640	3.4423	3.3286	25
30	6.1772	5.8294	5.5168	5.2347	4.9789	4.7463	4.5338	4.3391	4.1601	3.9950	3.8424	3.7009	3.5693	3.4466	3.3321	30
35	6.2153	5.8582	5.5386	5.2512	4.9915	4.7559	4.5411	4.3447	4.1644	3.9984	3.8450	3.7028	3.5708	3.4478	3.3330	35
40	6.2335	5.8713	5.5482	5.2582	4.9966	4.7596	4.5439	4.3467	4.1659	3.9995	3.8458	3.7034	3.5712	3.4481	3.3332	40
45	6.2421	5.8773	5.5523	5.2611	4.9986	4.7610	4.5449	4.3474	4.1664	3.9998	3.8460	3.7036	3.5714	3.4482	3.3332	45
50	6.2463	5.8801	5.5541	5.2623	4.9995	4.7616	4.5452	4.3477	4.1666	3.9999	3.8461	3.7037	3.5714	3.4483	3.3333	50

Appendix IV

Future value of an annuity of £1 at compound interest

Periods (n)	\multicolumn{18}{c}{Interest rate (i)}
	1	2	3	4	5	6	7	8	9	10	12	14	16	18	20	25	30	35
1	1.0000	1.0000	1.0000	1.0000	1.0000	1.0000	1.0000	1.0000	1.0000	1.0000	1.0000	1.0000	1.0000	1.0000	1.0000	1.0000	1.0000	1.0000
2	2.0100	2.0200	2.0300	2.0400	2.0500	2.0600	2.0700	2.0800	2.0900	2.1000	2.1200	2.1400	2.1600	2.1800	2.2000	2.2500	2.3000	2.3500
3	3.0301	3.0604	3.0909	3.1216	3.1525	3.1836	3.2149	3.2464	3.2781	3.3100	3.3744	3.4396	3.5056	3.5724	3.6400	3.8125	3.9900	4.1725
4	4.0604	4.1216	4.1836	4.2465	4.3101	4.3746	4.4399	4.5061	4.5731	4.6410	4.7793	4.9211	5.0665	5.2154	5.3680	5.7656	6.1870	6.6329
5	5.1010	5.2040	5.3091	5.4163	5.5256	5.6371	5.7507	5.8666	5.9847	6.1051	6.3528	6.6101	6.8771	7.1542	7.4416	8.2070	9.0431	9.9544
6	6.1520	6.3081	6.4684	6.6330	6.8019	6.9753	7.1533	7.3359	7.5233	7.7156	8.1152	8.5355	8.9775	9.4420	9.9299	11.2588	12.7560	14.4834
7	7.2135	7.4343	7.6625	7.8983	8.1420	8.3938	8.6540	8.9228	9.2004	9.4872	10.0890	10.7305	11.4139	12.1415	12.9159	15.0735	17.5828	20.4919
8	8.2857	8.5830	8.8923	9.2142	9.5491	9.8975	10.2598	10.6366	11.0285	11.4359	12.2997	13.2328	14.2401	15.3270	16.4991	19.8419	23.8577	28.6640
9	9.3685	9.7546	10.1591	10.5828	11.0266	11.4913	11.9780	12.4876	13.0210	13.5795	14.7757	16.0853	17.5185	19.0859	20.7989	25.8023	32.0150	39.6964
10	10.4622	10.9497	11.4639	12.0061	12.5779	13.1808	13.8164	14.4866	15.1929	15.9374	17.5487	19.3373	21.3215	23.5213	25.9587	33.2529	42.6195	54.5902
11	11.5668	12.1687	12.8078	13.4864	14.2068	14.9716	15.7836	16.6455	17.5603	18.5312	20.6546	23.0445	25.7329	28.7551	32.1504	42.5661	56.4053	74.6967
12	12.6825	13.4121	14.1920	15.0258	15.9171	16.8699	17.8885	18.9771	20.1407	21.3843	24.1331	27.2707	30.8502	34.9311	39.5805	54.2077	74.3270	101.841
13	13.8093	14.6803	15.6178	16.6268	17.7130	18.8821	20.1406	21.4953	22.9534	24.5227	28.0291	32.0887	36.7862	42.2187	48.4966	68.7596	97.6250	138.485
14	14.9474	15.9739	17.0863	18.2919	19.5986	21.0151	22.5505	24.2149	26.0192	27.9750	32.3926	37.5811	43.6720	50.8180	59.1959	86.9495	127.913	187.954
15	16.0969	17.2934	18.5989	20.0236	21.5786	23.2760	25.1290	27.1521	29.3609	31.7725	37.2797	43.8424	51.6595	60.9653	72.0351	109.687	167.286	254.738
16	17.2579	18.6393	20.1569	21.8245	23.6575	25.6725	27.8881	30.3243	33.0034	35.9497	42.7533	50.9804	60.9250	72.9390	87.4421	138.109	218.472	344.897
17	18.4304	20.0121	21.7616	23.6975	25.8404	28.2129	30.8402	33.7502	36.9737	40.5447	48.8837	59.1176	71.6730	87.0680	105.931	173.636	285.014	466.611
18	19.6147	21.4123	23.4144	25.6454	28.1324	30.9057	33.9990	37.4502	41.3013	45.5992	55.7497	68.3941	84.1407	103.740	128.117	218.045	371.518	630.925
19	20.8109	22.8406	25.1169	27.6712	30.5390	33.7600	37.3790	41.4463	46.0185	51.1591	63.4397	78.9692	98.6032	123.414	154.740	273.556	483.973	852.748
20	22.0190	24.2974	26.8704	29.7781	33.0660	36.7856	40.9955	45.7620	51.1601	57.2750	72.0524	91.0249	115.380	146.628	186.688	342.945	630.165	1152.21
25	28.2432	32.0303	36.4593	41.6459	47.7271	54.8645	63.2490	73.1059	84.7009	98.3471	133.334	181.871	249.214	342.603	471.981	1054.79	2348.80	5176.50
30	34.7849	40.5681	47.5754	56.0849	66.4388	79.0582	94.4608	113.283	136.308	164.494	241.333	356.787	530.312	790.948	1181.88	3227.17	8729.99	23221.6

CHAPTER 13
BOND VALUATION

Bonds, particularly those that are traded in liquid secondary markets, are priced according to supply and demand, and their prices can be volatile. The main influence is the general level of interest rates for securities of a similar risk level and length of time to maturity. As a bond approaches its maturity date, its market value grows closer to its nominal value, the amount that will be paid at maturity. This is known as the **pull to par**, **pull to maturity** or **pull to redemption**.

Irredeemable bonds

Take the case of a €1,000 irredeemable bond with an annual coupon of 8%. This financial asset offers to any potential purchaser a regular and fixed €80 per year in perpetuity (i.e. 8% of the par value of €1,000), but the actual price of the bond will fluctuate in response to the prevailing rate of interest. When the bond was issued, general interest rates for this risk class may well have been 8% and so the bond may have been sold at €1,000. However, interest rates change over time and the €80 coupon may not remain sufficient to maintain the bond price at €1,000.

Suppose that the current rate of interest is now 10%. Investors will no longer be willing to pay €1,000 for an instrument that yields only €80 per year. The current market value of the bond will fall to €800 – the current value of the irredeemable bond is given by dividing the coupon rate by the current rate of interest, €80/0.10. This is the maximum amount needed to pay for similar bonds given the current interest rate of 10%. We say that the bond is trading at a 'discount' to its nominal value because it is trading below €1,000.

If the coupon rate is more than the current market interest rate, the bond price will be greater than the nominal (par) value. Thus, if market rates are 6%, the irredeemable bond will be priced at €1,333.33 (€80/0.06). We say that it is trading at a 'premium' to its nominal value, i.e. at more than €1,000.

The formula relating the price of an irredeemable bond, the coupon and the market rate of interest is:

$$P_D = \frac{C}{k_D}$$

where P_D = price of bond, D stands for debt

C = nominal annual income (the coupon rate × nominal (par) value of the bond)

k_D = market discount rate, the annual return required on bonds of similar risk and characteristics.

Also:

$$V_D = \frac{I}{k_D}$$

where V_D = total market value of all of the bonds of this type

I = total annual nominal interest of all the bonds of this type.

We may wish to establish the market rate of interest represented by the market price of the bond. For example, if an irredeemable bond offers an annual coupon of 9.5% and is currently trading at £87.50, with the next coupon due in one year, the rate of return is:

$$k_D = \frac{C}{P_D} = \frac{£9.5}{£87.5} \times 100 = 10.86\%$$

Note this formula can be used only if the next coupon is payable one year from the time of valuation. If there are coupons before then they need to be discounted separately, adding to the overall value.

Redeemable bonds

A purchaser of a redeemable bond buys two types of income promise: first the coupon, second the redemption payment. The amount that an investor will pay depends on the amount these income flows are presently worth when discounted at the current rate of return required on that risk class of debt. The relationships are expressed in the following formulae:

$$P_D = \frac{C_1}{1+k_D} + \frac{C_2}{(1+k_D)^2} + \frac{C_3}{(1+k_D)^3} + \frac{C_4}{(1+k_D)^4} + \ldots + \frac{C_n}{(1+k_D)^n} + \frac{R_n}{(1+k_D)^n}$$

and:

$$V_D = \frac{I_1}{1+k_D} + \frac{I_2}{(1+k_D)^2} + \frac{I_3}{(1+k_D)^3} + \frac{I_4}{(1+k_D)^4} + \dots + \frac{I_n}{(1+k_D)^n} + \frac{R_n^*}{(1+k_D)^n}$$

where C_1, C_2, C_3 and C_4 = nominal interest per bond in years 1, 2, 3 and 4 up to n years

I_1, I_2, I_3 and I_4 = total nominal interest in years 1, 2, 3 and 4 up to n years

R_n and R_n^* = redemption value of a single bond, and total redemption value of all bonds in issue in year n, the redemption date or maturity date.

The following examples illustrate the valuation of a bond when the market redemption yield is given.

Example 13.1

Blackaby plc issued a bond with a par value of £100 in September 2014, redeemable in September 2020 at par. The coupon is 8% payable annually in September. Therefore:

- the bond has a par value of £100 but this may not be what investors will pay for it
- the annual cash payment will be £8 (8% of par)
- in September 2020, £100 will be handed over to the bond holder (in the absence of default by the issuer).

The price investors will pay for this bond at the time of issue if the current market rate of interest for a security in this risk class is 7% can be worked out as follows (computers and financial calculators will perform the task quicker, but by doing it the old-fashioned way you gain a greater understanding of what is going on inside the 'black box' of the machine):

The present value of an £8 annuity for 6 years when discounted at 7%: First obtain the present value of six lots of £1 paid at annual intervals. This is given in the annuity table. Look along the '6' period row and down the '7' interest rate column to obtain 4.7665. This bond pays £8 per year, not £1, so we need to multiply this annuity factor by 8.	4.7665 × £8 =	£38.13
This bond also gives the holder £100 in six years from now. We need to add the present value of this £100 to the present value of all the coupons	$\dfrac{100}{(1+0.07)^6}$ =	£66.63
P_D	=	£104.77

Example 13.2

It is now three years later. What is the value of Blackaby's bond in the secondary market in September 2017 if market interest rates rise by 200 basis points (i.e. for this risk class they rise to 9%)? (Assume the next coupon payment is in one year.)

£8 annuity for 3 years @ 9% = 2.5313 × £8	=	£20.25
+ $\dfrac{100}{(1+0.09)^3}$	=	£77.22
P_D	=	£97.47

If we need to calculate the rate of return demanded by investors from a particular bond when we know the market price they are paying and coupon amounts, we can compute the internal rate of return (IRR)[1] – see Example 13.3.

Example 13.3

Bluebird plc issued a bond many years ago that is due for redemption at £100 par in three years. The annual coupon is 6% (next one payable in one year) and the market price is £91. The rate of return now offered in the market by this bond is found by solving for k_D:

$$P_D = \frac{C_1}{1+k_D} + \frac{C_2}{(1+k_D)^2} + \frac{C_3}{(1+k_D)^3} + \frac{R_3}{(1+k_D)^3}$$

$$91 = \frac{6}{1+k_D} + \frac{6}{(1+k_D)^2} + \frac{6}{(1+k_D)^3} + \frac{100}{(1+k_D)^3}$$

We'll solve this problem through iteration, i.e. trial and error, by trying one interest rate after another on paper. First we will try 9%, as this seems roughly right given the capital gain of around 3% per year over the three years (i.e. £9 overall) plus the 6% coupon.

---

[1] If you would like a refresher on IRR and other discounted cash flow calculations consult Chapter 2 of Arnold, G. (2012) *Corporate Financial Management*.

At an interest rate (k_D) of 9%, the right side of the equation amounts to £92.41:

£6 annuity for 3 years @ 9% = 2.5313 × £6		=	£15.19
+	$\dfrac{100}{(1+0.09)^3}$	=	£77.22
P_D		=	£92.41

This is more than the £91 on the left side of the equation, so we conclude that we are not discounting the cash flows on the right side of the equation by a sufficiently high rate of return. At an interest rate of 10% the right-hand side of the equation amounts to £90.05:

£6 annuity for 3 years @ 10% = 2.4869 × £6		=	£14.92
+	$\dfrac{100}{(1+0.10)^3}$	=	£75.13
P_D		=	£90.05

This is less than the £91 we are aiming at, so the internal rate of return lies somewhere between 9% and 10%. We can be more precise using linear interpolation:

Interest rate	9%	k_D	10%
Value of discounted cash flows	£92.41	91	£90.05
	a ⟶	b	⟶ c

We are trying to find the value of k_D, where the cash flows are discounted at just the right rate to equal the amount paid for the bond (£91). k_D is 9% plus the fraction formed by the difference between points 'a' and 'b', that is 92.41 – 91, divided by the difference between points 'a' and 'c', that is 92.41 – 90.05, multiplied by the number of percentage points between a and c, that is 10 – 9, one percentage point:

$$k_D = 9\% + \frac{92.41 - 91}{92.41 - 90.05} \times (10 - 9) = 9.59\%$$

Thus the cash flows offered on this bond represent an average annual rate of return of 9.59% on a £91 investment if the bond is held to maturity and the coupon payments are reinvested at 9.59% before then. This is the yield to maturity or YTM discussed in the next section.

Excel offers formulae, IRR and NPV, for these calculations – see below:

	A	B	C	D	E	F	G
1	Calculating rate of return offered by the Bluebird bond						
2							
3	Year	zero	1	2	3		
4	Current bond price	−91					
5	Coupon payments		6	6	6		
6	Redemption value in year 3				100		
7							
8		−91	6	6	106		
9							
10	**The rate of return (IRR) offered by the bond is**				**9.59%**		
11							
12							
13	**Sensitivity of bond prices to changes in rate of return**						
14							
15	Rate of return	5.0%	6%	7%	8%	9%	10%
16							
17	**Current bond price (NPV)**	102.72	100.00	97.38	94.85	92.41	90.05

Using the above figures, format a cell (in this case E10) in Excel as a percentage and type in

=IRR(B8:E8)

and 9.59% will appear in cell E10.

To understand the sensitivity of bond prices to changes in the rate of return, type into a cell (in this case B17)

=NPV(B15,$C8:$E8)

and 102.72 will appear in cell B17, which is the market price if the rate of return is 5%. (**NPV** is the **net present value** of all the cash inflows, ignoring the initial outflow to buy the bond.) The figures for 6%, 7%, 8%, 9% and 10% can be worked out in the same fashion, or by copying B17 and pasting in C17, D17, E17, F17 and G17.

The two types of yield

The current yield[2] is the gross (before tax) interest amount divided by the current market price of the bond expressed as a percentage:

$$\frac{\text{Gross interest (coupon)}}{\text{Market price}} \times 100$$

Thus, for a holder of Bluebird's bonds in Example 13.3 the current yield is:

$$\frac{£6}{£91} \times 100 = 6.59\%$$

This is a gross yield. The after-tax yield will be influenced by the investor's tax position.

$$\text{Net interest yield} = \text{Gross yield } (1 - T)$$

where T = the tax rate applicable to the bond holder.

At a time when interest rates are higher than 6.59% for that risk class it is obvious that any potential purchaser of Bluebird bonds will be looking for a return other than from the coupon. That additional return comes in the form of a capital gain over three years of £100 – £91 = £9. A rough estimate of this annual gain is (9/91) ÷ 3 = 3.3% per year. When this is added to the current yield we have an approximation to the second type of yield, the yield to maturity (the redemption yield).

The yield to maturity of a bond is the discount rate such that the present value of all the cash inflows from the bond (interest plus principal) is equal to the bond's current market price. The rough estimate of 9.89% (6.59% + 3.3%) has not taken into account the precise timing of the investor's income flows. When this is adjusted for, the yield to maturity is 9.59% – the internal rate of return calculated in Example 13.3.

Return on selling before maturity

It is important to note that many investors sell their bonds before the redemption date. The price received depends on market conditions. If general interest

---

[2] Also known as the interest yield, flat yield, income yield, simple yield, annual yield and running yield.

rates have risen over the holding period, the bond could well be worth less than if market interest rates remained constant or declined. This will have a depressing effect on the rate of return received even though coupons have been paid during the time the bonds were owned – see Example 13.4.

Example 13.4

If an investor bought Bluebird's three-year bonds at £91 and sells them one year later when the rate of return on two-year bonds of this risk level in the market has risen to 10%, instead of receiving the original 9.59% yield to maturity he/she will achieve a rate of return of only 8.86% over the year of holding, as explained below:

After one year of holding there are only two cash inflows left owing to a buyer: £6 to be received in one year and £106 to be received in two years (£6 coupon plus £100 nominal value):

$$\text{Market value of bond after 1 year} = \frac{6}{1+0.1} + \frac{106}{(1+0.1)^2} = 93.06$$

Thus the return (r) to our investor is:

$$r = \frac{C + (P_{t+1} - P_t)}{P_t} \times 100$$

where C = coupon received

P_{t+1} = price of bond after one year

P_t = price of bond at the start.

There is an interest element (C/P_t) plus a capital gain or loss $((P_{t+1} - P_t)/P_t)$ element to the rate of return:

$$r = \frac{6 + (93.06 - 91)}{91} \times 100 = 8.86\%$$

Semi-annual interest

The example of Bluebird is based on the assumption of annual interest payments. This makes initial understanding easier and reflects the reality for many types of bond, particularly internationally traded bonds. However, many companies and governments around the world issue domestic bonds with semi-annual interest payments. The rate of return calculation on these bonds is slightly more complicated.

Example 13.5

Redwing has an 11% bond outstanding that pays interest semi-annually. It will be redeemed in two years at €100 and has a current market price of €96, with the next interest payment due in six months. The yield to maturity on this bond is calculated as follows:

Cash flows

Point in time (years)	0.5	1	1.5	2.0
Cash flow	€5.50	€5.50	€5.50	€5.50 + €100

Taking the capital gain (€100 − €96 over two years) as about 2% per year, the IRR/2 would be roughly 5.5% plus 1%, 6.5% for six months. To obtain a more accurate yield to maturity figure we need to solve for k_D allowing for the semi-annual compounding of interest received:

$$96 = \frac{5.50}{1+\frac{k_D}{2}} + \frac{5.50}{\left(1+\frac{k_D}{2}\right)^2} + \frac{5.50}{\left(1+\frac{k_D}{2}\right)^3} + \frac{105.50}{\left(1+\frac{k_D}{2}\right)^4}$$

More precisely, at a rate of 7% for $k_D/2$, P_D equals €94.920:

€5.50 × 4-period annuity @ 7% = 3.3872 × €5.50		=	€18.63
+	$\dfrac{100}{(1+0.07)^4}$	=	€76.29
P_D		=	€94.92

At a rate of 6% for $k_D/2$, P_D equals €98.267:

€5.50 × 4-period annuity @ 6% = 3.4651 × €5.50		=	€19.058
+	$\dfrac{100}{(1+0.06)^4}$	=	€79.209
P_D		=	€98.267

The IRR of the cash flow equals:

$$6\% + \frac{98.267 - 96}{98.267 - 94.92} \times (7 - 6) = 6.6773\%$$

The IRR needs to be converted from a half-yearly cash flow basis to an annual basis (an effective annual yield).

The relationship between semi-annual interest and annual interest is:

$$(1 + s)^2 = (1 + i)$$

where s is the semi-annual rate and i is the annual rate, i.e. interest received at the half year is compounded.

Thus:

$$(1 + s)^2 - 1 = i$$

In the case of Redwing:

$$i = (1 + 0.066773)^2 - 1 = 0.138 \text{ or } 13.80\%$$

Yield to maturity versus rate of return

It is important to understand the difference between yield to maturity and rate of return.

The yield to maturity is the return that would be received given the current rate of coupon and market price, and assuming the bond is held until maturity.

The rate of return is the rate that an investor actually receives between the purchase and when their bond is sold before maturity, or on reaching maturity.

Yield to maturity and rate of return are only the same if the time to maturity is the same as the holding period.

We can illustrate this as follows.

Example 13.6

Assume that Tom has just bought four bonds. The maturity dates are 1 year from now, 5 years from now, 10 years from now and 20 years from now. For the sake of simplicity assume that all the bonds are trading in the secondary market at €1,000, which is also their par values to be paid at maturity, and that they each offer a yield to maturity of 6% (annual coupons are €60).

Tom is planning to sell all of the bonds in a year from now. The question is, what rate of return will he receive if between now and then the yield to maturity that investors demand in the secondary market on these bonds rises from 6% to 10%, or falls to 2%? (Again, assume for the sake of simplicity that the yield to maturity of 10% or 2% is the same regardless of whether the bond has a short or a long time until maturity – there is a 'flat yield curve' as discussed later.)

We'll concentrate on the 10% interest rate level first.

One-year bond

In the case of the one-year bond Tom does not have to sell in the secondary market; the issuer redeems the bond at its par value of €1,000. Tom also receives the coupon of €60, so the rate of return he gains is 6% (60/1000). This is the same as the yield to maturity when he bought the bond.

Five-year bond

$$\text{Rate of return over the one-year holding perioid } r = \frac{C + (P_{t+1} - P_t)}{P_t} \times 100$$

where C = coupon rate

P_{t+1} = price of bond after one year

P_t = price of bond at the start.

To calculate P_{t+1}:

P_{t+1} = four annual coupons discounted to time t + 1 (€60 × annuity factor for four years at 10%) plus the redemption amount discounted back to t + 1:

€60 annuity for 4 years @ 10% = 3.1699 × €60		=	€190.19
+	$\dfrac{1000}{(1+0.10)^4}$	=	€683.01
P_{t+1}		=	€873.20

$$\text{Rate of return over one year } r = \frac{60 + (873.20 - 1000)}{1000} \times 100 = -6.7\%$$

So, while the yield to maturity at time t was 6%, the rate of return over the one-year holding period was −6.7% because of the large capital loss on the bond.

It is even worse for the 10-year and 20-year bonds. If yields to maturity rise from 6% to 10% over the holding year then these bonds can be sold for only €769.64 and €665.40 at time t + 1:

Ten-year bond

Rate of return $r = \dfrac{C + (P_{t+1} - P_t)}{P_t} \times 100$

P_{t+1} with nine annual coupons, 10% discount rate:

€60 annuity for 9 years @ 10% = 5.759 × €60		=	€345.54
+	$\dfrac{1000}{(1+0.10)^9}$	=	€424.10
P_{t+1}		=	€769.64

Rate of return over one year $r = \dfrac{60 + (769.64 - 1000)}{1000} \times 100 = -17\%$

Twenty-year bond

Rate of return $r = \dfrac{C + (P_{t+1} - P_t)}{P_t} \times 100$

P_{t+1} with 19 annual coupons, 10% discount rate:

€60 annuity for 19 years @ 10% = 8.3649 × €60		=	€501.89
+	$\dfrac{1000}{(1+0.10)^{19}}$	=	€163.51
P_{t+1}		=	€665.40

Rate of return over one year $r = \dfrac{60 + (665.40 - 1000)}{1000} \times 100 = -27.5\%$

So far, poor Tom. Because interest rates have risen, the value of all his bonds (except the one-year bond) has fallen and he ends up with a considerable capital loss, €691.76 in total.

If, however, interest rates fall by 4% points to 2%, then Tom is in luck. Each of his bonds (except the one-year bond) is worth far more, giving him a gain of €1105.93 on top of his coupon at the end of one year. The individual bond returns are shown in Table 13.1, for both a rise in interest rates to 10% or a fall to 2%. An interest rate change of 4% is quite dramatic; typically interest rates change by far smaller amounts, but this example demonstrates the different volatility of bond prices and how important it is to understand bond pricing.

Of course, if each of the bonds *is* held until maturity Tom will receive a 6% rate of return on all of them, because they will then be redeemed at their par value.

Table 13.1 Rates of return on Tom's bonds given market interest rate changes and sale after one year

Years to maturity when first bought	Initial yield to maturity (coupon on bond)	Current rate of interest	Price at time *t*	Price at time *t* + 1	Capital gain/loss		Rate of return	
					+	–	% +	% –
1	6%	10%	€ 1,000	€ 1,000.00			6.0	
1	6%	2%	€ 1,000	€ 1,000.00			6.0	
5	6%	10%	€ 1,000	€ 873.20		–€ 126.80		–6.7
5	6%	2%	€ 1,000	€ 1,152.31	€ 152.31		21.2	
10	6%	10%	€ 1,000	€ 769.64		–€ 230.36		–17.0
10	6%	2%	€ 1,000	€ 1,326.49	€ 326.49		38.6	
20	6%	10%	€ 1,000	€ 665.40		–€ 334.60		–27.5
20	6%	2%	€ 1,000	€ 1,627.14	€ 627.14		68.7	

Again, we have an illustration of the inverse relationship between the price of a bond and the yield to maturity. We also have the (when first encountered) counter-intuitive result that a rise in interest rates results in a poor bond investment – Tom will not be happy with the return on his bonds if interest rates rise, but if they fall he will benefit.

Volatility of bond returns

The Tom example also demonstrates how volatility changes with time to maturity. The most volatile bond is the one stretching for 20 years – its price is very sensitive to market interest rates, there is a large amount of interest rate risk. The degree of price change is much smaller for the five-year bond and non-existent for the one-year bond (although there would be some impact from market interest rate changes if the one-year bond was sold in a few months rather than after the whole year is out).

> In general, rates of returns and prices for long-term bonds are more volatile than they are for short-term bonds.

This means that if the investor has a time horizon of only a year or two, long-term bonds may be seen as risky investments – even if they have very low default risk, they have high interest rate risk. It is not uncommon for bonds to lose or gain a significant percentage of their value in a year, even if they are reputable government bonds. This is illustrated in Chapter 1 (Figure 1.3) by the returns on UK gilts for every year going back to 1900. On many occasions an investor who purchased bonds at the beginning of the year and sold at the end lost *more than* 10%, despite receiving coupons.

Duration

To gain a measure of interest rate risk and volatility for a bond relative to others, bond market participants often use duration. The **duration**[3] metric is a summary measure of how far into the future is the average date of the cash flows to be received, when the cash flows are weighted by their size after they have been discounted.

In other words,

> the duration of a bond is the weighted average maturity time of all pay-ments (coupons and principal) to be received from owning a bond, where the weights are the discounted present values of the payments.

So, for zero coupon bonds the effective duration is the same as its actual term to maturity – the 'average' maturity time is the same as the final payout, the only cash flow received. A three-year zero coupon bond has a duration of three years.

For coupon-paying bonds the duration is shorter than the stated term to maturity because as the years go by the investor receives income from the bond which pushes the weighted average timing of income flows more towards the start date than is the case on a zero coupon bond.

A three-year coupon-paying bond offering £7 per year (with the first in one year from now) and £100 on maturity can be seen as having cash flows equal to the following three zero coupon bonds:

A one-year zero coupon bond paying £7 in one year's time

A two-year zero coupon bond paying £7 in two years' time

A three-year zero coupon bond paying £107 in three years' time

If the present yields to maturity for bonds of this risk class are also 7% then the duration can be calculated – see Table 13.2 – where the present value

$$PV = \frac{C_t}{(1 + k_D)^t}$$

---

[3]   Often referred to as Macaulay's duration after Frederick Macaulay who formulated it in the 1930s.

Table 13.2 Calculating duration on a three-year 7% coupon bond

Period	Coupon and principal	PV (7% discount rate, the current market YTM)	Weights (PV + total PV as a percentage)		Weighted maturity value (period × weights + 100) in years	
1	£7	£6.542	(£6.542 ÷ £100) × 100 =	6.542%	1 × 6.542 ÷ 100 =	0.0654
2	£7	£6.114	(£6.114 ÷ £100) × 100 =	6.114%	2 × 6.114 ÷ 100 =	0.1223
3	£107	£87.344	(£87.344 ÷ £100) × 100 =	87.344%	3 × 87.344 ÷ 100 =	2.6203
	Total PV	£100.00		100.00%	Duration =	2.808 years

As we might expect, the duration of 2.808 years is almost as much as the time to maturity but it is lowered from the full three years because some of the income is received before the end of three years. This three-year 7% coupon bond has the same duration as a 2.808-year zero coupon bond also yielding 7%.

Duration if the term to maturity is lengthened

If we now look at a four-year bond offering £7 per year when the yield to maturity is 7% we expect to find its duration greater than that on the three-year bond – see Table 13.3.

This illustrates a general rule:

> Holding other factors constant, the longer the term to maturity of a bond, the longer its duration.

Table 13.3 Calculating duration on a four-year 7% coupon bond

Period	Coupon and principal	PV (7% discount rate, the current market YTM)	Weights (PV + total PV as a percentage)		Weighted maturity value (period × weights + 100) in years	
1	£7	£6.542	(£6.542 ÷ £100) × 100 =	6.542%	1 × 6.54 ÷ 100 =	0.0654
2	£7	£6.114	(£6.114 ÷ £100) × 100 =	6.114%	2 × 6.11 ÷ 100 =	0.1223
3	£7	£5.714	(£5.714 ÷ £100) × 100 =	5.714%	3 × 5.714 ÷ 100 =	0.1714
4	£107	£81.630	(£81.63 ÷ £100) × 100 =	81.630%	4 × 81.63 ÷ 100 =	3.2652
	Total PV	£100.00		100.00%	Duration =	3.6243 years

Article 13.1 illustrates the importance of length to maturity in creating increased interest rate risk related to duration – sometimes investors are very concerned about it, other times they are more sanguine.

Article 13.1

Investors lap up ultra-long corporate bonds

By Vivianne Rodrigues

Financial Times June 11, 2014

Global sales of corporate bonds maturing in 50 years have jumped to record levels this year as investors are flocking to the securities, lured by the higher yields offered by the debt.

Total issuance of ultra-long corporate debt jumped to $56.5bn in 2013, a rise of 84% from 2012.

Strong demand has boosted total returns on the debt, with investors for now leaving aside concerns about duration exposure – a measure of the sensitivity of bond prices to changes in interest rates – in their bond portfolios.

Longer-dated bonds are more sensitive to duration risks.

In spite of rising expectations of higher US bond yields, which may hurt long-dated corporate debt, there has been no shortage of buyers for 50-year dollar bonds sold in 2014 by companies such as Caterpillar, South Carolina Electric & Gas, Volkswagen and EDF.

'For people who are comfortable with some duration exposure, these bonds offer a good opportunity to capture 20 or sometimes even 30 basis points in additional yield,' said Adrian Miller, at GMP Securities.

'For high-grade companies, this is a great chance to raise very long-term funding at low costs.'

On Tuesday, building-supply maker Johnson Controls sold $450m in 50-year bonds as part of a $1.7bn offering. Demand for the 50-year tranche surpassed the $3bn mark, according to people familiar with the sale. The 50-year bonds offered yields 30 basis points higher than those offered by the company's 30-year debt.

However, a turn higher in rates still stands to hurt those investors chasing the higher yields on longer-dated debt . . . the clock is ticking for long-term interest rates.

Duration and changes in yield to maturity

The time to maturity of a bond is not enough on its own to tell you what its volatility level is. Thus all four-year bonds do not have the same duration (say, 3.6243 years). This can be illustrated using the four-year bond example again, keeping everything the same except that the yield to maturity is now 10%. Thus, we discount the future cash flows at the higher discount rate of 10%, not 7% – see Table 13.4.

Table 13.4 Calculating duration on a four-year 7% coupon bond when the yield to maturity is 10%

Period	Coupon and principal	PV (10% discount rate, the current market YTM)	Weights (PV ÷ total PV as a percentage)		Weighted maturity value (period × weights ÷ 100) in years	
1	£7	£6.36	(£6.36 ÷ £90.49) × 100 =	7.03%	1 × 7.03 ÷ 100 =	0.0703
2	£7	£5.79	(£5.79 ÷ £90.49) × 100 =	6.40%	2 × 6.40 ÷ 100 =	0.1280
3	£7	£5.26	(£5.26 ÷ £90.49) × 100 =	5.81%	3 × 5.81 ÷ 100 =	0.1743
4	£107	£73.08	(£73.08 ÷ £90.49) × 100 =	80.76%	4 × 80.76 ÷ 100 =	3.2304
	Total PV	£90.49		100.00%	Duration =	3.6030 years

With the interest rate at 10%, duration has fallen from 3.6243 years to 3.603 years. This is because at the higher interest rate the more distant cash flows are discounted more heavily and thus comprise a lower overall proportion of the overall discounted cash flows – the nearer-term cash flows gain relative weight as the duration reduces.

This illustrates another rule:

If interest rates rise, the duration falls (keeping everything else constant).

Article 13.2 discusses how the difference in yield between investment-grade and junk bonds causes significantly greater interest rate risk for investment-grade securities.

Article 13.2

Investors bet on junk bonds to outperform

By Vivianne Rodrigues and Michael Mackenzie

Financial Times July 30, 2013

The average junk yield, which moves inversely to prices, has dipped below 6% this month, a big turnround in sentiment when the 10-year Treasury yield of 2.60% remains just shy of its June peak.

The total return for an index of US junk bonds in July stands at 2%, according to Barclays. Year-to-date, high yield has returned 3.4%. While investment-grade bonds have rallied 1% in July, the sector has posted a negative 2.4% total return for the year.

The contrast in performance between junk and investment grade reflects a stark difference in the sensitivity of bonds in an environment of rising interest rates.

Investment-grade bonds tend to carry lower coupons over longer maturities, which in turn helps increase the bonds' so-called duration – a measure of how sensitive bond prices are to changes in interest rates.

For example the average duration for junk debt stands at 4.2 years, below the average of 6.9 years for investment-grade bonds for the respective Barclays bond indices that are followed by money managers.

The lower a bond's duration, the less its price reacts to change in underlying interest rates.

Duration if coupons increase

If we take two bonds with the same yield to maturity, but one has higher coupons, then duration will be lower on that bond, resulting in a bond with less volatility or interest rate risk. To illustrate we can go back to the example of the four-year bond above with a yield to maturity of 7% (Table 13.3). We can compare its duration with that for another bond with the same yield to maturity but with the following pattern of cash flows:

Current market price = £144.03

Four annual coupons of £20

Par (nominal) value to be redeemed in four years = £100

Table 13.5 Calculating duration on a four-year 20% coupon bond when the yield to maturity remains at 7%

Period	Coupon and principal	PV (7% discount rate, the current market YTM)	Weights (PV ÷ total PV as a percentage)		Weighted maturity value (period × weights ÷ 100) in years	
1	£20	£18.69	(£18.69 ÷ £144.03) × 100 =	12.98%	1 × 12.98 ÷ 100 =	0.1298
2	£20	£17.47	(£17.47 ÷ £144.03) × 100 =	12.13%	2 × 12.13 ÷ 100 =	0.2426
3	£20	£16.32	(£16.32 ÷ £144.03) × 100 =	11.33%	3 × 11.33 ÷ 100 =	0.3399
4	£120	£91.55	(£91.55 ÷ £144.03) × 100 =	63.56%	4 × 63.56 ÷ 100 =	2.5424
	Total PV	£144.03		100.00%	Duration =	3.2547 years

The bond with £20 coupons has a shorter duration, at 3.2547 years, than the bond with the £7 coupon, at 3.6243 years, despite the yield to maturity and time to maturity remaining the same. Thus we come to another rule:

The higher the coupon rate on the bond, the shorter the bond's duration.

Using duration as a guide to interest rate risk

As duration increases, the percentage change in the market value of a bond increases for a given change in interest rates, i.e. interest rate risk rises with duration. Thus we can use duration as a measure of interest rate risk. It is not a perfect measure, but it does provide a good approximation, when interest rate changes are small, of the extent to which the price of a bond will change if yields to maturity rise or fall – as expressed in the following formula:

$$\text{Percentage change in bond price from one period to the next} \approx -\text{Duration} \times \frac{\text{change in YTM}}{1 + \text{YTM}} \times 100$$

The negative sign in front of Duration is due to the inverse relationship between bond prices and interest rates.

For example, if an investor is holding the four-year bond yielding 7% at time t in Table 10.3 with a duration of 3.6243 years, you could ask: how much would the price of the bond change if interest rates (YTM) rose by 1%?

Answer:

Change in interest rate = 0.01

Current YTM = 0.07

Change in bond price $\approx -3.6243 \times \dfrac{0.01}{1+0.07} \times 100 = -3.39\%$

Thus, for a 1 percentage point change in market interest rates this bond's price moves by roughly 3.39%. (Note that this formula can only be used for small changes in yield to maturity of one percentage point or less, and even then it is only an approximation. It slightly overestimates price declines and underestimates price increases – see convexity discussion later.) We can compare this degree of sensitivity to interest rate changes with other bonds. Let us take the four-year bond in Table 13.5 offering 20% coupons with YTM of 7%. It has a duration of 3.2547 years.

Change in bond price $\approx -3.2547 \times \dfrac{0.01}{1+0.07} \times 100 = -3.04\%$

Clearly, this bond carries less interest rate risk than the 7% coupon bond, as its price changes by only 3.04% when yields change by 1 percentage point. The lower duration and therefore lower interest rate risk, but same yield to maturity, on the 20% coupon bond may induce an investor to switch investment funds from the more risky bond (7% coupon) to this less risky one.

Convexity

In the section discussing the effect of duration on interest rate risk we noted that the formula, while roughly correct, produces errors for the influence of interest rate changes on bond pricing. This is because it assumes a linear relationship between interest rate changes and bond price changes – this is shown by the straight diagonal line in Figure 13.1. The exact valuation relationship is curved, and the curvature around some interest rate level is measured by **convexity**. The true relationship line is tangential to the straight line assumption only at a zero interest rate change, i.e. it has the same slope, therefore for very small interest rate changes the duration approach gives the true answer. However, if we test large interest movements the true bond price changes are different to that determined by the duration-based calculation we used earlier.

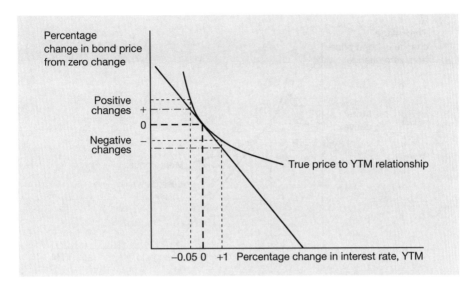

Figure 13.1 The linear assumption for the relationship between bond price and YTM

This can be illustrated using the same example above, where we calculated a change in bond price of –3.39% for a 1% increase in yield to maturity. We can now calculate the actual change for an increase in 1%. At the interest rate of 7% the four-year bond was priced at £100. If interest rates rise to 8% then the price changes to £96.6877:

Four-year annuity@ 8% for £7 per year = 3.3121 × £7 = £23.1847

Present value of the principal payment $\dfrac{£100}{(1+0.08)^4}$ = £73.5030

£23.1847 + £73.5030 = £96.6877

This is a –3.3123% change ((100 – 96.6877) ÷ 100), a true percentage change resulting from the rise in YTM. Compare this with the approximation provided by using a duration of –3.39%. When interest rates rise, the true decline in price is less than the fall implied using duration.

Bond market participants often want to use duration to estimate sensitivity of price to YTM changes. This can be done more accurately if they allow for the extent of convexity. More precisely, they need to measure the curve at that particular interest rate because slopes alter with the starting point for YTM changes. This involves formidable calculations which are beyond the scope of this book. Bond traders do not always need to carry out these calculations to make decisions because they develop an ability to gain a 'good enough' idea of

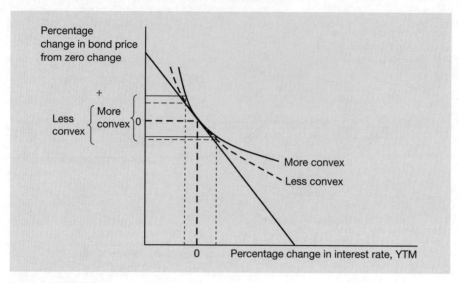

Figure 13.2 High convexity versus low convexity

bond price changes given the maturity and coupon rate to form a view of the ball-park movements in various scenarios. Besides, modern computer systems calculate duration and convexity automatically and display them on trading screens.

For bond investors, high convexity is usually a desirable quality and so they pay premiums to hold such bonds. This can be understood by examining Figure 13.2. Two bonds are shown, each with the same duration at point '0' (no change in interest rate), but one has greater convexity. If interest rates increase, the one with the greater convexity will experience a lower percentage decrease in price than the bond with lower convexity. However, if rates decline, the high convexity bond will have a greater uplift in value than the low convexity bond.

The term structure of interest rates

It is not safe to assume that the yield to maturity on a bond will remain the same regardless of the length of time of the loan (holding all else constant). So, if the interest rate on a three-year bond is 7% per year, it may or may not be 7% on a five-year bond of the same risk class and liquidity class. Lenders in the financial markets demand different interest rates on loans of differing lengths of time to maturity – that is, there is a **term structure of the interest rates**. Four of these relationships are shown in Figure 13.3 for lending to the UK, US,

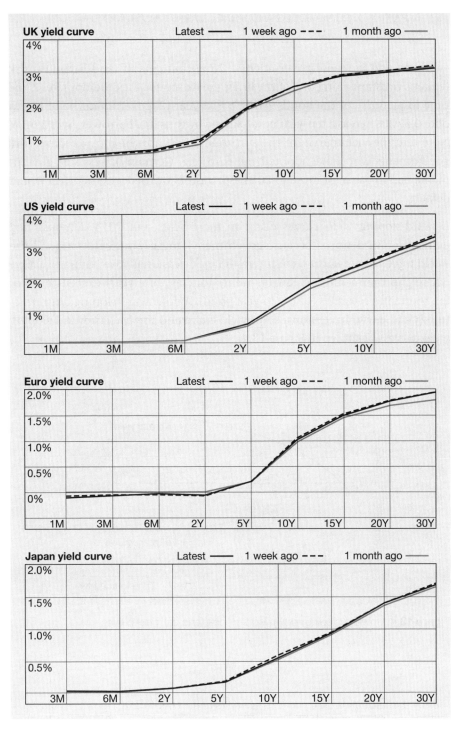

Figure 13.3 Yield curves for the UK, US, eurozone and Japanese government bills and bonds (The 'Latest' shows the current rates for different maturities. Also shown is the range of rates as calculated one week before and one month before)

Source: *The Financial Times*

eurozone and Japanese governments.[4] Note that default (and liquidity) risk remains constant along one of the lines; the reason for the different rates is the time to maturity of the bonds. Thus, a two-year US government bond has to offer 0.57% whereas a ten-year bond offered by the same borrower gives 2.62%. Note that the yield curve for the eurozone is only for the most creditworthy governments who have adopted the euro (e.g. Germany). Less safe governments had to pay a lot more in 2014 as investors worried whether they would default.

Upward-sloping yield curves occur in most years, but 2014 demonstrated extreme upward slopes because governments and central banks around the world forced down short-term interest rates. Occasionally we have a situation where short-term interest rates (lending for, say, one year) exceed those of long-term interest rates (say, a 20-year bond). A downward-sloping term structure (**yield curve inversion**), a flat yield curve and the usual upward-sloping yield curves are shown in Figure 13.4.

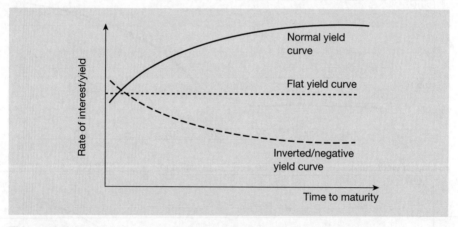

Figure 13.4 Upward-sloping, downward-sloping and flat yield curves

---

[4] Using the benchmark yield curves as examples of the term structure of interest rates may offend theoretical purity (because we should be using zero coupon, e.g. STRIPS, rather than those with coupons that have to be reinvested before the redemption date – we do not know the reinvestment rate), but they are handy approximate measures and help illustrate this section.

Three main hypotheses have been advanced to explain the shape of the yield curve (these are not mutually exclusive – all three can operate at the same time to influence the curve):

a The expectations hypothesis.

b The liquidity-preference hypothesis.

c The market-segmentation hypothesis.

The expectations hypothesis

The **expectations hypothesis** focuses on the changes in interest rates over time. To understand the expectations hypothesis you need to know what is meant by a **spot rate of interest**. The spot rate is an interest rate fixed today on a loan that is made today. So a corporation, Hype plc, might issue one-year bonds at a spot rate of, say, 8%, two-year bonds at a spot rate of 8.995% and three-year bonds at a spot rate of 9.5%. This yield curve for Hype is shown in Figure 13.5. The interest rates payable by Hype are bound to be greater than for the UK government across the yield curve because of the additional default risk on these corporate bonds compared with safe government bonds.

Spot rates change over time. The market may have allowed Hype to issue one-year bonds yielding 8% at a point in time in 2014 but a year later (time 2015) the one-year spot rate may have changed to become 10%. If investors expect that one-year spot rates will become 10% at time 2015 they will have a theoretical limit on the yield that they require from a two-year bond when

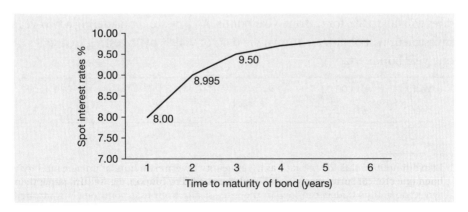

Figure 13.5 The term structure of interest rates for Hype plc at time 2014

viewed from time 2014. Imagine that an investor (lender) wishes to lend £1,000 for a two-year period and is contemplating two alternative approaches:

1 Buy a one-year bond at a spot rate of 8%; after one year has passed the bond will come to maturity. The released funds can then be invested in another one-year bond at a spot rate of 10%, expected to be the going rate for bonds of this risk class at time 2015.[5]

2 Buy a two-year bond at the spot rate at time 2014.

Under the first option the lender will have a sum of £1,188 at the end of two years:

| Year 1 | £1,000.00 | × | (1 + 0.08) | = | £1,080.00 |
| Year 2 | £1,080.00 | × | (1 + 0.10) | = | £1,188.00 |

Given the anticipated change in one-year spot rates to 10% the investor will buy the two-year bond only if it gives the same average annual yield over two years as a series of one-year bonds (the first option). The annual interest required will be:

$$£1,000 (1 + k_D)^2 = £1,188$$

$$k_D = \sqrt{(1,188/1,000)} - 1 = 0.08995, \text{ or } 8.995\%$$

which is the spot rate quoted for a two-year bond in 2014 in the second option.

Thus, it is the expectation of spot interest rates changing that determines the shape of the yield curve according to the expectations hypothesis.

Now consider a downward-sloping yield curve where the spot rate on a one-year instrument is 11% and the expectation is that one year from now spot rates will fall to 8% for the one-year bonds. An investor considering a two-year investment will obtain an annual yield (k) of 9.49% by investing in a series of one-year bonds, viz:

| Year 1 | £1,000.00 | × | (1+0.11) | = | £1,110.00 |
| Year 2 | £1,110.00 | × | (1+0.08) | = | £1,198.80 |

---

[5] I have simplified this to spot rates only. In reality investors in bonds can agree to buy a bond one year (or more years) from now, a **forward**. The price of the forward purchase is agreed now, thus traders can lock in the interest rate from that point on. This **implied forward rate** can be interpreted as the market's consensus of the spot rates in one year from now.

or £1,000 (1.11) (1.08) = £1198.80

$$k_D = \sqrt{(1198.8/1000)} - 1 = 0.0949, \text{ or } 9.49\% \text{ per year}$$

or $\sqrt{(1.08)(1.11)} - 1 = 0.0949$

With this expectation for movements in one-year spot rates, lenders will demand an annual rate of return of 9.49% from two-year bonds of the same risk class.

Thus in circumstances where short-term spot interest rates are expected to fall, the yield curve will be downward sloping.

Example 13.7

Spot rates

If the present spot rate for a one-year bond is 5% and for a two-year bond is 6.5%, what is the expected one-year spot rate in a year's time?

Answer

If the two-year rate is set to equal the rate on a series of one-year spot rates then:

$$x = \frac{(1+0.065)^2}{1+0.05} - 1 = 0.0802 \text{ or } 8.02\%$$

The liquidity-preference hypothesis

The expectations hypothesis does not adequately explain why the most common shape of the yield curve is upward sloping. The **liquidity-preference hypothesis (liquidity premium theory)** helps explain the upward slope by pointing out that investors require an extra return for lending on a long-term basis. Lenders demand a premium return on long-term bonds compared with short-term instruments because of greater interest rate risk and the risk of misjudging future interest rates. Putting your money into a ten-year bond on the anticipation of particular levels of interest rates exposes you to the possibility that rates will rise above the rate offered on the bond at some point in its long life. Thus, if five years later interest rates double, say because of a rise in inflation expectations, the market price of the bond will fall substantially, leaving the holder with a large capital loss if they sell. By investing in a series of one-year bonds, however, the investor can take advantage of rising interest rates as they occur. The ten-year bond locks in a fixed rate for the full ten years if held to maturity. Investors prefer short-term bonds so that they can benefit from rising rates and so will accept a lower return on short-dated instruments.

The liquidity-preference theory focuses on a different type of risk attaching to long-dated debt instruments other than default risk – a risk related to uncertainty over future interest rates. A suggested reinforcing factor to the upward slope is that borrowers usually prefer long-term debt because of the fear of having to repay short-term debt at inopportune moments. Thus borrowers increase the supply of long-term debt instruments, adding to the tendency for long-term rates to be higher than short-term rates.

A further factor is that in many bond markets there is a greater volume of trading for short-dated instruments than longer-dated ones, i.e. there is greater liquidity, an increased speed and ease of the sale of an asset. In bond markets where there is high liquidity for both short- and long-term bonds, the title 'liquidity-preference theory' seems incorrectly used because there is no problem of illiquidity for long-term bonds. For example, for government bonds, sale in the secondary market is often as quick and easy as for short-term bonds. In the bond markets where liquidity is fairly constant along the yield curve, the premium for long-term bonds is generally compensation for the extra risk of capital loss; 'term premium' might be a better title for the hypothesis.

The market-segmentation hypothesis

The **market-segmentation hypothesis** argues that the debt market is not one homogeneous whole but that there are, in fact, a number of sub-markets defined by maturity range. The yield curve is therefore created (or at least influenced) by the supply and demand conditions in each of these sub-markets. For example, banks tend to be active in the short-term end of the market and pension funds to be buyers in the long-dated segment.

If banks need to borrow large quantities quickly they will sell some of their short-term instruments, increasing the supply on the market, so pushing down the price and raising the yield. Meanwhile, pension funds may be flush with cash and may buy large quantities of 20-year bonds, helping to temporarily move yields downward at the long end of the market. At other times banks, pension funds and the buying and selling pressures of a multitude of other financial institutions will influence the supply and demand position in the opposite direction. The point is that the players in the different parts of the yield curve tend to be different. This hypothesis helps to explain the often lumpy or humped yield curve.

A final thought on the term structure of interest rates

It is sometimes believed that in circumstances of a steeply rising yield curve it would be advantageous to borrow short term rather than long term. However, this can be a dangerous strategy because long-term debt may be trading at a higher rate of interest because of the expected rise in spot short-term rates and so when the borrower comes to refinance in, say, a year's time, the short-term interest rate is much higher than the long-term rate and this high rate has to be paid out of the second year's cash flows, which may not be convenient.

Additional reading

Bodie, Z., Kane, A. and Marcus, A.J. (2014) *Investments*. McGraw-Hill.

Chisholm, A.M. (2009) *An Introduction to International Capital Markets*. 2nd edition. John Wiley & Sons.

Choudry, M. (2010) *An Introduction to Bond Markets*. 4th edition. John Wiley & Sons.

Fabozzi, F.J. (2012) *Bond Markets, Analysis and Strategies*. 8th edition. Prentice Hall.

Veronesi, P. (2010) *Fixed Income Securities*. John Wiley & Sons.

CHAPTER 14
MONEY MARKET SECURITIES VALUATION

Vast amounts of money in a wide variety of currencies are traded on the money markets daily. Most of this huge volume of short-term instruments is traded on a **discount** basis; there is no regular coupon payment, the instruments are bought at a discount to their face value; any return for investors comes from the difference between the price at which they were purchased and the payout received when they reach maturity or are sold in the secondary market before then.

There are two important considerations to take note of when undertaking any calculations associated with money market securities:

- day count convention
- the difference between bond equivalent yield and discount yield.

Day count convention

For supposed ease of calculation or simply because of long-established habit, some countries/markets use a 30-day month and 360-day year, rather than the actual variable days in a month and a 365-day year, or 366 in a leap year. This can get complicated when the repayment date falls on the 31st of a month, and there are various methods for dealing with this. Other markets use the precise number of days until redemption of the instrument and the real number of days in a year. Great care must always be taken to check which day count convention is being used and to understand terminology, e.g. actual/360, 360/360, actual/actual, actual/365 and so on; it is imperative that an investor/issuer knows which convention is being used and how it works.

Converting from a 365-day basis to a 360-day basis

To compare interest rates calculated with different day count conventions we need to convert all rates to a common basis. This can be done using the following formula:

Interest rate on comparison basis

$$= \text{interest rate on quoted basis} \left(\frac{\text{number of days in comparison}}{\text{number of days in quoted year}} \right)$$

If you wanted to compare a 5.5% interest quoted on a 365-day year basis with another instrument calculated on the basis of a 360-day year, the calculation would be:

$$\text{Comparison interest rate} = 5.5 \times \left(\frac{360}{365} \right) = 5.424657\%$$

When the rate offered on a 360-day convention is 5.424657%, then the effective annual rate of interest for the year is 5.5%. This difference may seem small, but when trading is done in millions it can be a significant amount. For example, on an investment of £100 million, the difference in interest rates is worth £75,343:

£100 million × 5.5%   = £5,500,000

£100 million × 5.424657% = £5,424,657

Difference   £75,343

A dealer thinking 5.424657% represented an actual annual rate of interest and investing £100 million at this rate, would end up £75,343 out of pocket.

If the rate quoted is presented for a 360-day year then to compare with other effective annual yield rates we need to adjust upwards. This time the comparison rate is based on 365-days.

Interest rate on comparison basis

$$= \text{interest rate on quoted basis} \left(\frac{\text{number of days in comparison}}{\text{number of days in quoted year}} \right)$$

Let us assume the 360-day rate is 10%. To compare with other rates on a 365-day basis:

$$\text{Comparison interest rate} = 10.0 \times \left(\frac{365}{360}\right) = 10.138889\%$$

Bond equivalent yield (bey) and discount (d) yield compared

Any investor/issuer needs to be able to compare returns with other investments and so it is important that they understand the figures and the basis on which they are calculated, and that they are able to work out the bond equivalent yield (bey).

The **bond equivalent yield** (also known as **equivalent bond yield**) is the yield that is usually quoted in newspapers and it allows a comparison between fixed-income securities whose payments are not annual and securities that have annual yields. So a wide variety of debt instrument yields is expressed in the same annual terms, whether they mature in a matter of days, have interest paid every three months or have one yearly interest payment. The bey uses the actual number of days in a year (365 or 366).

Example 14.1

Bond equivalent rate

Imagine a 12-month £100 UK Treasury bill was sold at a discount of 2%, i.e. at £98, the purchase price or market price. We recognise that the investment made is £98 and we gain £2 when it is redeemed in one year. Thus we know that the true rate of return is slightly over 2%.

To be more accurate we calculate the bey:

$$\frac{\text{Discount (Face value − Purchase price)}}{\text{Purchase price}} \times \frac{\text{Days in year}}{\text{Days to maturity}} \times 100$$

Given that there is a full year to maturity we know this is going to be the annual rate:

$$\text{bey} = \frac{100 - 98}{98} \times \frac{365}{365} \times 100 = 2.04\%$$

So although the bill was discounted at 2%, the actual return is more than this because the investor did not pay the face value.

The **discount yiel** (**bank-discount basis** or **discount rate**) is the yield when using the face value as the base rather than the actual amount invested by the buyer. Discount yields are often calculated using a 360-day year count convention (e.g. in US, German, Dutch, French and Italian T-bills), but the UK uses a 365-day year in its calculations.

To calculate the discount yield:

$$\frac{\text{Discount (Face value} - \text{Purchase price)}}{\text{Face value}} \times \frac{\text{Days in year}}{\text{Days to maturity}}$$

Example 14.2

Discount yield

For a UK T-bill issued at £98 when the face value is £100 and the time to maturity is one year, when there are 365-days in the year:

$$d = \frac{\text{(Face value} - \text{Purchase price)}}{\text{Face value}} \times \frac{\text{Days in year}}{\text{Days to maturity}} \times 100$$

$$d = \frac{(100 - 98)}{100} \times \frac{365}{365} \times 100 = 2\%$$

Treasury bills

We shall use examples from the UK and US Treasury bills to explain how these instruments are valued and how the returns on them are calculated.

Table 14.1 shows the results from the four sales of UK Treasury bills which took place weekly during March 2014, on the 7th, 14th, 21st and 28th. As different bidders pay different prices, a bill's tender results are averaged. Each bidder therefore must work out their own results to give them accurate information about their investment.

Table 14.1 DMO Treasury bill tender results 1 March 2014 to 31 March 2014

Tender date	Issue date	Redemption date	Nominal amount (£m)	Bid to cover ratio	Average yield (%)	Average price (£)
1 month						
07-Mar-14	10-Mar-14	07-Apr-14	2,000	2.21	0.393578%	99.969817
14-Mar-14	17-Mar-14	14-Apr-14	2,000	3.30	0.364505%	99.972046
21-Mar-14	24-Mar-14	22-Apr-14	2,000	1.85	0.381211%	99.969721
28-Mar-14	31-Mar-14	28-Apr-14	2,000	1.62	0.407344%	99.968761
3 months						
07-Mar-14	10-Mar-14	09-Jun-14	1,500	2.64	0.363186%	99.909534
14-Mar-14	17-Mar-14	16-Jun-14	2,000	3.09	0.379104%	99.905573
21-Mar-14	24-Mar-14	23-Jun-14	2,000	1.95	0.390464%	99.902746
28-Mar-14	31-Mar-14	30-Jun-14	2,000	1.51	0.421457%	99.895035
6 months						
07-Mar-14	10-Mar-14	08-Sep-14	1,500	2.87	0.409168%	99.796392
14-Mar-14	17-Mar-14	15-Sep-14	1,500	3.23	0.394030%	99.803910
21-Mar-14	24-Mar-14	22-Sep-14	1,500	2.17	0.400866%	99.800515
28-Mar-14	31-Mar-14	29-Sep-14	1,500	1.70	0.422876%	99.789585

Source: www.dmo.gov.uk

Example 14.3

UK three-month Treasury bill

If we take the three-month Treasury bill sold at tender on 24 March at a discount price of £99.902746, we can work out the discount yield (d), yield (bey) and purchase price. Note that the time difference between the date of purchase and redemption is only 91 days in this case and we must express these interest rates in annual terms, so we multiply by 365/91.

Discount yield

$$d = \frac{(\text{Face value} - \text{Purchase price})}{\text{Face value}} \times \frac{\text{Days in year}}{\text{Days to maturity}} \times 100 = \text{annual rate}$$

$$d = \frac{(100 - 99.902746)}{100} \times \frac{365}{91} \times 100 = 0.390085\% \text{ per annum}$$

Yield (bey) (on the purchase price)

$$\text{bey} = \frac{(\text{Face value} - \text{Purchase price})}{\text{Purchase price}} \times \frac{365}{91} \times 100$$

$$\text{bey} = \frac{100 - 99.902746}{99.902746} \times \frac{\text{Days in year}}{\text{Days to maturity}} \times 100 = 0.390464\% \text{ per annum}$$

This is the 'average yield' shown in Table 14.1.

Effective annual rate

To be really precise we need to note that this is not the effective annual rate (EAR) because we have failed to allow for the fact that after one-quarter of a year we receive £100 (after investing £99.902746) and this can be reinvested for a second, third and fourth three-month period within the year. Interest can be earned accumulatively on each subsequent three-month period and added to the original capital invested. In other words, the original investment is compounded more than once in the year. To calculate the EAR (if we can assume that in the next three quarterly periods the interest rate is the same as in the first three months):

$$\left[1 + \frac{0.00390464}{365/91}\right]^{365/91} - 1 \times 100 = 0.391037\%$$

Another example

You invest for three months and receive a 'simple' annual yield of 3%. This is an annual rate that does not take into account compounding over the year – i.e. interest received on interest, added after each quarter. With compounding the effective annual rate is:

$$\left[1 + \frac{0.03}{4/1}\right]^{4/1} - 1 \times 100 = 3.0339\%$$

Thus, over a period of one year you receive an extra 0.0339% because after the first three-month period you reinvest the maturity amount, including interest from the first investment, in an identical investment for the next three of the remaining nine months. And do the same after six months and nine months. Thus you receive interest on interest received of 0.0339%. This is, of course, assuming identical investments every three months. While this is unrealistic, at least the EAR provides a gauge of the 'true' annual rate offered on short-term securities.

Purchase price

To calculate the price to be paid if the discount yield is 0.390085% we need to start with the face value and take away the discount that applies when the term is only one-quarter of the year or, more strictly, for 91/365th of the year.

The annualised rate of discount of 0.390085 is decreased by multiplying by 91/365.

The purchase price is the face value of 100 multiplied by 1 minus the discount for this portion of the year:

$$\text{Purchase price} = \text{Face value} \times \left[1 - \left(\frac{\text{Discount} \times \text{Days to maturity}}{\text{Days in Year}}\right)\right]$$

$$\text{Purchase price} = 100 \times \left[1 - \left(\frac{0.00390085 \times 91}{365}\right)\right] = £99.902746$$

Note that the purchase price is often called the **settlement amount**. This is because the bill is paid for on the settlement day rather than the transaction or bargain day, which is usually one day earlier in the secondary market.

The results for the tender of this 24 March bill are in Table 14.2. The actual bids from buyers varied from a yield (bey) of 0.33% to a high of 0.418% with an average yield of 0.390464%.

A bidder tendering the lowest accepted yield, 0.33%, would have paid £99.9177936 for their bills:

If:

$$\text{bey} = \frac{(\text{Face value} - \text{Purchase price})}{\text{Purchase price}} \times \frac{365}{91} \times 100$$

Then:

$$\text{Purchase price} = \frac{\text{Face value}}{1 + \left(\frac{\text{bey}}{100} \times \frac{91}{365}\right)}$$

Table 14.2 Results of tender on three-month T-bill

3 months Treasury bill maturing on 23-Jun-2014, ISIN CODE: GB00B7P4VP73	
Lowest accepted yield	0.330000
Average yield	0.390464
Highest accepted yield	0.418000 (about 88.10% allotted)
Average rate of discount (%)	0.390085
Average price per £100 nominal (£)	99.902746
Amount tendered for (£)	3,894,400,000.00
Amount on offer (£)	2,000,000,000.00
Bid to cover ratio	1.95
Amount allocated (£)	2,000,000,000.00

Source: www.dmo.gov.uk

For this example:

$$\text{Purchase price} = \frac{100}{1+\left(\dfrac{0.33}{100}\times\dfrac{91}{365}\right)} = \text{£99.9177936}$$

And a bidder tendering the highest yield, 0.418%, would have paid £99.89589479:

$$\text{Purchase price} = \frac{\text{Face value}}{1+\left(\dfrac{\text{bey}}{100}\times\dfrac{91}{365}\right)}$$

$$\text{Purchase price} = \frac{100}{1+\left(\dfrac{0.418}{100}\times\dfrac{91}{365}\right)} = \text{£99.89589479}$$

During the life of a bill, its value fluctuates daily as it is traded between investors – see Table 14.3, which gives the daily March and April 2014 figures for this particular bill.

Table 14.3 Data for Treasury bill GB00B7P4VP73, 21 March to 16 April 2014

ISIN code	Redemption date	Close of business date	Price (£)	Yield (%)
GB00B7P4VP73	23-Jun-14	21-Mar-14	99.903464	0.388
GB00B7P4VP73	23-Jun-14	24-Mar-14	99.905141	0.385
GB00B7P4VP73	23-Jun-14	25-Mar-14	99.906352	0.384
GB00B7P4VP73	23-Jun-14	26-Mar-14	99.907558	0.384
GB00B7P4VP73	23-Jun-14	27-Mar-14	99.908762	0.383
GB00B7P4VP73	23-Jun-14	28-Mar-14	99.911712	0.384
GB00B7P4VP73	23-Jun-14	31-Mar-14	99.913389	0.381
GB00B7P4VP73	23-Jun-14	01-Apr-14	99.914615	0.380
GB00B7P4VP73	23-Jun-14	02-Apr-14	99.915802	0.380
GB00B7P4VP73	23-Jun-14	03-Apr-14	99.916987	0.379
GB00B7P4VP73	23-Jun-14	04-Apr-14	99.919921	0.380
GB00B7P4VP73	23-Jun-14	07-Apr-14	99.921688	0.376
GB00B7P4VP73	23-Jun-14	08-Apr-14	99.922855	0.376
GB00B7P4VP73	23-Jun-14	09-Apr-14	99.924018	0.375
GB00B7P4VP73	23-Jun-14	10-Apr-14	99.925176	0.374
GB00B7P4VP73	23-Jun-14	11-Apr-14	99.926169	0.385
GB00B7P4VP73	23-Jun-14	14-Apr-14	99.929775	0.372
GB00B7P4VP73	23-Jun-14	15-Apr-14	99.930889	0.371
GB00B7P4VP73	23-Jun-14	16-Apr-14	99.932055	0.370

Source: www.dmo.gov.uk

The price increases as the days to maturity decrease (all else remaining the same) and on redemption day, in this case 23 June 2014, the holder will receive the face value of £100. The yield in Table 14.3 is the (annual) return (bey) that a purchaser in the secondary market will achieve between purchase date (the settlement date is one day after the close of business transaction date) and maturity date. We can check these figures, using 8 April as the purchase date:

$$\text{bey} = \frac{100 - 99.922855}{99.922855} \times \frac{365}{75} \times 100 = 0.376\%$$

US Treasury bills

While in many countries bills are bought in the primary market (from the government) at the bidding price, in the US *all* bidders, competitive and non-competitive, receive the same discount rate, and therefore the same yield, as the highest accepted bid and so pay the same purchase price for their bills. Table 14.4 gives the results of US T-bill auctions held during March 2014.

If we take the 26-week T-bill that was auctioned on 17 March 2014 below its par value at $99.959556, we can work out the figures in Example 14.4.

Table 14.4 US Treasury bills auctioned March 2014

CUSIP	Security term	Auction date	Issue date	Maturity date	Price per $100	Average/ median discount rate	Bid to cover ratio
912796DE6	13-week	03/31/14	04/03/14	07/03/14	99.988625	0.04%	4.83
912796DX4	26-week	03/31/14	04/03/14	10/02/14	99.967139	0.06%	5.18
912796CJ6	4-week	03/25/14	03/27/14	04/24/14	99.996500	0.04%	4.65
912796BP3	13-week	03/24/14	03/27/14	06/26/14	99.987361	0.04%	4.61
912796DW6	26-week	03/24/14	03/27/14	09/25/14	99.962083	0.07%	5.05
912796CH0	4-week	03/18/14	03/20/14	04/17/14	99.995333	0.06%	4.27
912796DD8	13-week	03/17/14	03/20/14	06/19/14	99.987361	0.05%	4.42
912796CB3	26-week	03/17/14	03/20/14	09/18/14	99.959556	0.08%	4.86
912796CG2	4-week	03/11/14	03/13/14	04/10/14	99.995722	0.05%	4.11
912796DC0	13-week	03/10/14	03/13/14	06/12/14	99.987361	0.05%	4.76
912796DV8	26-week	03/10/14	03/13/14	09/11/14	99.959556	0.08%	4.97
912796BA6	4-week	03/04/14	03/06/14	03/04/14	99.996500	0.04%	3.93
912796DP1	52-week	03/04/14	03/06/14	03/05/15	99.878667	0.12%	4.85
912796DA4	13-week	03/03/14	03/06/14	06/05/14	99.987361	0.04%	5.02
912796DS5	26-week	03/03/14	03/06/14	09/04/14	99.959556	0.08%	4.46

Source: www.treasurydirect.gov

Example 14.4

US Treasury bill

For US short-term investments (less than one year) the day count is actual/360. To calculate the discount yield, d, on the 26-week (182 days) US T-bill sold on 20 March 2014 at a discount price of $99.959556:

$$d = \frac{(\text{Face value} - \text{Purchase price})}{\text{Face value}} \times \frac{\text{Days in year}}{\text{Days to maturity}} \times 100$$

$$d = \frac{(100 - 99.959556)}{100} \times \frac{360}{182} \times 100 = 0.08\%$$

To calculate the purchase price of the same bill:

$$\text{Purchase price} = \text{Face value} \times \left[1 - \left(\frac{\text{Discount} \times \text{Days to maturity}}{\text{Days in year}}\right)\right]$$

$$\text{Purchase price} = 100 \times \left[1 - \left(\frac{0.0008 \times 182}{360}\right)\right] = £99.959556$$

To calculate the bey from this bill, a 365-day (366 in a leap year) year is used (because a 360-day year would underestimate the return):

$$\text{bey} = \frac{\text{Face value} - \text{Purchase price}}{\text{Purchase price}} \times \frac{\text{Days in year}}{\text{Days to maturity}} \times 100$$

$$\text{bey} = \frac{100 - 99.959556}{99.959556} \times \frac{365}{182} \times 100 = 0.081143\% \text{ per annum}$$

The effective annual rate (over a 12-month investment period) assuming compounding after reinvesting at day 182 with the same bey on this T-bill is:

$$\text{EAR} = \left(1 + \frac{0.00081143}{365/182}\right)^{365/182} - 1 = 0.08116\%$$

Commercial paper

After T-bills, commercial paper is the most common money market instrument. It is a very popular way of raising money for large, well-regarded companies.

Example 14.5

Commercial paper

A dealer buys $2,000,000 worth of Eurodollar commercial paper from a company requiring liquidity, with a 60-day maturity, at a discounted price of $1,994,874. For Eurodollar (and most other Eurocurrency) deals interest is calculated using an actual/360-day count convention (the same as in the US).

The **discount yield** (using an actual/360-day count) is:

$$d = \frac{(\text{Face value} - \text{Purchase price})}{\text{Face value}} \times \frac{\text{Days in year}}{\text{Days to maturity}} \times 100$$

$$= \frac{(2,000,000 - 1,994,874)}{2,000,000} \times \frac{360}{60} \times 100 = 1.5378\% \text{ per annum}$$

The bey using an actual/365-day count is:

$$\text{bey} = \frac{(\text{Face value} - \text{Purchase price})}{\text{Purchase price}} \times \frac{\text{Days in year}}{\text{Days to maturity}} \times 100$$

$$\text{bey} = \frac{(2,000,000 - 1,994,874)}{1,994,874} \times \frac{365}{60} \times 100 = 1.5632\% \text{ per annum}$$

The effective annual rate is:

$$\text{EAR} = \left(1 + \frac{0.015632}{365/60}\right)^{365/60} - 1 = 1.57345\%$$

For UK commercial paper the day count convention is actual/365 days.

Repurchase agreements

Repurchase agreements (repos) and reverse repos are collateralised agreements used mainly by banks to borrow from or lend to each other with cash that is available for a short time (usually overnight or for a few days). Repo rates are calculated for a variety of maturities.

Example 14.6

Repurchase agreement

A high street bank has the need to borrow £6 million for 14 days. It agrees to sell a portfolio of its financial assets, in this case government bonds, to a lender for £6 million. An agreement is drawn up (a repo) by which the bank agrees to repurchase the portfolio (or an equivalent portfolio) 14 days later for £6,001,219.73. The extra amount of £1,219.73 represents the interest on £6 million over 14 days at an annual rate of 0.53%. Using an actual/365-day count convention, the calculation is:

$$\text{Interest} = \text{Selling price} \times \text{Interest rate} \times \frac{\text{Days to maturity}}{\text{Days in year}}$$

$$\text{Interest} = 6,000,000 \times \frac{0.53}{100} \times \frac{14}{365} = £1,219.73$$

Note that the agreement is to 'sell' securities and thereby borrow on a particular date. The **value date** is when the transaction acquires value. This is not always the same as the **settlement date** – when the amounts are actually transferred, i.e. 'settled' or 'cleared' – because the value date may fall on a non-business day such as a weekend.

Example 14.7

Repo bond equivalent yield

A financial institution borrows £26 million through a repo for 14 days. The difference between the amounts in the first and second legs is £5,285.48, therefore the annual rate of interest (bey) is:

$$\text{bey} = \frac{\text{Repurchase amount minus selling amount}}{\text{Amount of cash received in first leg}} \times \frac{\text{Days in year}}{\text{Days to maturity}} \times 100$$

$$\text{bey} = \frac{5,285.48}{26,000,000} \times \frac{365}{14} \times 100 = 0.53\%$$

In some markets, e.g. the US, the **repo yield** or **repo rate of interest** is calculated based on a 360-day year:

$$\text{Repo yield} = \frac{\text{Repurchase amount minus selling amount}}{\text{Amount of cash received in first leg}} \times \frac{360}{\text{Days to maturity}} \times 100$$

Of course, this is not the bond equivalent yield, but merely the convention used in some places to work out yields and prices of repurchases, strangely enough. The repo rate is the one that will be most quoted in these markets, so you need to remember that this is not even close to the true annualised interest rate.

Example 14.8

Repo interest paid

A bank lends £45 million overnight at an annual bey rate of 0.42%. The actual amount of interest is:

$$\text{Amount of interest} = \text{Amount lent} \times \frac{\text{interest rate (annualised, bey)}}{100} \times \frac{\text{Days to maturity}}{\text{Days in year}}$$

$$\text{Amount of interest} = 45,000,000 \times \frac{0.42}{100} \times \frac{1}{365} = £517.81$$

Example 14.9

A repo buy-back amount

A company owning £20 million worth of Treasury bills wishes to raise cash on 28 February and enters into an agreement to sell the bills and buy them back in one week's time. The agreed buy-back price would be £20 million plus the accrued interest. The bond equivalent yield on 28 February for a one-week repo is 0.52167%:

$$\text{Buy-back price} = \text{Selling price} + \left(\text{Selling price} \times \text{Interest rate} \times \frac{\text{Days to maturity}}{\text{Days in year}} \right)$$

$$\text{Buy-back price} = 20,000,000 + \left(20,000,000 \times \frac{0.52167}{100} \times \frac{7}{365} \right) = £20,002,000.93$$

This is not quite what happens in the markets because they impose 'haircuts'.

Haircuts

Haircuts counteract the possibility of loss due to a drop in value of the securities involved in a repo (and illiquidity and counterparty risk) by reducing the cash received by the seller for a given quantity of collateral. The lender makes sure that there is more collateral than the amount actually lent, also called margin or over-collateralisation.

Example 14.10

A repo with a haircut

If a company has ownership of £20 million of gilts and wishes to raise money for 7 days through the repo market it can do so, but not all of the £20 million can be borrowed. If a 0.95% haircut is imposed on £20 million, given a bond equivalent yield of 0.52167%, the seller receives £19,810,000 in return for £20 million worth of securities being sold in the first leg to the lender. Note that the repo interest is only applied to the lesser amount.

The buyer (lender) pays out £19,810,000, but has securities worth £20 million, and receives interest on the amount of cash actually lent. The buy-back price of a repo with a haircut can then be calculated:

Buy-back price

$$= \text{Selling price} + \left[(\text{Selling price} - \text{Haircut}) \times \text{Interest rate} \times \frac{\text{Days to maturity}}{\text{Days in year}} \right]$$

Buy-back price = 20,000,000 +

$$\left[\left(20,000,000 - \left\{ 20,000,000 \times \frac{0.95}{100} \right\} \right) \times \frac{0.52167}{100} \times \frac{7}{365} \right] = £20,001,981.92$$

Certificates of deposit (CDs)

In some places CDs are issued at face value and interest is charged on them, so that at maturity the holder will receive the face value plus interest. In other places the value at maturity is called the face value.

Example 14.11

Certificate of deposit

A £75,000 CD is issued on 15 March for two months at 1.04% (expressed as an annual rate, even though the money is deposited for a mere two months, often called the coupon rate). Using an actual/365-day count, this means that the holder will receive the following at maturity, including accumulated interest:

$$\text{Value at maturity} = \text{Face value} + \left(\text{Face value} \times \frac{\text{Interest}}{100} \times \frac{\text{Days to maturity}}{\text{Days in year}} \right)$$

$$\text{Value at maturity} = 75{,}000 + \left(75{,}000 \times \frac{1.04}{100} \times \frac{61}{365} \right) = £75{,}130.36$$

If the CD is sold to another investor with 16 days left to maturity, its present value (at the time of sale) if annual rates of interest on 16-day CDs are 1.04% is:

$$\text{Present value} = \frac{\text{Value at maturity}}{1 + \left(\dfrac{\text{Interest}}{100} \times \dfrac{\text{Days to maturity}}{\text{Days in year}} \right)}$$

$$\text{Present value} = \frac{75{,}130.36}{1 + \left(\dfrac{1.04}{100} \times \dfrac{16}{365} \right)} = £75{,}096.12$$

Thus, the second holder of the CD will pay £75,096.12 now and receive £75,130.36 from the holder if they keep it for another 16 days.

The annualised yield to maturity of this CD held for 16 days is:

$$\text{Yield to maturity} = \frac{\text{Value at maturity} - \text{Present value}}{\text{Present value}} \times \frac{\text{Days in year}}{\text{Days to maturity}} \times 100$$

$$\text{Yield to maturity} = \frac{75{,}130.36 - 75{,}096.12}{75{,}096.12} \times \frac{365}{16} \times 100 = 1.04\% \text{ per annum}$$

For Eurocurrency CDs a 360-day year convention is used, thus the future value at maturity is given by the following formula:

$$\text{Value at maturity} = \text{Face value} + \left(\text{Face value} \times \frac{\text{Interest}}{100} \times \frac{\text{Days to maturity}}{360} \right)$$

It is important to remember that the interest (coupon rate) quoted in these markets is based on the 360-day convention and is not the same as the yield to maturity based on a 365-day year.

Example 14.12

Eurocurrency CD

If the quoted rate based on a 360-day year is 3% for a CD with a present value of $10 million with 92 days to maturity, the value at maturity is:

$$\text{Value at maturity} = \$10m + \left(\$10m \times \frac{3}{100} \times \frac{92}{360} \right) = \$10.076667m$$

Bill of exchange

Bills of exchange are used by companies to facilitate trading by granting a credit period to a customer. The customer signs a bill (accepts it) promising to pay a sum of money to the seller at a set date.

Example 14.13

Bill of exchange

A customer has accepted a bill of exchange which commits it to pay £400,000 in 180 days. The supplier needs to raise cash immediately and so sells the bill to a discount house or bank for £390,000. The discounter will, after 180 days, realise a profit of £10,000 on a £390,000 asset. To calculate the effective rate of interest over 180 days:

$$\text{Interest} = \frac{\text{Discount}}{\text{Discounted price}} \times 100$$

$$\text{Interest} = \frac{10,000}{390,000} \times 100 = 2.5641\%$$

To calculate the annual rate of interest, the bond equivalent yield, this equates to:

$$\text{bey} = \frac{\text{Discount}}{\text{Discounted price}} \times 100 \times \frac{\text{Days in year}}{\text{Days to maturity}}$$

$$\text{bey} = \frac{10,000}{390,000} \times 100 \times \frac{365}{180} = 5.1994\%$$

Through this arrangement the customer has the benefit of the goods on 180 days' credit, the supplier has made a sale and immediately receives cash from the discount house amounting to 97.4359% of the total due. The discounter, if it can borrow its funds at less than 2.5641% over 180 days, turns in a healthy profit.

Banker's acceptance

With banker's acceptances it is a bank that takes on the liability to pay a sum of money on a fixed date.

Example 14.14

The use of a banker's acceptance

A German company purchases €8.5 million of goods from a Swiss company. It draws up a document promising to pay for the goods in 90 days' time, which its bank accepts, that is, it is obliged to pay €8.5 million when it is due.

By stamping 'accepted' on the document, the document becomes more valuable than if the promise to pay was given by the buying company only. Also it is a negotiable (sellable) instrument.

Twenty days after the Swiss exporter receives the banker's acceptance (BA) it decides to sell it in the money market to raise some extra short-term finance. It is sold at a discount of 0.95%. To calculate how much (the selling price) it receives:

Selling price = Face value − (Face value × Discount percentage)

$$\text{Selling price} = 8,500,000 - \left(8,500,000 \times \frac{0.95}{100} \right)$$

$$= €8,419,250, \text{ a discount of } €80,750$$

To calculate the annual rate of interest, the bond equivalent yield, which this is costing them:

$$\text{bey} = \frac{\text{Discount amount}}{\text{Discounted price}} \times 100 \times \frac{\text{Days in year}}{\text{Days to maturity}}$$

$$\text{bey} = \frac{80,750}{8,419,250} \times 100 \times \frac{365}{70} = 5.0011\%$$

The exporter can shield itself from the risk of exchange rates shifting over the remaining 70 days until the BA pays out by discounting the acceptance, receiving euros and then converting these to Swiss francs. And, of course, the exporter is not exposed to the credit risk of the importer because it has the guarantee from the importer's bank.

The 360-day convention

A point of potential confusion: bear in mind that in the US and many other money markets the rate of discount is quoted as an annualised rate based on a 360-day year.

Example 14.15

A US banker's acceptance

If an institution sells a BA with a face value of $10 million when the rate of discount is quoted at 3.05% based on a 360-day convention and the length of time to maturity is 60 days, the amount to be received is:

$$\text{Selling price} = \text{Face value} - \left(\text{Face value} \times \text{Discount percentage} \times \frac{\text{Days to maturity}}{360} \right)$$

$$\text{Selling price} = 10{,}000{,}000 - \left(10{,}000{,}000 \times \frac{3.05}{100} \times \frac{60}{360} \right) = \$9{,}949{,}166.67$$

PART 5
SOME VARIATIONS ON A BOND THEME

CHAPTER 15
SECURITISATION

In the strange world of modern finance you sometimes need to ask yourself who ends up with your money when you pay your monthly mortgage, or your credit card bill or the instalment payment on your car. In the old days you would have found that it was the organisation from which you originally borrowed and whose name is at the top of the monthly statement. Today you cannot be so sure because there is now a thriving market in repackaged debt – debt that is tied up in the bond markets.

Asset-backed securities

In this market a mortgage lender, for example, collects together a few thousand of its mortgage 'claims' (the right of the lender to receive regular interest and capital from the borrowers); it then sells those claims in a collective package as bonds to other institutions, or participants in the market generally. This permits the replacement of long-term illiquid assets with immediate cash (improving liquidity and financial gearing), which can then be used to generate more mortgages. It may also allow a profit on the difference between the interest on the mortgages and the interest on the bonds. The mortgages might be generating 6% interest, but the bonds secured on the cash flow from the mortgages might pay a coupon of only 5%. The 5% is known as the **pass-through** rate, the rate that is passed through to investors once fees and commission have been deducted.

The borrower is usually unaware that the mortgage is no longer owned by the original lender and everything appears as it did before, with the mortgage company acting as a collecting agent for the buyer of the mortgages. The mortgage company is usually said to be a seller of **asset-backed securities (ABS)** to other institutions (the 'assets' are the claim on the mortgage interest and capital) and so this form of finance is often called **asset securitisation**.

Rather than selling bonds in the mortgage company itself, a new company is established, called a **special purpose vehicle (SPV)** or **special purpose entity (SPE)**. This new entity is then given the right to collect the cash flows from the mortgages. It has to pay the mortgage company for this. To make this payment it sells bonds secured against the assets of the SPV (e.g. mortgage claims). By creating an SPV there is a separation of the creditworthiness of the assets involved from the general creditworthiness of the parent company.

Asset-backed securitisation involves the pooling and repackaging of relatively small, homogeneous and illiquid financial assets into liquid securities.

The sale of the financial claims can be either 'non-recourse', in which case the buyer of the securitised bonds (the lender to the SPV) bears the risk of non-payment by the mortgage holders, or 'with recourse' to the mortgage lender should the mortgage payment fall short (with recourse the bonds might be said to have 'credit enhancement').

Example 15.1

Car loan securitisation

GM Financial, the subsidiary of General Motors responsible for administering car loans, which regularly securitises its loans, explains securitisation on its website. Notice the recourse to GM if some customers do not pay – it suffers any 'credit losses':

> The securitization named 2007-D-F has an average customer interest rate of 16.9 percent, but we are only required to pay the investors approximately 5.5 percent. Therefore, GM Financial will earn a 11.4 percent net interest margin (16.9 percent minus 5.5 percent) on these loans before covering credit losses, operating expenses and any fees associated with the securitization. Utilizing a securitization locks in the net interest margin for the company for the entire life of the securitization, removing exposure to changes in interest rates for these specific loans.

> As net interest margin is generated, cash is available to the company to cover operating costs, credit losses and taxes. Anything left over is GM Financial's profit. This can be reinvested in new loans. Then, we start the cycle again – originating new loans, funding our dealers and transferring loans to warehouse lines or securitization trusts.

Source: www.gmfinancial.com

A wide variety of securitised bonds

The assets used in securitisations vary enormously. Securitisation has even reached the world of rock. Iron Maiden issued a long-dated $30 million asset-backed bond securitised on future earnings from royalties. It followed David Bowie's $55 million bond securitised on the income from his earlier albums. Tussauds has securitised ticket and merchandise sales, Keele University has securitised the rental income from student accommodation, and Arsenal Football Club has securitised £260 million future ticket sales at the Emirates Stadium. Loans to Hong Kong taxi drivers have been securitised, as have the cash flows from UK funeral fees. In the US, the **Student Loan Marketing Association (Sallie Mae)** is a publicly traded company which both provides student loans and buys them from other providers, then sells bonds collateralised (secured) on these loans.

The securitisation desks of investment banks are nothing if not innovative. Recent ideas include securitising the cash flows from solar panel output and from rents on houses – see Article 15.1.

Article 15.1

Sunshine-backed bond to go on sale

By Tracy Alloway

Financial Times November 4, 2013

The world's first sunshine-backed bond could be sold in the coming weeks after securing a coveted credit rating that should make it palatable to large investors.

SolarCity said on Monday it would sell a $54.4m bond backed by cashflows from the rooftop solar panels leased to US home owners, who can then claim certain tax breaks from the government. Credit Suisse is bookrunner for the securitisation, which will only be eligible to be sold to big, qualified investors.

According to people familiar with the proposed deal, the bonds have secured a credit rating from Standard & Poor's and pre-marketing of the private placement began on Friday.

Bankers have been experimenting with new assets that can be bundled and sold to investors, as they take advantage of resurgent demand for higher-yielding, sliced-and-diced securitisations. For instance, this week bankers also began selling another type of securitisation backed by foreclosed houses that have been turned into rental homes.

Deutsche Bank, Credit Suisse and JPMorgan are marketing the 'Reo-to-rental' after securing a surprise triple-A rating from Moody's, Morningstar and Kroll for the bonds, which are backed by single-family rental properties owned by Blackstone.

Bankers involved in the solar panel deal had a tougher time convincing rating agencies to evaluate the bonds, according to people familiar with the transaction, after struggling to put together a deal for many months.

As talks with rating agencies about the potential deal deepened this year they hit repeated structural snags. Rating agencies usually rely on historical data to judge the risks of bonds defaulting. In the case of solar panel installations, such data is lacking, making it difficult for the agencies to assess the probability of solar panel lessors missing out on their payments.

Some bankers said that despite the risks of investing in a new asset class, the solar bonds could attract interest from investors keen to place money into environmentally friendly assets that can also generate decent returns.

'There is a pool of capital that wants to invest in these types of assets,' said one banker at a large US investment bank. 'People love to talk about clean technology and renewables, because at some level most institutional investors want to invest in things they can put in their annual report with glossy pictures.'

Solar panel companies will also be hoping that a successful sale of the bonds will provide them with an additional source of capital to finance solar panel installations. To date they have mostly relied on financing from big investment banks to help fund their growth.

With additional reporting by Arash Massoudi.

Source: Alloway, T. (2013) Sunshine-backed bond to go on sale, *Financial Times*, 4 November.
© The Financial Times Limited 2013. All Rights Reserved.

Why securitise?

Securitisation permits banks, etc. to focus on the aspects of the lending process where they have a competitive edge. Some, for example, are better at originating loans than funding them, so they sell the loans they have created, raising cash to originate more loans. Other motives include the need to change the risk profile of the bank's assets (e.g. reduce its exposure to the housing market) or to reduce the need for reserve capital: if the loans are removed from the asset side of the bank's balance sheet it does not need to retain the same quantity of reserves – the released reserve capital can then be used in more productive ways (There is more on capital reserves in Chapter 16.)

A further motive is to adjust the extent of a bank's maturity mismatch. Banking is a business with large amounts of maturity mismatching, that is, they generally borrow short-term money, e.g. deposits from you and me or interbank loans, which might have to be repaid in hours or days, and lend long term, e.g. for 5 or 25 years. Sometimes a bank reduces the risks inherent in such a mismatch by placing a group of its long-term loans, say mortgages, in an SPV and then receiving cash from the sale of securitised bonds.

The process of securitisation

In the most common type of securitisation the **originator**, the bank or other firm that supplies the assets to be securitised, places them in an **issuer**, usually an SPV, a company set up for the securitisation – see Figure 15.1. Thus the assets are not vulnerable to the insolvency of the originator, they are **bankruptcy-remote**.

Credit enhancement is usually sought, which is often a guarantee from a highly rated organisation, e.g. an insurance company, that timely payments on bonds will be made. The credit enhancement when combined with the positive effect of the ring-fencing of assets from the originator frequently allows the securitised bonds to be issued with a triple-A rating. This rating is usually a higher rating than for the originator itself.

The SPV must be a separate entity to be bankruptcy-remote from the originator, even in those cases where the originator has some degree of ownership of the SPV. To make sure, the regulators insist on features such as:

1 The SPV is in existence for securitisation only.

2 It has a board of directors separate from the originator, with independent directors having special powers over when the SPV may place itself in liquidation.

3 The SPV maintains separate assets, bank accounts and record keeping.

4 The SPV pays its own expenses.

5 The originator publicly acknowledges that the SPV's assets are separate and not available to its creditors.

6 There are no inter-company guarantees between originator and the SPV.

7 All business between originator and SPV is conducted on an arm's length basis.

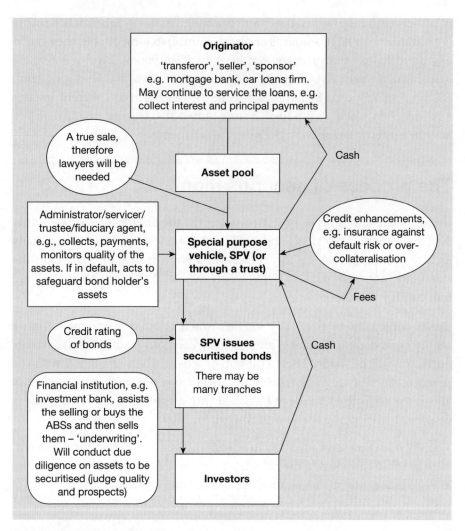

Figure 15.1 The securitisation process

There are different ways of paying bond investors:

● *Amortising (pass-through) structure.* As the interest and principal on the underlying assets are received the SPV passes these on in regular payments to the bond holders. Thus, as say mortgagees pay off their mortgages, i.e. the principal is repaid, the size of the asset pool gets smaller – there are fewer outstanding mortgages left in the SPV. This structure is commonly used for home, car and student loan assets. There may be a **pre-payment risk** with these because the bond holders do not know the proportion of borrowers who will repay their loans earlier than expected. By repaying earlier than expected the overall length of time to maturity of the pool of assets is curtailed.

● *Revolving structures*. The asset pool is topped up with new assets as principal is paid on older ones. In other words, when borrowers pay off their debt principal, the SPV then has cash which can be used to buy, say, more car loans, credit card debt, etc., but only if they fulfil key criteria in terms of quality of the financial asset. Interest payments made by the borrowers is regularly passed on to the SPV bond holders. The replacement of maturing loans carries on in the **revolving period**, but when the time comes for the **amortisation period** principal payments are paid to bond holders either periodically or in a single lump sum (**bullet** or **slug** methods).

● *Master trust*. Many batches of securitised bonds can be issued from the same SPV. A large number of mortgages, say, are sold to the SPV, which act as the collateral for a number of securitisations. ABS sold with this collateral backing in a single trust have a variety of different maturities and redemptions. The originator can replenish the asset pool by transferring new mortgages of a comparable credit quality that meet certain pre-defined minimum standards to the trust. Then additional series of ABS, identified by specific dates, can be issued. Thus a recurring process is created with numerous rounds of ABS (often called **certificates**) issues all backed by a single pool of assets. This is particularly useful where the assets are receivables with a short life, such as credit card receivables that may be paid off in a matter of days or months by the credit card borrowers. New cardholder receivables can take over from the old ones in providing cash flow and security for the ABS. Some of the ABS issued under the master trust may be of lower credit quality (offering high yields) than others.

In the UK, most mortgage-based securitised bonds, **RMBS (residential mortgage-backed securities)**, are from master trusts – see Article 15.2 – with periodic issuing of new bonds and top-ups with new mortgages. In other countries a specific bundle of ring-fenced mortgages is created, against which bonds can be issued.

Article 15.2

Recent deals signal market's reopening in the same old style

By Jennifer Hughes

Financial Times October 29, 2009

When Northern Rock decided to wind down its Granite master trust – now to be placed in the lender's 'bad bank' rump – industry insiders predicted the death of a structure that had helped the UK dominate the European mortgage-backed market.

The Granite decision, in November 2008, put all bondholders in a queue for repayments that could take years, regardless of the maturity date of the paper they held.

Investors warned that they would demand far simpler structures before venturing near the sector again.

Less than a year later, however, two master-trust-backed deals in the last month have signalled the reopening of the market in the same old style.

They have reignited a debate about how best to structure an instrument considered crucial for boosting economic growth but which represents the very complexity that triggered the crisis.

Policymakers in Europe and the US have called for simpler, more transparent structures. The industry has responded with guidelines and templates for providing more data that many big issuers have agreed to follow.

But the UK, responsible for about half the total European market before the crisis, is a particular challenge because its biggest lenders use a different structure from the rest of the world.

Most mortgage-backed securitisations are based around stand-alone, ring-fenced bundles of loans.

Bonds are backed by the loans in deals known as 'pass-throughs' because the mortgage repayments are passed to the bondholders almost as they happen.

This leaves investors with the risk of pre-payment – where the loans are repaid earlier than expected, meaning investors end up with extra cash they must reinvest – or of extension risk, where the bonds mature more slowly than expected.

In the UK, bankers have instead created master trusts – vast pools of mortgages which the lender would periodically top up with new loans and from which it would issue different bonds at different times.

The advantage was that this constant pool allowed the trust to issue the exact bonds investors wanted, such as ones with set maturity dates.

Investors were thereby freed from prepayment and extension risk and left only with credit risk, and the impact of any bad loans would be cushioned by the size of the whole giant mortgage pool.

Master trusts enabled the UK market to expand rapidly. Swathes of the bonds were sold overseas because it was far easier to arrange currency swaps on paper with set maturity dates than it would have been on a pass-through deal with its uncertain quarterly payments.

Investors liked the apparent relative simplicity of the deals. By buying bonds backed by a pool of known quality, they saved on the effort of analysing each deal in great depth.

But the upshot of the simple front was the complexity that lurked behind the master trust. 'They have got many strong positives but one big negative, and that's the complexity,' said one expert, summing up the industry's dilemma.

'Either we have a complex security or a simple-looking security backed by a complex structure.'

Some investors favour the former. 'Master trusts create concentration problems,' says Chris Ames, head of asset-backed securities at Schroders. 'If I own a 2005 bond and a 2006 bond from the same master trust, then I've simply doubled up my exposure to the exact same pool of mortgages.

'Furthermore, you lose a lot of information in a master trust pool. Because new loans are added to the existing collateral pool when new bonds are issued, the performance statistics of the older loans are diluted by the new loans.'

Steve Swallow, head of European asset-backed securities at CQS, the hedge fund, believes investors are prepared – or should be – to do the extra work required to analyse stand-alone deals.

'Providing the investor community with a proposition that requires more diligence and more consideration of risk can only be a good thing, and in the long term, the transparency will encourage more investors into the market,' he said.

Investors are unhappy at the way the structure leaves them at the mercy of the lender's treasury team, which can decide, under certain circumstances, not to repay the bonds until their legal maturity date.

This is further into the future than the set maturity date and reflects the long-term nature of mortgages.

In effect, this happened with Granite, where Northern Rock decided to no longer support the trust with new mortgages and where it will instead simply pay out on the existing bonds when the underlying mortgages are repaid.

'Before the crisis, people took complexity for granted since what would get them into trouble was so far-fetched, but now that's actually happened with Granite,' said one investor. 'Everyone is comfortable with credit risk, but it's really also extension risk they've taken. It's not always at the issuer's discretion. They might have to extend if certain things happen.'

Investor unhappiness does not appear to have yet held back the market.

Last month's £4bn ($6.5bn) deal from Lloyds was snapped up by investors who returned this week to take £3.5bn of paper offered by Nationwide, a deal even more notable because its Silverstone master trust was new to investors.

Bankers expect more deals to follow.

'We've talked to the core investor base and most of them said we want "master trusts",' said one banker on the Nationwide transaction.

David Basra, head of debt financing at Citigroup, argues that the UK structure is safer for investors. He helped structure the first master trust for Bank of Scotland.

'I'd argue that stand-alone pass-through transactions may expose investors to greater credit risk, depending of course on which mortgages back their underlying bonds,' he said.

'I think investors may find that they lose more over the cycle on some stand-alone deals because there is a greater chance they'll end up exposed to poorly under-written risk.'

 Source: Hughes, J. (2009) Recent deals signal market's reopening in the same old style, *Financial* Times, 29 October.
© The Financial Times Limited 2009. All Rights Reserved.

Article 15.3 describes the securitisation of Dunkin' Donuts' royalties received from its hundreds of franchises around the world – a steady source of income.

Article 15.3

Securitisation: it's all a question of packaging

By Richard Beales

Financial Times July 25, 2007

In a corporate securitisation, assets and related cash flows are carved out from a business into special purpose entities (SPEs) and repackaged. Debt is then raised against the SPEs alone.

'Securitisation isolates a cash flow and insulates it from extraneous events,' says Ted Yarbrough, head of global securitised products at Citigroup.

Depending on the credit quality and the quantum of borrowing, part or all the debt may be highly rated, and there is sometimes a low-rated or unrated subordinated slice of debt as well.

A financing structured this way can achieve higher credit ratings than the business on its own. This partly reflects the structural aspects – for example, the fact that the SPEs can survive a bankruptcy of the umbrella group – and partly the fact that the securities issued are often 'wrapped', or guaranteed, by highly-rated bond insurers such as Ambac, FGIC or MBIA in return for a fee.

This is a complex and costly exercise, but can result in much cheaper debt. Once established, a securitisation can be tapped again later if a business grows.

Sometimes securitisation is best suited to part of a business rather than the whole. When applied to an entire business, as with Dunkin' Brands or Domino's, the new financing typically replaces all traditional debt.

Rob Krugel, head of the esoteric asset-backed securities business at Lehman Brothers, says: 'Generally, the constituencies – rating agencies and bond insurers – require that all pre-existing debt is refinanced. There is flexibility on a go-forward basis to issue debt outside the securitisation as well as additional securitisation debt. We generally find that securitisation is so efficient there's no reason to issue debt outside the structure.'

While a securitisation does involve financial constraints, they can be fewer and less onerous than with traditional bank and bond debt. Managers would, for example, have greater flexibility to pay dividends or buy back stock.

This reflects the fact that financiers in a securitisation look only to the specific assets and cash flows held within the SPEs. But Eric Hedman, analyst at Standard & Poor's in New York, notes there can be a trade-off in terms of operational flexibility. 'Prior to the securitisation, Dunkin' was an owner operator. Now, the company is no longer the franchisor, there's an SPE. Any new store agreement is for the benefit of the securitisation.' The company's management also does not have sole discretion over advertising spending, for example.

And the Dunkin' Donuts brand is no longer owned by the company. 'The sign on the wall says "Copyright DD IP Holder LLC". That's a bankruptcy-remote SPE set up for the benefit of noteholders [in the securitisation],' Mr Hedman says.

This kind of shift might not suit all managers. But for some executives – particularly those focused on maximising cash returns to shareholders – such considerations can be outweighed by the financial benefits.

Private equity owners also like the fact that securitisations are 'portable' – they can stay in place through a change of ownership. 'That's a big hook from the point of view of sponsors,' says John Miller, US head of financial sponsors at Lehman.

But Mr Yarbrough concedes that the structural demands of securitising their entire business may not suit even the majority of companies. 'I don't know how many businesses are really going to completely fit that model,' he says. 'But what you will see is securitisation increasingly becoming a part of a financing solution.'

With the help of bond insurers, corporate securitisations can achieve triple-A or at least investment grade ratings, even if the company concerned could not have done so.

This attracts the broadest possible range of investors, including pension funds and fund managers at the most highly-rated end, and hedge funds lower down the capital structure.

Mr Krugel says the magic is in the legal separation of the assets and the creation of a tailored package for securitised investors. 'You're not fundamentally changing the operational risk of the business, but you're putting in place a lot of protections in downside cases.'

He says it is also crucial that the SPEs are bankruptcy-remote. He points to the test case of US car rental group Alamo National.

A securitised financing put in place before the group went bankrupt in 2001 survived the bankruptcy process, and was used for acquisition finance when the company was acquired by private equity firm Cerberus in 2003.

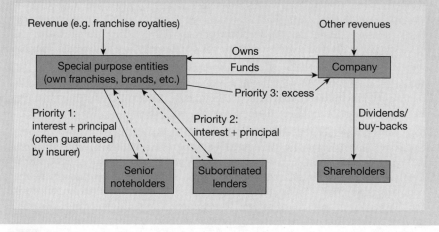

Source: Beales, R. (2007) Secularisation: it's all a question of packaging, *Financial Times*, 25 July.
© The Financial Times Limited 2007. All Rights Reserved.

The giants in the US market

The really big players in the securitisation market are the US quasi-government bodies of Fannie Mae, the Federal National Mortgage Association (FNMA), and Freddie Mac, the Federal Home Loan Mortgage Corporation (FHLMC), both 'government sponsored enterprises' (GSEs). They were privately (shareholder) owned companies acting in accordance with US government mandates to provide funding for the housing market. Even then there was an implicit subsidy from the government because everyone knew that bond holders would be bailed out by the government if anything went wrong, thus they could borrow cheaply, being regarded as virtually risk free. Sure enough, in 2008 the government had to bail them out with a $187.5 billion injection of US taxpayers' money. The value of the old shares was wiped out and Fannie and Freddie went into conservatorship, meaning they are owned by the government and profits go to the government.

Fannie and Freddie buy collections of mortgages from mortgage providers and issue bonds backed by the security of these mortgages (**mortgage bonds** or **mortgage-backed securities (MBS)**), thereby creating a secondary mortgage market. They guarantee that the interest and principal on the MBS are paid, thus the ultimate lenders have recourse to the GSE.

Ginnie Mae, the **Government National Mortgage Association (GNMA)**, also guarantees the timely payment of principal and interest payments on residential MBS backed by federally insured or guaranteed loans sold to institutional investors. These are mainly loans insured by the Federal Housing Administration (FHA) or guaranteed by the Department of Veterans Affairs (VA). Other guarantors or issuers of loans eligible as collateral for Ginnie Mae MBS include the Department of Agriculture's Rural Development (RD). Unlike Freddie Mac and Fannie Mae, Ginnie Mae neither originates nor purchases mortgage loans.

US mortgage bonds guaranteed by government-owned or sponsored enterprises are known as **agency MBS**. They make up by far the largest section of the US MBS market – they underwrite more than 80% of new US mortgages. **Non-agency MBS** are issued by banks or financial institutions, and rely on the quality of the collateral for their credit rating.

The sub-prime crisis

In the old days the government-sponsored enterprises Fannie Mae and Freddie Mac would not take just any old mortgage. They usually insisted that the house owner owed no more than 80% of the value of the house (loan-to-value ratio (LTV)) and the maximum size of mortgage was $417,000. They also investigated the borrower's income, state of employment, history of bad debts (if any) and amounts of other assets. In other words, this system was pretty safe because only the most creditworthy entered it. It was for **prime mortgages** only.

Now for some innovation: in the early 1990s new lenders emerged who were willing to lend to people who did not qualify as prime borrowers. They would often employ independent firms of mortgage brokers to persuade families to take out a mortgage. The brokers received a commission for each one sold. The number of sub-prime lenders grew significantly over the 12 years to 2005 and the proportion of mortgages that were sub-prime rose to over 20%. The rise of this market attracted the interest of the big names on Wall Street (e.g. Goldman Sachs, Merrill Lynch, Lehman Brothers, Bear Stearns and Morgan Stanley), which bought up sub-prime lenders. These borrowers could be charged higher interest rates than prime borrowers. They could also be charged large fees for setting up the loan. The sub-prime market boomed. By 2005 the largest US mortgage provider was the sub-prime lender Countrywide Financial, which had grown fast from 1980s' obscurity.

A key characteristic of the new lenders was that they lent at different interest rates to different groups of mortgagees classified on the basis of statistical models of likelihood of default. These relied heavily on the borrower's **credit score**. This score was calculated by examining a number of borrower characteristics, the most important of which became the absence (or low incidence) of missed or delayed payments on previous debts. The statisticians had discovered a high correlation between credit scores and defaults on mortgages in the 1990s and so it made sense to them to carry on with them in the 2000s. The problem was that the statisticians had not fully taken on board the extent to which mortgages in the 2000s were different to mortgages in the 1990s, particularly at the sub-prime end of the market.

Many of the 2000s mortgages required much less documentation than in the 1990s. People were often not even required to prove their level of income; they could just state their income. Nor was it necessary to pay for an independent valuation of the house; borrowers could just state the value of the house. **Stated income loans** were convenient for those without regular work, but anyone with common sense can see the potential temptation to overstating income to speculate on rising prices (they quickly became known as **liar loans** on the street – a clue that the mathematicians could have picked up on if they had taken time to glance up from the algebra).

Another change was the help given with the deposit on the house. Whereas traditionally households would have to find 10–20% of the house value as a down payment, in the new era brokers could offer a second mortgage (called a **piggyback**) which could be used as the deposit, so 100% of the value of the house could be borrowed. Taking things a stage further, the UK's Northern Rock offered mortgages that were 125% of the value of the house.

A further change was the increasing use of mortgages that had very low interest rates for the first two years (**teaser rates**), but after that they carried rates significantly higher than normal – 600 basis points above Libor was merely the average, many paid much more, i.e. well into double figures.

The more rational players in this market allowed for the qualitative changes that had taken place in the housing markets in the noughties, rather than simplistically using a mathematical model developed in the 1990s for estimating default likelihood. Those wedded to quantified data in the statistical series had difficulties adjusting to the new reality.

Originate-and-hold to originate-and-distribute

Traditionally, if a bank grants a mortgage it keeps it on its books until it is repaid. This is called the **originate-and-hold model**. In this way banks have every incentive to ensure that the mortgagee can repay and can help those few who have temporary problems along the way. Fewer and fewer banks kept mortgages on the books in the 2000s. They preferred the **originate-and-distribute model**, selling them to other investors, usually through securitisations. Alongside this development was the movement of investment banks to use their own money to invest in securities rather than only provide (lower-risk) advice and other fee-based activities.

In the 1990s only around one-quarter of sub-prime mortgages were packaged up into securitisation vehicles and sold to bond investors. By the mid-2000s three-quarters were. In the good old days Freddie and Fannie dominated this market; in the boom of the mid-2000s the private firms overtook the GSEs and issued vast quantities of mortgage-based securities – over $1,000 billion per year, cumulating to $11,000 billion by 2007. The leaders of this pack included the Wall Street investment banks as well as Countrywide and Washington Mutual.

Pressure was applied to the mortgage brokers to generate more mortgages which could then be repackaged so that the investment banks could generate fees and other profits from the transaction. The mortgage brokers were only too happy to oblige, so they ran after people to sign up for mortgages to receive commission. No job, no deposit, on welfare benefits? Don't worry, we have just the mortgage for you!

Despite losing their lead the GSEs still participated. Apart from holding hundreds of billions of dollars worth of MBS they had created, they also bought more than $1,000 billion of MBS issued by the private firms. They felt safe because they had put in place 'safeguards'. First, if the loans were at more than 80% of LTV they insisted on insurance being purchased from private insurance firms that paid out in the event of default. Second, the credit rating agencies had checked out the default likelihood on the private MBS they bought and had concluded that they should be granted AAA status. What could go wrong? Well, much of the insurance proved to be worthless as insurance companies went bust, overwhelmed by the sub-prime losses, and credit

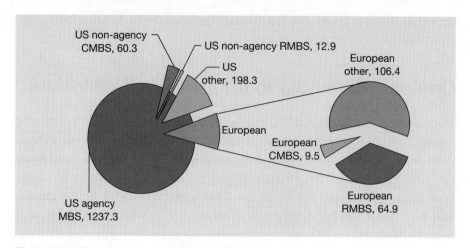

Figure 15.2 Securitisation issuance, 2013, €bn

Source: Data from European Securitisation Forum Securitisation Data Report

rating agencies looked foolish in granting high credit scores. Even they got caught up in the rose-tinted vision of the time. (Or did they, as some people suggest, have an incentive to rate excessively high? The debate rumbles on.)

The volume of mortgage payment defaults was too much for Fannie Mae and Freddie Mac and they had to be taken under government supervision in 2008 (they were too big to be allowed to fail) and government guarantees were put in place to try to restore public confidence. Fannie Mae and Freddie Mac, along with Ginnie Mae, still have an enormous slice of the ABS market – see Figure 15.2. Thus, in the land of the free (markets) most mortgage bonds are guaranteed by the government, squeezing out the private securitisation market and producing large profits. The flows of interest and principal payments for **commercial mortgage-backed securities (CMBS)** shown in Figure 15.2 come from companies paying off mortgages on commercial property (offices, factories, etc.).

European securitisation

The European asset-backed securities market is less than a quarter of the size of the US market. It has always been smaller, but it faltered particularly badly after the 2008 debacle. Also banks are currently not interested in increasing volumes of lending and so do not need to securitise, especially when they can borrow cheap money from the European Central Bank or the Bank of England – see Article 15.4.

Article 15.4

Banks shun packaged UK mortgage deals

By Christopher Thompson

Financial Times October 9, 2014

A former landfill site 10 minutes' drive from Nottingham's town centre is an unlikely symbol for the fortunes of the UK's struggling mortgage-backed securities market.

In the centre of the Showcase Cinema leisure park, amid knee-high weeds and broken bottles, stands a barn-sized building which used to house the city's biggest nightclub, called Isis. In 2009, amid a deepening recession, police ordered its closure after an R&B music night when a clubber was stabbed. It was not long before the club's owner, James Eftekhari, fell behind on his mortgage repayments.

The Isis mortgage was one of 27 'sliced and diced' commercial property mortgages that had been rolled up into London & Regional Debt Securitization No 2, a £256m MBS that subsequently defaulted. Five years later, in an echo of the wider sluggishness in the UK MBS market, the nightclub still stands vacant.

Volumes of UK MBS, whereby banks package together commercial and residential mortgages for sale to fixed-income investors, have traditionally been among the biggest in Europe. But volumes of $5.1bn for the year to date are poised to plumb the lowest annual total since the crisis in 2009.

'Issuance has gone off a cliff since 2011,' says Ganesh Rajendra at Royal Bank of Scotland.

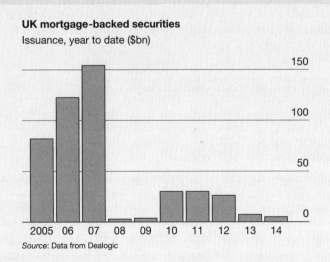

UK mortgage-backed securities
Issuance, year to date ($bn)

Source: Data from Dealogic

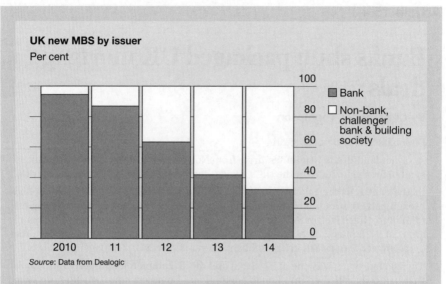

UK new MBS by issuer
Per cent

Source: Data from Dealogic

The primary reason for the fall is simple: banks do not need the funding. After volumes rose in the wake of the crisis – 2010 saw a nearly tenfold increase in ABS issuance year-on-year to $30bn – they declined sharply in 2012 after the Bank of England's 'funding for lending' scheme (FLS), which offered banks cheaper funding than selling ABS on the open market.

'Banks' need for securitisation funding has been diminished,' says Neal Shah at Moody's. 'Banks have been deleveraging their balance sheets over the past few years, and at the same time have had access to various forms of relatively cheap liquidity, including FLS.'

Even as volumes shrank investor demand remained robust. The result is that spreads – the amount of interest paid over the London Interbank Offered Rate – have declined markedly.

'Expectations of new issuance collapsed,' says Dipesh Mehta, a research analyst at Barclays. 'Before FLS a senior tranche of a residential mortgage-backed security priced at 150 basis points over Libor – now the same senior RMBS tranche is trading at between 30–50 basis points over Libor.'

As the big high street banks cut back volumes, challenger banks such as Virgin Money and Aldermore picked up some of the slack, albeit with smaller issues. In 2010 smaller banks and building societies accounted for 5% of MBS issuance. This year they account for two-thirds, according to research by RBS.

Source: Thompson, C. (2014) Banks shun packaged UK mortgage deals, *Financial Times*, 9 October.

You can see in Article 15.5 that the US market has remained extremely strong, with a blip in 2008. Investor confidence grew as it became clear in 2009–2010 that most pre-crisis securitised bonds, e.g. prime mortgage, car loan, credit card securitisations and student loans, were performing as they were supposed to through a recession. This led to high demand from insurance companies, banks, hedge funds and pension funds.

Article 15.5

Sliced and diced debt deals make roaring comeback

By Tracy Alloway

Financial Times June 4, 2014

In early June 2009, the world's securitisation bankers congregated at a London hotel on Edgware Road, not far from the prison cells at Paddington Green police station.

It was a location symbolic of the state of the securitisation industry in the aftermath of the financial crisis, when the bankers who had sliced and diced loans into bonds were in the collective doghouse. 'Regroup and rebuild' was the humble slogan for that year's 'Global ABS', or asset-backed securities, conference.

Five years later and bankers are heading to the sunnier climes of Barcelona for the annual ABS gathering. The location is, once again, suggestive of the wider state of securitisation markets – one that features a much brighter outlook.

Certain securitisation deals have roared back in the US. The European market could soon come back to life after a prolonged hibernation.

In the US, the resurgence has been swift. While the kind of subprime mortgage-backed securities that played a prominent role in the build-up to the financial crisis remain dormant, other securitisation deals have rebounded thanks to investors' hunger for yield and low corporate default rates.

Issuance of commercial mortgage-backed securities totalled $102bn in 2013, according to Dealogic data, the highest since the $231bn sold just before the crisis.

In the US investors, such as insurers and pension funds, have long been buyers of ABS. By contrast, much of the pre-crisis demand in Europe for such securities came from local banks and related structured investment vehicles which disappeared in the crisis.

'[In the US] there was continuous demand for fixed-rate product, whereas in the European market demand was much more dependent on the sale of floating-rate paper,' says Doug Tiesi, chief executive of Silverpeak.

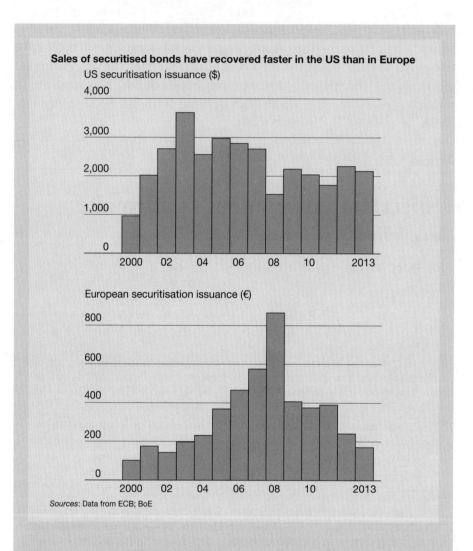

Sales of securitised bonds have recovered faster in the US than in Europe

US securitisation issuance ($)

European securitisation issuance (€)

Sources: Data from ECB; BoE

Nevertheless, there are critics who warn that the industry has yet to learn the lessons of the crisis. Adam Ashcraft, head of credit risk management at the Federal Reserve Bank of New York, warned at a conference last year: 'We haven't done anything meaningful to prevent the securitisation market from doing what it just did.'

Bankers are conscious the industry still needs to rebuild its reputation following the excesses of the past.

Source: Alloway, T. (2014) Sliced and diced debt deals make roaring comeback, *Financial Times*, 4 June.

It is hoped that the European securitisation market can grow strongly, not least because the European Central Bank and the Bank of England are helping to promote a 'high-quality' packaged debt market – see Article 15.6.

Article 15.6

Asset-backed securities: back from disgrace

By Christopher Thompson and Claire Jones

Financial Times September 30, 2014

When Ian Bell visited the European Commission in the dark days after the global financial crisis to lobby for 'high-quality' asset-backed securities, the veteran financial analyst was given short shrift. The packages of loans that were sliced and diced and sold off to investors had become one of the symbols of the type of financial engineering that brought on the worst economic crisis since the Great Depression.

'They would listen politely and say, "thanks for coming – don't call us, we'll call you",' says Mr Bell, the head of the Prime Collateralised Securities secretariat, a body set up in London to monitor the quality of ABS after the crisis.

By late 2013, however, the policy makers were inviting him back to Brussels. 'When I arrived they were sitting in a room with pads and pens saying, "high-quality securitisation – how can we make it work?"' The reason for the volte-face is simple enough: two years on from the promise by Mario Draghi, president of the European Central Bank, to do 'whatever it takes' to save the euro.

Mr Draghi gave the eurozone a much-needed respite, pushing euro borrowing costs for banks and governments to record lows. But as concerns have grown in recent months about deflation, Mr Draghi has realised that more radical intervention is needed. He says a reinvigorated ABS market will allow banks to start lending again to struggling small- and medium-sized businesses.

The ECB is expected to announce details on Thursday in Naples of an ambitious plan to buy hundreds of billions of euros of repackaged debt in order to kick-start bank lending.

'Assets only recently branded as toxic are being heralded as potential saviours,' says Andrew Jackson at Cairn Capital.

Supporters say a revival in the eurozone's moribund ABS market would allow banks to trim their bloated balance sheets and free up capital for lending. This would allow smaller companies to borrow money to invest in their businesses. But it would also entail unprecedented levels of credit exposure for the ECB. Mortgage-backed securities account for about two-thirds of the ABS market.

'The ECB is taking a bet on the credit market, and by opening to mortgage-backed purchases, especially the housing market, which has potentially powerful fiscal implications for the eurozone area,' says Carlo Altomonte, a professor at Bocconi University.

The plan has powerful critics. Last week, Wolfgang Schäuble, Germany's finance minister, voiced his unease. 'I am not particularly happy about the debate started by the ECB about the purchase of securitisation products.'

The ECB and Bank of England consider a revival of the market as a way of transforming European finance from a system based on bank loans to a US-style system weighted more in favour of capital markets.

Europe's bank dependence is stark: banks account for nearly 80% of corporate loans compared with about 50% in the US. With a greater variety of non-bank sources of finance, businesses' access to credit is not solely tied to the fortunes of their high street bank. Proponents of the plan point to the US programme of asset purchases as evidence that it can work in Europe.

The US Federal Reserve has $1.7tn in mortgage-backed securities on its balance sheet as a result of its buying programme since 2009, leading to a sharp rebound in US ABS volumes. The ability to sell historic debts has given banks more lending capacity. Commercial and industrial loans, for example, have risen by 45% to $1.74tn since late 2010.

'The key takeaway [from the US] is "build it and they will come",' says Jim Caron at Morgan Stanley. 'There were many questions about who would invest and would it work. But once the government started to buy [MBS] it kick-started other forms of lending and moved collateral away from banks to non-banks.'

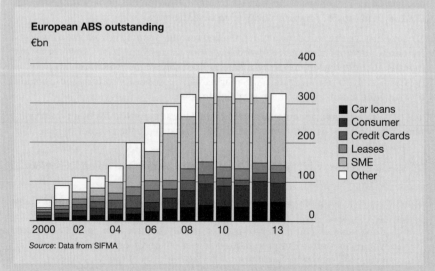

European ABS outstanding

€bn

Car loans
Consumer
Credit Cards
Leases
SME
Other

Source: Data from SIFMA

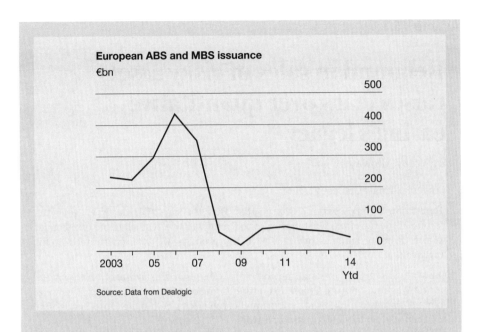

European ABS and MBS issuance
€bn

Source: Data from Dealogic

There is also evidence that Europe's inventory of ABS is in better condition than that of the US, where default rates were much worse. Of more than 9,000 European ABS notes issued during the past decade, only 2% have defaulted or are likely to realise future losses, according to Moody's Investors Service, compared with about a fifth of US ABS.

Mr Draghi said the ECB would only buy products that were 'simple, transparent and real'.

The ECB could start with ABS backed by SME, consumer and car loans, of which there is €300bn outstanding. Most existing ABS are held by banks as collateral in exchange for ECB loans. If the ECB included all banks' outstanding loans and mortgages that could be feasibly packaged, the potential ABS could be €3tn.

Source: Thompson, C. and Jones, C. (2014) Asset-backed securities: back from disgrace, *Financial Times*, 30 September.
© The Financial Times Limited 2014. All Rights Reserved.

Even sub-prime is making a come-back in the US, with bonds securitised on sub-prime car loans selling particularly well – see Article 15.7. Quantitative easing is discussed in Chapter 16.

Article 15.7

Rebound in sales of risky assets raises fears over quantitative easing's legacy

By Tracy Alloway

Financial Times October 27, 2014

'Bankruptcy? Repossession? Charge-offs? Buy the car YOU deserve,' says the banner at the top of the Washington Auto Credit website. A stock photo of a woman with a beaming smile is overlaid with the promise of '100% guaranteed credit approval'.

On Wall Street they are smiling too, salivating over the prospect of borrowers taking Washington Auto Credit up on its enticing offer of auto financing. Every car loan advanced to a high-risk, subprime borrower can be bundled into bonds that are then sold on to yield-hungry investors.

These subprime auto 'asset-backed securities' have, like a host of other risky assets, been beneficiaries of six years of quantitative easing.

When the Fed began asset purchases in late 2008 the premise was simple: unleash a tidal wave of liquidity to force nervous investors to move out of safe investments and into riskier assets.

It is hard to argue that the tactic did not work; half a decade of low interest rates and QE appears to have sparked an intense scrum for riskier securities as investors struggle to make their return targets. Wall Street's securitisation machine has kicked back into gear to churn out bonds that package together corporate loans, commercial mortgages and, of course, subprime auto loans.

The question now is whether the rebound in sales of risky assets will prove to be a toxic legacy of QE in a similar way that the popularity of subprime mortgage-backed securities was partly spurred by years of low interest rates before the financial crisis.

'QE has flooded the system with cash and you're really competing with an entity with an unlimited balance sheet,' says Manish Kapoor of West Wheelock Capital. 'This has enhanced the search for yield and caused risk appetites to increase.'

The subprime auto loan market is a case in point. Lured by the higher returns on offer from investing in subprime auto ABS, investors have flocked to buy the securities.

Washington Auto Credit, just one of many similar companies in a burgeoning industry, helps would-be car owners find financing for their vehicle purchases by connecting them with a growing crop of subprime car lenders. On its website, it lists Flagship Credit Acceptance, a relatively new auto lender backed by the private equity firm Perella Weinberg, as one of its partners.

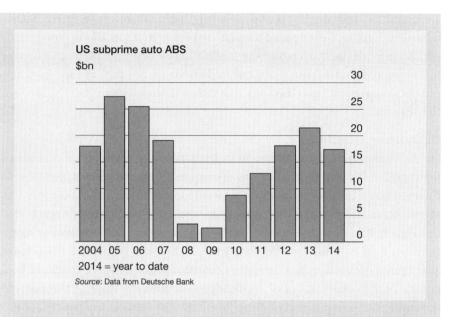

US subprime auto ABS
$bn

2014 = year to date

Source: Data from Deutsche Bank

Like other subprime auto lenders, Flagship has been able to grow its business by tapping strong investor demand for subprime auto ABS. So strong is that demand that Flagship has been marketing ABS with a 'prefunding' feature – in effect selling securitised bundles of auto loans before the loans have even been made.

Such prefunding features were a hallmark of securitisation markets before the crisis, when demand for residential mortgage-backed securities was so high that it outstripped supply of new loans. Now a similar dynamic appears in play, prompting concerns that investors' relentless search for yield will once again end poorly.

There remains a lingering unease that investors are being herded into asset classes that may not be adequately compensating them for the risks involved. Some are already leveraging their portfolio and using derivatives to help amplify their returns during a period of unprecedented low interest rates.

Source: Alloway, T. (2014) Rebound in sales of risky assets raises fears over quantitative easing's legacy, *Financial Times*, 27 October.

Covered bonds

Covered bonds are similar to the securitised asset-based bonds described above, in that a specific group of assets, e.g. mortgage receivables, is used to back up the claims of the bond holders. But covered bonds give investors extra layers of protection compared with other types of ABS. First, only banks are permitted to issue them and investors have full recourse to the bank's resources. This applies even for those issued through a special purpose vehicle which on-lends the proceeds to the originating bank (either through a loan or by buying its bonds). Thus if the covered bonds do not pay on time investors can obtain payment from the bank that issued them, albeit indirectly, through the SPV.

Furthermore, if the issuer goes bust, covered bond holders have priority claims on the assets (mortgages, etc.) held in the **cover asset pool**. This is always a segregated collection of financial assets, separate from the assets of the bank. Covered bond holders rank above unsecured creditors of the bank in being able to claim the assets in the pool. Thus covered bond holders are protected from the failure of the bank because they have a group of ring-fenced assets they can turn to, while, at the same time, if the bank is fine but the pool of assets turns out to be a dud, investors can turn to the assets of the bank held outside of the cover asset pool. In most jurisdictions the value of the assets in the cover pool is required at all times to exceed the value of the covered bonds by a prescribed amount: over-collateralisation – see Figure 15.3.

There is also the protection offered of **dynamic cover pool maintenance**, meaning that the bank has an ongoing obligation to maintain sufficient high-quality assets in the cover pool as collateral to satisfy the claims of

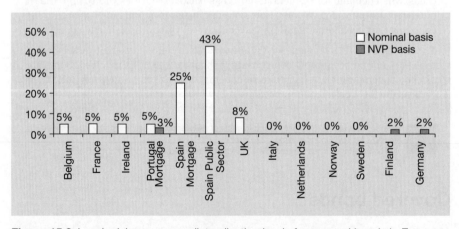

Figure 15.3 Legal minimum over-collateralisation levels for covered bonds in Europe

Source: European Covered Bond Council http://ecbc.hypo.org European Covered Bond Fact Book 2014, European Covered Bond Council http://ecbc.hypo.org/Content/default.asp?PageID=501

covered bond holders at all times. Under this the bank is required to add further assets to the cover pool to compensate for matured or defaulted assets (e.g. house owner not paying his mortgage). This contrasts with most securitisations, where the sponsoring institution is not obliged to replace defaulted assets, so the losses are borne by the bond investors.

On top of that protection, covered bonds can be issued only in strict legal and supervisory settings. Supervision typically includes:

- a special **cover pool monitor**
- periodic audits of the cover pool by the cover pool monitor
- arrangements for ongoing management and maintenance of the cover pool should the bank become insolvent to ensure continued payments to covered bond holders.

In most of the 29 countries with covered bond markets the monitor is a public authority, e.g. the banking supervisory authority. In other countries the issuing organisation (e.g. bank, SPV) appoints an external auditor (outside its control) to regularly audit the cover pool, as well as an external trustee to safeguard bond holders' interests.

The financial assets held within the cover pool include loans and bonds. There might also be derivatives designed to hedge interest rate and currency risk, but equities, property and commodities cannot be included. The most common pool asset is mortgage loans secured on residential or commercial property, but in many countries there is a large market in covered bonds where the underlying assets are loans to public entities such as regional or local authorities. Ship loans comes in a distant third.

Figure 15.4 shows the growth of this market, which in 2013 had more than €2.5 trillion outstanding, with an increasing shift towards mortgage-backed covered bonds and a decrease in the importance of public sector CBs.

We can see clearly from Figure 15.5 that the covered bond market is more significant in some European countries than others. Germany takes nearly 20% of the outstanding covered bond market (its covered bonds are called **Pfandbriefe**). Spain, Denmark and France all have around €350 billion outstanding. The UK accounts for 5% (nearly €137 billion), while the US, with less than 0.3% of the market, is only just getting going.

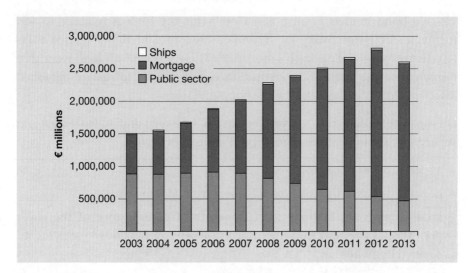

Figure 15.4 Total outstanding covered bonds outstanding bonds, 2003–2013

Source: Data from European Covered Bond Council http://ecbc.hypo.org European Covered Bond Fact Book 2014, European Covered Bond Council http://ecbc.hypo.org/Content/default.asp?PageID=501

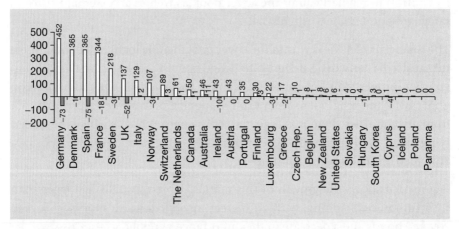

Figure 15.5 Outstanding covered bonds by country as well as change versus 2012 in billions of euros

Source: European Covered Bond Council http://ecbc.hypo.org European Covered Bond Fact Book 2014, European Covered Bond Council http://ecbc.hypo.org/Content/default.asp?PageID501

About three-quarters of covered bonds are denominated in euros, with US dollar and UK pound issues accounting for only a small fraction of the total. More than 97% in a typical year are issued with fixed-rate coupons, rather than floating rates.

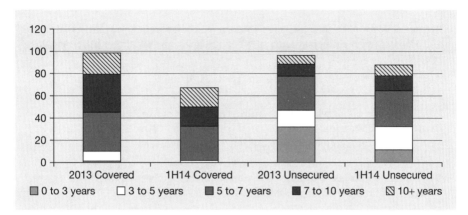

Figure 15.6 Covered bond and senior unsecured euro new issues by maturity, billions of euros

Source: European Covered Bond Council http://ecbc.hypo.org European Covered Bond Fact Book 2014, European Covered Bond Council http://ecbc.hypo.org/Content/default.asp?PageID=501

Some are short bonds, but most are medium-term bonds – see Figure 15.6.

Because of their high level of backing, covered bonds are usually given high credit ratings (AAA) and are therefore a relatively low-cost way for financial institutions to raise money. Having said that, the AAA rating is far from automatic – see Article 15.8.

Article 15.8

Moody's risk alert sparks covered bond dispute

By Tracy Alloway

Financial Times July 20, 2011

An unlikely dispute has blown up over one of the finance world's oldest and safest assets, drawing in Danish banks, rating agencies and even a George Soros venture.

Rarely do Danish covered bonds, which have their roots in the reconstruction following the 1795 fire that devastated Copenhagen, generate controversy.

But Moody's unsettled the 200-year-old market last month by warning that the bonds were carrying a higher refinancing risk.

The rating agency demanded that Danish issuers top up the debt with billions of extra funds to maintain the top ratings.

'Denmark is one of the biggest, most liquid, most transparent bond markets around and Moody's are picking on them,' says Alan Boyce, chief executive of the Absalon Project.

At the heart of the rating agency's stance is its assertion that Danish covered bonds – which pool together mortgages – are changing.

Where once the bonds were almost entirely composed of fixed-rate loans, now more than half of outstanding Danish covered bonds – some DKr1,217bn ($231bn) worth – are for financing adjustable-rate mortgage (Arm) loans, says Denmark's central bank.

But Danish banks have to reissue the bonds before the underlying loans expire, creating a refinancing risk, according to Moody's.

The interest rate that borrowers pay on their loan also changes every time the bond is refinanced, meaning they may have to pay a higher rate if the rollover comes at a time of financial stress for the issuing bank.

'Typically, Arm loans mature after 20 to 30 years while the covered bonds mature every one to three years,' Moody's says. 'Hence there is refinancing risk and the issuers' dependence on regular market access to issue covered bonds has increased with the growing volume of Arm loans.'

Covered bond issuers counter by arguing that unique features of the Danish mortgage market mitigate risk. Mortgages are capped at 80% loan-to-value and the bonds stay on bank balance sheets, aligning the interests of borrowers and the issuing banks, says renowned financier Mr Soros.

Issuers say the debt has never defaulted – not even during Denmark's early 19th century bankruptcy – and also survived the 2008 financial crisis relatively well.

Denmark now has over DKr2,300bn in outstanding mortgage bonds, more than four times the country's government bond market.

But Moody's says the refinancing risk for Danish covered bonds may still be up due to the so-called 'bail-in' rules introduced for failed banks last year by Denmark's government.

The new rules allow banks to fail and impose losses on creditors and have raised Danish banks' funding costs in recent months.

Danske Bank, which issues covered bonds through its Realkredit Danmark business, says it dropped Moody's after the agency estimated it would have to surrender an additional DKr32.5bn of collateral to maintain the triple A rating on its debt.

Smaller issuers say they will turn to other rating agencies such as Standard & Poor's or Fitch, according to Jan Knøsgaard, deputy director-general of the Association of Danish Mortgage Banks. 'The issuers can't understand Moody's decision; they find it very mechanical and very different to the position of other rating agencies,' he adds.

Danish banks have started spreading their refinancing dates throughout the year to limit the risk of big pressure points.

➡

Nykredit Realkredit, Denmark's largest mortgage lender, says it will hive off its funding for adjustable rate mortgages into a separate unit to protect the ratings on its fixed-rate covered bonds. 'The mortgage bonds have already traded back up since the Moody's announcement, and this is in an environment where everything else in Europe has widened out,' says Mr Boyce.

'If Moody's want to play hardball, they should look at some other European covered bonds, things like German Public Pfandbriefe, which are stuffed with exposure to eurozone peripherals but still retain their triple A ratings.'

 Source: Alloway, T. (2011) Moody's risk alert sparks covered bond dispute, *Financial Times*, 20 July.
© The Financial Times Limited 2011. All Rights Reserved.

The main investors in covered bonds are banks and investment funds, but there are many others – see Figure 15.7.

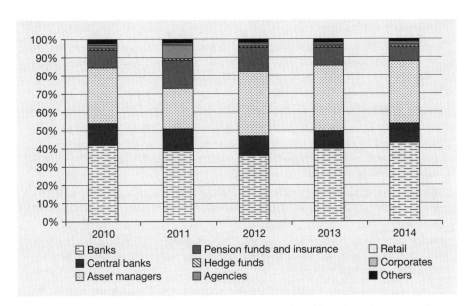

Figure 15.7 Allocation of euro-denominated covered bond benchmark issuance by investor type

Source: European Covered Bond Council http://ecbc.hypo.org European Covered Bond Fact Book 2014, European Covered Bond Council http://ecbc.hypo.org/Content/default.asp?PageID=501

Covered bonds originated in 18th-century Prussia, and Europe remains the strongest market for these bonds, where they are well understood by both investors and issuers, see Article 15.9.

Article 15.9

'Periphery' bank bonds are the comeback assets

By Christopher Thompson, Rachel Sanderson and Miles Johnson

Financial Times October 17, 2013

Banco Popolare was one of three mid-tier Italian banks which together sold €2.75bn of covered bonds last week.

Weakened mid-tier banks in the eurozone 'periphery' economies are widely seen as holding back the continent's broader economic and financial market recovery.

Yet in spite of limited capital, depressed profitability and bulky books of non-performing loans, some are returning to favour among investors.

Analysts say Italy's midsized banks are ratcheting up their bond issuances having seen an opening in the market amid indications that Italy's crippling two-year recession is coming to an end.

Last week UBI Banca, Banca Popolare dell'Emilia Romagna and Mediobanca – three mid-tier Italian banks – issued covered bonds, collectively raising €2.75bn. It was the largest weekly issue ever from Italian non-national champion banks.

With one eye on the European Banking Authority's stress tests next year, other peripheral banks are expected to follow suit.

'It's about boosting market credibility,' said Ralf Grossmann, head of covered bonds at Société Générale. 'There is the best potential [for debt issuance] in the periphery because they have been absent from the market for some time and they want to show investors that "we can do this".'

Much of the capital raising has been done using covered bonds – those backed by specific, high-quality assets held by the issuing bank – which are seen as a low-risk form of lending.

Banks in peripheral countries account for more than a third – or $31.7bn – of eurozone banks' covered bond issuance so far this year, the highest proportion since 2006, according to Dealogic, the data provider.

By contrast, senior unsecured debt issuance, viewed as a bank's bread and butter funding, has fallen in the periphery year-on-year since 2009.

Since the intervention of Mario Draghi, president of the European Central Bank, Spanish banks have been able to once again issue debt – a process started by BBVA, the country's second-largest lender by assets, which issued a five-year covered bond back in November last year.

Little wonder they are eager to flaunt their capital raising prowess.

It's not all plain sailing. Banco Popular [the Spanish bank] struggled to attract significant demand for a €750m bond it issued at the start of September, a sale not helped by uncertainty over US monetary policy at the time.

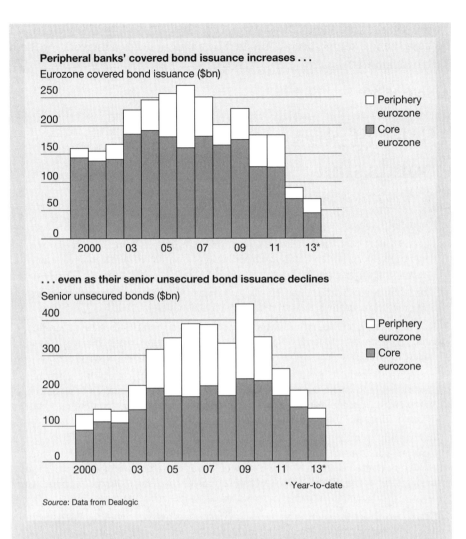

Peripheral banks' covered bond issuance increases . . .

Eurozone covered bond issuance ($bn)

☐ Periphery eurozone

■ Core eurozone

. . . even as their senior unsecured bond issuance declines

Senior unsecured bonds ($bn)

☐ Periphery eurozone

■ Core eurozone

* Year-to-date

Source: Data from Dealogic

Moreover, non-performing loans as a proportion of total bank lending continue to rise in Portugal, Ireland, Italy, Greece and Spain, according to research by Royal Bank of Scotland. Mid-tier banks bear the most exposure to bad loans and also to wider sovereign interest rate spreads.

Nevertheless, Oliver Burrows, a credit research analyst at Rabobank, believes the recent deals show the market is increasingly willing to take a punt on the periphery.

'The fact they're issuing shows there is a thawing in the market,' he said. 'It's not just covered bonds now; we've seen a flood of issuance across the capital and credit quality spectrum.'

FT | *Source*: Thompson, C., Sanderson, R. and Johnson, M. (2013) 'Periphery' bank bonds are the comeback assets, *Financial Times*, 17 October.
© The Financial Times Limited 2013. All Rights Reserved.

In the US, covered bonds make up a very small part of the bond universe because the market has been hampered by a lack of legal framework for them – see Article 15.10.

Article 15.10

Sales of ultra-safe US covered bonds stall

By Tracy Alloway and Vivianne Rodrigues

Financial Times October 14, 2013

Legend has it that Frederick the Great, the 18th century King of Prussia, sent a sword to George Washington inscribed with the words: 'From the oldest general in the world to the greatest.'

More than two centuries later, efforts to export to the US one of Frederick's oldest and greatest inventions – covered bonds – have completely stalled.

It is a far cry from the situation in July 2008, when then-US Treasury Secretary Henry Paulson recommended the specially-structured mortgage bonds as a way of offsetting the sputtering of Wall Street's loan securitisation machine.

Six years after the US government first raised the possibility of writing new rules that would help US banks sell the special debt, that legal framework is no closer. When bankers and investors gather in New York this week for a conference about covered bonds in 'the Americas' there is likely to be little excitement about the prospect of Washington – still in gridlock – creating new legislation for the debt.

Covered bonds have been a feature of the wider European debt market since Frederick crafted them in 1769 as a way of easing a credit shortage following the devastating Seven Years' War. Early iterations of the bonds allowed creditors to acquire direct claims over Prussian estates, as well as a claim on the debtor.

Giving investors the right to a specific pool of assets differentiated the bonds from so-called 'unsecured' debt which is not backed by any specific collateral.

This extra recourse remains one of the defining features of modern covered bonds. Even more important is the specially-designed law that accompanies covered bonds in many countries, and which gives investors in the debt added legal protections in the event that the issuing bank goes bust.

While those added protections have made the bonds popular with ultra-conservative investors, they have also impeded the debt's march into the US market. The Federal Deposit Insurance Corporation (FDIC) is still said to be concerned about the bonds' potential to hoover up assets from a failed or failing bank – making the government agency a key sticking point to new legislation.

The lack of a covered bond framework has not stopped the mortgage bonds from being sold in the US. For years, non-US banks, especially Canadian lenders, have been distributing 'yankee' covered bonds denominated in dollars.

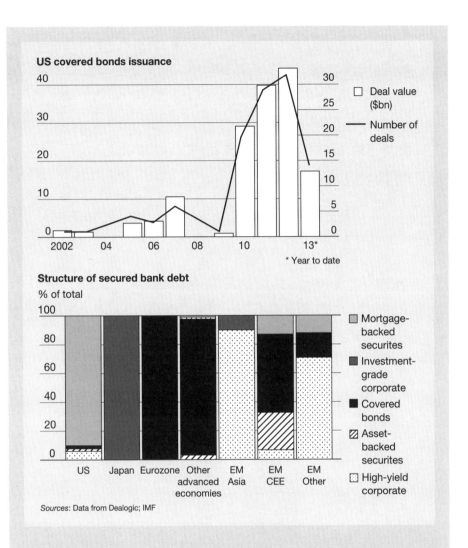

US covered bonds issuance

Structure of secured bank debt

% of total

Sources: Data from Dealogic; IMF

But sales in the US of such bonds have slumped to $17bn so far this year. That is down from $45bn in 2012 and $40bn in 2011, according to data from Dealogic.

The slower-than-expected march of covered bonds into the US is a disappointment for the debt's proponents, who still view the bonds as an elegant solution to the problem of encouraging private investors into a mortgage market which is still largely propped up by government-sponsored enterprises (GSEs).

Some in the market are now looking at alternative ways to make covered bonds work in the US and give banks an opportunity to tap an alternative source of financing, even without new legislation.

FT   Source: Alloway, T. and Rodrigues, V. (2013) Sales of ultra-safe US covered bonds stall, *Financial Times*, 14 October.

CHAPTER 16
CENTRAL BANKING INFLUENCE ON INTEREST RATES

To appreciate the influence of central banks on interest rates we need to first look at how money is created. It may surprise you to learn that, for the most part, money is not created by the actions of the central bank, it is mostly created by the commercial banks lending to people and business.

We then need to tackle the constraints on that money creation, which come largely from prudential self-restraint, with a helping hand from the central banking authorities. Because a commercial bank knows it is sensible to keep a proportion of the assets it owns in a highly liquid form, but at the same time knows that it is tempting to lend long term to gain higher interest, there is a tension within a bank on the quantity of money to hold in reserve. The central bank can influence interest rates through its supply of cash reserves, its interest rate on money borrowed from it, the level of interest it pays on money deposited with it, and its purchases and sales of money market and bond securities.

Following the 2008 financial crisis central banks significantly changed the way in which they influence interest rates in the wider economy, not least through quantitative easing. Thus we need to discuss both the 'normal' monetary policy approaches and the more recent interventions.

The start of modern banking

Imagine you are a wealthy Londoner in the 17th century. You have a problem: much of your wealth is in metal coins and you need somewhere safe to keep these. You have heard of a group of merchants known as goldsmiths who have long experience, strong vaults, high reputation and the latest technology to keep valuables safe. They've been dealing in gold for decades. You could strike up a deal with them whereby they looked after your gold and silver for a small fee.

The goldsmith gives you a written receipt. This piece of paper states the value of the coins deposited. If you wanted to buy something in a shop you could take your piece of paper to your goldsmith to receive coins to spend. But what happened next led to the development of goldsmiths as banks. The shop keeper, as likely as not, would deposit your coins with a goldsmith for safekeeping, receiving a receipt in return. It did not take long for shopkeepers to realise that a receipt from a reputable goldsmith was worth taking from a customer rather than insisting on the usual merry-go-round of collecting coin and depositing it again. The shopkeeper could simply accept the receipt and collect the coins at a later date (or get them transferred to their account at the goldsmith). The paper receipts increasingly became accepted as a form of money.

These private depositories of coin got a real boost when the rival depository, the Royal Mint, on Tower Hill, was raided by Charles I at the start of the civil war. He decided to 'borrow' the huge sum of £200,000. He later repaid, but the damage was done, trust was gone. The goldsmiths not only had higher reputations but paid interest.

Fractional-reserve banking

Goldsmiths noticed that most of the deposited coins were never taken out. On a typical day, or even a typical month, only a very small proportion of depositors turned up to demand their coins. So, reasoned the bankers, if for every £100 deposited only around £20 would need to be kept in the vault to satisfy those who turned up at the bank, why not lend out the other £80 and gain some interest? Hence only a fraction of the money deposited is held in reserve: **fractional-reserve banking**.

Money creation

Now we can move to another stage, we can actually create money. The borrowers of the money from goldsmiths were usually content to take a piece of paper – call it a **bank note** – instead of taking coins out of the bank. They could then use that as currency to buy things. The goldsmith could just create these pieces of paper off their own bat. Thus, a goldsmith-bank might have a total of, say,

£1,000 deposited, but hand out £500 of the coin as loans and issue another £5,000 or £6,000 of new paper money to borrowers.

You can see the obvious danger here: depositors might all come at the same time to demand their money – they want £1,000 back when there is only £500 in the vault. Illiquidity! But what are the chances of a high proportion of depositors wanting cash back at the same time? Minuscule, thought the bankers, and so they carried on lending beyond their **deposit base** – and this is what bankers do today. They create money out of thin air (just so long as there is a deposit base on which to build) – see Figure 16.1. Initially there is only £100, after seven actions there is £100 + £80 + £64 + £51.20 = £295.20 in the economy.

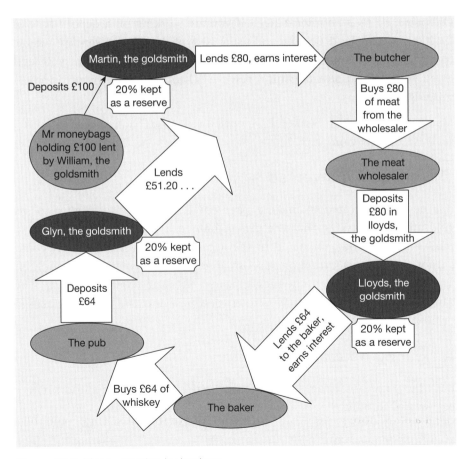

Figure 16.1 Money creation by bankers

This new money is actually debt. And it works only if people are willing to accept **bankers' promissory notes**. They do this because these notes are perceived as being 'payable on demand'. If you turned up at a bank you would have been able to swap your notes for coins. Today UK notes still state 'I promise to pay the bearer on demand the sum of twenty pounds'. However, unlike in the 17th century, if you went to collect from the Bank of England today you would only get another note in exchange – we have moved right over to pure **fiat money**. Paper money is called fiat money – it is money simply because it is declared as such by a government to be legal tender. It is money without intrinsic value other than the potential for others to trust it and accept it as money. To be useful the notes issued then and now have to carry a legally enforceable unconditional right to payment. Also, they should be negotiable – that is, transferable – between people.

Of course, there is another danger: if you are working off a deposit base of £1,000 and you lend £4,000, and then 30% of your borrowers are unable to pay, you are bankrupt. This thought should limit the amount you lend given your deposit base (a **capital reserve** is kept), but bankers occasionally misjudge this.

Many of the goldsmith-bankers developed into famous banking firms of today, such as Coutts & Company.

The cheque is invented

If a depositor wanted to make a payment he could write a letter to his goldsmith-bank asking that the person named in the letter be allowed to receive in cash the sum stated in the letter. Alternatively, the letter could authorise the transfer from one deposit account at the goldsmith to another. The earliest handwritten **cheques** appeared after the English civil war. The early 1700s saw the first fully printed cheques, and the first personalised printed cheques were produced in 1810.

A clearing house

But what if the payee banks with another goldsmith-bank? Then there had to be a way of communicating between the two. At first this process would have been laborious, as clerks from each bank would visit all the other banks to exchange cheques and then settle between them, but in 1770 the London bankers got together in one place (a tavern) to handle the cheques from many banks. This eventually became the **Bankers' Clearing House** in the early 19th century. When the railways linked up the rest of the country in the 1840s the cheque system really took off, linking up more than 150 banks.

More on fiat money

The first modern fiat paper money issued by a government was by Massachusetts in 1690. To pay off soldiers who had contributed to the latest round of plundering expeditions in Quebec, £7,000 was printed. The pieces of paper handed out were to be redeemed in gold or silver out of tax receipts in a 'few years' (in fact, they had to wait 40 years). Massachusetts' politicians loved this way of paying for things and so kept issuing paper – by 1748 there was £2.5 million in circulation. By the late 1750s all the other colonies had followed suit. It was only natural that the Continental Congress chose the tool of fiat paper money to finance the Revolutionary War (1775).

Paper money in the UK

Britain was somewhat slower in gaining government control over the issue of paper money. In 1694 the Bank of England (BoE) was founded but at this stage its job was to act as the government's banker (managing its account) and to raise money for it. It immediately raised £1.2 million for the government by getting people to subscribe to a share issue to set up the new bank (the government needed to pay for a war with France). The subscribers became the Governor and the Company of the Bank of England. While other banks were restricted in size by being limited to six partners (if they were to issue currency), the BoE, being a joint-stock company with shareholder limited liability, could issue shares to investors around the country to raise capital. Also, being so big and strong it attracted plenty of deposits. Its strength meant that by the 1780s it was acting as banker to other banks.

During the Napoleonic wars the government was borrowing so much paper money from the BoE that it ran out of gold to back the notes. The government thus declared that the notes need no longer be convertible to gold. The result of all this spending and the creation of so much fiat money was high inflation. The lesson was learned: you need to limit the quantity of paper money.

There continued to be many small banks issuing bank notes. Many were unsound, irresponsibly creating notes. In 1844 the BoE was emphasised as the main issuer of notes. From then on, there were to be no new issuers of notes and those whose issues lapsed, or that were taken over, forfeited their right to issue. Other issuers gradually died out. The notes issued by the BoE were mostly backed by its holdings of gold or silver bullion, but another £14 million was permitted (equal to the BoE capital raised from shareholders). The backing of gold (the **gold standard**) created a long period of price stability. However, today in most countries currency notes are not backed by anything other than a promise to pay – pure fiat systems.

In addition to the issue of notes and being banker to the government the BoE took on roles such as being **lender of last resort** to the banking system and was called on to stabilise the banking system in crises, which happened pretty often.

The key elements of banking

Bankers must avoid lending out via long-term loans a very high proportion of the money they attract without regard for the potential of depositors and other creditors to suddenly demand their money back. That is, banks must prudentially retain reserves of cash (and other liquid assets) to satisfy creditors as the need arises. Yet holding too much cash leads to the loss of opportunities to lend that money (acquire assets) to earn higher interest. This **liquidity management** involves a delicate balance.

Second, banks must protect themselves against the possibility of their assets falling below liabilities (what the bank owes depositors and other creditors of the bank). Such an eventuality would make a bank insolvent and unable to carry on. This might happen, for instance, if, say, 10% of the loans it has made to businesses go sour and are never repaid (as happened with HBOS following the financial crisis). If a bank was to play it ultra-safe it would always hold assets worth at least 20% more than its liabilities. This level of safety is being called for by some experts in the wake of the 2008 financial crisis, but very few banks come anywhere near that level; more typical levels are 3–5%.

This **capital management** is a much debated topic. The fundamentals are that a bank starts out with some money put in by its owners to pay for buildings, equipment, etc. Shareholders' funds, obtained by the selling of shares in the bank, have the advantage that the shareholders do not have the right to withdraw their money from the company – it is **permanent capital** (although they might sell their shares to other investors). As well as paying for the initial set-up, shareholders' capital provides a buffer acting as a safety margin against the event of a significant number of the loans granted to borrowers going wrong. The buffer is referred to as **capital** and loans made are **assets** of the bank. Deposits (and other loans to the bank) are **liabilities**:

Total assets = Total liabilities + Capital

In addition to capital being raised at the foundation of the business it can be augmented over the years through the bank making profits and deciding to keep those profits within the business rather than distributing them as dividends to shareholders – **retained earnings**. It can also be increased by selling more shares. Capital is also called **net worth** or **equity capital**.

A closer look at liquidity risk

A bank keeps a proportion of the money it raises in the form of cash (and near cash) rather than lending it all to lower **liquidity risk**, running out of liquid assets. Let us assume for now that a bank, BarcSan, is required by the central bank (its regulator) to hold 8% of the value of its deposits in reserves. These are the regulatory **required reserves**. However, the bank may judge that 8% is not enough and decide to add another 4% of the value of its current account liabilities as **excess reserves**. Reserves consist of both the cash that the bank is required to hold in its account with the central bank and cash that it has on its own premises, referred to as **vault cash**. Note that we are referring here to cash reserves and not the capital reserves (the difference between assets and liabilities). Cash reserves are there to avoid running out of cash, a short-term phenomenon, whereas capital reserves are there to avoid running out of net assets (assets minus liabilities).

Cash reserves of 12% are unusually high, but useful for illustration. A more normal figure is 1–3% of overall liabilities (not just deposit liabilities) held in cash, but another 10% or so might be held in assets that can quickly be converted to cash, such as very short-term loans to other banks, certificates of deposit for money placed with other banks in tradable form and government Treasury bills – these are termed near cash. The term for reserves that includes near cash is **liquid reserves**.

To understand the working of a bank we will start with a very simple example of a change in the cash held by a bank. Imagine that Mrs Rich deposits £1,000 of cash into her current account at the BarcSan Bank. This has affected the bank's balance sheet. It has an increase of cash, and therefore reserves, of £1,000. This is an asset of the bank. At the same time it has increased its liabilities because the bank owes Mrs Rich £1,000, which she can withdraw any time. We can illustrate the changes by looking at that part of the balance sheet that deals with this transaction. In the T-account below, the asset (cash) is shown on the left and the increased liability is shown on the right.

BarcSan partial balance sheet

Assets	Liabilities
Vault cash (part of reserves) £1,000	Current account £1,000

This increase in reserves could also have come about through Mrs Rich paying in a £1,000 cheque drawn on an account at, say, HSBC. When BarcSan receives the cheque it deposits it at the central bank, which then collects £1,000 from HSBC's account with the central bank and transfers it to BarcSan's account at the central bank, increasing its reserves. Remember: cash reserves include both those held at the central bank and those in the bank vault, tills, ATMs, etc.

Given that BarcSan has required reserves at 8% of current account deposits, following the receipt of £1,000 it has increased assets of £80 in required reserves and £920 in excess reserves.

BarcSan partial balance sheet

Assets	Liabilities
Required reserves £80 Excess reserves £920	Current account £1,000

These reserves are not paying a high interest to BarcSan.[1] What is even more troubling is that the bank is providing an expensive service to Mrs Rich with bank branch convenience, cheque books, statements, etc. This money has to be put to use – at least as much of it as is prudent. One way of making a profit

---

[1] Many central banks now do pay interest on those reserves deposited with them, but it can be quite low. In May 2014 the US Federal Reserve paid 0.25% (annual rate), for example. The BoE paid 0.5%.

is to lend most of the money. It does this by lending to a business for five years. Thus the bank borrows on a short-term basis (instant access for Mrs Rich) and lends long (five-year term loan). The bank decides to lend £880 because this would allow it to maintain its required reserve ratio of 8% and its target excess reserve of 4%.

BarcSan partial balance sheet

Assets	Liabilities
Required reserves £80 Excess reserves £40 Loan £880	Current account £1,000

Liquidity management and reserves

There may be times when a large volume of cash is withdrawn by depositors and the bank has to be ready for that. Let us look at the (simplified) balance sheet for BarcSan as a whole, all its assets and all its liabilities. We will assume that it keeps 8% of deposits as required reserves and aims to have a further 4% as excess reserves (either at the central bank or as vault cash). As well as £10 billion in deposits the bank has £900 million in capital accumulated mostly through retaining past profits. It has lent £5.7 billion and bought £3.1 billion of marketable securities such as government bonds and bills.

BarcSan's balance sheet

Assets	Liabilities
Required reserves £800m Excess reserves £1,300m Loans £5,700m Securities £3,100m	Deposits £10,000m Bank capital £900m

To satisfy its own rule of 12% of current account deposits held as reserves it needs only £1.2 billion but it currently has £2.1 billion (£800m + £1,300m). It has a 'spare' £900 million. If there is a sudden rise in withdrawals from bank accounts as people worry about the bank system collapsing and not being able to repay its deposit liabilities (as with Northern Rock in 2007, or Cypriot banks in 2013), this will have an impact on BarcSan. If £900 million of cash is withdrawn from BarcSan, its balance changes to:

BarcSan's balance sheet after a sudden withdrawal of £900 million

Assets	Liabilities
Required reserves £728m Excess reserves £472m Loans £5,700m Securities £3,100m	Deposits £9,100m Bank capital £900m

The bank still has cash reserves above its target because 12% of £9,100 million is £1,092 million (this apportioned as required reserves, 8% of £9,100m = £728m, and excess reserves, 4% of £9,100m = £364m), but the bank has £1,200 million (required reserves of £728 million plus excess reserves of £472 million). Because it started with plentiful reserves the public panic to withdraw funds has not affected the other elements in BarcSan's balance sheet.

Now take a different case, where BarcSan has already lent out any reserves above its prudential level of 12% of deposits.

BarcSan's balance sheet if actual reserves equal target reserves

Assets	Liabilities
Required reserves £800m Excess reserves £400m Loans £6,600m Securities £3,100m	Deposits £10,000m Bank capital £900m

Now imagine a financial panic: many depositors rush to the bank's branches to take out their money. In one day £900 million is withdrawn. At the end of the day the balance sheet is looking far from healthy.

BarcSan's balance sheet after £900 million is withdrawn (after the bank just met its reserve target)

Assets	Liabilities
Required reserves £300m Excess reserves £0m Loans £6,600m Securities £3,100m	Deposits £9,100m Bank capital £900m

Another day like that and it might be wiped out. It is required to hold 8% of £9,100 million as reserves, £728 million, but now has only £300 million. Where is it going to get the shortfall from? There are four possibilities.

1 *Borrow from other banks and other organisations.* The active markets in inter-bank loans, repos, commercial paper or certificates of deposit could be useful to raise the £428 million.

BarcSan's balance sheet if it borrows £428 million from the markets

Assets	Liabilities
Required reserves £728m Excess reserves £0m Loans £6,600m Securities £3,100m	Deposits £9,100m Borrowed from banks and firms £428m Bank capital £900m

However, given the cause of the crisis was a system-wide loss of confidence, BarcSan may have difficulty raising money in these markets at this time. This was a problem that beset many banks around the world in 2008, and then many eurozone banks in Greece, Cyprus, Portugal and Spain in 2011–2013. They had grown used to quickly obtaining cash to cover shortfalls from other banks. But in the calamitous loss of confidence following the sub-prime debacle and the eurozone crisis, banks simply stopped lending – those that were caught with insufficient reserves failed or were bailed out by governments.

2 *Securities could be sold.* Of the securities bought by a bank, most are traded in very active markets where it is possible to sell a large quantity without moving the price. Let us assume that the bank sells £428 million of government Treasury bills and bonds to move its reserves back to 8% of deposits.

BarcSan's balance sheet if it sells £428 million of securities

Assets	Liabilities
Required reserves £728m Excess reserves £0m Loans £6,600m Securities £2,672m	Deposits £9,100m Bank capital £900m

The short-term securities issued by respectable (safe) governments held by banks are classified as **secondary reserves** because they tend to be very easy to sell quickly, at low transaction cost and without moving the market price, even if sold in fairly high volume. Other securities held by the bank will have higher transaction costs of sale and are less easy to sell and so are not classed as secondary reserves.

3 *Borrowing from the central bank.* One of the major duties of a central bank is to act as lender of last resort. It stands ready to lend to banks that lack cash reserves. However, it will do this at a high price only (high interest rate) to deter banks from calling on it in trivial circumstances.[2] If BarcSan borrows the £428 million shortfall from the central bank to take it back to the regulator's minimum of 8%, its balance sheet now looks like this:

BarcSan's balance sheet if it borrows £428 million from the central bank

Assets	Liabilities
Required reserves £728m	Deposits £9,100m
Excess reserves £0m	Borrowings from central bank £428m
Loans £6,600m	Bank capital £900m
Securities £3,100m	

4 *Reducing lending.* Banks receive principal repayments on loans every day as the periods of various loan agreements come to an end, or as portions of loans are repaid during the term of the loan. To raise some money the bank could simply refuse any more loans for a period. I was on the sharp end of this in February 2007 when trying to complete a business property deal. Suddenly Halifax Bank of Scotland refused to lend on what was a pretty safe deal for them. I was nonplussed. What were they playing at? Didn't they know they would lose my company as a customer? Of course, with hindsight we all know that this was the start of the crisis when HBOS was desperately short of cash (it avoided complete annihilation only by allowing itself to be bought by Lloyds). Another possibility is to sell off some of the loan book to another bank – but the purchasers are unlikely to pay full value, especially in uncertain times. An even more drastic solution is to insist that borrowers repay their loans immediately. This is possible with some types of loans such as overdrafts, but it results in much resentment and damage to long-term relationships. If BarcSan raised £428 million in one of these ways its balance sheet would look like this:

---

[2] Interest charged by central banks is normally at penalty rates, but in 2014 many central banks were charging very low rates to assist banks and encourage lending.

BarcSan balance sheet after reducing loans by £428 million

Assets	Liabilities
Required reserves £728m Excess reserves £0m Loans £6,172m Securities £3,100m	Deposits £9,100m Bank capital £900m

Of course, there are a few more moves that need to be made if the bank wants to reach its target of 12% reserves, rather than simply get to 8%, but after such a crisis in the financial markets this may take a few years to achieve.

A difficult balance

A bank has a trade-off to manage. If it ties up a very high proportion of its money in reserves it loses the opportunity to lend that money to gain a decent return, but the managers can feel very safe, as they are unlikely to run out of cash. Yet if it goes for maximum interest by lending the vast majority of the money deposited long term, it could run out of cash. Thus it has to have enough reserves to avoid one or more of the following costly actions to quickly raise money: (a) borrowing from other banks; (b) selling securities; (c) borrowing from the central bank; or (d) reducing its loans. Required and excess reserves provide insurance against incurring liquidity problems due to deposit outflows, but like all insurance it comes at a high price.

Capital adequacy management

How much capital should the bank hold? In deciding this managers need to trade off the risk of bank failure by not being able to satisfy its creditors (depositors, wholesale market lenders, etc.) against the attraction of increasing the return to the bank's owners by having as little capital as possible relative to the asset base. The fear here is of **insolvency** – an inability to repay obligations over the longer course of events – rather than illiquidity, which is insufficient liquid assets to repay obligations falling due if there is a sudden outflow of cash (e.g. large depositor withdrawals on a particular day, unexpectedly drawing down on lines of credit, or large payments under derivative deals). To understand the difficulty with this trade-off we can compare BarcSan's situation with a less well-capitalised bank, Mercurial.

BarcSan's opening balance sheet

Assets	Liabilities
Required reserves £800m Excess reserves £1,300m Loans £5,700m Securities £3,100m	Deposits £10,000m Bank capital £900m

BarcSan's capital to assets ratio is £900m/£10,900 = 8.3%. Mercurial has exactly the same assets as BarcSan, but it has only £400 million in capital. It has an extra £500 million in deposits. Its ratio of capital to assets is 3.7% (£400m/£10,900m).

Mercurial's opening balance sheet

Assets	Liabilities
Required reserves £800m Excess reserves £1,300m Loans £5,700m Securities £3,100m	Deposits £10,500m Bank capital £400m

Now consider what happens if we assume a situation similar to that in southern Europe in 2013. Both banks invested £500 million in bonds issued by Cypriot financial institutions. These now become worthless as the borrowers stop paying.[3] BarcSan can withstand the loss in assets because it maintained a conservative stance on its capital ratio.

BarcSan's balance sheet after £500 million losses on Cypriot bonds

Assets	Liabilities
Required reserves £800m Excess reserves £1,300m Loans £5,700m Securities £2,600m	Deposits £10,000m Bank capital £400m

---

[3] This case illustrates a domino effect. The Cypriot banks ended up in trouble and unable to pay their debts because a few years earlier they had bought a lot of bonds issued by Greek banks. Then the eurozone 'bailout' of Greece was agreed, which resulted in default on the Greek bank bonds – they lost 70% of their value. This wiped out a tremendous proportion of assets from the Cypriot banks' balance sheets.

Its **capital to assets ratio** has fallen to a less conservative 3.8% (£400m/£10,400m), but this is a level that still affords some sense of safety for its providers of funds. (Some writers refer to the capital to assets ratio as the **leverage ratio**, others take its inverse as the leverage ratio.)

Mercurial is insolvent. Its assets of £10,400 are less than the amount owed to depositors.

Mercurial's balance sheet after £500 million losses on Cypriot bonds

Assets	Liabilities
Required reserves £800m Excess reserves £1,300m Loans £5,700m Securities £2,600m	Deposits £10,500m Bank capital – £100m

A course of action is to write to depositors to tell them that it cannot repay the full amount that was deposited with the bank. They might panic, rush to the branch to obtain what they are owed in full. More likely is for the regulator to step in to close or rescue the bank. Occasionally the central bank organises a rescue by a group of other banks – they, too, have an interest in maintaining confidence in the banking system. In 2009 Royal Bank of Scotland and Lloyds Banking Group, following the sudden destruction of balance sheet reserves when the value of their loans and many securities turned out to be much less than what was shown on the balance sheet, were rescued by the UK government, which injected money into them by buying billions of new shares. This was enough new capital to save them from destruction, but the banks are still clawing their way back to health and still trying to rebuild capital reserves.

Why might banks sail close to the wind in aiming at a very low capital to assets ratio?

The motivation to lower the capital to assets ratio is to boost the returns to shareholders. To illustrate: imagine both BarcSan and Mercurial make profits after deduction of tax of £150 million per year and we can ignore extraordinary losses such as the sub-prime fiasco. A key measure of profitability is **return on assets (ROA)**.

$$ROA = \frac{\text{Net profit after tax}}{\text{Total assets}}$$

Given that both firms (in normal conditions) have the same profits and the same assets, we have a ROA of £150m/£10,900m = 1.376%.[4] This is a useful measure of bank efficiency in terms of how much profit is generated per pound of assets.

However, what shareholders are really interested in is the return for each pound that *they* place in the business. Assuming that the capital figures in the balance sheet are all provided by ordinary shareholders then the **return on equity (ROE)** is:

$$ROE = \frac{\text{Net profit after tax}}{\text{Equity capital}}$$

$$\text{For BarcSan: ROE} = \frac{£150m}{£900m} = 16.7\%$$

$$\text{For Mercurial: ROE} = \frac{£150m}{£400m} = 37.5\%$$

Mercurial appears to be super-profitable, simply because it obtained such a small proportion of its funds from shareholders. Many conservatively run banks were quizzed by their shareholders in the mid-2000s on why their returns to equity were low compared with those of other banks, and 'couldn't they just push up returns with a little less caution on the capital ratio?' Many were tempted to follow the crowd in the good times only to suffer very badly when bank capital levels were exposed as far too daring. You can understand the temptation, and that is why regulation is needed to insist on minimum levels of capital.

Monetary policy

If the interest rates in an economy are held at a level that is too low then inflation will start to take off. This can be disruptive to businesses in addition to destroying people's savings. It is especially problematic if inflation is high and fluctuating. The resulting uncertainty about future price levels is likely to inhibit economic growth, or, at the very least, penalise those who are not protected against inflation. Unpredictability makes planning very difficult.

Yet if interest rates are set at an excessively high level this will inhibit business activity, cause people to put off buying houses and reduce spending in the

---

[4] This is at the top end of the usual range of ROAs for commercial banks.

shops, leading to a recession with massive job losses. Clearly a society needs an organisation whose task it is to select the appropriate short-term interest rate for the economic conditions it faces: neither too high nor too low. That organisation is the central bank.[5]

Controlling reserve amounts

When the amount of money spent rises faster than the quantity of goods and services produced in the economy, the result is likely to be raised inflation. To understand how a central bank controls money supply and interest rates you need to focus on the fact that it acts as banker to the banks (including other depository institutions, e.g. building societies), holding commercial bank reserves in its accounts, which banks are either formally obliged to hold or feel informally obliged to hold because of the need to settle accounts between depository institutions when cheques and electronic payments are cleared at the central bank and for liquidity-safety reasons. A central bank might insist that, say, 2% or 10% of the amount deposited by customers be held as the **required reserve ratio**.[6]

Thus, one way to control money supply and interest rates is to use its special powers to insist that each bank leaves a certain proportion of the amount it has received as deposits from its customers (households, small businesses, etc.) at the central bank. If a bank's reserves at the central bank fall below the minimum required then it has to top this up.

Many central banks, e.g. the Bank of England, some time ago moved from a fixed daily level of reserves to target balances of reserves held at the central bank on average over 'maintenance periods'. In the case of the BoE the maintenance period ran from one meeting of the committee that sets interest rates (the Monetary Policy Committee) to the next, usually one month. Smaller banks may be exempt from the system.

A couple of years before the financial crisis the BoE removed its formal insistence for banks to achieve targeted levels of reserves to be held with it. It had a 'voluntary' system. However, when motivated by self-imposed prudential liquidity levels and the need to settle payments with other commercial banks, bankers want to hold reserves at the BoE.

---

[5] Occasionally called a reserve bank or national bank or monetary authority.
[6] Also called the cash reserve ratio.

Currently, even this voluntary reserves averaging system in the UK is described as 'suspended' (since March 2009). Because there may be a return to this system, and because it is used elsewhere in the world, we need to understand the system first. While there are no formal reserve requirements in the UK, Australia, New Zealand and Canada, elsewhere, such as the eurozone, Switzerland, the US and China have reserve requirements in proportion to the bank's holdings of deposits. After describing monetary policy under a reserves targeting system we'll look at how monetary policy changed over the last few years of crisis.

Banks and other depository institutions (henceforth 'banks') like to maintain an additional buffer beyond the required reserves at the central bank, excess reserves, to feel comfortable about the prospect of a sudden outflow of cash. The target amount of the excess reserves may, in fact, be largely dictated by the banking regulator (which is usually the central bank) and may be strongly influenced by international agreements on the appropriate amounts.

Monetary base

The central bank has a liability – it accepted deposits from banks. Another liability of a central bank is what you see written on notes (or coins) that you have in your wallet or purse; the central bank 'promises to pay the bearer on demand the sum of . . .'. As well as reserves at the central bank a typical commercial bank will hold some of its assets in the form of vault cash in hand. Finally, the economy has **currency in circulation**, that is, outside of banks. The combination of reserves and currency in circulation is the monetary base:

> **Monetary base** = currency in circulation + reserves
>
> **Reserves** = required reserves + vault cash (excess reserves)

It is important to note that the sole supplier of reserves – notes and coins, and balances at the central bank as liabilities of the central bank – is the central bank.

It is changes in these accounts that can have an influence on the size of a nation's money supply. The relationship between the amount of money in banks or the wider economy and changes in the monetary base or reserves is very far from a mechanical mathematical relationship – the downturn in 2008–2013 rammed that home – but nevertheless there is, holding all else constant, a relationship. If there is an increase in either the currency in circulation or reserves there is likely (but not always) to be an increase in the money supply. Normally, an increase in reserves, either cash deposited by a bank at the central bank or vault cash, leads to an increase in the level of loans and deposits and thus contributes to the money supply.

Central banks can conduct monetary policy by changing the country's monetary base.

The monetary base described above is sometimes referred to as M0, which is a very extreme form of **narrow money**, i.e. defining what money is in a very narrow way. Banks can use this base to create **broad money**, which is a multiple of the monetary base. The definitions of broad money vary from country to country, but generally include money that is held in the form of a current (checking) account or deposit account, and some money market instruments such as certificates of deposit. These broad money aggregates often have names such as M3 or M4. You can see why it is difficult to define money because banks can 'create money' – see the Example 16.1 below.

Example 16.1

Money creation – the deposit multiplier

Assume that all banks in a monetary system are required to keep 20% of deposits as reserves. Bank A has $100 million of deposits from customers. Because it is sticking to the reserve requirement, both required by the central bank and its own prudential reserves policy, it lends out only $80 million and keeps $20 million as cash or in its account with the central bank (assume no vault cash for simplicity).

Bank A's opening balance sheet

Assets	Liabilities
Reserves $20m Loans $80m	Deposits $100m

Now, if deposits in Bank A are increased by $5 million, the position changes (we'll look at where it got $5 million from in a minute – this is crucial). Deposits rise to $105 million and reserves rise to $25 million as the additional $5 million is initially held as reserves at the central bank.

Bank A: an increase in deposits – intermediate period

Assets	Liabilities
Reserves $25m Loans $80m	Deposits $105m

This means that the reserve ratio has risen to $25m ÷ $105m = 23.8%. The bank earns no or little interest from reserves, so it will wish to reduce it back to 20% by lending out the extra. The next balance sheet shows the amount of lending that leaves a 20% reserve ratio, $84 million.

Bank A: lending out just enough to attain minimum reserve ratio

Assets	Liabilities
Reserves $21m Loans $84m	Deposits $105m

Now let us bring in more banks. In lending an additional $4 million Bank A will have an impact on the rest of the banking system. If the $4 million is lent to a company and, initially at least, that company deposits the money in Bank B, then at the central bank, Bank A's account will be debited (reserves go down) and Bank B's account will be credited (reserves increase). Bank B will lend out 80% of the amount, or $3.2 million, keeping $800,000 in reserves to maintain its 20% ratio of reserves to deposits. The $3.2 million lent finds its way to Bank C, which, again, holds 20% as reserves and lends the rest . . . and so on. At each stage 80% of the deposit is lent out, increasing the deposits of other banks, encouraging them to lend.

The effect on the banking system of an injection of $5 million of money, under a reserve ratio of 20%

	Change in deposits, $m	Change in loans, $m	Change in reserves, $m
Bank A	5.00	4.00	1.00
Bank B	4.00	3.20	0.80
Bank C	3.20	2.56	0.64
Bank D	2.56	2.05	0.51
Bank E	2.05	1.64	0.41
Bank F	. . .	. . .	. . .
Bank G	. . .	. . .	. . .
Bank . . .			
Total of all banks	25	20	5

The deposit multiplier is a reciprocal of the reserve ratio, which in this case = 1 ÷ 0.20 = 5. Following an injection of $5 million into the financial system, the whole process ends when an additional $25 million of deposits have been created; equilibrium has been reached again. Broad money grows by $25 million.

Reality check: please note that the model is a simplification for illustrative purposes. In reality, there might be leakages from the system due to money flowing abroad, or people increasing currency holdings,[7] or buying government bonds rather than placing it in bank deposits. People and companies might be so shocked by an economic downturn that instead of borrowing more they repay old debt, thus working against the multiplier. Banks might also be in such turmoil that they would rather reduce their loan book than expand lending despite huge injections of deposits (they increase excess reserves). But for now we'll go along with the logic of the deposit or money multiplier in 'normal' times, with an assumed mathematically pure relationship between narrow and broad money.

The key point to remember is: the creator of the monetary base is the central bank because it has a monopoly on the issuance of currency. If it has control over this then it can influence the broader money supply (including deposits at banks) through the reserves requirements. So, once the system has settled down from the injection of a new deposit, it will be fairly stable – little money creation or removal.

Here is the crucial bit about the source of the additional deposits of $5 million: if it came from a customer who withdrew it from another bank then the example is null and void because while Bank A benefits from the $5 million deposit, the other bank, Bank X, sees a reduction in its reserves at the central bank by an equal amount. It can now lend less than it could before because it has to rebuild its reserves. Thus the stimulus effect of Bank A's deposit is exactly offset by the removal of money from the system by Bank X. If, however, the

---

[7] If none of the extra reserves finds its way into currency then the example, assuming all else equal, would be describing the **money multiplier**. However, the money multiplier is usually a much smaller number than the deposit multiplier because a significant proportion of the new reserves finds its way into currency and this does not lead to multiple deposit expansion.

$5 million came from the central bank purchasing Treasury bills from an investor who then put the newly created cash received into his account with Bank A, then we have new money coming into the system and we can expect something like the multiplier effect shown above. The central bank is the only player here that can create money out of thin air and pump it into the system if the system is at equilibrium.

Thus, despite commercial banks' ability to create money on the way to equilibrium, there is a limit to the amount that the system as a whole can go up to because for every dollar, pound, euro, etc. created there has to be a fraction held as a cash reserve. It is the central bank that controls the total volume of monetary base (reserves at the central bank plus cash in circulation and at deposit-taking institutions) and so the broader aggregates of money have an upper limit. Small changes in the monetary base can have a large impact on the amount of broad money in the system and so we often refer to the monetary base as **high-powered money**.

Central banks have three major tools they use to increase or decrease the money supply and interest rates:

● open market operations
● standing lending facilities/discount rate
● reserve requirement ratio changes.

Open market operations

This is the most important tool of monetary policy in most countries today. **Open market operations** means the buying and selling of government securities (Treasury bills and bonds) in the normal trading markets on a day-to-day basis. In purchasing government securities the central bank creates money to hand it over to those selling. It issues currency notes (as in your wallet/purse) or it writes a cheque in the name of the owner. When the cheque is drawn on, the central bank just creates an amount of credit for itself to satisfy the buyer – money from thin air. When the central bank sells some of its stock of previously market-bought government securities, the purchasers draw on their money in the banking system, which leads to a lowering of reserves.

To illustrate the creation of money by a central bank we can take Bank A's balance sheet from the example above. The starting position is:

Bank A: lending out just enough to attain minimum reserve ratio

Assets	Liabilities
Reserves $21m Loans $84m	Deposits $105m

The central bank wants to inject money into the financial system and lower interest rates. It offers to buy billions of dollars of government securities. One of the customers of Bank A sells $6 million of securities to the central bank. The central bank sends money to the customer of Bank A who deposits the newly created money (an electronic record rather than cash) in Bank A.[8] Bank A adds this $6 million to its reserve account at the central bank. Now Bank A's balance sheet looks like this:

Bank A balance sheet after an injection of $6 million

Assets	Liabilities
Reserves $27m Loans $84m	Deposits $111m

Bank A has a very high reserve level relative to its deposits, $27m ÷ $111m = 24.3%. The managers will want to employ the surplus money above that needed to maintain the target reserve ratio (20%) to earn higher interest by lending it. If banks are more willing to lend to businesses and individuals because of the central bank intervention then interest rates are likely to fall, along with new money flows into the financial system. If the central bank wanted to raise interest rates by draining money from the system through open market operations it would sell government securities to investors, which reduces the amount held by banks in their reserve accounts at the central bank or reduces vault cash. This would curb lending and raise interest rates.

Central banks tend to use Treasury securities to conduct open market operations because the secondary market in these securities is very liquid, there is a

---

[8] In many financial systems there is a select group of security dealers (often a wing of the major commercial and investment banks) with which the central bank buys and sells government securities. It is these security dealers' deposit accounts that are credited and debited.

large volume of these securities held by dealers and investors, meaning that the market can absorb a large number of buy and sell transactions. The main method used is a repurchase agreement. The BoE generally uses repos with an average maturity of one or two weeks, but will also target long-term repos (3–12 months). The assets eligible for repo are gilts and sterling Treasury bills, UK-government foreign currency debt, eligible bank and local authority bills, and certain sterling bonds issued by supranational organisations and by governments in the European Economic Area. Turkey uses the repo market – see Article 16.1.

Article 16.1

Turkey's central bank cuts rates despite mounting inflation

By Daniel Dombey

Financial Times May 22, 2014

Turkey's central bank has cut its benchmark interest rate by 50 basis points despite mounting inflation, a move likely to rekindle the debate about the bank's independence. But in a decision that took some economists by surprise, the central bank – which is formally independent – announced on Thursday that it was enacting a 'measured decrease' in the benchmark one week repo rate from 10% to 9.5%. The broader range of rates at which the central bank lends money to the banking sector remained unchanged.

Last January, the central bank defied [president of Turkey] Mr Erdoğan's calls for lower borrowing costs and increased the repo rate to 10%, during a midnight meeting. The move sparked rallies in both the lira and Turkish equity markets, after weeks in which the currency had slid against the dollar.

While the currency has recovered, Turkey's inflation has continued to rise, reaching a two year high of 9.4% in April. Economists expect prices will rise even faster this month.

In its statement on Thursday, the bank argued that a 'recent decline in uncertainties and improvement in the risk premium indicators' had led to a fall across the board in market interest rates. It insisted that 'the monetary policy stance will continue to be tight' despite the latest cut.

An alternative, used in many countries, is to lend or borrow in the interbank market to add or subtract reserves and influence rates of interest charged. In the US, for example, the Fed funds rate is targeted.

Repos and reverse repos are, by their nature, temporary interventions because the opposite transaction takes place on maturity, a few days after the first buy or sell. There are times when the central bank wants to effect a more permanent change in the money supply. Then it can go for an outright transaction, a purchase or a sale (of government bills and bonds), that is not destined to be reversed in a few days.

(An alternative way to increase the monetary base is for the central bank to lend money to a commercial bank. The central bank simply credits the commercial bank's account with electronically created reserves. The amount of monetary base is less controllable through this method than through open market operations because the banks may or may not borrow, even if the central bank offers enticing interest rates.)

The supply and demand of reserves

Banks trade surplus reserves with each other. They always have an incentive to lend – even if only for 24 hours – if they find themselves with too many reserves. Each day there will be dozens of other banks that find themselves temporarily below the reserve level they need and so they willingly borrow in the market. The main target for central banks is usually the overnight interest rate on loans of reserves from one bank to another. In the US this is the Federal funds rate, in the eurozone it is the overnight repo rate in euros, and in the UK it is the overnight sterling repo rate. Switzerland opts for the Swiss franc Libor target rate. Soon after the official rate changes (typically the same day) banks adjust their standard lending rates ('base rate' in the UK), usually by the exact amount of the policy changes. This is transmitted through money market rate changes, repos, interbank lending, etc. The impact on longer-term interest rates can go either way when the short-term rates are changed, depending on what the market perceives the future will bring in terms of inflation and additional rises or falls in the overnight interest rate. (A rise in the official rate could, for example, generate expectations of lower future interest rates, in which case long rates might fall in response to a rise in short-term rates.)

If we take the banking system as a whole, the demand for reserves falls as interest rates rise. That is, the quantity of reserves demanded by banks (holding all else constant) reduces if banks have a higher opportunity cost of keeping money in the form of reserves; they would rather lend it out to clients to achieve higher interest rates. This becomes more and more of a lost opportunity as rates in the short-term interest rate markets rise. Bankers increasingly start to think that they can economise on the excess reserves buffer if interest rates are high. Thus, the demand curve for reserves, D, slopes downwards in Figure 16.2.

The central bank usually has a continuous programme of lending into the general repo market and so there is a large quantity of money borrowed by banks from the central bank at any one time. It is through the adjustment to the amount of reserves outstanding that the central bank controls interest rates. The supply curve for reserves, S, is the amount of reserves from the central bank supplied through its open market operations (in more normal times, at least). Equilibrium occurs where the demand for reserves equals the quantity supplied. This occurs at an interest rate of A, providing the short-term interest rate in the market.

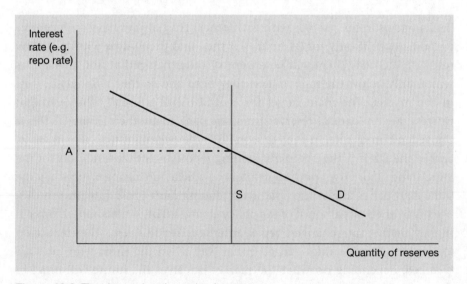

Figure 16.2 The demand and supply of reserves

Now imagine that the central bank wishes to lower interest rates. It does this by increasing its purchases of government securities in the repo market, providing a greater quantity of reserves. This pushes the supply curve in Figure 16.3 from S_1 to S_2, and moves the equilibrium interest rate from A to B. Obviously, if the central bank reduced its reserves outstanding to the banking system by selling additional securities, the supply curve would move to the left and the interest rate would rise.

So far we have discussed **dynamic open market operations**. That is, where the central bank takes the initiative to change the level of reserves and the monetary base within a reasonably static banking environment. However, many times the environment is not static because there are a number of factors changing demand for borrowed reserves, e.g. greater or lesser banker confidence in the economy and thus the potential for low-risk lending. Thus, it intervenes – a **defensive open market operation** – to offset the other factors influencing reserves.

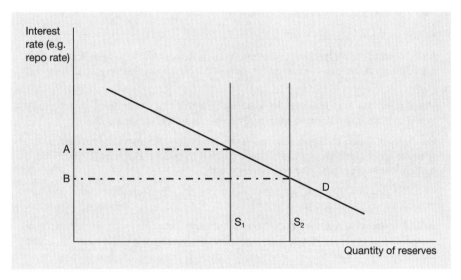

Figure 16.3 An open market increase in the supply of reserves

When the central bank wants to change short-term interest rates it can often do so merely by announcing its new target rate and threatening to undertake open market operations to achieve it rather than actually intervening. The money market participants know that if they do not immediately move to the new rate they will encounter difficulties. For example, if the central bank shifts to target an interest rate lower than previously (i.e. it will lend on the repo market at a new lower rate), then any bank wanting to borrow will be foolish to borrow at a higher rate. Conversely, if the central bank announces a new higher target rate, any bank wanting to lend will be foolish to accept a lower rate than the central bank's target because it stands ready to trade at its stated rate. India targets the repo rate – see Article 16.2.

Article 16.2

India cuts interest rate to revive growth

By Amy Kazmin

Financial Times March 19, 2013

India's central bank has lowered a key interest rate by 0.25% as it seeks to revive an economy that has slowed to the same pace as during the global financial crisis.

The Reserve Bank of India cut its key repo rate to 7.5%, as concerns about India's faltering economy outweigh worries about persistently high inflation.

But in its outlook, the central bank warned that the 'headroom for further easing remains quite limited', with inflation expected to remain stuck at levels that are 'not conducive for sustained economic growth'.

The RBI also left the cash reserve ratio unchanged, disappointing many who had expected a slight reduction.

India's economy grew just 4.5% from October to December, the slowest pace in 15 quarters – sharply down from the near double-digit growth rates recorded earlier in the decade.

Indian businesses have been complaining that high interest rates, coupled with policy gridlock on such issues as land acquisition policies, are constraining economic expansion.

Lending facility/discount rate changes

There is an option for banks to borrow additional reserves from the central bank, the **standing lending facility**. In some countries it is called **discount window borrowing**. The European Central Bank offers loans at the **marginal lending rate** in its **marginal lending facility**. In May 2014 when the **main refinancing rate** was 0.25%, if banks were forced to borrow under the marginal lending rate they paid 0.75%. In the US, the Federal Reserve offers (a) a **primary credit discount rate** for very short-term (usually overnight) lending to banks in sound condition, set in May 2014 at a level of 0.75% (at a time when the Fed Funds target was 0–0.25%); (b) a **secondary credit discount rate** for banks not in sound financial condition, where the interest rate is even higher at 1.25%; and (c) a **seasonal discount rate** for special situations. In the UK, with the target Bank Rate at 0.5% in May 2014, the BoE would lend to banks under the **operational standing lending facility** at 0.75%. In more normal times the standing lending facility/primary credit discount rates are usually 100 basis points above the target Bank Rate.

The BoE's operational standing lending facility is designed to allow banks a way of managing unexpected day-to-day shortages of reserves, which may arise due to technical problems in the commercial bank's own systems or in market-wide payments and settlement infrastructure. These funds are available in unlimited size. Standing lending facility borrowing is used by generally sound banks in normal market conditions on a short-term basis, typically overnight, at a rate above the normal open market target rate. But given the higher interest rate it is used sparingly.

For banks in severe shock there is usually another facility, which is even more expensive to borrow under. The BoE also has a **discount window facility**, which is aimed at banks experiencing firm-specific or market-wide shock. Rather than cash being borrowed from the BoE, the more usual form of borrowing is UK government bonds, gilts, which are lent for up to 30 days (or 364 days for an additional fee). The BoE hands over the gilts and receives in return less liquid collateral in a repo-type deal. These less liquid securities are much more risky than sovereign bonds, e.g. the collateral put up could be securitised bonds or a portfolio of corporate bonds. Once it is in receipt of the gilts the borrowing bank then obtains cash by lending them in the market – another repo. The discount window facility borrowing is designed only to address short-term liquidity shocks and the fees are set to ram home the extraordinary nature of this type of help with reserves. The BoE states that 'the fees are set to be unattractive in "normal" market conditions so that participants use the facility as back up rather than a regular source of liquidity'.

In normal conditions banks will be most interested in using the standing lending facility. This type of borrowing can allow an increase in reserves in the financial system and therefore an increase in the money supply. When the standing lending facility loans are repaid the total amount of reserves, the monetary base and the money supply will fall.

If the interest *premium* (above Bank Rate, Fed funds rate, etc.) charged in the standing lending facility falls then an increasing number of banks will be tempted to cut things fine on excess reserve levels, leading potentially to more borrowing at the lending facility rate. If the premium rises then few banks will borrow this way. Thus banks rein in their lending to customers for fear of having to borrow themselves at punitive interest rates. The standing lending facility rate acts as a back-stop for the open market target interest rate. The money market rate will not rise above the standing lending facility rate so long as the central bank remains willing to supply unlimited funds at the facility rate.

If we introduce the possibility of large volumes of supply of money (reserves) from the central bank at a high interest rate then we have the upside-down L-shaped supply curve shown in Figure 16.4. If the demand curve D_1 is the

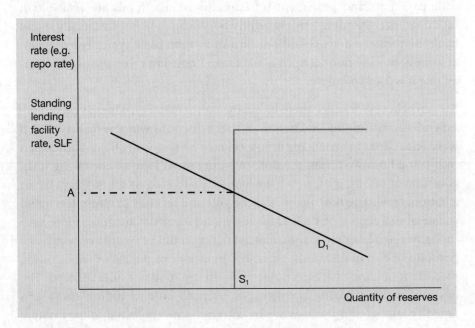

Figure 16.4 Standing lending facility availability changes the supply curve

relevant demand schedule for aggregate bank reserves then the horizontal portion of the curve – bank borrowing from the central bank at the standing lending facility rate – does not come into play. Banks will continue to borrow and lend in the money markets but not from the central bank,[9] and the equilibrium interest rate remains at A. This is the case most of the time: changes in the standing lending facility rate have no direct effect on the market interest rate.

Now, consider the case where there has been a shock to the system and banks increase their demand for reserves all the way along the curve – the demand curve has shifted to the right, from D_1 to D_2 in Figure 16.5. Indeed, it has shifted so much that banks now borrow from the central bank at the standing lending facility rate to top up their reserves – see demand curve D_2 intersecting the supply curve at the standing lending facility rate at point M. Now, if the central bank moves the lending facility rate up or down the point of intersection with the demand curve shifts and thus the market interest rates change. If the central bank wanted to lower interest rates it could move the lending facility rate from, say, F to G, leading to increased borrowing from the central bank and an increased money supply.

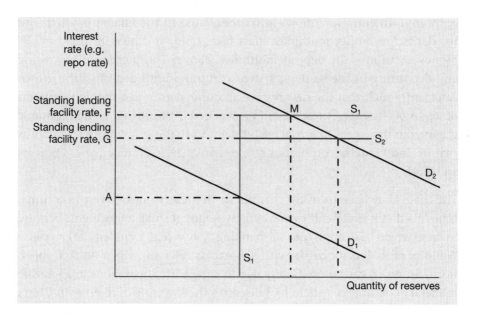

Figure 16.5 Standing lending facility rate lending

---

[9] Unless, of course, it too happens to be one of the buyers or sellers in the normal market.

A few decades ago adjusting the standard lending facility/discount rate was the main way in which many central banks effected monetary policy, but the problem with this approach became increasingly apparent. It is difficult to predict the quantity of lending facility/discount rate borrowing that will occur if the lending facility/discount rate is raised or lowered, and so it is difficult to accurately change the money supply. Today changes in this rate are used to signal to the market that the central bank would like to see higher or lower interest rates: a raising indicates that tighter monetary conditions are required with higher interest rates throughout; lowering it indicates that looser, more expansionary, monetary conditions are seen as necessary.

Reserve requirement ratio changes

The power to change the reserve requirement ratio is a further tool used by central banks to control a nation's money supply. A decrease in the reserve requirement ratio means that banks do not need to hold as much money at the central bank (the demand curve for reserves shifts to the left) and so they are able to lend out a greater percentage of their deposits, thus increasing the supply of money. The new loans result in consumption or investment in the economy, which raises inflows into other banks in the financial system and the deposit or money multiplier effect takes hold, as shown in the Example' Money creation – the deposit multiplier' above. The process of borrowing and depositing in the banking system continues until deposits have grown sufficiently such that the new reserve amounts permit just the right amount of deposits – the target reserve ratio is reached. At least that is the economic theory, but the recent financial crisis taught us that it is not quite as simple as that if individuals, corporations and banks lack confidence to borrow and lend.

The main drawback to using changes in the reserve ratio, even in 'normal times', is that it is difficult to make many frequent small adjustments because to do so would be disruptive to the banking system (e.g. a sudden rise can cause liquidity problems for banks with low excess reserves). Open market operations, however, can be used every day to cope with fluctuations in aggregate monetary conditions. Article 16.3 discusses the lowering of reserves in China to stimulate the economy.

Article 16.3

Chinese shares fall despite bank reserve ratio cut

By Gabriel Wildau and Patrick McGee

Financial Times February 5, 2015

Chinese equities fell despite early gains on Thursday after the People's Bank of China loosened policy earlier than anticipated during London trading hours on Wednesday.

China's central bank cut the required reserve ratio for its banks as it stepped up efforts to counter the impact of capital outflows and encourage banks to boost lending amid fresh data showing a weakening economy.

The Shanghai Composite lost 1.2%, having jumped 2.3% at the open on Thursday.

A survey published on Sunday revealed that China's manufacturing sector – a key growth driver – contracted in January for the first time in more than two years. This followed news last month that China experienced its weakest GDP growth in 24 years last year.

In addition, China suffered its largest capital outflow on record in the fourth quarter last year, according to balance of payments data released on Tuesday. The deficit of $91bn on the capital and financial accounts was the worst since quarterly data were first compiled in 1998. China's foreign exchange reserves also fell as investors sold renminbi and bought foreign currency.

'The most important reason for the cut is liquidity demand in the banking system,' said Haibin Zhu, chief China economist at JPMorgan in Hong Kong ...

The required reserve ratio, known as the RRR, specifies the portion of a commercial bank's deposits that must be held on reserve at China's central bank, where it is unavailable for loans and other investments.

For most of the past decade, 'twin surpluses' on both the current and capital accounts swelled China's foreign exchange reserves and its domestic money supply. In response, the People's Bank of China (PBOC) raised the RRR steadily as a way to sterilise these inflows and prevent inflation. The RRR for China's biggest banks rose from 8% in 2005 to a high of 20.5% in late 2012.

Wednesday's cut of 0.5% brings that rate down to 19.5% – although this is still much higher than any other major economy. With inflows now reversing, economists expect at least one more RRR cut this year.

In depth

The central bank has tried to tread a fine line over the past year by providing a targeted stimulus to support the slowing economy, without exacerbating financial risks by unleashing a new credit binge like the one deployed in response to the 2008 financial crisis.

The central bank's latest easing move followed a cut in benchmark interest rates in November and a series of targeted easing measures last year, which included direct loans worth more than $80bn to specific banks, and RRR cuts for small lenders.

In addition to Wednesday's broad-based cut, the PBOC announced further targeted cuts for so-called city commercial banks, whose loan books tilt towards small business and the agricultural sector – two areas that have long complained of difficulty obtaining credit.

In addition to responding to domestic conditions, economists say the PBOC's move is also a reaction to moves by central banks in other countries, including the recent decision by the European Central Bank to pursue an ambitious programme of quantitative easing.

'Various countries are raising the stakes when it comes to monetary policy easing,' said Cao Yang, an analyst at Shanghai Pudong Development Bank. 'China's RRR cut is a move to keep pace.'

Source: Wildau, G. and McGee, P. (2015) Chinese shares fall despite bank reserve ratio cut, *Financial Times*, 5 February.
© The Financial Times Limited 2015. All Rights Reserved.

Choosing between targeting the quantity of reserves and targeting an interest rate level

Which is more likely to lead to stable monetary conditions: (a) targeting a fixed aggregate supply of money, or (b) targeting a particular overnight interest rate? Or consider an alternative question leading to a similar conclusion: is it possible to target both the quantity of reserves and the interest rate simultaneously?

To provide answers, examine the situation in Figure 16.6. The central bank expects the aggregate demand curve to be as described by the solid demand line, D_2. However, the reality is that the authorities have only a vague idea of where the demand schedule is. It might fluctuate up to the higher dashed line or down to the lower one as, say, unexpected changes in deposit levels increase or decrease commercial banks' desire to hold excess reserves. Thus, if the central bank rigidly maintains the supply schedule, S, the result could be that from one day to the next overnight interest rates could be quite volatile, fluctuating

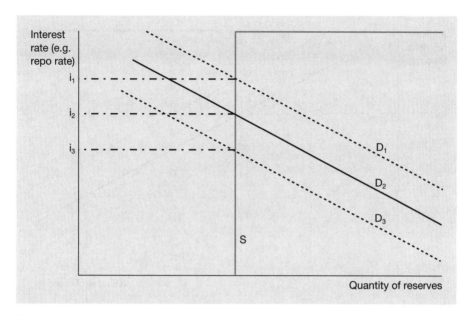

Figure 16.6 Targeting reserve levels

from, say, i_1 to i_3, as the demand curve moves left and right. Such a rapidly shifting overnight rate can be disruptive.

The alternative approach is to target the overnight interest rate and to therefore fine-tune the supply of reserves to achieve the desired interest rate stability – see Figure 16.7. Here the reserves demand curve fluctuations can be accommodated by the central bank response of quickly implementing open market operations to pump in or drain reserves. If the D_1 curve comes into play with higher reserves demanded at each interest rate then the central bank can increase supply to S_3 by buying securities, achieving equilibrium at interest rate, i. If demand for reserves is low, D_3, then the central bank can move to supply only S_1, leaving equilibrium at i. It can do this by selling securities or simply not supplying fresh reserves as repo positions come to an end. Thus, the supply of reserves is determined by the commercial banks' aggregate demand for reserves, which is accommodated by the central bank through open market operations in targeting the price of credit.

Interest rate targeting is generally preferred because the central bank can quickly observe changes in the rate, whereas measuring aggregate quantities of reserves involves a time lag. It can also intervene quickly to control the interest

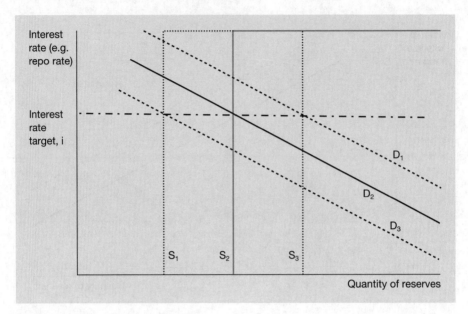

Figure 16.7 Targeting the interest rate

rate, whereas reserves are not completely controllable. Also, central banks have generally concluded that there is a closer link between interest rates and the goal of the inflation level in the economy than that between monetary aggregates and inflation. For these reasons central banks generally target short-term interest rates.

Following the logic of targeting the overnight interest rate, some monetary economists emphasise that it is the price of credit that determines the quantity of broad money created by banks. So, rather than targeting a deposit multiplier through altering the quantity of the monetary base in an assumed stable ratio of broad money to narrow money, central banks set overnight interbank interest rates, which affect other interest rates. The level of interest rates throughout the economy (mortgages, deposit interest, etc.) creates the demand for broad money – banks may become more or less willing to lend, borrowers become more or less willing to borrow, pay down debt or spend, depending on the interest rates. The impact on broad money then has an impact on the quantity of base money demanded. Thus the demand for reserves is a *consequence* rather than a cause of banks making loans and creating broad money. Commercial bank decisions on the amount they make available for loans depends on the perceived profitability of lending, which in turn depends on a number of factors, including degree of confidence in a growing economy and the cost of funds that banks face, which is influenced strongly by the interest rate paid on reserves at the central bank.

A central bank decision to lower overnight interest rates is likely to increase the amount of broad money, as long-term loan rates fall and the volume of loans rises. The larger volume of spending and broad money in the economy is likely to cause banks and customers to demand more reserves and currency. Thus the deposit or money multiplier is seen as working in a reverse way to that described earlier. However, bear in mind that whichever direction the causation goes, broad money has to backed up with reserves. Thus the reserves level can limit changes in the amount of broad money. Interest rates, reserves and long-term bank lending are intimately linked, and controllable, to some extent, by the central bank.

Quantitative easing

In extreme circumstances a central bank may find that interest rates have been reduced to the lowest level they could go and yet still economic activity does not pick up. People are so shocked by the crisis – increased chance of unemployment, lower house prices, lower business profits – that they cut down their consumption and investment regardless of being able to borrow at very low interest rates. This happened in 2009–2014. Annualised short-term interest rates in eurozone countries were less than 0.1%, in the UK they were 0.5% and in the US they were between 0% and 0.25%. Clearly, low short-term interest rates were not enough to get the economy moving, even with the additional boost of government deficit spending to the extent that up to one-eighth of all spending was from government borrowing.

In response, another policy tool was devised: **quantitative easing**. This involves the central bank electronically creating money ('printing money', but without any more bank notes) which is then used to buy assets from non-bank investors in the market. Thus pension funds, insurance companies and other non-financial firms can sell assets, mostly long-term government bonds (but can include mortgage-backed securities and corporate bonds), and their bank accounts are credited with newly created money (broad money increases). This raises bank reserves. More significantly, the increased demand for government bonds raises their prices and lowers interest rates along the yield curve – so the main influence is on interest rates for medium- and long-term bonds. Also, it is hoped that the new cash will be used to invest in other assets such as shares pushing up equity issuance, prices and lowering required returns on these assets, thus stimulating investment in companies.

In the UK the BoE bought so many bonds in 2009–2013 that it now owns about one-third of all gilts, pushing ten-year yields at times to only 1.5%. Between 2008 and 2014 the Fed bought more than $3.5 trillion bonds (mostly mortgage-backed and government). However, central banks are increasingly anxious about the consequences of ceasing quantitative easing – interest rates might rebound dramatically and devastatingly. Some economists are also worried that inflation might take off at some point given all the extra cash floating about (optimists argue that the central bank can just sell the bonds or wait until redemption to suck cash out of the system, others are not so sure). Japan launched the most audacious quantitative easing plan in 2013: $1.4 trillion in less than one year – see Article 16.4. Many suspect that bubbles are being created in bond and other asset markets.

Article 16.4

Bank of Japan opens floodgates

Financial Times April 5, 2013

This week, Haruhiko Kuroda, the new governor of the Bank of Japan, launched perhaps the boldest ever experiment by the central bank of an important country. It is not a revolution in monetary policy, since the BoJ is following the intellectual lead of Ben Bernanke's Federal Reserve. But it is a revolution in Japanese thinking and in the magnitude of the planned action. The Bank of Japan risks doing too much. But Japan already knows well the costs of doing too little. That lesson is one the European Central Bank may yet learn.

The BoJ has promised to turn Japan's slow-motion deflation into inflation of 2% within two years. To achieve this transformation it has now promised to raise purchases of government bonds from a monthly rate of Y2tn ($21bn) to one of Y7tn, to double the average maturity of new bond purchases to seven years and to double the monetary base to Y270tn by the end of 2014.

This is still monetary policy, since the BoJ intends to reverse the purchases. The aim is to force holders of government liabilities to move into riskier assets. The result, it is hoped, will be higher prices for riskier assets, including equities; a weak yen, a stronger economy and so higher inflation.

The floor system

Over the decades central banks have tried all sorts of levers to control inflation, money supply and interest rates. Currently, a popular approach is the floor system. This has been prompted by the pressures caused by the enormous amounts of money pumped in to counteract depressed appetite to invest, borrow and lend.

With quantitative easing the central bank is creating large quantities of reserves far beyond that needed to achieve its target interest rate. Not only this, but the quantity of money goes up in large increments, so the supply curve is all over the place – view the supply curve in Figure 16.8 as moving frequently left to right and back again.

This could lead to uncertainty. To put a floor under the fluctuations the central bank introduces a policy of paying its target Bank Rate of interest (0.5% in the UK) to all reserves lodged by banks with it (even excess reserves). Because commercial banks will not lend their surplus reserves to each other at rates lower than can be obtained by depositing them at the central bank, this has the effect of flattening the demand curve for reserves after the point where there

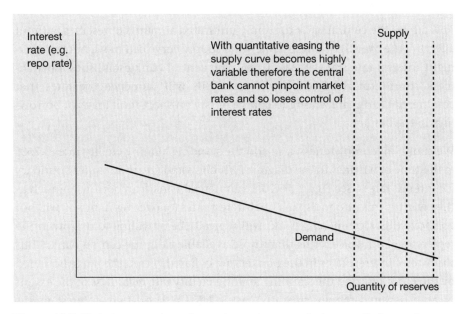

Figure 16.8 First change: extraordinary circumstances calls for quantitative easing

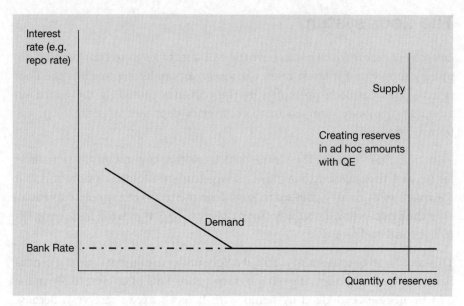

Figure 16.9 Second change: a floor system, where all bank reserves held at the central bank are remunerated at Bank Rate (Fed Funds rate, etc.)

are sufficient reserves in the system for banks to manage their day-to-day liquidity needs – see Figure 16.9.

This allows the central bank to supply unlimited amounts of reserves without affecting the overnight interest rate – the supply curve can move but the overnight interest rate stays at, say, 0.5%. The central bank establishes a benchmark short-term risk-free interest rate. This will influence the rates that commercial banks are willing to charge or pay on short-term loans or borrowings in the market.

We could, for completeness, also add the standing lending facility rate (0.75% at the time of writing) to the diagram, which would create an upper boundary for interest rates – see Figure 16.10. Commercial banks can borrow as much as they want at this rate and so market interest rates for overnight money will not go above this. Commercial banks will typically be unwilling to borrow in the repo market on worse terms than those available from the central bank. Thus short-term interest rates in the markets are collared within the range bounded by the Bank Rate and the standing lending facility rate regardless of the extent of high-powered money creation. In the UK the short-term interest rate is

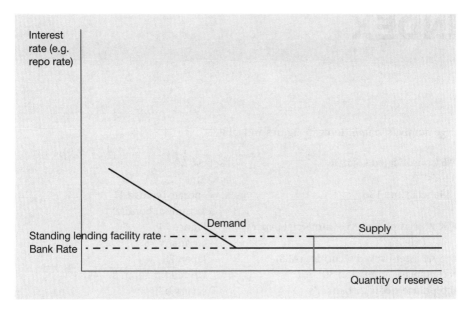

Figure 16.10 A floor system combined with a standing lending facility

unlikely to be lifted higher than the Bank Rate given the sheer quantity of reserves sloshing about the banking system, where there are plenty of banks willing to lend overnight to other banks at 0.5%. Collectively, banks would need to come under severe strain for the upper limit of the corridor (0.75%) to be tested.

INDEX

Page numbers in *italic* indicate figures and tables.

Do you want your people to be the very best at what they do?

Talk to us about how we can help.

As the world's leading learning company, we know a lot about what your people need in order to be better at what they do.

Whatever subject or skills you've got in mind (from presenting or persuasion to coaching or communication skills), and at whatever level (from new-starters through to top executives) we can help you deliver tried-and-tested, essential learning straight to your workforce – whatever they need, whenever they need it and wherever they are.

Talk to us today about how we can:

- Complement and support your existing learning and development programmes
- Enhance and augment your people's learning experience
- Match your needs to the best of our content
- Customise, brand and change it to make a better fit
- Deliver cost-effective, great value learning content that's proven to work.

Contact us today:
corporate.enquiries@pearson.com